The Comparative Politics of Education

Public education is critically important to the human capital, social well-being, and economic prosperity of nations. It is also an intensely political realm of public policy that is heavily shaped by power and special interests. Yet political scientists rarely study education, and education researchers rarely study politics. This volume attempts to change that by promoting the development of a coherent, thriving field on the comparative politics of education. As an opening wedge, the authors carry out an 11-nation comparative study of the political role of teachers unions showing that, as education systems everywhere became institutionalized, teachers unions pursued their interests by becoming well-organized, politically active, highly influential – and during the modern era, the main opponents of neoliberal reform. Across diverse nations, the commonalities are striking. The challenge going forward is to expand on this study's scope, theory, and evidence to bring education into the heart of comparative politics.

Terry M. Moe is the William Bennett Munro Professor of Political Science at Stanford University and a senior fellow at the Hoover Institution. He has written extensively on the presidency, public bureaucracy, and the American political system, as well as the theory of political institutions more generally. He has also written extensively on the politics of education and the role of power and special interests in shaping education systems. His books include *Relic* (2016, with William Howell), *Special Interest: Teachers Unions and America's Public Schools* (2011), and *Politics, Markets, and America's Schools* (1990, with John Chubb).

Susanne Wiborg is Reader in Education at the UCL Institute of Education and a member of the LLAKES centre. She is the leader of the MA programme in Comparative Education at UCL. She has published widely on the comparative history of education, focusing particularly on the policy and politics of secondary education in Scandinavia and Europe. She is the author of *Education and Social Integration: Comprehensive Schooling in Europe* (2009).

The Comparative Politics of Education
Teachers Unions and Education Systems Around the World

Edited by

TERRY M. MOE
Stanford University

SUSANNE WIBORG
UCL Institute of Education

CAMBRIDGE
UNIVERSITY PRESS

University Printing House, Cambridge, CB2 8BS, United Kingdom

Cambridge University Press is part of the University of Cambridge.

It furthers the University's mission by disseminating knowledge in the pursuit of education, learning and research at the highest international levels of excellence.

www.cambridge.org
Information on this title: www.cambridge.org/9781107168886

© Cambridge University Press 2017

This publication is in copyright. Subject to statutory exception and to the provisions of relevant collective licensing agreements, no reproduction of any part may take place without the written permission of Cambridge University Press.

First published 2017

Printed in the United Kingdom by Clays, St Ives plc

A catalogue record for this publication is available from the British Library

Library of Congress Cataloging-in-Publication data
Names: Moe, Terry M., editor. | Wiborg, Susanne, editor.
Title: The comparative politics of education : teachers unions and education systems around the world / edited by Terry M. Moe, Stanford University; Susanne Wiborg, UCL Institute of Education.
Description: Cambridge, United Kingdom; New York: Cambridge University Press, 2017. | Includes bibliographical references and index.
Identifiers: LCCN 2016026760| ISBN 9781107168886 (hardback) | ISBN 9781316619766 (paperback)
Subjects: LCSH: Teachers' unions–Cross-cultural studies. | Comparative education. | BISAC: POLITICAL SCIENCE / General.
Classification: LCC LB2844.52 C66 2016 | DDC 331.88/113711–dc23
LC record available at https://lccn.loc.gov/2016026760

ISBN 978-1-107-16888-6 Hardback
ISBN 978-1-316-61976-6 Paperback

Cambridge University Press has no responsibility for the persistence or accuracy of URLs for external or third-party internet websites referred to in this publication, and does not guarantee that any content on such websites is, or will remain, accurate or appropriate.

Contents

List of Contributors		page vi
1	Introduction *Terry M. Moe and Susanne Wiborg*	1
2	Teachers Unions in the United States: The Politics of Blocking *Terry M. Moe*	24
3	Teacher Unions in England: The End is Nigh? *Susanne Wiborg*	56
4	Teacher Unionism in France: Making Fundamental Reform an Impossible Quest? *Michael Dobbins*	87
5	Teacher Unionism in Germany: Fragmented Competitors *Rita Nikolai, Kendra Briken, and Dennis Niemann*	114
6	Teachers Unions in the Nordic Countries: Solidarity and the Politics of Self-Interest *Susanne Wiborg*	144
7	Teachers' Unions in Japan: The Frustration of Permanent Opposition *Robert W. Aspinall*	192
8	Teachers' Unions in Mexico: The Politics of Patronage *Christopher Chambers-Ju and Leslie Finger*	215
9	Teacher Unions in India: Diverse and Powerful *Tara Béteille, Geeta Gandhi Kingdon, and Mohammad Muzammil*	239
10	The Comparative Politics of Education: Teachers Unions and Education Systems Around the World *Terry M. Moe*	269
Index		325

Contributors

Robert W. Aspinall, Doshisha University
Tara Béteille, World Bank
Kendra Briken, University of Strathclyde
Christopher Chambers-Ju, University of California, Berkeley
Michael Dobbins, Goethe University of Frankfurt
Leslie Finger, Harvard University
Geeta Gandhi Kingdon, UCL Institute of Education
Terry M. Moe, Stanford University
Mohammad Muzammil, Agra University
Dennis Niemann, Bremen University
Rita Nikolai, Humboldt-University Berlin
Susanne Wiborg, UCL Institute of Education

1

Introduction

Terry M. Moe and Susanne Wiborg

Education is a basic function of government everywhere in the world. Part of the reason, of course, is that all nations want their children to learn how to read, write, and do arithmetic. But there is much more to the story than that. For education systems can serve many other purposes as well—with far-reaching consequences for societies, their citizens, and the governments that operate them.

An education system can be a means of boosting human capital and economic growth. But as a prime source of money and jobs in the hands of politicians, it can also fuel the fires of patronage and corruption—and stifle productivity. It can be a means of advancing social equity and upward mobility, but also of entrenching the existing class structure. It can be a means of integrating immigrants into the nation's culture, but also of imposing a common culture on diverse ethnic groups that don't want it. It can be a means of socializing citizens to democratic norms, but also of socializing them to authoritarian ideology and control. It can be a means of promoting religious tolerance and secularism, but also of privileging one religion at the expense of others (see, e.g., Cremin, 1961; Goldin and Katz, 2009; Green, 2013; Hanushek and Woessmann, 2015; Kosack, 2012).

Education, then, is an institutional arena of enormous potential, a shaper of the fundamentals of human society. Precisely because this is so, governments have strong incentives to put this potential to use by getting actively involved in the design, control, and operation of education systems for their societies—and these systems, as a result, cannot help but be profoundly influenced by the political processes through which governmental decisions get made. In great measure, education systems are what they are, and indeed, the schools are what they are—everywhere in the world, regardless of the nation—because politics makes them that way.

The United States was a late bloomer in building a public education system. While Prussia and France began building their systems more than 200 years ago, the American system did not take shape until the early 1900s, when Progressive-era reforms—achieved through political battles that lasted decades—purged American education of party machines and patronage and created a system based on bureaucratic administration, expertise, and nonpartisan local democracy: a more "rational" structure far better suited to socializing the nation's new waves of immigrants, preparing young people for the workforce, and providing free and easy access to secondary education and pathways to upward mobility. Although the US was not a leader in developing a public education system, it *was* a leader in developing a system that (for its time) achieved remarkable equity—bringing schools to the masses in a way that far exceeded what was then happening in most of Europe (not to mention the less-developed world), where, well into mid-century, nations were still fighting political battles about bringing "comprehensive education" to their own systems (Cremin, 1961; Green, 2013; Tyack, 1974).

As Goldin and Katz (2009) have argued, the US system of extending education to the masses, and doing it early, was consequential for more than social equity. It also had enormous consequences for the national economy—providing valuable reserves of human capital that would give this country great advantages over others, and serve as an engine of economic growth that propelled the US to economic dominance during the 1900s. Whether other (or many) nations saw this connection between education and economic growth early on is unclear. But it is clear that social equity was a burning political issue, that parties of the left were committed to it, that many parents and children wanted new opportunities—and that, over time, other nations throughout the world followed roughly the same path that America did in expanding their public school systems to include ever-larger populations of children.

This era of expansion, which occupied not only the more advanced nations, but also, increasingly, the less developed ones, was essentially a worldwide era of institutional formation in which virtually all nations were building, staffing, funding, and expanding their educational institutions for the first time. In the process, over a period of many years, those institutions became established as the institutional status quo (e.g., Archer, 1979; Green, 2013; Meyer *et al.*, 1992). From that point on, nations would find themselves on set institutional paths that, for reasons that political scientists well understand—having to do with path dependence, including the protective role of powerful political constituencies—would be very difficult to depart from should governments decide that these institutions needed to be changed (Pierson, 2004).

And that is what happened. The 1970s and 1980s saw the dawning of a new era for public education, but also for government in general. Two developments were mainly responsible. First, nations were collectively plunged into a shockingly new and different international environment of globalization, technological innovation, and intense economic competition. In the realm of education, this new environment led them to see human capital as crucial to their ability to compete in the new "knowledge economy," and to demand from their education systems much higher levels of academic achievement. Second, and at roughly the same time, the developed world was faced with the so-called "crisis of the welfare state," the onset of fiscal austerity, demands for governmental efficiency, and rising disaffection with centralized, bureaucratic modes of governance—which led to pressures for neoliberal reforms of governmental institutions in general, and education systems in particular, that put a premium on decentralization, accountability, and markets: sharp departures from the institutional past.

As this new era took hold, then, the sheer quantity of education was no longer enough. The emphasis now was on performance—on academic excellence—which the existing institutions were not specifically designed to provide, at least at the levels the modern world required. The stage was set, then, for a new type of education politics. For this was an era in which reformers would seek major change in entrenched institutions inherited from the past—and thus, inevitably, would face political resistance from the defenders of the institutional status quo. Other issues would remain, of course, regarding equity, race, religion, and myriad other lines of social cleavage, depending on the nation. But across the world, what was distinctive about the modern era—which continues to the present day—is its historically new emphasis on performance and the political pursuit of institutions that might be capable of providing it. The politics of the modern era would be a politics of performance-based reform (e.g., Blossing *et al.*, 2014; Jakobi *et al.*, 2010; Wiborg, 2013).

These are the broad outlines of what we see as the two major eras in worldwide systems of public education: the era of institutional formation and the era of performance-based reform. Distinguishing between these two eras, and appreciating why they are different and distinctive, is essential for understanding their politics and, in particular, for understanding how politics through time has driven processes of institutional development and reform in the realm of education. This is a vast subject matter that one book can only begin to explore. Our strategy here, given the enormity of the challenge, is to focus on certain aspects that we think are especially important—key pieces of a much larger puzzle—and in so doing, to construct a useful foundation that other scholars can build upon going forward.

More specifically, this book focuses on elementary and secondary school systems—the basic education systems that virtually all governments provide—and explores key features of their politics in 11 nations across the globe. Obviously, the details vary from country to country, often quite dramatically. The politics of education is starkly different in Sweden than in Mexico or France, and their education systems reflect those differences. That said, politics in all nations is heavily shaped by *power* and by the *interests* of those that exercise it—and in every chapter of the book, the politics of education will be approached from the standpoint of this common analytic framing, lending a measure of structure and unity to chapters whose substantive contents are in some ways quite different (Korpi, 2006; Moe, 2005; Pierson, 2015).

Any serious effort to understand the world's education systems needs to study, for any given nation, how power is structured within the politics of education—who wields political power, how they wield it, what their interests are, what the relevant coalitions are, how their power and interests connect with the party system and the larger apparatus of government, and more generally, how the type of political system and its institutions shape the way power and interests find expression in the political process. And all this needs to be done, of course, across nations and over time in order to provide for an enlightening comparative understanding of education systems throughout the world.

The scholarly literature at this point is almost a *tabula rasa* on these scores, and has not viewed its agenda as one of systematically exploring the politics of education and the structure of power and interests that drive it (see, e.g., the review in Busemeyer and Trampusch, 2011). This book is an attempt to change that. Here at the outset, there are many ways such a new research program might be pursued. We have chosen one tack—a focus on the political role of teachers unions—that we believe stands to be especially productive as a basis for future progress. Here is why.

Teachers Unions, Politics, and Vested Interests

Anyone who follows education in the United States knows that the teachers unions have played a central role in that nation's politics of education for decades. Yet scholars rarely study them as political actors. An exception is Moe's *Special Interest* (2011), which seeks to understand the American politics of education through the theoretical lens of power and interests, and marshals evidence to show that the teachers unions—since their first emergence as key actors during the 1960s, 1970s, and 1980s—have exercised great power in the American educational arena, and have been the leading opponents of education reform.

Informed observers may disagree about just how powerful the teachers unions are. In recent times, moreover, the unions have lost some important political battles—the stand-out being No Child Left Behind in 2001—and are clearly on the defensive. But there is plenty of hard evidence to show that, by any reasonable account, the teachers unions are major political forces at all levels of American government when official decisions are made about the policies, organization, funding, and reform of the public schools. The unions are not the only political actors that matter. But they are absolutely central to the political controversies, struggles, and decisions that make the public schools what they are—and in particular, they are absolutely central to the politics of performance-based reform that has so consumed the modern era.

That being so, scholars who seek to understand the American politics of education need to pay serious, careful attention to them. A different way to put this is that scholars who do study the teachers unions will learn a great deal about how the American politics of education works, why it works as it does, and what it implies for the education system more generally. That, in fact, is a key argument of Moe's *Special Interest*—which isn't just a book about teachers unions per se, but rather a book about how the American politics of education can be understood.

As we look across nations, there is good reason to believe that the United States is not an outlier with respect to the prominent political role of its teachers unions. American government and society may be exceptional in many ways, and American exceptionalism is a long-standing theme in the study of comparative politics. But in our view, the fact that its teachers unions are highly organized, politically very active, and play central roles in the politics of education is likely to be an exceedingly common fact of political life across all nations (aside from authoritarian or very poor ones), however diverse they may be and however different from America in other respects. By studying the teachers unions, then, we believe we are studying something of universal importance to the worldwide politics of education.

There is a strong theoretical basis for this belief (see Moe, 2015). The place to begin is by recognizing that educational institutions are not unique. In fundamental respects, they are just like all other government institutions. And most important from the standpoint of our analysis, all government institutions—across all areas of public policy, everywhere in the world—naturally and inevitably generate *vested interests*. This happens, and is literally unavoidable—whether it is in health care, defense, agriculture, transportation, international trade, or public education—simply because certain people and groups receive benefits, often in very different ways, from what specific government institutions do. The benefits may take the form of services, public jobs, business revenues, power, status, or simple opportunities for corruption, nepotism, and patronage. But wherever there are government institutions, there are people and groups with vested interests in what those institutions do, in their structure and operation, in their funding, and, indeed, in their very existence.

In ordinary language, the term vested interest tends to be used when the intent is to convey something negative. To label groups as vested interests is to criticize them, to voice disapproval of their behavior. But this negative connotation is entirely unnecessary, and it is not at all what we are getting at here. To say that a group has a vested interest in a particular issue or institution, or to say that the group "is" a vested interest (a common word-usage that we will often employ here, for convenience), is to say something that is entirely objective, and also important and revealing, about the nature of those interests. On purely scientific grounds, the concept of vested interest has great analytic value as a basis for theory—and as a basis for progress in understanding why the politics of government institutions works as it does.

What is distinctive about vested interests, and what is distinctively valuable about their theoretical role, is that they arise from the very institutions whose development, stability, and change we want to explain. They are not just special interests. They are rooted in specific institutions, they benefit from those institutions, and they have incentives to get organized—if the stakes are high enough, and if they can overcome their collective action problems—to seek active and powerful roles in politics in order to protect and enhance their benefits. These roles may involve pressuring for new programs and spending, and thus for expansions of their institutions. But they may also involve—and almost always do involve, especially in an era of reform—taking action to oppose reforms that, by bringing change to the status quo, would threaten their institutions and benefits.

In the politics that surround government institutions, then, *vested interests are likely to be key players*. If the institutions are of any size and consequence, moreover, at least some of the vested interests associated with them are likely to have enormously valuable stakes in those institutions—and incentives to invest especially heavily in the requisites of political power, far more so than other groups. There is a reason why, in the lore and scholarship of politics, vested interests have reputations for political power. The reality is, they often *are* powerful. They have strong incentives to be (e.g., Lowi, 1969; McConnell, 1966; Olson, 1984).

All of this applies across the board to education systems. They, too, automatically generate vested interests. The most obvious are those of parents and children, who have vested interests in the services being provided; but children are inherently powerless, and except in affluent niches, parents are too atomized and weakly motivated to overcome the formidable collective action problems that stand in the way of political organization. Another source of vested interests is the government bureaucracies responsible for running the schools, for they are filled with public officials whose jobs, authority, status, and perquisites are rooted in the existing systems—and, unlike parents, they are already organized and in positions to exercise influence.

Outside the bureaucracy, arguably the most valuable and motivating benefits that educational institutions generate, in terms of deep-seated material stakes, are the jobs they provide for *teachers*: which translate into incomes, careers, security, and the material foundations of teachers' lives. These are very positive things, of course, for individual teachers, and it is only natural and normal that they put great value on them. We are not saying, moreover, that teachers—as human beings—only care about their jobs and nothing else, for they surely care about children, their communities, their families, and all sorts of other things, just as other human beings do. The point to be made here, rather, is an analytical one: that as employees of education systems, teachers have *vested interests in their jobs*—and accordingly, they have strong incentives to get organized, mobilize resources, and exercise power in the politics of education in order to protect and advance *those* interests. The teachers unions are their specialized means of doing that—of protecting and advancing their job interests, and not all the other concerns and values that they may have as human beings.

The way to understand the teachers unions, then, is that they arise from these vested interests, are founded on them and oriented by them, and are the organized means by which they are protected and pursued. And because we can expect education systems everywhere, throughout the world, to generate these *same* vested interests, we should expect teachers unions to be a force in the politics of education in *every* nation where teachers are allowed to organize or have the capacity to. Whether they can be expected to be more powerful than government bureaucrats—in any given nation at any given time—is a complex matter, needless to say; and any good answer would presumably vary with specific conditions. That said, it is important to note that, in every nation, teachers will tend to outnumber government bureaucrats by many orders of magnitude and are guaranteed to be a massive presence. In addition, they will tend to be geographically distributed across the entire country and well anchored in local communities—wherever there are kids, there are teachers—giving them important political advantages that bureaucrats don't have. At the very least, then, however these considerations of relative power shake out, we should expect teachers unions to be central players in the politics of education everywhere in the world. (Again, for a more detailed argument, see Moe, 2015.)

Because, as we will soon see, teachers unions are often allied with parties of the left, and because their rhetoric and issue positions tend to square with that of their leftist coalition partners—calling, for example, for greater social equity, higher government spending and taxation, expanded social programs, and so on—it is easy to see them in ideological terms and to infer that they are primarily motivated by ideology. But there are good theoretical reasons for thinking otherwise. Their leaders may sometimes be ideological, and the unions surely do participate in ideological coalitions. But the bedrock of their organizations is formed by the job interests of their members, and we should expect these job interests to be given top priority and to be the driving force behind the unions' politics and their approach to institutional reform. The teachers unions are interest groups, their fundamental interests are in jobs, and that is the key to understanding their behavior.

Scholars, as we've said, have rarely studied education from the standpoint of political power, and even less often have studied the teachers unions as political actors. The literature does contain two books that provide useful surveys of teachers unions across nations, but they were written long ago, before the modern era of performance-based reform had really taken hold, and they do not offer the kind of political perspective that we will be providing here. The first is Lawn's *The Politics of Teacher Unionism* (1985). It focuses on politics, but it is quite dated now (through no fault of its own), and its chapter-authors "were asked to explore sympathetically the development of a teachers union or a contemporary problem in educational work" (p. 3), consistent with Lawn's concern for providing "a useful source of experience for the necessary defense of teachers and teaching" (book jacket material). Its approach is thus shaped by these normative concerns rather than being strictly theoretical and empirical.

The second is Cooper's *Labor Relations in Education* (1992). This book is mainly, as the title suggests, about how collective bargaining and other aspects of labor relations in education differ across countries. It is not centrally about politics, nor does it explore issues of power and interest. Some of its chapters, moreover, were written by union representatives rather than by professional researchers. The US chapter was written by Al Shanker, president of the American Federation of Teachers, and the Germany chapter was coauthored by Deiter Wunder, president of the GEW (the largest German teachers union). Both books are informative, however, especially in the histories they provide (before the modern era), and we recommend them to our readers.

Of the scant work that has been carried out on teachers unions in politics, there is a high quality literature on Latin America that stands out. It does deal directly with issues of power and interest—and vested interests—and what it finds is very much in line with Moe's (2011) analysis of the United States: that the teachers unions are indeed quite central to the politics of education, that they are fundamentally motivated by the job interests of their members, and that they are the leading opponents of reform (e.g., Bruns and Luque, 2014; Grindle, 2004; Murillo, 1999, 2001). Here is a summary assessment by Merilee Grindle (2004, p. 139), whose *Despite the Odds* examines the efforts of Latin American governments to pursue education reform during the 1990s.

With very few exceptions, teachers unions formed the core of resistance to the education reforms of the 1990s. They were powerful political opponents, even if they had seen their influence diminish over the course of the 1980s and 1990s. Institutionally, they continued to be well positioned to confront government policies, making their demands known through strikes and protest actions and using their links to ministries of education and political parties to challenge the power of the reformers. They had the capacity to bring national ministries and school systems to a halt. They marshaled significant numbers of votes. Their close connections to political parties meant that their leaders were frequently important figures in party decision making and the distribution of government largess when those parties were in power.

A very recent survey and analysis of the overall literature on education reform in Latin American by Bruns and Luque (2014, p. 47) offers the same basic assessment. As they summarize it:

Teachers are ... the most powerful stakeholder in the process of education reform. No other education actor is as highly organized, visible, and politically influential. Because of their unique autonomy behind the closed door of the classroom, teachers also have profound power over the extent to which new policies can be implemented successfully.

By studying teachers unions and their political activities, then, we are likely to learn a lot about the politics of education generally, the power and interests that drive it, the roles of governments and parties, and the broader consequences for education systems. Theory suggests that, for the great majority of governments throughout the world, the teachers unions aren't likely to be just marginal players or interesting in their own right. They are likely to be organized, active, and at the heart of things—and we should expect that, by studying them and exploring their role in education politics, particularly in the modern reform era, we can gain perspective on the larger whole and generate new ideas for moving the research agenda forward. In a very meaningful sense, the teachers unions offer us a window into the world of education. And as scholars, we can take advantage of it in deepening our understanding of how that world works.

The Literature

Given the profound importance of education to nations and their citizens, and given the inevitable role of politics in shaping education systems in all their aspects, there ought to be a lively, well developed body of social science on the topic, exploring how the politics of education actually works and what its various determinants are. But political scientists have never shown much interest in studying these things. As Gift and Wibbels (2014: 292) recently observed

One could argue that no single policy domain lies more clearly at the heart of the key social, political, and economic dynamics of our age [...] In academia, the salience of education is reflected in booming research programs in economics and sociology [...] Political science, however, is oddly underrepresented among social science disciplines in the study of education. It is hard to identify a community of political scientists who are dedicated to the comparative study of education.

The vast literature on comparative politics has been animated by grander issues—the rise of the welfare state, the onset of retrenchment and austerity, the role of party systems and their left-right dynamics, the role of unions and businesses in shaping the "varieties of capitalism," and so on. Elementary and secondary education, as a specific realm of comparative political study, has largely been off the field's radar screen (but not entirely, of course—see, e.g., Ansell, 2010; Ansell and Lindvall, 2015 Busemeyer, 2009, 2014; Iversen and Stephens 2008; Klitgaard, 2007; Kosack, 2012; Stasavage, 2005; Wiborg, 2009). To the extent that education and its politics have been central to the comparative politics literature, the focus has been on vocational education, job training, and higher education (Busemeyer, 2014; Busemeyer and Trampusch, 2012; Dobbins and Busemeyer, 2014; Iversen and Stephens, 2008; Thelen, 2004).

In the field of American politics, political scientists have given education short shrift. Aside from rather small and sequestered literatures on the politics of urban education reform (Henig *et al.*, 2001; Stone *et al.*, 2001; Reckhow, 2012), No Child Left Behind (Manna, 2006; McGuinn, 2006; Rhodes, 2012), and governance (Henig, 2013; Manna and McGuinn, 2013), education has not been an integral part of the political science mainstream and has essentially been pushed to the periphery.

The other social science of obvious relevance here—the field of education research—has generated a voluminous body of work on education in general. But little of it deals with the actual policy process, elections, special interests, power, and other matters that explain how politics shapes public education (for an exception, see, e.g., Kirst and Wirt, 2009). When it does deal with politics, the analysis is often a mixture of empirical, normative, and aspirational components—focusing, for example, on issues of inequity, poverty, and social justice, and arguing that political leaders should do more to promote better social outcomes (e.g., Freire, 1996). There is a growing literature on globalization and neoliberalism that is very much in this vein, criticizing the apparent impacts of these forces on education systems and social equality and arguing, among other things, that the political power of business is behind them (e.g., Burbules and Torres, 2002; Zadja, 2015).

For the most part, however, the education literature is so focused on schools, students, and teachers, and it views the larger political system as so remote from the immediate subject matter of schooling, that the role of politics and power in shaping the education system hasn't been subjected to serious empirical examination. When education scholars look beyond schools to study matters of government, they tend to study "policy" and its impacts—much as labor economists do more generally. The focus is typically on whether policy X has impact Y, not on the politics—and power—that would explain why X was adopted and how it was implemented.

Across all these fields of study, two recent books deserve special mention as pioneering efforts to bring education into the political science mainstream. The first is Busemeyer's (2014) *Skills and Inequality*, which attempts to integrate education into the larger literature on the welfare state by showing that key lines of theoretical thinking central to that literature—arising from Esping-Anderson's three models of welfare capitalism and theories of partisan politics—help to explain why particular countries developed the distinctive systems of vocational and higher education that they did. The second is the edited volume by Jakobi *et al.* (2010), *Education in Political Science*, which is an explicit attempt to make education a more serious topic of research within political science, and uses a "governance" perspective to explore a broad and eclectic range of educational topics and issues, mostly related to higher education and international organizations. Neither book brings elementary and secondary education—the most fundamental and universal of all educational institutions across nations—to center stage. But both deserve high praise as agenda-setting moves to put education squarely on the political science map.

We also want to highlight a recent article by Ansell and Lindvall (2015), which brings quantitative evidence to bear on the historical evolution of primary education. This is an innovative analysis that is especially promising as a basis for future research. Ansell and Lindvall explore the political and societal factors—for example, control by social democratic parties, the presence of an established church—to explain why the emerging education systems of 19 of

Introduction

today's modern welfare states took on the institutional forms that they did, with attention to three key dimensions: centralization, secularization, and subsidies to private schools. This is the most analytically sophisticated study yet of the formative period of modern educational institutions, and a significant step forward in our understanding of why different nations took off on very different paths—and remain on different paths today.

Aside from these exemplary works, what does the broader literature on the comparative politics of education consist of, and how might it be characterized overall as a distinctive body of social science? A recent review by Busemeyer and Trampusch (2011, pp. 413–14) is helpful—and revealing (see also Gift and Wibbels, 2014). To date, this is the most comprehensive review of the literature available, and their theme is that the comparative politics of education is an exciting subfield on an upward trajectory. "The past twenty-five years," they say, "have seen an upsurge in political science work on issues such as the partisan politics of education reform, the comparative political economy of skill formation, institutional complementarities between education and the welfare state, and the internationalization of education."

We agree that there has been an upsurge of sorts. But what kind of literature has been generated in the process? From our own standpoint, their review is quite enlightening in providing perspective on this body of work; but one of the things it reveals along the way (although the authors do not argue as much) is that this is a very sparse, thin, and heterogeneous literature indeed—as our discussion above tends to suggest—to the point that it may not warrant being considered a genuine literature at all. Here are some of its basic features.

(1) Much of the work deals with higher education, not with elementary and secondary education. Yet it is the latter, not the former, that is by far the most relevant to all children and families throughout the world, is a far more fundamental function of governments everywhere, and is of far greater salience to public policy and politics—even more so in modern times, with the performance-based pressures of globalization and PISA tests. The comparative politics of education needs to deal, first and foremost, with the politics of elementary and secondary education. To this point it doesn't do that—and indeed, it often makes no distinction between the two types of systems in building its corpus of theory and research. These are *very* different systems with very different politics, and the literature needs to recognize as much. (See Jakobi *et al.*, 2010.)

(2) Much more central to the field of comparative politics is the study of "skill formation"—which involves the distinctive stakes and incentives of businesses, unions, and workers as major determinants of the "varieties of capitalism." But this line of work, important though it is to a larger understanding of the origins and structure of the welfare state, is about vocational education, on-the-job training, and other institutions of worker skill formation, not the politics of elementary and secondary

education (Busemeyer, 2014; Busemeyer and Trampusch, 2012; Dobbins and Busemeyer, 2014; Hall and Soskice, 2001; Iversen and Stephens, 2008; Thelen, 2004). Although these two realms tend to overlap, with vocational education often a part of upper secondary education, they are mostly very different realms indeed.

(3) Another line of political science research, unlike the others, has actually put the spotlight on elementary and secondary education—and, in particular, on the politics behind its expansion to the middle and lower classes, the levels of financial support that governments provide, and the implications for social equity. We've already discussed Ansell and Lindvall (2015). Another notable contribution is Kosack (2012), which focuses on three developing nations and provides an in-depth look at how their political dynamics play out in bringing primary education to the poor. Besides these works, there is a fair amount of research that takes spending as its dependent variable, and uses spending data to explore some of the themes arising from the larger literature on the welfare state—having to do, for example, with whether greater funding for education is particularly associated with parties of the left and democratization (Ansell, 2010; Stasavage, 2005). Exploring these issues is essential for understanding the politics of education. But the focus on spending is narrow, and it limits what this line of work can ultimately tell us.

Finally, we want to reiterate that an especially productive body of comparative research on the politics of elementary and secondary education has been carried out on countries in Latin America. This work, spearheaded by the pioneering research efforts of Murillo (1999, 2001) and Grindle (2004), tackles issues of power and special interest head on in explaining why education reform in those contexts is so difficult—pointing, above all, to the role of teachers unions in opposing government efforts to bring about change, and placing these conflicts in historical and political context. As a basis for understanding the politics of education and building a strong literature, these studies of Latin America are exceptional contributions; yet they are not included in Busemeyer and Trampusch's (2011) review of the literature.

We want to be clear that, in our view, Busemeyer and Trampusch are to be applauded for bringing together a vast number of diverse studies that deal (in some fashion) with the politics of education, and for trying to impose order and perspective on a very diverse collection of scholarly work. The problem lies with the literature itself, and with the fact that, at least for now, there really isn't a there there. No substantive focus. No theoretical coherence. Little or no connection between the various strands of research.

Obviously, these are deficiencies that cannot be eliminated right away. It will take time and a great deal of new research. Our purpose here is help move the ball forward—in substance, in theory, in focus—and in so doing, to take

Introduction

constructive steps toward a stronger, more coherent, more illuminating literature on the comparative politics of education.

Authors and Countries

Literatures are created by scholars. But they also attract scholars—who build upon one another's work, generate scholarly communities, and help ensure that, when new research agendas are pursued within their realms of inquiry, there will be many experts to draw upon. Without a real literature, however, none of this happens. And that is the situation we faced as we sought to make this book a reality. For any given country, we needed to find scholars who were knowledgeable about its politics of elementary and secondary education, the structure and operation of both its political system and its education system, and the role of the teachers unions. Yet political scientists rarely study education, and education researchers rarely study politics, so locating and recruiting scholars whose expertise covered the relevant terrain was a challenge.

It took a while, but this challenge was more than met, and we are very proud of the team we were able to assemble. All of our contributors have strong academic backgrounds, and all but one (who is a researcher at the World Bank) hold positions at universities. Beyond that, they are intellectually diverse, with backgrounds that range from political science to economics to sociology to education. They are an interdisciplinary group. They do not, therefore, come at this subject with a common set of preconceptions. Nor do they have a common rooting in a particular literature. What they have in common is that they are all professional researchers with extensive knowledge about the politics of education of specific countries, and about the political role of teachers unions in those countries.

Our plan in organizing this project was to focus mainly on the developed nations, and to include as well a smaller number of less-developed nations. We sought out experts accordingly, and the team we've assembled provides coverage of 11 nations in total, nine developed and two less-developed. The nine developed nations are the United States, England, Germany, France, Japan, and the Nordic countries—Sweden, Norway, Denmark, and Finland. The two less-developed nations are Mexico and India.

At this early stage of research, we think an initial focus on the developed nations makes good sense. These countries have long been central to theory and research in comparative politics, particularly the influential work on the welfare state, and little is known about how politics, power, and the teachers unions have shaped their education systems. As we begin to explore this new terrain, the large existing literature on these nations provides a helpful foundation for moving forward. The research we present here, in turn, contributes to that literature by filling in some yawning empirical gaps, speaking to important theoretical issues, and offering new findings and ideas.

The nine developed nations we study have much in common: they are prosperous, stable, and democratic, with modern administrative systems possessed of high capacity (relative to those of other nations) to deliver public services like education. As such, at least during the postwar era, they represent institutional contexts in which many of the fundamentals likely to shape the politics of education and the role of teachers unions are much the same, and thus are essentially controlled. The politics of education is free to play out on democratic terms, teachers are free to organize and take political action, education systems are bureaucratic and professional. *Within* these common contexts, however, the developed nations we explore are different in many ways that are potentially of great consequence—including, among other things, their specific governmental arrangements, their party systems, their political cultures, their historical trajectories, and more generally, their type of welfare-state regime: social democratic (the Nordic states), conservative-corporatist (Germany, France), and liberal (US, England). There is great diversity across these developed nations, and a key question is how—and whether—that diversity ultimately matters.

There is even more diversity, needless to say, when we include the two less-developed nations, Mexico and India. Their contexts not only lack the kinds of resources and well-functioning democratic and bureaucratic institutions of the developed nations, but are fraught with clientelism, patronage, and corruption—which are common problems in the less developed world. How do these stark differences show up in the politics of education and in the role that teachers unions play? And is it possible that, in at least some important ways, these nations actually turn out to look very similar to those that are far better developed?

This book is a first foray into a new and complicated realm of politics, and our aim here is not to proliferate variables, to disentangle all the relevant influences at work, or to explore all the theoretical avenues that might be of interest. We leave that for others in future work. Ours is an early attempt to get the lay of the land—and thus, above all else, to provide *basic information* that can help fill in some of the many unknowns. This is what each individual country-chapter is designed to do. As things now stand, not nearly enough is known—in terms of sheer facts—about the politics of education in the various nations across the world, and even less is known about the power and political activities of their teachers unions. These chapters go a long way toward changing that.

They also do much more. For when viewed together, they provide a very useful empirical basis for making comparisons, identifying patterns, and otherwise gaining perspective on basic features of education politics and the role of teachers unions across the world—and thus for pointing the way toward a larger understanding that goes well beyond the details of individual countries. This is a task—of summary, of interpretation, of comparative analysis—that is taken up in the book's final chapter. Again, our aim is not to revel in complexity or to move off in countless "relevant" directions. Nor is it to link every aspect of our analysis to every part of the comparative literature—the broader work on labor unions, say, or on industrial relations or political economy—that our studies might well have relevance for. These are surely worthwhile endeavors for the future. But for now, as we just begin to chart new territory and make sense of it, our approach is nearly the opposite. It is to simplify, to clarify, to establish some basic findings of comparative interest and theoretical value—and to strive for coherence and intellectual order in providing a foundation for future work on the comparative politics of education.

A Brief Summary of the Findings

Here is a brief sketch of the perspective that will be fleshed out in the final chapter, highlighting some of the key patterns and findings that arise from the country-chapters.

The Era of Institutional Formation

During the era of institutional formation, which saw the emergence, expansion, and institutionalization of public education systems as well as (in developed nations) the welfare state more generally, teachers unions arose in all the nations we've studied here—although the United States was very much a laggard, its unions failing to get organized until the 1960s and 1970s. Ultimately, teachers succeeded—everywhere—in overcoming their collective action problems to form organizations. Indeed, they attracted between 80 and 100 percent of teachers in most of Europe, Scandinavia, and Mexico, and somewhat lower but still high levels in the other nations.

In the early going, teachers unions in most nations were highly fragmented along various lines, reflecting school type (primary, secondary), religion, gender, ideology, region, and more. Over time, however, they became much more unified organizationally (except in India, where even today they remain highly fragmented). In a few countries—Finland, Mexico—this process of consolidation led to one monopoly teachers union, but in all the rest it did not. In some of the latter nations, one union represents elementary (and lower secondary) teachers and another represents (upper) secondary teachers, with the former almost always the more powerful and politically prominent. In the other nations, teachers are represented by two or more unions that are broadly based and compete for members—as is the case in the US, for example, with its National Education Association and American Federation of Teachers.

Once teachers unions got organized, they were able to wield a formidable array of political resources. They had mass memberships, they had money to fund political candidates and parties, they could mobilize voters, they could influence public opinion, and they could threaten strikes and other forms of disruption. With governments wanting peace and normalcy—and to win elections—the unions were thus positioned to exercise real political power in the realm of public education. This was the case everywhere. And in the exercise of that power, their behavior—uniformly, across all nations—focused largely on protecting and increasing the number of jobs, and on wages, benefits, transfers, promotions, working conditions, and other job-related issues. That is still true today. Most of what they do in politics can be explained by their members' vested interests in jobs.

In most countries, the teachers unions emerged and became politically active as their education systems were first becoming institutionalized, and they were essentially woven into the evolving institutional fabric of educational governance through various sorts of corporatist-like mechanisms. In the Nordic nations, the world's classic cases of corporatism, the unions were integrated along with other interest groups into decision structures designed to promote moderation and balance. In many other countries, corporatist-like inclusion of the teachers unions took place as well—yet it was not about balance at all, but rather about handing the unions extensive operational control over jobs and policy (but not wages). Only in the US, Japan, and India were the unions not ushered into government through insider corporatist status.

Politically, teachers unions were (and still are) usually allied with their nations' major left parties, which, during the institution-building era, either controlled the government or played influential roles in expanding the bureaucracy and constructing the welfare state. The unions were thus on the winning side as modern government was being created—and they were made integral to it. The left's center-right opponents, moreover, were not really opponents of the welfare state and not intent on undermining union power. Almost everywhere (Japan being the exception), this was a very good time for the teachers unions, when the politics and institutions of education worked very much to their advantage.

Throughout this early era, there were surely differences across nations in the politics of education and the role played by teachers unions. But what is most striking is that there was so much sameness across nations. As education systems emerged and developed, teachers unions acted on their vested interests to become organized, politically active, involved in government and policy making, and key shapers of their education systems. This happened in social democratic welfare states. It happened in corporatist-statist welfare states. It happened in liberal welfare states. It even happened in the less-developed nations. Details matter, of course. And differences matter. But there is extraordinary commonality here—driven by the power of vested interests that are present and profoundly consequential in every nation.

The Era of Performance-Based Reform

The modern era brought a radical shift in environment. In the late 1970s and 1980s, with the disruptive advance of globalization and technological innovation, together with the austerity, retrenchment, and restructuring associated with the "crisis of the welfare state," governments began demanding much higher levels of performance from their education systems. And they began pursuing institutional changes they hoped would bring it about. Broadly speaking, the approach to institutional reform—often labeled neoliberal—was much the same across nations: emphasizing some combination of decentralization, accountability, and school choice.

The teachers unions entered the modern era of performance-based reform as entrenched players in existing institutions, and the reforms now being pursued stood to undermine their traditional bases of power, their control over jobs and money, and the job security and working conditions of teachers. Major change was threatening to their vested interests. And in all countries, as a result, when governments pursued performance-based reforms of their education systems, teachers unions were opposed—and, indeed, were their main political adversaries.

To say as much is not to say that the unions were somehow the "bad guys" in these political sagas, as we take no position here on whether the neoliberal reforms in question were actually good ideas or socially advantageous. The key point about the unions is an objective one: they were major vested interests and, as we would expect on theoretical grounds, they were indeed threatened by institutional reform—and opposed to it. This imparted a distinctive and predictable *structure* to the modern politics of education in all countries.

These efforts at institutional reform played out very differently across nations, but here too there is a basic pattern to the results that makes good theoretical sense. And it is a pattern, interestingly enough, that has nothing to do with the regime types—social democratic, corporatist-statist, liberal—that have played such central roles in the comparative literature. The operative factor here is more generic: in any nation, regardless of regime type, the extent to which the political system puts formal *veto points* in the way of government action has a lot to do with the capacity of vested interests to block major reform. It is in political systems where governments are free from such constraints—thus empowering them to act, and reducing opportunities for vested interests to block—that real reform is most likely. In the developed nations covered in this book, the presence or absence of formal veto points is strongly related to whether governments were able to overcome the opposition of vested interests and bring about major reform to their education systems.

The stand-outs, by far, were England and Sweden. Although these are very different types of welfare states, government reformers in both were operating within a veto-free parliamentary system that fully empowered them to act. And in both—largely because Labour (in England) and the Social Democrats (in Sweden) moved toward the center to embrace neoliberal welfare-state reforms—successive governments proved committed to using that power over time to bring about major education reform. The result was profoundly transformative. Sweden moved from a centralized, corporatist, heavily bureaucratic system to one that is radically decentralized and makes extensive use of school choice. England moved from a system in which schools were controlled by local education authorities and local unions (often bound by a "social partnership") to one that subjects the locals to strict accountability requirements and removes huge numbers of schools (and kids) from their jurisdiction through an explosive expansion of school choice. In both countries, the teachers unions strongly resisted—and lost. Institutional change has left them (for the time being) weakened and marginalized, and the politics of education drastically different.

Norway and Denmark, also with one-house parliamentary systems, are in the process of transforming their education systems too—over the resistance of their unions—but it has taken them longer to do it by comparison to Sweden, and their reforms are so far less radical. The main reason is that, while their governments had the power to act, their leftist parties did not move to the center as quickly or as aggressively as Sweden's did, and for some time were more supportive of the unions in protecting traditional institutions. But the 2000s have seen the leftist parties become more centrist, and the pace of reform has picked up considerably. Here too, then, the teachers unions have been opposing reform all along—but after a modicum of success, they have been largely circumvented and weakened. There are signs in these nations, and in Sweden too, that the unions are beginning to re-establish their power by putting down political roots at the local level; but how successful that will be—absent the great advantages of centralization—remains to be seen.

Finland is like its Nordic cousins in having a one-house parliament, but its reform experience has been starkly different. Much as Sweden did, Finland took successful, aggressive action early on—under a conservative coalition government, against union resistance—to decentralize education, and the result was institutionally transformative. Yet unlike in Sweden, what the union most valued—the national bargaining arrangement for wages and benefits—was protected from those decentralizing reforms, and remained an important power base for the unions going forward. More generally, the corporatist decision structures that in Sweden had been weakened to circumvent union participation (and blocking), and that had also been temporarily weakened in Finland, were re-embraced over time by Finnish governments—which, from the mid-1990s until 2007, were broad multiparty coalitions that included both left and right, leading to a collaborative form of governance that allowed the unions to block any unwanted reforms.

What further distinguished Finland, however, was a unique and remarkable educational event. Quite out of the blue, the 2001 PISA tests of international student achievement revealed that Finland was the best of the best, a rock star among nations—convincing everyone, including the Finns, that their education system did not need reforming. Thus, during most of the 2000s, as other countries frantically sought to improve their schools, Finland was content with its status quo. The union had little to fight against, and its power remained substantial and intricately woven into the system. This unusual situation, however, is beginning to change. The 2012 PISA scores showed a marked decline in Finland's test scores (after a smaller decline in 2009), and political pressures are building for genuine reform. The union is suddenly playing defense.

Finland aside, then, the developed nations in our sample that do not put formal veto points in the way of government action—England, Sweden, Norway, Denmark—have been largely successful over time in overcoming union resistance and adopting major reforms of their education systems. The other developed countries in our sample—the United States, France, Germany, and Japan—all have political systems that put multiple veto points in the way of government action, and thus give vested interests ample opportunity to block. *In none of these countries did major education reform occur.* Indeed, their political systems actually leave them doubly disadvantaged when it comes to reform: for precisely because their multiple veto points make major change so difficult, their governments have reason *not even to attempt* the kind of transformative change that occurred in England and Sweden, but instead to scale back their efforts to incremental changes that at least stand a chance of being passed.

The US has made marginal progress in advancing school choice and accountability; but as of today, only 6 percent of students are in charter schools, No Child Left Behind has been eviscerated, and performance-based evaluations—while they have the look and sound of reform—have so far led, in practice, to almost every teacher being rated satisfactory. In France, governments have tried to decentralize their massive, centralized system many times, only to be defeated by union opposition and strikes. In Germany, governments went for many years doing next to nothing, and in the 2000s—thanks to PISA shock—managed to adopt some modest accountability reforms in the form of national standards and tests. In all three countries the basic structure of the school system remains the same as it was decades ago.

Among the multiple-veto nations, Japan is the outlier. But not because it achieved major change. It is an outlier because the Japanese Teachers Union (JTU) has literally been shut out of power and decisional involvement by the conservative LDP, which has basically held a monopoly on the control of Japanese government (with minor departures) since 1955. Teachers do have vested interests in their jobs; the JTU has been very organized and very active in protecting them; it has opposed neoliberal reforms when they have been pursued; and in the more distant past, it was reasonably successful (despite its outsider status) at using its powers of disruption to block changes it didn't like. That said, the main explanation for Japan's limited pursuit of neoliberal education reforms has less to do with the teachers unions than with the powerful national ministry of education—which has deep vested interests in maintaining its own central control, and has long stood in the way of major change.

And then, finally, there are the developing nations of Mexico and India. Both are desperately in need of far-reaching education reforms. Yet, unlike the developed nations, they are saddled with political systems mired in clientelism and corruption. To politicians and union leaders alike, education is an irresistible source of jobs, money, and power that enables rent-seekers to prosper—and in so doing, ensures that the existing education institutions, however unproductive, will be well protected in politics. The details have worked out differently in these two countries, but the themes are much the same. In Mexico, beginning in the late 1930s, a single monopoly union has wielded extraordinary political power—in elections, legislatures, and bureaucracies at both federal and state levels—to exercise considerable control over jobs and policy, and, indeed, over politicians. In India, the teachers unions are numerous and fragmented, but even so they are extremely active in electoral politics, they are heavily represented in state legislatures (indeed, they are constitutionally guaranteed at least 12 percent of the seats in state upper chambers), and they are engaged in corrupt connections with politicians in brokering job favors for members. In both nations, outrages abound. In Mexico, for example, teachers buy and sell their jobs or pass them on to their children. In India, some 25 percent of teachers don't even show up for work on any given day.

The prospects for these two countries are not bright. India faces many obstacles in the coming decades. The system is too fragmented, too unwieldy, too lubricated by the jobs and money that make rent-seeking so profitable and worth protecting. Mexico appears to have a better chance of making genuine gains, but it will not be easy. There are signs, with the election of President Pena Nieto in 2012—who, with the backing of a growing middle class and business sector, has taken on the monopoly teachers union and championed education reform—that Mexico may be on the verge of the kind of Progressive movement that restructured American government 100 years ago. The question is: can this nascent reform movement in Mexico succeed in overcoming the powerful vested interests that have governed that nation's education system for well over half a century?

Other developing nations around the world almost surely face the very same core challenge as Mexico and India. Yes, their citizens could benefit enormously if education could be thoroughly overhauled and improved. But their political and education systems are stacked against it. And most of the people in power do not want it.

The Road Ahead

In this book, we use the teachers unions as an opening wedge in advancing a larger scholarly agenda. As this summary can only suggest, the various chapters cover a great deal of ground and are highly informative about the histories, politics, unions, and institutions of individual countries. Even more important, when taken together they point to a whole that is much greater than the simple sum of its parts in what it conveys: not only about teachers unions, but also about the bigger picture of education politics worldwide—and about the key theoretical roles of vested interests and government veto points in shaping how that politics plays out in national contexts.

Given how little is currently known about the politics of education, this is a useful step forward. But it is only one step in what needs to be an ongoing process of study and exploration that goes well beyond what we are able to accomplish in this one book. Our hope is that the information and analysis we provide here will help to bring the study of politics—and power—to center stage in theory and research on education, activate the involvement of a much larger scholarly community, and serve as a foundation on which others can build.

References

Ansell, Ben W. 2010. *From the Ballot to the Blackboard: The Redistributive Political Economy of Education*. Cambridge University Press.

Ansell, Ben W., and Johannes Lindvall. 2015. The political origins of primary education systems: Ideology, institutions, and interdenominational conflict. *American Political Science Review* 107.3: 505–22.

Archer, Margaret S. 1979. *Social Origins of Educational Systems*. Routledge.

Blossing, Ulf, Gunn Imsen, and Lejf Moos, eds, 2014. *The Nordic Education Model: 'A School for All' Encounters Neo-Liberal Policy*. Springer.

Bruns, Barbara, and Javier Luque. 2014. *Great Teachers: How to Raise Student Learning in Latin America and the Caribbean*. World Bank Group.

Burbules, Nicholas C., and Carlos Alberto Torres, eds, 2002. *Globalization and Education: Critical Perspectives*. Routledge.

Busemeyer, Marius R. 2009. Social Democrats and the new partisan politics of public investment in education. *Journal of European Public Policy* 16.1: 107–26.

2014. *Skills and Inequality: Partisan Politics and the Political Economy of Education Reforms in Western Welfare States*. Cambridge University Press.

Busemeyer, Marius R., and Christine Trampusch. 2011. Review article: Comparative political science and the study of education. *British Journal of Political Science* 41.2: 413–43.

2012. *The Political Economy of Collective Skill Formation*. Oxford University Press.

Cooper. Bruce S. 1992. *Labor Relations in Education: An International Perspective*. Greenwood Press.

Cremin, Lawrence Arthur. 1961. *The Transformation of the School: Progressivism in American Education, 1876–1957*. Knopf.

Dobbins, Michael, and Marius R. Busemeyer. 2014. Socio-economic institutions, organized interests and partisan politics: The development of vocational education in Denmark and Sweden. *Socio-Economic Review* 13.2 (2015): 259–84.

Freire, Paulo. 1996. *Pedagogy of the Oppressed*. 2nd ed. Penguin.

Gift, Thomas, and Erik Wibbels. 2014. Reading, writing, and the regrettable status of education research in comparative politics. *Annual Review of Political Science* 17: 291–312.

Goldin, Claudia Dale, and Lawrence F. Katz. 2009. *The Race Between Education and Technology*. Harvard University Press.

Green, Andy. 2013. *Education and State Formation: Europe, East Asia, and the USA*. 2nd ed. Palgrave McMillan.

Grindle, Merilee S. 2004. *Despite the Odds: The Contentious Politics of Education Reform*. Princeton University Press.

Hall, Peter A., and David Soskice, eds, 2001. *Varieties of Capitalism: The Institutional Foundations of Comparative Advantage*. Oxford University Press.

Hanushek, Eric A., and Ludger Woessmann. 2015. *The Knowledge Capital of Nations: Education and the Economics of Growth*. MIT Press.

Henig, Jeffrey R., Richard C. Hula, Marion Orr, and Desiree S. Pedescleaux. 2001. *The Color of School Reform: Race, Politics, and the Challenge of Urban Education*. Princeton University Press.

Henig, Jeffrey R. 2013. *The End of Exceptionalism in American Education: The Changing Politics of School Reform*. Harvard Education Press.

Iversen, Torben, and John D. Stephens. 2008. Partisan politics, the welfare state, and three worlds of human capital formation. *Comparative Political Studies* 41.4–5: 600–37.

Jakobi, Anja P., Kersten Martens, and Klaus Dieter Wolf. 2010. *Education in Political Science: Discovering a Neglected Field*. Routledge.

Kirst, Michael W., and Frederick M. Wirt. 2009. *The Political Dynamics of American Education*. 4th ed. McCutchan.

Klitgaard, Michael Baggesen. 2007. Do welfare state regimes determine public sector reforms? Choice reforms in American, Swedish and German schools. *Scandinavian Political Studies* 30.4: 444–68.

Korpi, Walter. 2006. The Power Resources Model. In Christopher Pierson and Francis G. Castles, eds, *The Welfare State Reader*. Polity: 77–89.

Kosack, Stephen. 2012. *The Education of Nations: How the Political Organization of the Poor, Not Democracy, Led Governments to Invest in Mass Education*. Oxford University Press.

Lawn, Martin, ed., 1985. *The Politics of Teacher Unionism: International Perspectives*. Croom Helm.

Lowi, Theodore J. 1969. *The End of Liberalism: Ideology, Policy, and the Crisis of Public Authority*. Norton.

Manna, Paul. 2006. *School's In: Federalism and the National Education Agenda*. Georgetown University Press.

Manna, Paul, and Patrick J. McGuinn, eds, 2013. *Education Governance for the Twenty-First Century: Overcoming the Structural Barriers to School Reform*. Brookings Institution Press.

McConnell, Grant. 1966. *Private Power and American Democracy*. Knopf.

McGuinn, Patrick. 2006. *No Child Left Behind and the Transformation of Federal Education Policy*. University of Kansas Press.

Meyer, John W., Francisco O. Ramirez, and Yasemin Nuhoğlu Soysal. 1992. World Expansion of Mass Education, 1870–1980. In J. Meyer, *Sociology of Education* 65.2: 128–49.

Moe, Terry M. 2005. Power and political institutions. *Perspectives on Politics* 3.1: 215–33.

2011. *Special Interest: Teachers Unions and America's Public Schools*. Brookings Institution Press.

2015. Vested interests and political institutions. *Political Science Quarterly* 130.2: 277–318.
Murillo, Maria Victoria. 1999. Recovering political dynamics: Teachers' unions and the decentralization of education in Argentina and Mexico. *Journal of Interamerican Studies and World Affairs* 41.1: 31–57.
2001. *Labor Unions, Partisan Coalitions, and Market Reforms in Latin America*. Cambridge University Press.
Olson, Mancur. 1984. *The Rise and Decline of Nations: Economic Growth, Stagflation, and Social Rigidities*. Yale University Press.
Pierson, Paul. 2004. *Politics in Time: History, Institutions, and Social Analysis*. Princeton University Press.
2015. Power and Path Dependence. In James Mahoney and Kathleen Thelen, eds, *Advances in Comparative-Historical Analysis*. Cambridge University Press.
Reckhow, Sarah. 2012. *Follow the Money: How Foundation Dollars Change Public School Politics*. Oxford University Press.
Rhodes, Jesse. 2012. *An Education in Politics: The Origins and Evolution of No Child Left Behind*. Cornell University Press.
Stasavage, David. 2005. Democracy and education spending in Africa. *American Journal of Political Science* 49.2: 343–58.
Stone, Clarence N., Jeffrey R. Henig, Bryan D. Jones, and Carol Pierannunzi. 2001. *Building Civic Capacity: The Politics of Reforming Urban Schools. Studies in Government and Public Policy*. University Press of Kansas.
Thelen, Kathleen. 2004. *How Institutions Evolve: The Political Economy of Skills in Germany, Britain, the United States, and Japan*. Cambridge University Press.
Tyack, David B. 1974. *The One Best System: A History of American Urban Education*. Harvard University Press.
Wiborg, Susanne. 2009 *Education and Social Integration: Comprehensive Schooling in Europe*. Palgrave Macmillan.
2013. Neo-liberalism and universal state education: The cases of Denmark, Norway and Sweden 1980–2011. *Comparative Education* 49.4: 407–23.
Zadja, Joseph, ed. 2015. *Second International Handbook of Globalization, Education, and Policy Research*. Springer.

2

Teachers Unions in the United States
The Politics of Blocking

Terry M. Moe

The teachers unions are a powerful force in American education. They shape the public schools from the bottom up through collective bargaining, and shape them from the top down through their extensive involvement in state and national politics. In combining these bottom-up and top-down sources of power, and in combining them as potently as they do, the teachers unions are unique among all actors in the educational arena.

In this chapter, I will discuss the unions' historical rise to power, how they have exercised that power in collective bargaining and politics, and the constraining effects they have had on more than a quarter century of attempted reform. Throughout, I will take advantage of the theoretical framing set out in the Introduction, emphasizing the key importance of vested interests and institutional veto points, to offer perspective on why these developments have occurred as they have.[1]

The Formative Era of American Education—and the Late Rise of Union Power

The American public school system began to emerge in roughly its present form a little over 100 years ago, an outgrowth of the Progressive movement during the early 1900s to bureaucratize and professionalize American government at all levels. The national government was not the driving force behind this new education system. Under the Constitution, all responsibilities not specifically assigned to the federal government are reserved to the states—and public education is one of these. From the beginning, the American education system has been radically decentralized, with the states holding primary authority and

---

[1] For a much more extensive treatment of many of the issues covered in this chapter, see Moe (2011). On vested interests and their theoretical importance for understanding all political institutions, including those in education, see Moe (2015).

using it to set up local districts with much discretion to staff, organize, and operate the schools.

Teachers in this new system clearly had vested interests in their jobs, with strong incentives to get organized in protecting those interests. Yet throughout the school system's era of institutional formation and expansion—lasting roughly half a century—hardly any teachers got organized into unions, and there was no collective bargaining. In this respect, the United States was unique among Western nations, where teachers universally got organized into unions as their education systems developed. The prime reason for American exceptionalism is that in the US, collective bargaining for public sector workers—of all types, not just teachers—was typically prohibited by law and practice, and the political environment for the unionization of public workers was quite hostile.

During that formative era, the power-holders in public education were its administrative professionals, notably the local superintendents, as well as the local elected school boards that appointed them. Many teachers across the country belonged to the National Education Association (NEA), which was widely recognized as the most prominent organizational force in education. But the NEA was a professional association controlled by administrators, and it was avowedly *opposed* to unions and collective bargaining.[2]

Throughout this period of administrative hegemony, teachers had no organized means of pursuing their vested interests in jobs, and they were essentially powerless. It would be decades before the broader American labor movement and its political allies could bring about legal reforms that would pave the way for unionization, collective bargaining—and political power.

The watershed event for *private sector* workers came in 1935 with the adoption of the National Labor Relations Act (NLRA), a central component of President Franklin Roosevelt's New Deal. The NLRA was designed to make union organizing and collective bargaining much easier to achieve—through, for example, representation elections, exclusive representation, and the legal duty to bargain. The result was a massive surge in union membership, which in turn greatly enhanced the political power of private sector unions and gave the Democratic Party an invaluable core of organized political support.

As time went on, the Democrats and the beefed-up union movement combined forces to push for similar labor laws in the states for *public sector* workers—who had deliberately been excluded from the National Labor Relations Act. Beginning with Wisconsin in 1959, most of the states (outside the South) adopted public-sector labor laws during the 1960s and 1970s, and these legal changes fueled dramatic increases in public-sector union membership and collective bargaining (Freeman, 1986; Di Salvo, 2015; Moe, 2011).

They also triggered a transformation of the NEA, which, beginning in the early 1960s, found itself competing with the American Federation of Teachers

---

[2] On the history of the teachers unions' rise to power, see Moe (2011), chapter 2, from which this section's discussion is taken. See also Murphy (1990).

(AFT) to represent the nation's teachers. The AFT, although tiny at the time—with roughly 59,000 members in 1960 compared to about 750,000 for the NEA—was a union affiliated with the AFL-CIO; it had long-established locals in some of the country's biggest cities; and after its tumultuous 1962 strike in New York City, it initiated a national organizing drive. The NEA responded by turning itself into a teachers union. And with its huge advantage in members and geographic distribution, it soon became not only the biggest education union, but also the biggest union of *any* type in the entire country.

When the dust finally settled, the United States had two national teachers unions, each with its own state and local affiliates. And these affiliates had so carved up the educational terrain that, aided by the monopolizing effects of the states' collective bargaining laws (which required exclusive representation within each unionized district), there would be almost no turf competition between them going forward. An NEA district would stay an NEA district. An AFT district would stay an AFT district. The system quickly became stable and, outside the South, quite comprehensive.

Today, the NEA has somewhat more than three million members, while the AFT has about 1.5 million. These figures, especially for the AFT, include many members who are not classroom teachers: retirees, as well as secretaries, janitors, and other district employees who are not teachers at all. Also, the AFT is concentrated in big cities—places like New York City, Chicago, Boston—and some 30 percent of all its teacher-members appear to be located in the state of New York. The NEA, by comparison, organizes districts of all shapes and sizes throughout the country, and is representative of America's teachers in a way that the AFT is not. Even so, the AFT is a powerful force in many large cities, and its leaders, from Al Shanker to Randi Weingarten, have been key figures at the center of America's education debates (Moe, 2011).

The trajectory of change was stunning. The percentage of teachers covered by collective bargaining soared from near zero in 1960 to 65 percent in 1978—the southern and border states being the main exceptions—and the system settled into a steady state. Bargaining coverage stood at 65 percent in 1993, 64 percent in 2000, 65 percent in 2004, and 63 percent in 2008 (Moe, 2011). It appears to have fallen a few percentage points in the years since, but precise coverage data are as yet unavailable. Throughout the modern era, union membership levels have consistently been much higher, above 75 percent and stable for decades (Moe, 2011). They also seem to have declined a few percentage points in recent years. In part, these recent declines in both membership and coverage appear to be due to restrictive new labor legislation in a few states, notably Wisconsin and Michigan, controlled by an increasingly conservative Republican Party. The declines may also reflect a shift in US population to southern and border states, where unions are weaker.[3]

---

[3] The figures cited in the text are from the US Department of Education's Schools and Staffing Survey (SASS). For reasons I discuss in Moe (2011), this survey provides much better measures

The bigger picture is that, by the early 1980s, the teachers unions reigned supreme as the most powerful force in American education and its politics, with millions of members, far-flung armies of political activists, enormous wealth for campaign contributions and lobbying, and more. The rise of union power, in turn, transformed the world of American public education, creating what amounted to a new education system: one that has been in equilibrium now for roughly 30 years and is vigorously protected by the very union power that created it. In many ways, this new system looks very much like the original system of school boards, superintendents, and local democracy installed by Progressive reformers a century ago. But what the Progressives envisioned was a system run by professionals, not a system of union power that promotes the vested job interests of employees. This is a modern development, one that makes the modern system qualitatively different from the one it replaced.

Along with this transformation came a great historical irony. The most influential call to reform in the annals of American education—*A Nation at Risk*, the report of a presidential commission—burst onto the scene in 1983, warning of a "rising tide of mediocrity" in the nation's schools and setting off a frenzy of reform from coast to coast. This marked the beginning of the modern era of performance-based education reform in the United States. Yet here is the irony: *A Nation at Risk* came along just as the teachers unions were consolidating their power. From the very beginning of the modern reform era, then, the proponents of change were up against a powerful new foe—whose vested interests in jobs led them to resist major reform, and whose access to American government's multiple veto points gave them ample means to do it quite successfully.

Collective Bargaining and the Organization of Schools

In the politics of education, the great power wielders are the NEA and the AFT, along with their state affiliates. In California, for example, the state affiliate of the NEA is the California Teachers Association, and the state affiliate of the AFT is the California Federation of Teachers. Both are active in California politics and elections. Much the same can be said for every other state—except that the AFT, being more regionally concentrated and more centered in large cities, does not have affiliates in all 50 states. The NEA does.

---

than the Current Population Survey, whose figures for membership and coverage are consistently lower. The latter are available at www.unionstats.com. At the time of this writing, the most recent SASS figures are for 2011–12. I want to thank Eunice Han and Michael Hartney for providing me with breakdowns of these data. The coverage figures provided by SASS for 2008–09 and 2011–12 are flawed, and too low, because of confusing changes in the question wording on the survey (see Moe, 2011). I have corrected the 2008–09 figures, but do not have a correction for 2011–12.

These national and state union organizations are political powerhouses, extensively involved in elections and policy making processes throughout the country. But the primordial fact is that teachers join the *local* (school district) affiliates of these higher level unions, and it is the *local unions* that attract the members, the money, and the activists on which all higher level union power depends.

The ability of the local unions to attract these resources is aided immensely by collective bargaining, the bread-and-butter of all teachers unions, which is conducted within the local school districts. Survey data show that collective bargaining is what teachers care about most as union members (Moe, 2011). It is what ties them securely to their unions. Were it not for collective bargaining and its protected legal status, the national and state unions would not be nearly as *politically* powerful as they are, and not nearly as successful in resisting the forces for education reform unleashed by *A Nation at Risk*.

Collective bargaining is also profoundly important for another reason. Through local negotiations, the unions use their power to shape "working conditions" by pushing for forms of organization that benefit their members. There is no guarantee, however, that these forms of organization will actually promote more effective schooling. Indeed, there are straightforward theoretical grounds for expecting that, at least sometimes, they may undermine it. The teachers unions, after all, are special interest groups. They seek to protect teachers' jobs, increase their wages and benefits, expand their rights, and restrict managerial discretion. And in collective bargaining, they quite naturally pursue these job interests by trying to win restrictive contract rules that specify how the school districts must operate, spend their money, and allocate their resources. These rules then prescribe the organization of schooling—whether or not they are conducive to high levels of performance (Moe, 2011; Hess and West, 2006).

As collective bargaining has played out over several decades and many thousands of school districts, the teachers unions have heavily shaped the organization of America's schools. Here are a few examples of common contract provisions.[4]

(1) *Salary rules* that pay teachers on a formal schedule based on seniority and formal credits—thus ensuring that good and bad teachers are paid the same and that salary cannot be used as an incentive for productive behavior.

(2) *Transfer rules* that give senior teachers their choice of available jobs—thus making it impossible for districts to place teachers where they are

---

[4] For a more extensive discussion of these and other contract rules, see chapter 6 of Moe (2011). Note that the unions sometimes are able to use their political power to get their favored rules embedded in state law – which, for them, is much more effective than fighting for such provisions district by district.

needed most (by putting the best teachers in the most disadvantaged schools, for example).
(3) *Layoff rules* that require staffing reductions in reverse order of seniority—ensuring that excellent young teachers will automatically be let go, while low-performing teachers with lots of seniority will automatically be kept on.
(4) *Evaluation rules* that set out onerous procedures to be followed—for monitoring, reporting, mentoring, etc.—if a teacher is rated as unsatisfactory, thus giving principals strong incentives to rate all teachers as satisfactory even when their performance is inadequate. The best evidence is that 99 percent of the nation's teachers have traditionally received satisfactory ratings (see, e.g., Weisberg et al., 2009).[5]
(5) *Dismissal rules* that, together with evaluation rules and state tenure laws, spell out additional onerous procedures to be followed if a teacher is to be dismissed—thus making it virtually impossible to dismiss anyone. Studies suggest that it takes roughly two years and more than $200,000 just to dismiss one poorly performing teacher, and that it almost never happens.[6]

This book is about power and politics, and it is not an effort to explore school performance or its organizational determinants. The point to be made here is simply that these and many other union-favored contract rules are clearly not adopted because they are considered the best possible means of building effective organizations. They are adopted for other, job-related reasons. The schools, as a result, are literally *not designed* for effective performance—whatever that might require. There is a disconnect between what the public schools are supposed to do and how they are actually organized to do it, and this disconnect is a built-in feature of the modern American school system, a reflection of its underlying structure of power and vested interests.[7]

Local Governments as Weak Bargainers
The fragmented system of collective bargaining in American education is somewhat unusual by comparison to the way "wage bargaining" is handled in other

---

[5] As I will discuss later, this remains true despite new laws in many states requiring rigorous, performance-based evaluations.
[6] See, e.g., the detailed research of journalist Scott Reeder, covering an 18-year period in the state of Illinois. Available on his website at www.thehiddencostsoftenure.com
[7] There is a fair-sized quantitative literature that explores the causal impacts of collective bargaining on student achievement, but such studies are difficult to carry out for methodological reasons. The literature, most of it dated and of uneven quality, not surprisingly arrives at mixed conclusions. For an assessment of this literature, see Moe (2011). The studies that, in my view, are the most credible on methodological grounds tend to find that collective bargaining has a negative effect on student outcomes. See Hoxby (1996); Lovenheim and Willen (2015); Moe (2009); and Strunk (2011). For an exception, see Lovenheim (2009). More research is clearly needed for confident conclusions.

developed nations. In most of Europe and Scandinavia, teacher wage bargaining has traditionally been conducted at higher levels of government, often as part of much larger labor agreements covering many public occupations at once—arrangements that tend to encourage broader societal perspectives, trade-offs, and moderation, and give the teachers unions little scope for targeted influence. The US is at the other end of the continuum. Each local teachers union hammers out its own labor contract with its own school district, with incentives to push for all it can get, unconstrained by other occupational groups or larger societal concerns—leading to thousands upon thousands of distinctly different labor contracts, filled with various permutations of rules that shape the organization of schooling.

The US system would not be so problematic if, as is often the case in Europe and Scandinavia, the power of government were brought to bear in promoting broader social and educational interests. But that is precisely what American governments are unlikely to do—because, as I'll discuss in Chapter 10, they are weak by comparison to (most) parliamentary governments, and American politicians are far more open to parochial, special-interest influences. This is true at all levels of American government, including school districts.

The school districts are weak bargainers in their collective negotiations with the teachers unions. The prime reason is that the districts are governed by elected school boards, whose members must win local elections in which the teachers unions are typically the most organized, active, and powerful forces—knowing they are in a position to choose the very people they will be bargaining with. As a result, many board members are union allies. Others are reliably sympathetic. And the rest have reason to fear that, if they cross the unions, their jobs are at stake (Moe, 2005, 2006, 2011; Strunk and Grissom, 2010).

The districts are weak bargainers for other reasons as well. One is that the unions can unleash sanctions if dissatisfied, and no district wants a fight, a sick-out, or—much worse—a strike (which can occur even where strikes are illegal, because unions and their members are rarely prosecuted in practice). Another is that most work rules don't cost the districts anything in direct outlays, making it financially easy for them to make work-rule concessions, and thus concessions on organizational form. And another is that, as near-monopolies with a lock on kids and money, the districts have historically had little incentive—until recently—to insist on effective organization.

Over the last decade, districts have had their spines stiffened a bit. Accountability reforms—while still weak, as we will see—have put them under pressure to raise achievement; charter schools have proliferated (in some cities) to offer families exit options; and both have strengthened district incentives to fight restrictive union rules. The financial crisis that began in 2008, moreover, forced districts to be more confrontational with unions over money and organization—although with an improved economy, that source of pressure has diminished somewhat.

When districts have fought for effective organization, it has almost always occurred in cities where mayors control the schools. Mayoral control is not common, but where it has occurred it is potential trouble for unions. Mayors have more diverse constituencies than school board members do, have more resources for wielding power, and are more accountable for results. An "education mayor" can be a force for reform in a way that school boards rarely are (see, e.g., Viteritti, 2009).

The highest profile cases of districts fighting hard for effective organization have come in the mayor-controlled systems of New York City and Washington, DC. In both, the mayors were committed to major reform, and they appointed school chancellors—Joel Klein in New York City, Michelle Rhee in DC—willing to launch all-out assaults on restrictive work rules in the face of fierce union resistance. And they won major victories—especially far-reaching in Rhee's case—on seniority, performance pay, and teacher evaluations (Moe, 2011).

These victories were remarkable precisely because they were so unusual. They also took many years of agonizing struggle, were enormously expensive, and left many reform issues unaddressed. The Rhee and Klein experiences testify to how difficult it is, even when all the ducks are in a row, to make even partial progress in bringing new forms of organization to the schools. Their victories, moreover, were (and are) inherently vulnerable—because reformist mayors ultimately leave office.

In Washington DC, Mayor Adrian Fenty lost his 2010 re-election bid, Michelle Rhee quickly resigned, and the schools were soon in the hands of Vincent Gray, the union-supported candidate. Gray, surprisingly, did not torpedo Rhee's labor contract; indeed, he appointed her deputy, Kaya Henderson, as the new schools chief, and the two of them implemented the contract in a kinder, gentler way. In 2014, Gray himself was defeated by Muriel Bowser—who, since taking office in 2015, has continued to embrace reform. The continuity—and the unexpected behavior of Gray, in particular—is probably due to two factors. One, the reforms have clearly been working: scores from the National Assessment of Educational Progress (the nation's "report card") show that DC has recently been a star performer compared to other urban districts—which has bolstered political support for continued reform (Rich, 2013, 2015). Two, the local teachers union is the weakest urban teachers union in the country (outside New Orleans), largely because more than 40 percent of that district's children are in charter schools, and the union has suffered a dramatic drop in membership and money (Moe, 2011).

In New York City, the reforms achieved by Mayor Bloomberg and Joel Klein didn't fare nearly as well as Rhee's. After three terms in office, Bloomberg was succeeded in 2014 by Bill de Blasio, a staunch ally of the United Federation of Teachers (UFT)—perhaps the nation's most powerful local teachers union. Like the UFT, he was an ardent opponent of charter schools and accountability. He quickly appointed a very traditional, establishment-oriented school chancellor who shared his anti-reformist views, and soon all the reforms Bloomberg had worked to achieve during his 12 long years in office were on the chopping block. His accountability reforms and their reliance on data and rigorous assessments were essentially abandoned. The new mayor also targeted charter schools, his first move being a denial of physical space for some of Eva Moskowitz's high-achieving Success Academies. But Moskowitz and her allies fought back, to the point of orchestrating demonstrations in the state capital. With support from Governor Cuomo and a large, enthusiastic constituency of charter school supporters, Moskowitz was able to save her schools (see, e.g., Taylor, 2015).

There is a political lesson here. Accountability reforms are especially vulnerable to reversal because they create no vested interests that will protect them from attack. Charter school reforms *do* create vested interests—the schools and their parents—and those vested interests will fight back to try to prevent opponents from undoing the reforms.[8] The larger reality for any reform—whatever the realm of public policy—is that, once the reform is adopted, its political enemies don't just go away, but rather continue to look for opportunities to reinstate the status quo ante.

In addition to New York City and Washington DC, there are a few other districts where unusual changes are under way. One is Cleveland, where Democratic Mayor Frank Jackson partnered with a Republican state government to bring changes to that city's schools: basing layoffs and pay on performance rather than seniority, weakening tenure by allowing ineffective teachers to be dismissed, and allowing more funding for charter schools. Another is New Haven, where a thin contract has been adopted. But the reality in these and other places, once again, is that mayors come and go, leaving reforms vulnerable to reversal over time.

And finally, there is New Orleans, which is the exception that proves the rule. New Orleans is home to the most radically different school system in the entire country. More than 90 percent of students are in charter schools, all children choose the schools they attend, and test scores have risen dramatically. But all of this came about for a special reason. The city's traditional school system—corrupt, bureaucratic, and an abysmal performer long-resistant to change—was destroyed by Hurricane Katrina in 2005, as were the local teachers union (because all the district's teachers were let go) and the local school board (which had no schools to control). With the local power structure wiped out, state and local leaders then had virtually a free hand to truly transform the education system as they rebuilt it—and they did, creating a full-blown charter system that would never have had a political chance in any other school district in the nation, due to the power of vested interests that is invariably stacked against such a radical innovation.

What New Orleans shows, above all else, is the scope and magnitude of education reform that is possible *when the power of vested interests is*

---

[8] More generally, on the durability of reforms and the role of vested interests in their protection, see Patashnik (2008) and Moe (2015).

removed from the equation. Everywhere else in the United States, "reform" takes place in contexts where the power of vested interests is very much present. This is unavoidable, but its universal presence tends to guarantee that "reform," if it happens at all, will be highly constrained by power—and thus incremental, and orders of magnitude less than what happened in New Orleans. In effect, Katrina created a natural experiment, allowing us to see what reform can look like when there is no (or very little) vested interest power to resist it—a phenomenon that, under normal circumstances, we never get to see (Moe, 2011).

As we look across all the other American cities, then, we are wise not to interpret the various signs of change in those systems as monumental transformations. Yes, reformers are making gains here and there. But the big picture is that the teachers unions remain powerful, motivated by job interests, and opposed to major reform. Almost all change, everywhere, has been incremental, and has left the basic structure of the existing system intact.

The Politics of Blocking

Let's turn now to the politics of education at higher levels of government. By law, America's public schools are governed mainly by the states. From the late 1800s until the mid-1900s, the states allowed most schooling to be locally controlled through local school districts. But in the years since, mainly in response to court-ordered funding equalization and pressures to improve the schools, the states have reasserted some of their authority. Whatever the balance, school districts are ultimately state creations, and all of their essential features—their boundaries, organizations, funding, programs, collective bargaining—are subject to state authority. Any group that hopes to wield power over the public schools, therefore, needs to wield power in state politics. This is where the real action is (e.g., Kirst and Wirt, 2009; McGuinn and Manna, 2013).

The national government has also gotten more involved since mid-century. Its main vehicle has been the 1965 Elementary and Secondary Education Act (ESEA), which authorizes a variety of programs—particularly for disadvantaged children—and funnels billions of dollars through states to districts. In 2001 the feds moved aggressively into the reform era with No Child Left Behind (NCLB), a ground-breaking revision of ESEA that sought to create a nationwide system of school accountability. Still, the states continue to reign as the key authorities in public education.

For the teachers unions, politics can be enormously advantageous but also enormously threatening. Higher level governments can adopt virtually any work rules, education programs, or funding arrangements they want for the public schools, and the decisions automatically apply to all districts and schools in their jurisdictions. When the unions wield decisive power, all these advantages can be theirs. But reformers can do the same: by pushing for accountability, school choice, pay for performance, and other reforms the unions find threatening—and turning them into law. Either way, the stakes are huge. So for the unions, getting involved in politics is essential, and they have invested heavily in political organization.

For well over a quarter century, the NEA and the AFT have been the most powerful groups in the politics of education.[9] No other groups have even been in the same ballpark. Since the unions first got established, they have had millions of members (today, over four million). They have had astounding sums of money coming in regularly (mainly from dues) for campaign contributions and lobbying. They have had well-educated activists manning the electoral trenches—ringing doorbells, making phone calls. They have been able to orchestrate well-financed media campaigns on any topic or candidate. And their organizations have blanketed the nation, allowing them to coordinate all these resources toward their political ends.

Most aspects of the union power formula are difficult to quantify. But good information is available on their campaign contributions, and they consistently rank among the very top contributors—compared to other interest groups *of all types*—at the national level and in virtually all of the states. They dwarf other education groups. In ballot-measure campaigns, moreover, they are consistently the top contributors on their side of the issue, even on matters of taxation and spending that have nothing directly to do with education.[10]

Superior power does not mean that the teachers unions always get the policies they want. The nation's multiple veto points ensure that shepherding new laws through the political process is extremely difficult, because victories must be won at every step along the way to overcome all the hurdles. The flip side is that *blocking* new laws is much easier, because opponents need to succeed at just *one* veto point to win. American governments are designed to make defending the status quo far easier than taking positive action (Tsebelis, 2002; Baumgartner et al., 2009). And this is how the teachers unions have used their political power in shaping the nation's schools: not by imposing the policies they want, but by blocking or weakening those they don't want—most importantly, major reforms of the system.

Throughout, they have relied on their alliance with the Democrats, America's left party (although it is more centrist than many European left parties).

---

[9] See Moe (2011). There are two notable literatures on education politics, but neither sheds much light on the teachers unions or their power. One literature centers on "No Child Left Behind," whose national-level politics are simply not representative of the broader—mainly state and local—politics that shape American education generally. See, e.g., McGuinn (2006) and Rhodes (2012). The second is concerned with urban education reform, and derives much of its theoretical orientation from the concepts of "civic capacity" and "regimes." See, e.g., Stone et al., (2001) and Henig et al. (1999). For discussion of these literatures, see Moe (2015).

[10] The 2010 Citizens United decision by the Supreme Court blew the lid off of "independent" political spending and made this money difficult to track. The data on contributions directly to candidates and parties, however, shows teachers unions to be in the very top tier of group contributors. See Moe (2011), chapter 9. See also the Center for Responsive Politics, at www.opensecrets.org, for national spending figures; and the National Institute on Money in State Politics, at www.followthemoney.org, for state spending figures.

Democratic candidates receive almost all of the unions' campaign contributions, their electoral manpower, and their public relations support. These are resources of enormous political value. In return, the unions can usually count on the Democrats to go to bat for them in the policy process: by insisting on job protections, bigger budgets, higher salaries and benefits, restrictive work rules, and other union-favored objectives—and above all, by opposing efforts to bring major reform. The teachers unions have been the raw power behind the politics of blocking. The Democrats have done the blocking (Moe, 2011).

The Reform Movement

The movement to reform America's schools was initiated by the publication of *A Nation at Risk* in the early 1980s. The timing was no accident, because forces were then being unleashed all around the world—associated with globalization, international competition, and the "crisis of the welfare state"— that launched a tumultuous new era of performance-based education reform affecting a great many countries. *A Nation at Risk* was an explicitly American reaction to these same international forces, arguing that education reform was desperately needed because "Our once unchallenged preeminence in commerce, industry, science, and technological innovation is being overtaken by competitors throughout the world" (National Commission on Excellence in Education, 1983, p. 113).

The report proved to be a bombshell, generating nationwide reform efforts that, within the first decade or so, coalesced into two distinctly neoliberal movements for institutional change: the movement for school accountability and the movement for school choice. Before discussing how their politics have played over time, however, I want to address an issue that looms large in much that has been written on education reform, and is best dealt with explicitly and up front: the role of corporate political power in advancing a neoliberal agenda for education.

From the time of *A Nation at Risk*, business groups like the Chamber of Commerce and the Business Roundtable (and their state affiliates) have clearly been concerned about the country's international competitiveness, have pointed to its lagging public school system as a threat to human capital and economic growth, and called for significant improvements. For these and related reasons, representatives of the business community at both the state and the national levels have been important supporters of American education reform.

Yet the true role of "business" is easily misconstrued. The business sector is astoundingly fragmented by industry, geography, and many other factors; and as research on American interest groups has long demonstrated, business is represented by hundreds of specialized groups—a constellation that makes a mockery of any notion that the "business community" is organized for unified action in pursuit of common interests (e.g., Schlozman, 2010). In education, moreover, the material interests of business firms are quite indirect—and they pale by comparison to the deep vested interests that teacher unions and school districts have in the existing education system. The typical owner of a business firm is not staying up at night worrying about education reform. And general business organizations like the Chamber of Commerce—which care about countless dimensions of economic policy, and have very diverse memberships—are typically unwilling to invest heavily in education reform at the expense of everything else they need to do (Moe, 2011).

Any notion that America's business community is foisting a neoliberal agenda on the nation's public schools, then, is wide of the mark. The fact is, the key reformers coming out of the business sector are typically *individuals* who simply have *personal* reasons for wanting to bring about education reform, and who have nothing material to gain. They may want to help disadvantaged kids, for example, or to provide the nation with better schools. Although they are especially well-heeled, they are classic political activists who seek to promote what they see as the public good. The best examples are business leaders turned philanthropists—people like Bill Gates, Eli Broad, John Walton, and Walter Annenberg—who have used their money and foundations to promote education reform. Over the years, they or people like them have bankrolled much of the education reform movement (Reckhow, 2012).

These moneyed activists have often supported neoliberal reforms that involve major doses of accountability and choice. They have done so not to make money off them, but because they—like many other reformers around the world—genuinely think these lines of reform are the ones most likely to work. They may be wrong about that. And their own thinking about the most productive paths to reform may well be influenced by their business backgrounds. But whatever the case may be, they are not acting on behalf of some orchestrated corporate drive to impose a neoliberal agenda. They are individual do-gooders, acting on their own, trying to bring improvement to what they see as a mediocre system.

If the theme in understanding the role of "business" is one of fragmentation and diversity, the same is true—in spades—of education reformers more generally. In the US, the reform side of the political equation is populated by activists, organizations, and interest groups of every imaginable sort—representing (depending on the time and place) minorities, the disadvantaged, churches, parents, conservatives, youthful subversives (from Teach for America, notably), rebellious Democrats (such as Democrats for Education Reform), think tanks, homeschoolers, and many more. This is a movement with no organizational core. No one is in charge. And most certainly, "business" is not in charge. There are just lots of reformers, typically with nothing material to gain—and they generate lots of activity, usually with little or no coordination, in states and districts all over the country.[11]

---

[11] Although it is not the norm, some reformers do have material interests at stake. For example, churches would benefit from vouchers and tax credits, which would bring money to church-run

USA: The Politics of Blocking

In the American context, then, the politics of education reform has a distinctive structure. On the reform side, there is nothing like a united neoliberal army. There is instead a vibrant, diverse, uncoordinated, often chaotic population of activists and interest groups, and they push for change wherever they might be able to get it. On the other side are the opponents of reform. They are far better organized and funded. They have a powerful leader—the teachers unions—with deep vested interests in the institutional status quo, and a political reach that extends to all decision venues at all levels. And because the American political system is filled with veto points, they have enormous advantages in blocking or weakening what the reformist legions are trying to pull off.

This imbalance has been true from the beginning. And although the reformers have gained some ground in recent years—as I'll discuss—imbalance remains the fundamental reality of education politics in the US today. Bringing institutional change to American education is a long, hard slog, with results that are at best incremental. The teachers unions and their allies simply hold most of the cards, playing a political game that is stacked in their favor.

Mainstream Reforms

How, then, did reform unfold in the wake of *A Nation at Risk*? During the 1980s, as the movement got under way, the key drivers were business groups and state governors. Business groups, as we just discussed, saw the moribund education system as a serious impediment to growth and productivity in an era of growing international competition, and they called for political action. They found allies in the nation's governors—who, as executives with broad political constituencies, were far less susceptible to vested-interest pressures than legislators, far more responsible for the economic well-being of their states, and eager to take on leading roles in improving their schools.

In the early going, the reform ideas that gained traction were essentially just common sense, the obvious things to do. They were also decidedly incremental: spending more money, raising teacher salaries, adopting more rigorous curricula, training teachers better, and other mainstream reforms that fit comfortably within the existing system—and posed little or no threat to the teachers unions. Indeed, the unions saw the new reform environment as an opportunity to push for spending and salary objectives they had long yearned to advance anyway (e.g., Toch, 1991).

These reforms did nothing to change the structure of the system or its incentives. National spending shot up by 74 percent between the 1982–83 and 1989–90 school years, providing schools with 35 percent more money per student in real dollars. Yet the money would be spent by the same districts

---

schools. And charter schools have vested interests in charter programs and the funding attached to them. But for the most part, the reform movement is made up of activists with nothing material to gain.

that had spent money so unproductively in the past, and their incentives were as weak as ever. Teacher salaries were raised substantially across the board, increasing 52 percent during this same period, for a gain of 17 percent in real dollars. Yet good and bad teachers were still paid the same, and no one was being held accountable for student learning.

This was a turbulent time, and much bolder ideas—for school choice, pay for performance, and more—were finding their way into policy debates. But precisely because these reforms were threatening to the traditional structure of jobs, the unions used their power (with the help of allies) to derail them. The level of reform activity triggered by *A Nation at Risk* was unprecedented. But it was an inside-the-box affair, stifled by the politics of blocking.

As the 1980s came to an end, these early efforts had clearly failed, and the talk among reformers turned to fundamental change (e.g., O'Day and Smith, 1993; Toch, 1991). Support surged for two major movements that soon amassed political power of their own: the choice movement and the accountability movement. Even so, states continued to invest heavily in mainstream reforms. Indeed, the reforms they pursued during the 1990s and into the 2000s were mostly the *same* kinds of reforms they pursued during the 1980s—more spending, stricter requirements, more training—all with great fanfare, as though this time their recycled efforts would pay off (Hess, 2010; Tyack and Cuban, 1995).

A number of "new" mainstream reforms gained traction along the way. Of these the most popular was class size reduction, heavily promoted by President Clinton via his effort to fund 100,000 new teachers for the public schools. It was also aggressively pursued in certain states, notably California, which was the pioneer in 1996; and Florida, where a 2002 ballot measure required drastic reductions in class size. The teachers unions were strongly supportive, for teachers like the reduced workload, and it could only be implemented by hiring lots more of them, thus increasing union membership and power. But like the other mainstream reforms, class size reduction has proved a disappointment. It leaves teacher quality and incentives the same, and there is no evidence that it brings improvements in student learning beyond the first few years of school. Worse, it is among the most expensive of all possible reforms (Hanushek, 2003).

What is the problem here? Why, over the last quarter century, have the states invested so heavily in reforms that offer so little promise? The answer is that, in addition to having a superficial appeal that makes them an easy sell, these reforms are not threatening to the teachers unions, nor to their usual allies like the school districts—and the unions don't use their power to block. The political gates are swung open, and governments are allowed to take action in ways that fit comfortably with the status quo.

From the standpoint of politics and power, then, mainstream reforms are all pluses and no minuses. The only downside is that they don't work (Hanushek, 2003).

School Accountability

To reformers, the ideas behind accountability have obvious merit. If the school system is to promote academic excellence, it must have clear standards defining what students need to know. It must test students to measure how well the standards are being met. And it must hold educators accountable for results—and give them incentives to do their best—by attaching consequences to outcomes. Writ large, these are the principles of effective management that business leaders live by every day: setting goals, measuring performance, attaching consequences, creating incentives. Applying these same principles to the public schools—however, more concretely, that might best be done—is not an ideological matter, as most reformers see it, and not part of a larger neoliberal agenda. It is simply what needs to be done in any large organization, school districts included, to enable effective operation.

As the 1980s drew to a disappointing close, accountability offered a path to fundamental change. And because it was essentially a demand for effective management that business leaders, governors, and the public could readily understand, it attracted broad support. The teachers unions, however, saw it very differently. Historically, teachers had been granted autonomy behind classroom doors, and their pay and jobs had been secure regardless of how much their students learned. Genuine accountability meant that they would have new requirements thrust upon them, their performance seriously evaluated, consequences attached to their performance, and their jobs made less secure. These were radical departures from a performance-is-irrelevant past—and the unions were opposed (Moe, 2003).

They weren't alone. They had allies among many superintendents and school boards, who saw it as a threat to their local autonomy; among (some) civil rights groups, concerned that testing could lead to high failure rates for minority kids; among certain experts, who claimed that tests are flawed and culturally biased; and among certain Republican policy makers, who wanted to protect local control (Hess, 2003; Moe, 2011).

Yet this wasn't much of a coalition. Some superintendents eventually came to *support* accountability, because it gave them leverage for improving their schools. Key groups speaking for disadvantaged kids—Education Trust, for example—emerged as strong supporters of accountability as a means of improving urban education. Opinion surveys consistently showed that most parents and citizens supported accountability as well. Most experts believed that test scores could be put to valid, reliable use. And many Republicans—even those resistant to *national* accountability efforts—came to believe that, through state and local action, educators need to be held accountable.[12]

---

[12] Most scholarly accounts overly emphasize Republican resistance to accountability. This is because these studies focus on NCLB and its attempt to nationalize accountability, rather than on accountability more generally and its state-level politics. See Moe (2011, 2015). See also Hess (2003).

In addition, the various members of the anti-accountability coalition have long been grossly unequal in terms of numbers, organization, money, and political clout. Except when it comes to national v. state accountability (which mobilizes Republican policy makers), the teachers unions really *are* the coalition. Without them, the whole thing would collapse in a heap, and the opposition to accountability (at the state level) would lack sufficient power to stand in the way of true reform (Moe, 2011; Williams, 2006).

From the beginning, the unions could have drawn a line in the sand. Yet because this reform was so broadly popular, they opted for a more sophisticated strategy: to publicly support the *idea* of accountability, but to participate in the design of actual accountability programs with the aim of watering them down. This was their approach throughout the 1990s, when many states actually adopted some (usually weak) form of accountability. And it continued during the 2000s in the wake of No Child Left Behind.

A key part of the union strategy has been the embrace of stronger curriculum standards—which, in themselves, are not threatening to teachers. It is the testing and the consequences for poor performance that the unions have sought to weaken and render ineffectual.[13]

The science of testing is the most sophisticated component of the academic field of education. The unions' concern is that tests provide concrete evidence on the performance of teachers, not just of students. If tests show that kids aren't learning, the publicity will inevitably bring public complaints, pressures to improve, and consequences. A rigorous testing system, moreover, would quickly reveal that some teachers are much better than others and that some are very bad. Indeed, that is precisely what the research literature does reveal (Hanushek and Rivkin, 2006). Were such information routinely available, there would be objective grounds for removing bad teachers from classrooms. There would be objective grounds for giving better teachers higher pay. Accountability would begin to have real teeth.

The unions, accordingly, have long acted to prevent test scores from being put to serious use in evaluating teachers.[14] In New York City, for example, Joel Klein sought in 2008 to improve teacher quality by bringing student scores to bear—along with much other relevant information—in evaluating teachers for tenure. The United Federation of Teachers reacted by playing its trump card: getting its allies in the state legislature to enact a new law prohibiting any

---

[13] Note that, in recent years, the NEA and AFT were publicly supportive of Common Core national standards, but turned against them when—as tests were developed and put to use in evaluating teacher performance—they became threatening to teachers.

[14] Recently, under intense pressure—and sometimes in response to money (in Race to the Top, as well as in landing big philanthropic grants for their districts)—the unions have indicated a willingness to consider at least some role for test scores in evaluating teachers. But these are strategic concessions, not an indication that the unions are truly embracing this line of reform. Their underlying opposition remains the same. And as time goes on, they can be expected to try to minimize the role that test scores are allowed to play. See Moe (2011), chapter 8 and chapter 10.

district in New York from using test scores in tenure evaluations. The information was available, but the unions had made it illegal to take the information into account.

The New York case highlights the data challenge that the unions are up against nationwide. The rise of information technology has dramatically enhanced the ability of state governments to collect data on students, schools, teachers, finances, and other aspects of the education system; to store this information in "data warehouses"; and to employ it in better managing their schools. Reformers believe that nothing could be more basic to school improvement than good information. Yet the unions see good information as a threat—because it gives states and districts the capacity to link the evaluation, pay, and job security of teachers to student performance (Moe and Chubb, 2009).

In legislatures around the country—Texas, Colorado, California, and elsewhere—they fought these data battles over and over again during the 2000s. They pressured policy makers not to authorize teacher identifiers that can be linked to student identifiers in state data systems. And if they lost on that score, they pushed for laws that (as in New York) simply prohibited the linked data from being used in the evaluation or compensation of teachers. For many years, they were quite successful. Until Race to the Top intervened in 2009–10 to induce states to take down their "firewalls," only 18 states had data systems that were even capable of connecting teacher data to student data. Now these data systems are much more widespread, but the unions continue to use their political power to prevent them from being used. In California, for example, the data firewall was taken down so that the state could compete for Race to the Top—but since then, the state's Democratic government has defunded the teacher portion of the data system, thus defeating its use as an evaluation tool.

The unions' ultimate goal, however, is not to eliminate data or testing per se. It is to ensure that there are *no negative consequences* for teachers—so that no one loses a job, no one's pay suffers, and no schools are shut down or reconstituted due to poor performance. Unions attack test scores and data systems because they provide the evidentiary basis for such negative consequences. But it is the negative consequences that are truly threatening.

The unions have been quite successful at blocking these consequences. Until very recently, even the most basic reforms went nowhere. It would have been simple, for example, for states to relax their tenure laws so that low-performing teachers could be removed from the classroom. But for years this obvious reform was rarely even considered. An exception occurred in Georgia, when Democratic Governor Roy Barnes eliminated tenure for incoming teachers in 2000. But he was quickly reminded of why other politicians around the country hadn't done that: the state teachers union targeted him in the 2002 elections—and was widely credited with his defeat.

The story isn't much different for performance-based evaluations, performance-based pay, the reconstitution of failing schools, and other reforms that would put teeth into accountability. For the greater part of 20 years, as accountability systems were being adopted in state after state—and then nationally via NCLB—the specific reforms promising to make accountability real were not adopted. The politics of blocking saw to it that the states would have accountability systems that were literally *not designed to hold anyone accountable.*

The unions' blocking power is not uniform across the states. They tend to be weaker in the South, for instance, and that is why some of the pioneering accountability efforts have come from states like Texas, North Carolina, Kentucky, and Florida. Union power also tends to be weaker at the national level than at the state level, because national politicians have larger, more diverse constituencies, and the unions have more competition from other groups.

It was due to the unions' national-level disadvantage, plus the fact that the political stars happened to line up just right for reformers—with Republican President George W. Bush leading the way (and local-control Republicans temporarily following him), with key Democrats on board (in part, out of concern that Republicans might become the "education party"), and with key advocates for the disadvantaged on board as well—that the teachers unions lost control of the politics of No Child Left Behind. With the enactment of this legislation, the unions suffered their biggest defeat of the entire reform era (McGuinn, 2006; Rhodes, 2012).

The adoption of No Child Left Behind was a watershed event, initiating a radical shift in the federal government's role in public education. It required all states to test students annually in math and reading, with the goal of getting 100 percent of students to proficiency by 2014; to disaggregate scores by social subgroups (ethnicity, poverty, and more) so that no child would be left behind; to evaluate schools based on "adequate yearly progress" for all subgroups; and to subject failing schools to consequences intended to turn them around. In so doing, NCLB imposed a uniform regime of accountability on America's schools for the first time—seeking to significantly improve the quality of education, especially for disadvantaged students.

Yet NCLB's vision was not to be realized. A big reason is that the act itself was weak from the outset. Some of this weakness was due to technical problems that needed to be corrected. It measured the schools' "adequate yearly progress," for example, in a way that didn't provide valid assessments of their true performance; and as a result, a fair number were classified—very publicly—as failing when they really weren't. But the act was also weak by design, because the teachers unions and their allies won important concessions during the legislative process that watered it down. Most important, they succeeded in making it almost devoid of enforceable consequences. The major remedies for egregiously low-performing schools—reconstitution, for example, or conversion to charter schools—contained enough loopholes to ensure that they would rarely be carried out. And for teachers, there were really no consequences at all.

Indeed, the act did not even try to measure their success at getting kids to learn (Hess and Finn, 2007; Hoxby, 2005; Resnick, 2011; Williams, 2007).

These built-in weaknesses were just the beginning of NCLB's saga of turmoil. The unions pivoted from their loss in Congress to launch a years-long campaign to destroy it. The NEA went to court to try to have it declared illegal. Both the NEA and the AFT, meantime, relentlessly railed in the media against "over testing" to convince Americans that NCLB was bad policy (a strategy much aided by NCLB's very real flaws), and they put intense pressure on Democrats to overturn it. Their ace in the hole, however, was that Republicans—normally their arch-enemies—were jumping ship for their own reasons. In 2001, many had violated local control in order to support their president's signature legislation. But as the years passed, and with the Tea Party brewing, they increasingly closed ranks against what they called "federal overreach"—thus powerfully aiding the unions' cause.

As the years passed, Democrats and Republicans in Congress both heaped criticisms on NCLB, but there was no consensus on precisely what should replace it. The result was gridlock. NCLB was supposed to come up for reauthorization, and thus to be revisited and reassessed, in 2007. But 2007 came and went, and NCLB lived on for another eight agonizing years—unpopular and flawed, but encased in legislative concrete.

President Obama, who was legally responsible for the act's implementation, reacted to its flaws and political opposition by choosing not to fully enforce its provisions. Instead, in 2012 he began granting the states waivers, using criteria that encouraged them to pursue certain reforms—among them, performance-based evaluations of teachers and Common Core national standards—that were favored by his administration *but not actually part of NCLB at all*. Throughout most of Obama's second term in office, as a result, the nation's accountability policy was being made through presidential discretion, not through Congressional legislation. Republicans were irate at his ramped-up exercise in "federal overreach." The unions were irate at the content of his reforms (see, e.g., Strauss, 2014).

When the Republicans took control of Congress after the 2014 elections, the destruction of NCLB became a priority. A de facto alliance between the Republicans and the teachers unions, whose power brought along many Democrats, quickly led in December 2015 to passage of the Every Student Succeeds Act (ESSA). Under the new law, students would still be tested annually and the results made public. But the essentials of accountability—what the academic standards would be, how performance would be measured, how schools would be evaluated, what consequences would be imposed on those that were failing—would now be entirely in the hands of state and local governments. The federal government, moreover, was specifically prohibited from promoting national academic standards or requiring that the states evaluate the performance of teachers.

As is par for the course, the ESSA was heralded in Congress with much lofty language about the wonders of local control. According to the act's key architect, Republican Senator Lamar Alexander, the ESSA "will unleash a flood of excitement and innovation and student achievement that we haven't seen in a long time. But it will come community by community, state by state, rather than through Washington, D.C." (Huetteman, 2015).

Reality argues otherwise. In the 1980s, the federal government took on the challenge of improving America's schools precisely because so many state and local governments had done a poor job of running their own education systems. It is no coincidence, moreover, that the key vested interests in public education—the teachers unions and the school districts—are much stronger at the state and local levels, where they are embedded in the institutional woodwork and have enormous political clout, than they are at the national level. Shifting all authority to the state and local governments, then, is a guarantee that school accountability in the years ahead will prove to be weak and ineffective.

In the grander scheme of things, NCLB's death spiral should come as no surprise. NCLB had its problems, to be sure—but they were fixable. Its real problem was political. For its adoption did nothing to weaken or dislodge the powerful defenders of the status quo ante, who simply regrouped and marshaled their troops to destroy it. And it did nothing to create *new* vested interests with a stake in supporting the new accountability regime and battling the onslaughts of opponents. If there was a surprise—a bad one for reformers—it was that the Republicans who helped enact the original legislation took a sharp turn to the right in later years, creating a bizarre coalition in which the teachers unions gained the support of their eternal Republican foes to bring NCLB down (Moe, 2015; Patashnik, 2008).

A workable, uniform, well designed system of accountability for America's public schools never really had a chance.

School Choice

Accountability is a reformist effort to make the traditional top-down system of schooling work more effectively through better management. School choice is very different and potentially more transformative. In its most developed form, it aims to move away from top-down government control in favor of a radically decentralized system of largely autonomous schools among which families would choose.

To its supporters, choice has obvious advantages. Most important, it allows parents to leave bad schools: an empowerment especially valuable to poor and minority children, who are often trapped in the nation's worst schools. Choice also shapes incentives. The public schools have traditionally had their kids and money guaranteed, regardless of how well they perform—but with choice, the guarantees evaporate. If schools don't do their jobs, they stand to lose children and resources. There are consequences for ineffective behavior, giving schools stronger incentives to perform and innovate (Chubb and Moe, 1990).

Choice was first proposed in the 1950s by economist Milton Friedman, who advocated vouchers and envisioned a free market in education. Yet the modern American choice movement, which picked up steam around 1990 (when accountability did), is not mainly driven by an ideology of free markets. Libertarians are supportive, of course. But most proponents recognize that unfettered choice can generate problems—of equal access, parent information, transportation, accountability—and that government needs to address these problems by setting up appropriate rules to shape and guide how a choice system would operate (Moe, 2008).

To the teachers unions, choice is very threatening. When families are given new options, the regular public schools lose children and money. And jobs. Indeed, were choice widely adopted, it could trigger a plunge in union membership, resources, and power; and many teachers could find their work lives and career paths disrupted. So the unions do not want families to have alternatives to the schools where their members teach. This is true even if the children are desperately poor and trapped in chronically bad schools.

The teachers unions are the nation's leading opponents of choice. But they also have allies. The school districts oppose choice because they want to protect their own enrollments, money, and control. The NAACP has long seen choice as a veiled opportunity for whites to flee blacks; it also wants to protect jobs, because urban school systems are a prime source of minority jobs and upward mobility. The American Civil Liberties Union and the People for the American Way see vouchers for private schools (many of them religious) as a breach in the "wall of separation" between church and state. Liberals tend to be supportive of government, suspicious of markets, and worried that the poor cannot make good choices. And Democrat officials—who do the actual blocking—tend to be liberal in belief and electorally dependent on the unions.

The choice movement has long been weaker than its opponents. Unlike the accountability movement, moreover, it has never benefited from broad business support. A few wealthy individuals (like the late John Walton) have been major contributors, but most business leaders have seen education reform as a management problem—which is not surprising, perhaps, because management is what they do for a living, and it is how they view problems of ineffective organization. Throughout the 1980s, as a result, the choice movement was fueled by conservative activists, churches, private schools, parent groups, and the like: an enthusiastic lot, but hardly the kind of power base necessary to take on the unions and other choice opponents. To have any hope, the movement needed to broaden its constituency (Hill and Jochim, 2009; Moe, 2001; Morken and Formicola, 1999).

It did that by taking a left-hand turn from its libertarian roots. The signal event came in 1990, when minority parents in inner city Milwaukee rose up to demand vouchers as a means of escaping their abysmal public schools. With pivotal support from Wisconsin's Republican governor, Tommy Thompson, they won a surprising victory—a small pilot program—over strident union opposition. Since 1990, choice advocates have largely focused on poor, minority, and other disadvantaged students (for example, those with learning and physical disabilities), usually in urban areas. The modern arguments for vouchers have less to do with free markets than with social equality, and opinion polls have consistently shown that its greatest supporters are black and Hispanic parents (e.g., Howell et al., 2009; Moe, 2001).

Voucher supporters have eked out occasional victories despite all-out union opposition. The Milwaukee program has been vastly expanded, and there are now many other voucher programs as well—almost all of them small, some just recently adopted—for low-income children in Cleveland, Washington, DC, Ohio, Louisiana, Indiana, and Racine (WI). There are also voucher programs for special needs children in Florida, Ohio, Utah, Georgia, Ohio, Oklahoma, and Louisiana. There are voucher-like programs that, through tax credits and nonprofit foundations, provide scholarships for low-income children (Florida, Arizona, Indiana, Iowa, Pennsylvania, and Rhode Island), for special needs kids (Arizona and North Carolina), and children generally (Arizona, Georgia, Louisiana, Illinois, Iowa, and Minnesota). And there are "education savings accounts" that allow parents to use government money to pay for a variety of educational options, including private school tuition, in such states as Arizona and Nevada (Friedman Foundation, 2015).

Yet the battles never end, because the unions want all voucher and tax credit programs eliminated. When Utah passed a voucher bill in 2007, the unions overturned it by putting it on the ballot and spending heavily to defeat it. They attacked the Milwaukee and Cleveland programs for years in the courts—leading to the landmark Zelman decision in 2002, which ruled, in a union loss, that including religious schools in a voucher program is constitutional. They have gotten the courts to invalidate some of these programs—in Colorado and Florida, for example—and created legal uncertainty for many others. When the Democrats gained control of Congress and the presidency in 2009, they took swift action to kill the Washington, DC, voucher program for disadvantaged kids—which supporters were able to reinstate in 2011 as part of a high-stakes budget deal. And these are just a few highlights.

The voucher programs left standing are impressive victories over a powerful opposition. Even so, they are hardly transformative. Of roughly 55 million elementary and secondary students in the United States (public and private), only 300,000–400,000 are receiving vouchers or tax-credit scholarships. This is a drop in the bucket. And most enrollments are due to just a few (relatively) large programs: the Milwaukee voucher program (26,056), the Florida McKay scholarship program for special education kids (28,957), the Arizona tax credit program (25,720), the Florida tax credit program (69,671), and the Pennsylvania tax credit program (38,278) (Friedman Foundation, 2015). Nationwide, vouchers and tax credits today provide little choice, little competition for public schools, and few new incentives. The bottom line is that the teachers unions have been extremely successful at preventing these reform efforts from altering the educational status quo.

The idea of vouchers and tax credits is an old one. The other seminal idea for expanding choice came along much later—again, around 1990. This was the idea of charter schools: public schools of choice that would operate independently of district control and most state regulations. For many policy makers, especially Democrats, charters offered a politically attractive middle ground. With charters they could support *public sector* choice for disadvantaged (and other) families—thus responding to demands for new options—yet they could also appease the unions by opposing vouchers, and also by burying charters in union-favored restrictions. The unions, for their part, preferred charters to vouchers because charters were potentially easier to control through politics. But the threat was much the same: charters allow kids to leave the regular public schools, taking money and jobs with them.[15]

The unions put up intense opposition, but they failed to stem the tide completely. In 1991 Minnesota adopted the first charter law (authorizing just eight schools statewide), followed by California in 1992 (with a ceiling of just 100 charters in a state with some 7,000 regular public schools). By 2003, 40 states (including Washington, DC) had adopted charter legislation. As the dominoes were falling all across the nation, charters became America's most widely accepted approach to school choice. They grew increasingly popular with parents and students, especially in urban areas with underperforming public schools. They spawned some stunningly effective schools for disadvantaged kids—most famously, the KIPP schools (which now number 162 nationwide). They gained considerable positive attention in the media and were featured in widely seen films (such as *Waiting for Superman*). They attracted support from prominent Democrats—including, during the 1990s, President Bill Clinton and Vice President Al Gore. And in recent years, President Barack Obama and his secretary of education, Arne Duncan, made charter reform a key part of their Race to the Top.

These are important developments. Yet throughout this time, the teachers unions fought to keep charters weak, and their Democratic allies talked a better game of charter "support" than they actually played. The result was "reform" legislation high on symbolism and weak on substance. Among the usual restrictions: low ceilings on the number of charters allowed statewide, lower per-pupil funding than the regular public schools (by an average of 23 percent), districts as the sole chartering authorities (because they have incentives to refuse), no charter access to district buildings, and no seed money to fund initial organization. The result is that almost all charter systems have

---

[15] On the politics of charters, see Moe (2011). For other accounts, see Finn *et al.* (2001); Morken and Formicola (1999); and Vergari (2007).

been designed, quite purposely, to provide families with very little choice and the public schools with very little competition (Hill, 2006).

Once these programs are in place, moreover, the unions try to weaken them further. One line of attack is through public relations: they regularly generate claims, reports, and studies attacking charter performance and aiming to shrink their popularity. Another line of attack is through the courts, where the unions have taken action—in New York, New Jersey, Minnesota, Ohio, and elsewhere—to argue that charter schools violate state constitutions.

In certain cities, the situation has gotten away from them, and charters have made impressive gains. In New Orleans, charters now enrol more than 90 percent of students—but this, as I have discussed, is due to the unique effects of Katrina. The charter "market share" is also quite high, however, in Washington, DC (44 percent), Detroit (53 percent), Kansas City (41 percent), Philadelphia (33 percent), Cleveland (30 percent), and a number of other urban districts, where they are clearly offering families many new choices and creating meaningful competition for the regular public schools (National Alliance for Public Charter Schools, 2015).

Reformers have been far less successful in the rest of the country. Eight states do not even have charter laws. And in those that do, there are very few charter schools and only small percentages of kids attend them. Here are some "charter states" and their enrollments: Connecticut (1.3 percent), Iowa (0.1 percent), Kansas (0.5 percent), Maine (0.2 percent), Virginia (0 percent), Oklahoma (2.0 percent), Missouri (2.1 percent), and Tennessee (1.6 percent). Nationwide, *after a quarter century of reformist effort*, there are only 6,000-plus charter schools in a population of more than 95,000 public schools, and they enroll only 6 percent of the nation's public school children.[16]

Tiny enrollments are no indication of the underlying demand. Charters often have long waiting lists of children eager to get in. In Harlem, for instance, charter schools are enormously popular, enrolling nearly 25 percent of local public school kids; but many more are clamoring to get in and can't, because there aren't nearly enough charters to take them. In the spring of 2010, some 14,000 Harlem children submitted applications for just 2,700 open slots, and more than 11,000 were turned away (Brill, 2010). Nationwide, an estimated 920,000 children are on waiting lists, hoping to get into schools that do not have room to take them.[17]

With 42 states now having adopted charter laws, it is natural to think that charters must be making great progress almost everywhere. But this is far from the truth. Most charter laws are filled with restrictions designed to limit the

---

[16] The figures are for 2012–13, the most recent available nationwide, taken from the "dashboard" data compiled by the National Alliance for Public Charter Schools, available at: www.dashboard.publiccharters.org/dashboard/home

[17] As of 2013–14, from data in Table 216.90 of the *Digest of Education Statistics* 2015, National Center for Education Statistics.

spread of charters and keep enrollments down. The real winner here is not the charter movement or the many American families seeking new alternatives for their kids. The real winner is the politics of blocking.

Recent Developments

In recent years, the teachers unions have been on the defensive like never before: blamed for obstructing reform, defending bad teachers, and undermining effective organization. Reformers are gaining strength. The unions seem to be getting weaker. What is going on?

Part of the story is that, with the onset of the Great Recession, the states were plunged into financial crisis—leading to teacher layoffs, drops in union membership and finances, and thus a partial erosion of the unions' power base. Yet these effects were temporary. The economy is improving, and the unions are benefiting from that.

The unions face a more serious threat from the growing assertiveness of conservatives. Republicans now control more than half of state governments, and they have taken aim at unions and collective bargaining. Wisconsin's Act 10, passed in 2011, drastically limited collective bargaining for teachers and imposed right to work (meaning, nonmembers cannot be required to pay "fair share" fees in support of the union), thus undercutting the incentives for membership—which has plummeted. In 2013 right to work legislation was passed in Michigan, traditionally a heavily unionized state, leading to significant drops in membership there as well. Similar Republican attempts are under way elsewhere. Indeed, a conservative Supreme Court very nearly ruled in 2016, in Friedrichs v. California Teachers Association, that "fair share" fees for unions are unconstitutional, which would have imposed right to work on public sector unions in all states—leading, almost surely, to future drops in union membership, money, and political power (Semuels, 2016). The death of conservative Justice Antonin Scalia, however, left the court evenly divided at 4–4 and unable to make a decision. The unions had dodged a bullet.

The impact of this conservative opposition should not be exaggerated. Most Republican governments are unlikely to pass major anti-labor legislation, because they fear massive political blowback from still-powerful unions. Republican control of state governments, moreover, will surely recede in the years ahead (it is now at its historical peak), and Democrats and unions will have opportunities to reverse their losses (although checks and balances will put Republicans in a position to block.) If the Supreme Court imposes right to work, however, the unions will move into the future with *permanently* lower levels of membership, money, and power—a potentially big handicap for them.

The teachers unions, moreover, are not just threatened by conservatives. They are also threatened by a loss of support among Democrats and liberals. With many urban schools under-performing, with accountability laying bare these miserable outcomes, and with school choice offering attractive options, advocacy groups for the disadvantaged have become major supporters of institutional change—and overtly critical of the teachers unions for obstructing it. Moderate and liberal opinion leaders—writing in *Time*, the *Washington Post*, and other respected outlets—regularly excoriate the unions for putting job interests ahead of children. A new group (formed in 2007), the Democrats for Education Reform, has attracted a bevy of high-profile Democrats and is taking forceful action in elections, legislatures, and the media to combat the teachers unions (Brill, 2011).

Energizing this new movement is a growing network of progressive activists, who are increasingly occupying influential positions in politics and education—and are openly critical of the unions. The most vibrant source of this activism is Teach for America, whose alumni have immersed themselves in the cause of educational change. Working side by side with these activists are deep-pocketed philanthropic foundations—Gates, Broad, Walton—that have poured big money into reforms the unions have long opposed (Hess and Henig, 2015; Reckhow, 2012).

This ferment hasn't converted most Democratic officeholders, who remain union allies. Yet during the 2008 presidential primaries, one Democratic candidate did *not* toe the union line; and that candidate, Barack Obama, managed to become president. Once in office, he and his secretary of education, Arne Duncan, proved to be reformers—producing (among other things) the 2009–10 Race to the Top (RTT), in which states competed for shares of $4.35 billion by embracing, or saying they would embrace, system-challenging reforms such as performance-based evaluations and pay, charter schools, and state data systems. Whether the results have substance remains to be seen, and they continue to be fiercely resisted in politics and on the ground. But the sheer level of RTT-induced reform has been striking (Moe, 2011; National Council on Teacher Quality, 2014).

Performance-based evaluations have since become the centerpiece of the nation's reform agenda. As of 2015, 43 states have required that teachers be evaluated with some reference to objective measures of student achievement, and 35 have required that student achievement be a significant, or the most significant, factor (National Council on Teacher Quality, 2015). Part and parcel of these reforms is a weakening (potentially) of teacher tenure, as senior teachers who repeatedly fail to measure up are made subject to dismissal. In some states, moreover—Florida is one of them—new teachers are put on renewable contracts, and tenure protections are no longer in place. Tenure is also under attack in the courts, with the most spectacular reformist victory occurring in the 2014 Vergara case in California, where a lower state court declared that the state's tenure and seniority laws are unconstitutional.

These are stunning advances, and many reformers see them as evidence that a major transformation is coming soon. But almost all these victories are still on paper (as new laws) or temporary (like the Vergara decision, which was later overturned) and remain to be fully translated into action. As new laws are implemented, moreover, the devil is in the details—which will be worked out over a period of many years, usually through collaboration with unions intent on using their power in politics and collective bargaining to water the new policies down. Experience to date reveals that, despite the rigorous new criteria for evaluating teachers, and despite the potential for dismissing poorly performing senior teachers, almost all teachers are still getting satisfactory evaluations and almost no one is being dismissed for poor performance (Anderson, 2013; Sawchuk, 2013).

The Democrats' enthusiasm for change, moreover, only goes so far. The reason is that even reformist Democrats, from Obama and Duncan on down, have made it clear that they believe in unions and collective bargaining, and they have no intention of taking action to limit collective bargaining or weaken their power. They are serious about improving the nation's schools, but they intend to do it collaboratively, and thus within an education system filled with powerful unions that must somehow be accommodated and made "part of the solution."[18] This intention is strongly reinforced by a brute political fact: the power of the Democratic Party itself is highly dependent on the power of the unions, which provide extremely valuable electoral support for the party. And the continuation of collective bargaining is absolutely essential to union power. These are fundamentals, then, that almost no Democrat is willing to touch. Like Obama, they might well want to encourage reform, but they aren't going to upset their own applecart to do it.

Conclusion

Much has happened since *A Nation at Risk* first ushered the United States into the modern era of performance-based reform. But if we step back from it all, what do we see? We see a nation with a vibrant, enthusiastic, exceedingly active reform movement intent on bringing about major change and improvement to the public schools. And we see an education system that is heavily protected from reform by powerful vested interests—the teachers unions most prominent among them.

This sort of tension—between reformers who seek institutional change and the vested interests that resist it—is natural and universal. It happens in all political systems in all realms of public policy (Moe, 2015). But especially in the United States, with its proliferation of veto points, it is a tension whose resolution is stacked in favor of the vested interests and against those who seek change. That the teachers unions have been so successful for so long is not surprising. They are endowed with multiple sources of genuine power—millions of members, massive financial resources, large contingents of political activists,

---

[18] For a detailed discussion of this Democratic belief in "reform unionism," see Moe (2011), chapters 8 and 10.

expert lobbying operations—and they operate in a political system that works to their great advantage.

Conservative attacks, combined with the ferment among (some) Democrats, liberals, and moderates, have given reformers considerably more political clout in recent years. But the teachers unions remain genuinely powerful and the great likelihood in the near future is that America's reformers will continue to face stiff union opposition, and they will continue to settle for small victories—in the form of more serious evaluations of teachers, say, or more data, or more charter schools—that don't come close to transforming the system.

As I have written elsewhere, there are exogenous, Katrina-like forces at work as well—due to the worldwide revolution in information technology—that may have transformative impacts on American education over the longer term (Moe, 2011; Moe and Chubb, 2009). But any such breakthroughs will probably happen very slowly over the decades. For the foreseeable future, the reality is that the United States will probably continue to have an education system that fails to meet the nation's expectations: a system that reformers are frenetically trying to change—but that is well protected by the teachers unions.

References

Anderson, Jenny. 2013. Curious grade for teachers: Nearly all pass. *New York Times* (March 30).
Baumgartner, Frank R., Jeffrey M. Berry, Marie Hojnacki, David C. Kimball, and Beth L. Leech. 2009. *Lobbying and Policy Change: Who Wins, Who Loses, and Why*. University of Chicago Press.
Brill, Steven. 2010. Teachers unions' last stand. *New York Times Sunday Magazine* (May 17).
— 2011. *Class Conflict: Inside the Fight to Fix America's Schools*. New York: Simon and Schuster.
Chubb, John E., and Terry M. Moe. 1990. *Politics, Markets, and America's Schools*. Washington, DC: Brookings Institution.
Di Salvo, Daniel. 2015. *Government Against Itself: Public Sector Unions and American Democracy*. New York: Oxford University Press.
Finn, Chester E., Bruno V. Manno, and Gregg Vanourek. 2001. *Charter Schools in Action*. Princeton University Press.
Freeman, Richard B. 1986. Unionism comes to the public sector. *Journal of Economic Literature* 24.1 (March): 41–86.
Friedman Foundation. 2015. *The ABC's of School Choice, 2014 Edition*, available at: www.friedmanfoundation.org
Hanushek, Eric A. 2003. The failure of input-based schooling policies. *The Economic Journal* 113 (February): 64–98.
Hanushek, Eric A., and Steven Rivkin. 2006. Teacher Quality. In Eric A. Hanushek and Finis Welch, eds, *Handbook of the Economics of Education*. Amsterdam: Elsevier, 1051–78.

Henig, Jeffrey R., Richard C. Hula, Marion Orr, and Desiree S. Pedescleaux. 1999. *The Color of School Reform*. Princeton University Press.

Hess, Frederick M. 2003. Refining or Retreating? High-Stakes Accountability in the States. In Paul E. Peterson and Martin West, eds, *Leave No Child Behind? The Politics and Practices of School Accountability*. Washington, DC: Brookings Institution.

2010. *The Same Thing Over and Over Again*. Cambridge, MA: Harvard University Press.

Hess, Frederick M., and Chester E. Finn, Jr. 2007. Conclusion: Can This Law Be Fixed: A Hard Look at the NCLB Remedies. In Frederick M. Hess and Chester E. Finn, Jr., eds, *No Remedy Left Behind: Lessons From a Half-Decade of NCLB*. Washington, DC: AEI Press.

Hess, Frederick M., and Jeffrey R. Henig. 2015. *The New Education Philanthropy*. Cambridge, MA: Harvard Education Press.

Hess, Frederick M., and Martin R. West. 2006. *A Better Bargain: Overhauling Teacher Collective Bargaining for the 21st Century*. Program on Education Policy and Governance, Harvard University.

Hill, Paul T., ed. 2006. *Charter Schools Against the Odds*. Stanford, CA: Hoover Institution Press; Center for Education Reform.

Hill, Paul T., and Ashley E. Jochim. 2009. Political Perspectives on School Choice. In Mark Berends, Matthew G. Springer, Dale Ballou, and Herbert J. Walberg, eds, *Handbook of Research on School Choice*. New York: Routledge, 3–18.

Howell, William G., Paul E. Peterson, and Martin R. West. 2009. The persuadable public. *Education Next* 9 (Fall): 20–9.

Hoxby, Caroline M. 1996. How teachers unions affect education production. *Quarterly Journal of Economics* 111.3: 671–718.

2005. Inadequate yearly progress: Unlocking the secrets of NCLB. *Education Next* 5.3 (Summer).

Huetteman, Emmarie. 2015. Senate approves overhaul of No Child Left Behind. *New York Times* (December 9).

Kirst, Michael, and Frederick M. Wirt. 2009. *The Political Dynamics of American Education*, 4th ed. Richmond, CA: McCutchan.

Lovenheim, Michael. 2009. The effect of teachers' unions on education production: Evidence from union election certifications in three midwestern states. *Journal of Labor Economics*, 27.4, 525–87.

Lovenheim, Michael, and Alexander Willen. 2015. *The long-run effect of teachers unions on educational attainment and earnings*. Working Paper.

McGuinn, Patrick. 2006. *No Child Left Behind and the Transformation of Federal Education Policy*. University of Kansas Press.

McGuinn, Patrick, and Paul Manna, eds. 2013. *Educational Governance for the Twenty-First Century: Overcoming the Structural Barriers to School Reform*. Washington, DC: Brookings Institution.

Moe, Terry M. 2001. *Schools, Vouchers, and the American Public*. Washington, DC: Brookings Institution.

2003. Politics, Control, and the Future of School Accountability. In Paul E. Peterson and Martin West, eds, *Leave No Child Behind? The Politics and Practices of School Accountability*. Washington, DC: Brookings Institution.

2005. Teachers Unions and School Board Elections. In William G. Howell, ed., *Beseiged: School Boards and the Future of Education Politics*. Washington, DC: Brookings Institution Press.

2006. Political control and the power of the agent. *Journal of Law, Economics, and Organization* 22, 1–29.

2008. Beyond the free market: The structure of school choice. *Brigham Young University Law Review*. 2008.1: 557–92.

2009. Collective bargaining and the performance of the public schools. *American Journal of Political Science* 53.1: 156–74.

2011. *Special Interest: Teachers Unions and America's Public Schools*. Washington, DC: Brookings Institution.

2015. Vested interests and political institutions. *Political Science Quarterly* 130.2 (Summer): 277–318.

Moe, Terry M., and John E. Chubb. 2009. *Liberating Learning*. San Francisco: Jossey-Bass.

Morken, Hubert, and Jo Renee Formicola. 1999. *The Politics of School Choice*. London: Rowman and Littlefield.

Murphy Marjorie. 1990. *Blackboard Unions: The AFT and the NEA, 1900–1980*. Ithaca: Cornell University Press.

National Alliance for Public Charter Schools. 2015. A growing movement: America's largest charter school communities. www.publiccharters.org/publications/enrollment-share-10/

National Commission on Excellence in Education. 1983. A nation at risk: The imperative for educational reform. *The Elementary School Journal* 84.2: 113–130.

National Council on Teacher Quality. 2015. *State of the States: Evaluating Teaching, Leading and Learning*. Washington, DC: National Council on Teacher Quality.

O'Day, Jennifer A., and Marshall S. Smith (1993). Systemic School Reform and Educational Opportunity. In Susan Fuhrman, ed., *Designing Coherent Education Policy: Improving the System*. San Francisco: Jossey-Bass, 250–312.

Patashnik, Eric. 2008. *Reforms at Risk: What Happens After Major Policy Changes Are Enacted*. Princeton University Press.

Reckhow, Sarah. 2012. *Follow the Money: How Foundation Dollars Change Public School Politics*. Oxford University Press, USA.

Resnick, Brian. 2011. The mess of No Child Left Behind. *The Atlantic* (December 16) www.theatlantic.com/national/archive/2011/12/the-mess-of-no-child-left-behind/250076/

Rhodes, Jesse H. 2012. *An Education in Politics: The Origin and Evolution of No Child Left Behind*. Ithaca, NY: Cornell University Press.

Rich, Motoko. 2013. US reading and math scores show slight gains. *New York Times* (November 7).

2015. Nationwide test shows dip in students' math abilities. *New York Times* (October 28).

Sawchuk, Stephen. 2013. Teacher ratings still high despite new measures. *Education Week* (February 5).

Schlozman, Kay. 2010. Who Sings in the Heavenly Chorus: The Shape of the Organized Interest System. In L. Sandy Maisel, Jeffrey M. Berry, and George C. Edwards III, eds, *The Oxford Handbook of American Political Parties and Interest Groups*. New York: Oxford University Press.

Semuels, Alana. 2016. Why are unions so worried about an upcoming Supreme Court case? *The Atlantic* (January 8).

Stone, Clarence N., Jeffrey R. Henig, and Carol Pierannunzi. 2001. *Building Civic Capacity*. Lawrence, KS: University Press of Kansas.

Strauss, Valerie. 2014. GOP's Klein smacks Obama over NCLB waivers, says administration 'has not gotten the message' from elections. *Washington Post* (November 14).

Strunk, Katharine O. 2011. Are teachers' unions really to blame? Collective bargaining agreements and their relationships with district resource allocation and student performance in California. *Education Finance and Policy* 6.3: 354–98.

Strunk, Katharine O., and Jason A. Grissom. 2010. Do strong unions shape district policies? Collective bargaining, teacher contract restrictiveness, and the political power of teachers unions. *Educational Evaluation and Policy Analysis* 32.3: 389–406.

Taylor, Kate. 2015. Chancellor Carmen Fariña changes New York City schools' course. *New York Times* (February 6).

Toch, Thomas. 1991. *In the Name of Excellence*. New York: Oxford University Press.

Tsebelis, George. 2002. *Veto Players: How Political Institutions Work*. Princeton University Press.

Tyack, David, and Larry Cuban. 1995. *Tinkering Toward Utopia*. Cambridge, MA: Harvard University Press.

Vergari, Sandra. 2007. The politics of charter schools. *Educational Policy* 21.1: 15–39.

Viteritti, Joseph, ed. 2009. *When Mayors Take Charge: School Governance in the City*. Washington, DC: Brookings Institution Press.

Weisberg, D., Sexton, S., Mulhern, J., and Keeling, D. 2009. *The Widget Effect: Our National Failure to Acknowledge and Act on Differences in Teacher Effectiveness*. Brooklyn, NY: The New Teacher Project. www.widgeteffect.org/down-loads/TheWidgetEffect.pdf

Williams, Joe. 2006. *Echo Chamber: The National Education Association's Campaign against NCLB*, Education Sector, Connecting the Dots (July 2006) on Education Sector's website at: www.educationsector.org/publications/echo-chambernational-education- ssociations-campaign-against-nclb

2007. District Accountability: More Bark Than Bite? In Frederick M. Hess and Chester E. Finn, Jr., eds, *No Remedy Left Behind: Lessons From a Half-Decade of NCLB*. Washington, DC: AEI Press.

3

Teacher Unions in England
The End is Nigh?

Susanne Wiborg

Introduction

In striking contrast to organised teachers in Europe and the USA, the teacher unions in England have had a substantial amount of power removed from them during the last 30 years. Their power was brutally cut by Margaret Thatcher during her long premiership from 1979 to 1990, a blow from which the unions have never recovered. They lost access to policy formulation and their national bargaining rights were abolished. Prior to Thatcher, the teacher unions were an influential force in education politics, reaching their zenith of power in the 1960s and 1970s. The 'iron triangle' between organised teachers, local authorities and central government, which were in full operation throughout these two decades, enabled teacher unions to become intimately involved in education policy at both national and local levels. Their power-base was primarily concentrated at a local level, given that local authorities have been responsible for the planning and provision of education since 1944. Following Margaret Thatcher's arrival, a raft of policies were introduced to dismantle this 'iron triangle' and in its place the government launched a system which was, on the one hand, governed by a centralisation of power and, on the other hand, marketisation of education. Central government would thus control the framework within which schools would compete with one another for resources, teachers and students, and thus by extension, higher standards.

   This substantial reorganisation of English education is significant and has been subjected to a large number of studies seeking to understand why and how this change was brought about, along with its long-term effects. The dominant explanation provided by this literature is the political will of Margaret Thatcher and her forceful education secretaries, most notably Kenneth Baker; the reinvention of Victorian laissez-faire individualism; and the spreading of global neo-liberal ideology and austerity which were crucial in pushing through reforms (Ball 1990, 2008; Chitty 2004; Simon 1991; Tomlinson 2005; Whitty 1989, 2008).

However, the existing academic writing fails to add any analytical value to the fact that the curbing of vested interests opposing change resulted for the most part in rapid policy implementation. The Conservative government undermined the key institutional structure within which the teacher unions were closely integrated: the local authorities. This simply opened the gates for radical reform. The oversight of vested interests and their tremendous ability to block or alter policy may be due to scholars' preferences for offering a regrettable account of teacher unions' loss of power and emphasising the forces which might revive it (Barber 1992; Chitty 2004; Simon 1991; Stevenson 2007; Stevenson and Carter 2009).

This chapter will argue that reformers in English education since 1979 have not been heavily constrained by teacher unions and other interests, particularly the local authorities, and therefore have been bestowed with the power to radically overhaul the education system. The argument is also applicable to the subsequent governments. Despite pursuing somewhat different reforms, neither New Labour (1997–2010) nor the Coalition government (2010–15) were confronted with forces of such resilience that they had to shelve or considerably compromise their reform plans. A recent and striking example of this is the Coalition government, which in less than four years has removed more than half of all secondary schools – and many more will follow suit – from local authority control in order to grant these schools, now called Academies, self-governing status under direct central control. Extensive school autonomy on this massive scale appears to have cut the umbilical cord between local authorities, schools and teacher unions.

Teacher unions in England have retaliated with campaigns, strikes and occasional alliances with other interests, achieving some success in frustrating government plans; but on the whole they have been ineffectual. Their lack of clout in dealing with government is compounded by the fact that the unions are highly fragmented. English teachers are divided into six different unions, with approximately 84 per cent of all teachers members of a union in 2014. They have been notoriously incapable of mustering powerful alliances and have often found themselves in conflict with each other over union policy and tactics as well as in competition over recruitment of each other's members. The changing distribution of membership is the fuel which energises the continuing tensions and competition between unions themselves.

This chapter will explore the teacher unions' rise to and fall from power. The first part will describe the early beginnings of the teacher unions, particularly the National Union of Teachers (NUT) which is the largest and most influential union in England. Since their inception the teacher unions have been seeking to push remuneration demands, reduce workloads, and influence the design of school types, curriculum and exams – all of which were in the interests of teachers. The following part, covering the early interwar period until 1979, will address the ways in which the 'iron triangle' bestowed the unions with unprecedented power, and the benefits that were gained from this. The last and longest part of the chapter will focus on the period from 1979 until the present day, a period that witnessed the unions going into a relentless decline. The chapter will scrutinise decisive events in teacher union history that shed light on how interest politics and power distribution have fundamentally changed in the arena of education in England.

State, Class and Education: The Rise of Teacher Unionism

The Early Beginnings

The establishment of teacher unions should be considered in light of the interaction between the continuing process of educational provision, increased state regulation, and the English social structure of the last quarter of the nineteenth century. As public schools came to predominate over private and voluntary institutions, governments increased their influence on education. Whether through central or local authorities, the state increasingly controlled education through the allocation of funds, the inspection of schools, the recruitment, training and certification of teachers, and, to varying degrees, through the oversight of national certification and standard curricula. A full public system of elementary education was achieved with the 1870 Education Act although compulsory attendance was not achieved in most areas until the 1880s, and schools were not entirely free of charge until 1891.

The act laid the foundation on which a highly organised and strictly segregated system of education was constructed, and was designed specifically for the working classes. However, the British state, comprising the smallest central bureaucracy of any of the major Western nations and imbued with the Victorian belief in 'self-help' capacity, only provided education where voluntary provision was absent. Thus, the elementary school 'system' consisted of, on the one hand, the voluntary schools administered primarily by the Church of England and the rival Dissenting denominations; and, on the other hand, the board schools which were run by the School Boards, set up by the 1870 Education Act in order to 'fill up the gaps'. Voluntary schools were the most prevalent, enrolling over half of the school population. State secondary schools were established with the 1902 Education Act. Prior to this, only private secondary schools were available, such as the grammar schools which catered for the middle classes, and the elitist 'public' schools (such as Eton and Harrow) for the upper classes.[1] Although the state lagged behind countries such as Germany and France by around 50 years in setting up a national system of education

---

[1] During 1850–70 five Royal Commissions were established to examine and report on all levels of education, from Oxford and Cambridge universities to the elementary schools for the masses. Each of these commissions was followed by Acts of Parliament, resulting in the firm establishment of a hierarchical structure comprising five distinct levels according to social class. These ranged from the newly developed system of 'public schools' (modelled on the ancient nine public schools, including Eton and Harrow), through sets of schools (primarily grammar schools)

including both elementary and secondary education, this century witnessed the transition from an inconsistent educational provision at the beginning of the century to a structured 'system' relating to social class differences toward its close (Green 1990, 2013; Simon 1991).

Teachers organised themselves along the faultlines of this highly socially segregated education system, and the resulting organisations that sprang up were largely in competition with one another. This situation gave rise to rivalries, particularly between the different organisations that represented elementary and secondary school teachers. Victorian middle-class secondary teachers organised themselves into the Joint Four Secondary Associations, and three further unions, in order to defend their status and privileges against the rapidly expanding body of elementary school teachers, who were organised from 1870 in the form of the National Union of Elementary Teachers, NUET[2] (changed to the NUT in 1889) (Tropp 1957).

The NUET, which quickly became the largest teacher union, reflected vast differences in teachers' backgrounds. Most elementary school teachers had working class backgrounds, but deep cleavages ran between rural and urban teachers, and between teachers serving in the voluntary and the board schools – the latter gaining the upper hand due to their access to greater government funding. In particular, there were differences between teachers belonging to the Church of England and those belonging to the Dissenting denominations. These differences among teachers crystallised from the 1890s onwards and took the form of distinguishable internal (as well as external) pressure groups that strongly marked out the work of the teacher unions – such work revolving around the traditional union tenets of education policy, tenure, salaries, and conditions of service. In its quest to build a professional monopoly, the NUET sought control over who could enter the teaching profession by erecting barriers for uncertified persons, raising teacher training standards, and increasing the value of teachers' certificates.[3] The NUET sought through a great variety of means to exert pressure on Parliament, the education department, and on the 'employers' at the local School Boards.[4] As time went by they also resorted to militant actions and strikes (Tropp 1957; Ironside and Seifert 1995: 90–5).

---

designed to meet the needs of the three levels of the middle class (upper-middle class, middle-middle class, and lower-middle class), through to the elementary schools for the large working class (Simon 1991: 24).

[2] The NUET was made up of around 50 local teacher associations.

[3] The NUET did not have much success in this respect, and, in defeat, the union turned its attention to the training college system as a means of reducing the 'army of unqualified practitioners' and as a way of closing all 'side entrances' – hence its strong engagement with the teacher training sector in the latter part of the century.

[4] The union had several strategies ranging from local deputations to MPs in their constituencies, through to distribution of memos and other briefing materials (the union had also started to produce its own surveys) to provide information for teachers and known supporters in both parliamentary Houses, as well as attempts to canvas candidates during elections. The first successes

School Policy: Payment by Results

Since its inception, the NUT has strategically placed great importance on its dealings with national government. In his presidential address, the union leader, J.J. Graves, stated: 'there was no class of men whose daily duties and personal interests were more frequently interfered [with] by legislation and hence the teachers must by necessity unite to influence such legislation' (Tropp, 1957: 110). The first piece of legislation, which mobilised the union into action, was the Revised Code of 1862.[5]

The Revised Code – which came about as a result of the Victorian belief that the state should spend and regulate as little as possible in order to allow for the operation of the laws of demand and supply – brought an end to direct payments from the state to teachers, removed any rights they had to a pension, and abolished an array of grants that had previously been available to schools. Instead, it provided grants to be allocated directly to school managers, the total amount of which depended on the attendance of pupils, their exam results, and by non-teacher external inspectors in each of the 'three Rs'. The school manager, often the local vicar, was free to spend the money as he wished. Thus, a teacher's salary, tenure and working conditions were now in the hands of the school manager; while the curriculum, which 'his' teacher(s) instructed, was laid down nationally in the Code (Tropp 1957: 59, 129).

This caused uproar at the NUET, but the union was faced by a Department of Education that largely ignored its existence, an attitude succinctly encapsulated by one official who stated that 'teachers desiring to criticize the Code were as impertinent as chickens wishing to decide the kind of sauce in which they would be served' (Thompson 1927: 76). However, the union had some success in 'chipping' away at the Code through 'negotiations' with the Department, but it was not until 1895 – after 33 years of agitation – that the Code was abolished.[5]

Working Conditions and Pay

It was the local School Boards (after 1902, the Local Education Authorities), that became the primary arena for teacher union influence. The NUT felt at liberty to lobby School Boards directly, all over the country, if they felt they

---

of this new policy – which was decided at the 1877 NUET conference – were seen in 1893 when the general secretary and a leading member of the Union's executive were elected to Parliament. Both proved influential, particularly during the debate which preceded the 1902 Education Act. The union became increasingly involved in the major parliamentary commissions on education at the end of the century. The union deliberately avoided all strike action until late in the century, in line with its general reluctance to adopt 'trade union' methods during a period in which its primary goal was to engage in building a 'profession' of teachers that could be distinguished from 'ordinary' manual workers.

[5] In 1875 grants were made based on *class* proficiency rather than on individual attainment. This concept was revived, in a new form, in the 1980s.

were unfit for their position – that is, if they kept down the rates (money) paid to the school, acted in ways that made tenure insecure, paid low salaries, or imposed 'extraneous' duties on teachers. The union had its greatest successes in actions involving the larger urban boards – in London in particular – where it had obtained consultation status, sometimes with elements of bargaining power. The union also tried to get on to the School Boards by using its electoral weight. They canvassed support for their favorite candidates (teachers could stand until 1875) for School Board elections.[6] In the 1890s, as the radical labour movement intervened more effectively in local politics, the teachers' influence in School Board affairs became increasingly visible (Tropp 1957: 137–8, 144).

The NUT also campaigned for higher salaries for all elementary school teachers. Local wage bargaining meant that there was considerable variation in the remuneration of teachers across different locations. On the whole, teachers working for a large School Board were better paid than teachers in small voluntary schools in rural areas. There were also many instances of small School Boards that had been elected with the purpose of keeping the rates down, or that simply could not afford to pay anything other than meagre salaries.[7] The union also appealed to government to reinstate the pension, which had been abolished in 1862, and to ensure tenure of office for teachers.[8] An act on tenure would require notice of dismissal and a right of appeal in unjust cases. Although it gained the right of teachers to pensions in 1889, the union failed to secure a parliamentary act on tenure. As a result, the union set up a legal department to deal with the increasing number of 'capriciously' dismissed teachers. Offering this service had the positive effect of increasing membership[9] (Tropp 1957: 114–18, 145).

---

[6] The Code of 1875 prohibited the election of elementary teachers to School Boards. However, former teachers, permanent officials of the NUET, and private school teachers, were still eligible. The union's general secretary from 1873 was an elected member of the London School Board.

[7] The rural School Boards, often dominated by farmers, saw children as cheap labour and school therefore as a disruption. They often set out to deliberately keep rates down.

[8] By far the most important issue for the NUET was the issue of securing a pension. The withdrawal of the right to a pension by the Revised Code, galvanised the union into fierce action to win back its reinstatement. The pension was gradually reduced during the 1850s and finally withdrawn in 1862. This resulted in continued agitation, culminating in the huge campaign of 1892. In 1898, after several years of preparations, the House of Commons finally passed a bill that gave teachers the right to a pension. This act provides the basis for all legislation on teachers' superannuation (Tropp 1957, 123–6).

[9] On appointment, a new vicar would often dismiss the teacher, or if the teacher had refused to secure regular attendance or carry out extraneous duties. The mere knowledge that union members could draw on legal resources played an important part in the increase in membership from 1886 onwards. The union had more than doubled its members by the 1890s – and from 43,621 at the turn of the century, membership had reached 72,400 by 1911 (Tropp 1957: 145).

Onwards and Upwards: The Interwar Period

Rising Militancy and Policy Activism

The years up to the end of the First World War witnessed the rise of mass labour movements. Trade unionism spread, inspired by events in Russia, on a massive scale. Between 1888 and 1918 the unions grew at a faster rate than at any other time in their history, reaching more than six million members in 1918. This growth was a product of the extraordinary militancy of the pre-war years, which exploded in a huge wave of strikes (Hinton 1983: 24). The NUT likewise turned to the left and admitted uncertified teachers to increase its clout. It mustered united union support for militant action in pursuit of higher salaries. The transition to militancy resulted in the first NUT-initiated national campaign for salaries in 1913 (due to an increase in prices), which was subsequently followed by a series of local strikes – often in collaboration with other labour organisations – after the NUT decided that its members were unfairly paid or treated. The left wing of the NUT membership forced through a union policy that supported national payscales through collective bargaining. The fact that teachers' salaries were to be paid from the rates (local taxation) provided the NUT with the opportunity to bargain directly across the country. The union now wanted to move beyond this and gain national bargaining rights (Tropp 1957: 207; Barber 1992: 21).

Interestingly, the NUT's leftward turn and militancy over pay did not lead to a formal affiliation with the Labour Party – as was the case with the other trade unions – although many elementary school teachers did contribute to Labour's advance at the ballot box in 1919. In an NUT referendum, a two-thirds majority turned the proposal down, believing that the union should retain its independence to deal with whichever party was in government – a decision upheld ever since. Regardless of this, the more conservative among the male teachers split from the NUT to form the National Association of Schoolmasters (NAS); and women, believing that insufficient priority was being given to equal pay, broke away and established the National Union of Women Teachers (NUWT). As we shall see later, this split has haunted teacher union politics ever since.

Burnham: National Collective Bargaining Rights for Teachers

In the face of the teachers' unrest, Parliament began debating whether teachers should be given Civil Service status. The sense of neutrality was appealing, but the Board of Education was unwilling to expand its bureaucracy in the way that was necessary to manage the teachers; worse still, it feared it would step directly into the firing line of discontented teachers. Once Civil Service status was ruled out, a committee was established in 1919 – chaired by Lord Burnham – to inquire into the principles of national salary scales for teachers.

The basis of the settlement of the Burnham constitution was that pay for all teachers would be determined by bargaining between representatives of employers and employees. This committee had fixed membership proportional to the size of the unions, along with members of the Local Education Authorities (the LEAs, previously the local School Boards) – but the NUT enjoyed a comfortable majority.[10] This committee set national payscales for all teachers in the UK, with separate scales for men and women and for certified and non-certified teachers. Teacher pay was revised on an annual basis through the Burnham Committee, which operated in a collective bargaining context until 1986. Teachers' pay increased throughout the interwar period, although cuts were made during the depression of the 1930s. The seal on the NUT's national negotiation rights was set in 1926, when the Board of Education issued a regulation which required LEAs to pay the Burnham rates unless the Board approved a variation[11]. At a local level, the union had a working relationship with most LEAs, enabling issues concerning tenure or working conditions to be dealt with through formalised negotiations (Tropp 1957: 209–13; Barber 1992: 15–20; Seifert 1987: 28–53; Ironside and Seifert 1995: 23–9).

Reorganising the School Structure
During the interwar period secondary education expanded rapidly as a result of the 1902 Education Act. The act specified a state-aided, dual system of secondary education: the endowed grammar schools (which remained the preserve of the elite) and the new secondary schools (for the working classes and lower-middle classes). By 1939, 63.5 percent of pupils over 11 years of age were in some form of reorganised secondary education. This secondary school system, kept strictly separate from elementary education, raised the critical issue of moving from elementary to secondary school, since, for the first time in history, a very large number of children were embarking on secondary education. It was at this point that different vested interests clashed. In possession of their own individual unions, teachers, and other sectional interests, the elementary and secondary school sectors held conflicting views on how this transition ought to be organised. Ultimately, this was a fight about who should teach in which schools – in other words, a fight about jobs.

---

[10] In general, the union wished for larger district-controlling committees of managers. Only such authorities would be able to grant teachers security of tenure, free them from extraneous duties, and campaign for higher salaries. Prior to 1902 this was only possible in the urban School Boards. There were 2,500 such Boards, which had developed greatly in size and efficiency, and were increasingly difficult to deal with centrally. The act made county and county boroughs councils responsible for organisation of education via newly established Local Education Authorities (LEAs, of which there were a total of 318). These LEAs were to provide and coordinate elementary education, secondary education and teacher training. In conjunction with central government and the newly established Board of Education (which replaced the Education Department), they exercised control over education.
[11] On tenure, where the union representative and the LEA officer were in disagreement, LEAs organized formal inquires at which the teacher could be represented by counsel, provided normally by the union. At national level, the union had established a right to a hearing for teachers who believed they had been wronged by inspectors.

The organised secondary school teachers wanted to maintain a strict separation between primary and secondary establishments as this would maintain their 'superior' status and monopoly over middle-class education; whereas the NUT, prior to the 1902 Education Act, demanded that this separation be eliminated in favour of a three-step educational ladder. Specifically, the NUT campaigned for the so-called higher grade schools or higher tops (post-primary education) – with which the elementary school teachers were heavily involved – to form an intermediate stage between elementary and secondary education, thereby forming an educational ladder.

The more enterprising School Boards had already provided education at this post-primary level. In contrast to the grammar schools, the higher grade schools provided technical or commercial training and were widely attended by lower-middle class parents because of their occupational relevance. However, the Conservative government, galvanised by secondary teacher support, fought a forceful campaign in the 1890s against this kind of 'pseudo education', which they believed competed destructively with the 'honoured' grammar schools. Consequently, School Boards were prevented by the Department of Education from using funds for anything but elementary schools. However, some higher grade schools survived, but these were converted into secondary schools after 1902[12] (Robinson 2002; Simon 1965: 208; Simon 1974; Vlaeminke 2000).

What is important to highlight here is that the maintained division between elementary and secondary education, enacted by the 1902 Education Act, largely prevented elementary school teachers from entering the secondary school system. The NUT thus failed to obtain a stronghold in terms of member recruitment from secondary schools. This was also precipitated, as earlier mentioned, by the break-up of the NUT in 1919, which had resulted in two new unions: the NAS and AWT. The male teachers in the secondary schools would usually belong to the NAS, while the women joined the AWT (Beck 2009: 121). This rift between the NUT and the secondary school teachers' unions served to stiffen the elementary and secondary divide.

Teacher Self-Regulation and Training

The NUT made continued attempts to break down the divide, this time via the means of teachers' registration. In its pursuit of achieving self-regulation of the teaching profession, the NUT fought for a unified profession with a single teachers' register and a single scheme of education for elementary and

---

[12] Throughout the interwar period, the NUT continued to push for continuation schools for the working classes. The Fisher 1918 Education Act put forward a proposal to make provision for such schools, which would at least offer part-time education for most young people over 14 years of age. However, the plan was shelved due to spending cuts in the early 1920s. The union also tried to meet this aim by demanding the extension of the school leaving age to 15 (the Fisher Act had legislated it to 14). Bills to that effect were introduced in 1929 and 1931, but were successfully toppled by the religious lobby – the influence of the Anglican and Catholic churches was immense.

secondary teachers. The principle of registration, which was to be controlled by a general education council responsible for stipulating standards of entry, was accepted by all teacher unions. However, the secondary school teacher unions could not agree to a single register for *all* teachers for fear of being swamped by the much larger numbers of elementary teachers who were represented by the NUT. Refusing any attempt to define the exact status of an elementary teacher, the NUT retaliated against this by successfully fending off a series of bills aimed at establishing a separate register for secondary school teachers.[13]

A council for elementary school teachers was established in 1912, but it achieved no power beyond 'forming and keeping a register' of them. The purpose of this was defeated with the introduction of the 1944 Education Act, which conferred upon the minister of education the power to grant qualified teacher status. In 1949 the council was quietly closed down (Tropp 1957: 172). As for the unification of training for elementary and secondary teachers, the NUT proposed a university-based system. All teachers should acquire a secondary education before proceeding to university to obtain a diploma that would entail both academic study and practice-based training in schools. Some degree of success was achieved in bringing teachers to university, but the training of each category of teacher remained separate. Over the course of just ten years, from 1890 to 1900, 16 departments had been established – although only a minority of teachers received post-graduate diplomas (Gosden 1972: 256–7; Tropp 1957, 170–1).

Expanding the Reach of the Teacher Unions: 1944–79

The 'Iron Triangle'

During the first half of the post-war period the teacher unions were parachuted into power by a new institutional structure: the 'iron triangle'. In the context of English education, the triangle refers to the distribution of power between three parties: the Department of Education and Science[14], the local authorities, and the teacher unions – of which the NUT was the most significant. This 'iron triangle', which emerged in the interwar period and was consolidated by the 1944 Education Act, lasted until 1979.[15] In English education policy literature, the triangle is usually referred to as the 'social partnership' model or educational 'partnership' to demonstrate positive endorsement, although this depiction obscures the fact that, rather than promoting consensus, it provided

---

[13] The NUT referred to the fact that they were engaged in secondary education such as the higher grade schools, pupil-teacher centres, and science and art classes.

[14] Prior to 1964, the Ministry of Education.

[15] The first piece of legislation that can be said to be a direct result of the 'iron triangle' was the 1944 Education Act. The NUT's general secretary from 1931, Sir Frederic Mander, and the secretary of the AEC, Sir Percival Sharp, worked together to negotiate with the secretary of the Board of Education concerning the act's preparation, as well as the constituted Burnham Committee of 1945.

a formidable platform that enabled the unions to frustrate government education policies (Barber 1992; Cooper 1992; Salter and Tapper 1981; Stevenson 2007; Stevenson and Carter 2009).

The 'sharpest corner' in the triangle during this time in history was the local authorities, which maintained educational institutions and acted as the employer. Power was concentrated here at a local level – both in terms of the day-to-day running of the education system, and also with regard to the teacher unions. At a national level, the local authorities belonged to different associations.[16] These national associations represented the local authorities in their collective dealings with the Department of Education and Science, and together with the Department acted as 'employers' in national negotiations with the teacher unions.

The Department had long been willing to involve these associations – which it did formally through a set of permanent advisory committees established by or since the 1944 Education Act – and through working parties set up to consider certain issues; as well as informally through regular contact between the permanent officials of the Department and those of the local authority associations and the teacher unions. The most important working party was the Schools Council, set up in 1964 to assume responsibility for curriculum and examinations. The NUT, having initially opposed the Schools Council as an attempt at centralisation, went on to play a significant role in the planning of subject content and assessment, particularly with regard to adapting them to the comprehensive education system which was now under way (Barber 1992: 40).

Comprehensive Education

Contrary to the widely embraced view among education scholars, this process of triangular policy-making did not promote a consensus on comprehensive education – the biggest issue of the day. The Labour government (1964–76) initiated a reform in the mid-1960s to merge the tripartite system into comprehensive schools. The tripartite system introduced with the 1944 Education Act provided a system of three school types: grammar schools, secondary modern schools, and technical schools. Under this system pupils at the age of 11 were allocated to the next phase of education on the basis of entry exams and intelligence tests.[17] There had been a relatively high degree of consensus surrounding this tripartite system because the teacher unions relied heavily on particular teacher groupings from each of these school types, a fact that served to bolster the stratification of the system.

---

[16] The Association of Education Committees (AEC), and either the Association of Municipal Corporations (AMC) or the County Councils Association (CCA).
[17] The structure that emerged subsequently was, in reality, a bipartite system as the technical schools, focusing on vocational subjects, failed to take off. Less than 4 percent of the secondary school age group was enrolled in the technical schools (Chitty 2004: 25).

This consensus, however, broke down as a result of government intervention, but comprehensive schools were extremely slow to develop precisely because the entrenched vested interests within the education sector were able to oppose, alter or delay their introduction. However, the key literature dealing with comprehensive education attributes the slow progress of comprehensive education almost exclusively to government failure (Ball 2008; Benn and Chitty 1997; Benn and Simon 1972; Chitty 2004: 29; Simon 1991). The Labour government, so the explanation goes, was not fully committed to ending selection at 11-plus and thus only issued a circular (Circular 10/65), rather than trying to pass a parliamentary act; this circular requested rather than required LEAs to submit plans for reorganising secondary education in their areas along comprehensive lines. No single pattern of comprehensive organisation was laid down; instead the circular outlined several different models that local authorities could choose to phase out selective education. In the words of Ball (2008: 71) 'there was no national planning for the replacement of grammar and secondary modern schools with comprehensives, no set of articulated principles and little evidence of political will for thoroughgoing change'.

This interpretation needs to be modified for a number of reasons. First, the Labour government was acting within the confines of the administrative style of British government at the time, which refrained from centralising control and prescribing the educational content in detail, and entrusted the implementation of policies to nominated bodies (in this case, the LEAs). The Department for Education and Science usually supervised rather than controlled the LEAs, which in practice meant that the local authority could develop, within broadly defined parameters, educational provision that suited their local circumstances. Such devolution limited the degree of control that central government could assume, even though Labour won the 1966 General Election with a vast majority (Coates 1972: 7). It is in light of this that the secretary of state, Michael Stewart's, statement should be understood: 'It is the government's policy to reorganize secondary education on comprehensive lines. The method and timing of reorganization must vary from one area to another' (quoted in Simon 1991: 276).

Second, even if the government had enforced comprehensive education by law, the teacher unions with their much strengthened power base would still have been engaged in the politics of blocking in an effort to defend the status quo. In their quest to chronicle the march of comprehensive education as it steadily crushed all obstacles in its way, Benn and Chitty's seminal study (1997) fails to regard teacher unions as a reason for its slow, piecemeal and incoherent development, with little evidence of radical reform. In 1981, after 16 years of restructuring, 83 per cent of children were educated in a comprehensive school.

None of the teacher unions, whose teachers had long experience of assimilation within the divided system, wanted comprehensive schools for the simple reason that the reorganisation would threaten their professional interests – issues of salary, career prospects, redeployment, and so on. The NUT was not, as is often claimed, an active force in promoting comprehensive schools, even though it fought determinedly in its defence *after* the development appeared inevitable and was well under way (Barber 1992: 39; Simon 1991: 285). It simply changed its tune and its tactics in response to changes it perceived in education policy, a policy over which they sought influence.[18]

The unions' resistance to change hindered any radical transformation of the education system. LEAs – depending on political leadership and union penetration – either refused to convert their schools into comprehensives, or did so in piecemeal fashion, relying on persistent delaying tactics to hold up change. A common tactic was to relabel the old secondary modern schools as 'lower schools' and grammar schools as 'upper schools', and to turn junior schools or small secondary schools into 'middle schools' that would feed directly into the upper schools. While this model phased out selective education to satisfy government policy, it ensured that the schools were kept largely intact so as to minimise disruption to the old system. The birth of comprehensive schools as single institutions resulted in the old, divided system being replicated. For example, grammar school procedures relating to teaching, overall curricula, and exams, were transferred wholesale, and without serious modifications, into comprehensive schools (Simon 1991; Benn and Chitty 1997). As such, the structures of the divided system, including teacher categories and salary differentials, were recreated within the comprehensive schools and thus strongly fortified the lines of defence of the existing structures, and so too of the status quo. Over the years, these divisive structures were to soften in many schools, but a nationwide system of comprehensive education was never developed in England.

The fact that different teacher unions were united under 'one roof' did not result in collaboration, alliances or mergers. The strong reliance of each of the unions on particular groupings within the teaching labour force simply reinforced the tendency to emphasise policy differences and to accentuate sectional differences among their actual and potential memberships. This sectionalism permeated the entire set of relations that comprised teacher politics at both local and national levels – the national level focusing on negotiations with the Department of Education and national associations of LEAs. We shall now turn to those educational aspects that proved far more controversial for the unions than comprehensive education: self-government, working conditions and pay.

---

[18] The NUT's rejection was also caused by a change in its membership base. The union had become increasingly successful in poaching members from the secondary modern schools. These institutions, which in 1960 accounted for a quarter of the NUT's membership, wanted to retain their 'own' schools – arguing that it was only a matter of time before they would achieve a parity of esteem with the grammar and technical schools. Moreover, the small but disproportionately influential grammar school membership (6 percent of members) campaigned for the preservation of 'their' schools (Coates 1972: 3).

Self-Government

Both organisational unity and professional self-government were tactics perpetuated by the unions in the 1960s to strengthen their bargaining position with the Department for Education – this was achieved specifically through the creation of a coalition of the unions in the form of a teacher-dominated council with statutorily defined powers. The impetus for the creation of a single teachers' organisation originated in the NUT, which argued that a 'single voice' would enable the profession to make its representation felt to the fullest extent. Being the largest union, the NUT had the most to gain from organisational unification; it would enable it to dominate the unions and mute sectional voices from within.

Largely under the initiative of the NUT, talks were arranged between the teacher unions to put into action their unification plans – including putting an end to recruitment competition. However, these talks floundered due to differing views on the constitution, representation and distribution of power between the unions involved, and nothing came of it. Relations between the NUT and organised secondary school teachers – which were at their worst in the 1890s – had barely improved, so that that even in the 1960s this friction prevented the creation of a unified body of unions.[19]

Regardless of this massive failure, the NUT continued to advocate a Teachers' General Council. This body would control entry into the profession – including standards of entry to teacher training – manage professional discipline, and monopolise the award of 'qualified status' to teachers working in primary, secondary, further, and higher education. Such a council could not be achieved without legislation and the NUT therefore appealed to the Secretary of State to appoint an official working party. This was refused on the grounds that such matters should rest with the government. This attitude changed when an NUT-sponsored MP, Edward Short – a former teacher and member of the NUT – was appointed Education Minister in 1968 and set up a working party to explore the possibility of establishing a teaching council.

This was now endangered by inter-union rivalry. The NUT, more committed to its cause than the other unions, refused to participate in the working group unless its representation reflected its greater size. The deadlock was resolved thanks to Short, who was personally committed to such a council and gave the NUT increased representation by constructing it along the lines of Burnham. For the first time the unions were negotiating directly with a minister, resulting in a

---

[19] The secondary school teacher unions, the NAS chief among them, refused to enter a common association for fear of absorption. Further still, the four unions would lose both their representation on national bodies like the Burnham Committee, and their right of direct and separate access to the minister and to the Local Authority Associations. In other words, they were not prepared to surrender the autonomy that a continued separation of unions would ensure. All that remained of 60 years of recurrent negotiations was the Joint Committee of the four Secondary Associations, and a joint membership scheme between the NUT and the Association of Teachers in Technical Institutions (ATTI).

report in 1970 that outlined the constitution of a Teaching Council. The council would have a strong representation among the teacher unions and a separate advisory body on the training and supply of teachers. But by the time the report was ready to be ratified, the Labour government had lost the 1970 General Election. The secretary in the incoming Conservative administration refused to act without the unanimous support of the teacher unions, and the report was then surprisingly rejected by the NUT conference in 1971. A majority of members believed that it would be more effective to continue to seek organisational unity than to pursue measures aimed at professional self-government.

The teacher unions failed to develop professional unity under the aegis of a council, and, as we will see later, such opportunities faded considerably as conditions of employment became increasingly legislated and enforced through government rules and managerial control, rather than through professional discipline (Ironside and Seifert 1995: 84; Barber 1992: 38; Coates 1972: 52–7).

Militancy Over Work and Pay Conditions

During the 1960s and 1970s the unions resorted to militant tactics and strikes, with increasing frequency, as a means to win the level of income they believed would match their professional status. Teachers would, for instance, withdraw their labour, refuse to perform voluntary duties or teach oversized classes, or teach alongside unqualified teachers. By the early 1960s the teacher unions had never before called a national stoppage, but towards the end of the decade 100,000 teachers were on half-day and one-day strikes (Coates 1972: 61). This, even more so than organisational unity or professional self-government, increased their influence during these two decades. Strikes were based on the NUT's demand for a much-improved basic payscale and for the abolition of the primary–secondary differential. They also demanded action from government and LEAs in meeting union policy on school meals and unqualified teachers.

This militancy had some success for the NUT as it dealt with the opposing Local Authority Associations (LAAs) to reach an agreement on a marked reduction in the primary-secondary differential and a phasing out of unqualified teachers. After 1970 no LEA could employ temporary or occasional staff, and this was accepted by government (Coates 1972: 69–70). Fuelled by widespread strike action, mass rallies and protest marches, the Burnham Committee met to discuss a salary increase, resulting in tough negotiations and government intervention. Government authorised a salary increase, which was refused by the unions on the grounds that it would not have resulted in the same increase that other public sector workers received during this time. Teachers refused arbitration and insisted that negotiations be maintained in the Burnham Committee,[20]

---

[20] In 1944 it was made a statutory requirement for the LEAs to pay the rates agreed by the Burnham Committee, to cover both primary and secondary education (just as the NUT had hoped). In addition to the 16 NUT representatives, the Burnham Committee included four representatives from the Association of Teachers in Technical Institutions (ATTI, which later became

which took place against the backdrop of continued strike actions. During a day-long meeting of the Burnham Committee, nearly all of the teacher unions' initial demands were granted (Saran 1992; Seifert 1987).[21]

Thatcherism: 'Handbagging' the Teacher Unions

Radical Reforms

The election of a Conservative government in 1979 marked a watershed in English education. It heralded a new approach characterised by centralisation and the growth of markets in education. During the period 1979–88, the comprehensive enterprise was brought to an end, and a raft of policies were introduced to increase central control over education, particularly over the curriculum, testing and teachers. A 'market' for schools was created, enhancing their autonomy and encouraging competition to increase standards, giving parents the opportunity to choose between a diverse set of schools. This about-face in English education policy has been intensively researched, and focuses on many relevant factors relating primarily to the governments' changes of policy choices. There is a strong current of opinion running through this body of literature suggesting that the timing of Thatcher's arrival, her direct and persistent will, and the actions of forceful education secretaries imbued with a neo-liberal ideology, were the principal driving forces responsible for bringing these reforms about (Ball 1990, 2008; Chitty 2004; Simon 1991; Tomlinson 2005; Whitty 1989, 2008).

---

part of the National Association of Teachers in Further and Higher Education, NATFHE) and six from the Joint Four secondary associations. The NUT had a comfortable majority. However, in the 1960s, when the government wanted to enforce a 'pay pause', it sought a more direct influence by refusing to implement the settlement negotiated in the Burnham Committee. This was achieved through the 1965 Remuneration of Teachers Act which, with LEA endorsement, gave the government direct representation on Burnham, a right of veto over the global sum of any award, and a weighted vote over its distribution. It also gave the minister the right to vary the membership of the Burnham Committee (Barber 1992: 33).

[21] The consequences of the post-war baby-boom meant an increasing pressure on the education budget until the 1960s simply to maintain existing levels of teachers' salaries. Given steady post-war inflation on top of these pressures, teachers' salaries fell slightly in relative terms during the late 1940s and 1950s. The government was at this time increasingly turning instead to consultation with the Trade Union Congress (TUC) over economic issues. The teacher unions had remained outside the TUC, hostile as it was to some of its far-left political alignments. This prompted the NUT and the Joint Four, along with several other white-collar organisations, to establish the Conference of Professional and Public Service Organisations, COPPSO, in 1962. COPPSO sought representation on the National Economic Development Council, similar to that granted to the TUC. But the Conservative government insisted on consultation with the TUC only, which brought about COPPSO's collapse as organisations withdrew and affiliated with the TUC. The NUT followed suit in 1970, recognising that this was the only option if it were to achieve anything by influencing the government through legal enactments. The NUT was thus forced into a closer formal working relationship with the wider trade union movement (Ironside and Seifert 1995: 103).

However, the reason why these reforms were quickly implemented is missed by this interpretation of events. Vested interests, which are only treated in a cursory manner in the literature, in fact play a major role in understanding the reasoning behind these changes and associated legislation. The teacher unions, which prior to 1979 had served as a force for stability in education and the progress of slow-moving reform, were now being undermined to such an extent that radical reform was now able to bring about rapid changes to education. First, there were only a few constitutional constraints on Thatcher's leadership since her government had an overwhelming majority in Parliament. Once the government had decided on a policy change – the process for which the unions were entirely excluded from – it could simply force the necessary measures through. Second, the government curbed vested interests by dismantling the 'iron triangle'. The Schools Council, which had operated a system of interest representation that had hitherto placed the unions in a strong position, was abolished and never recalled.[22] At the local level, the influence of the teacher unions was severely reduced through the curbing of local authority power – primarily achieved via funding cuts and the outsourcing of schools to non-governmental bodies. Furthermore, industrial relations between the local authorities and teacher unions were seriously hampered by the centralisation of decision-making powers over pay and working conditions. The late 1980s thus witnessed the demise of local government and an unprecedented degree of centralisation, propelling the teacher unions into a long-term decline (Jones 1985).

Hollowing Out the Local Authorities

Central government, believing that local government was swollen, bureaucratic, ineffective and inordinately costly (it funded 60 per cent of local government expenditure) passed some 40 acts affecting local government finance and administration. One of these acts, passed in 1980, strengthened central control of spending by fixing local government expenses (the block grant) at the level deemed necessary to maintain a uniform national service.[23] Moreover, the power of local authorities to raise extra money through local taxation was abolished, and they were penalised if they exceeded spending targets (Rhodes 1992). Such funding arrangements progressively reduced each LEA's share of the aggregate school budget (the total sum available for schools and their administration), and instead gave the schools increased spending power to purchase services from contractors other than their own authority.[24] In

---

[22] The government also did away with a range of independent advisory groups and committees concerning the issue of teacher training. For instance, the Association of Local Authority Education Committees was closed down in 1983, as was the Advisory Committee on the Supply and Education of Teachers in 1985.

[23] Following an act in 1984 on grants and awards, the government could take control over local spending by taking money from the block grant and reallocating it to projects (Education Support Grants) considered important by the education secretary.

[24] Such services included ground and building maintenance, professional development and in-service education, and school meals.

addition, funding went directly to those schools which – enabled by the 1988 Education Reform Act – had opted out of LEA control, and now were called Grant Maintained schools, GMs. In 1997, some 1,000 out of 35,000 secondary schools – a great majority of them grammar schools – were grant-maintained (Tomlinson 2005: 60). Moreover, funds of £120 million were given to establish City Technology Colleges (CTCs) in order to provide more parental choice.[25]

The 1988 Education Reform Act linked admissions to resources via an age weighted *per capita* funding formula that determined school budgets.[26] GMs controlled their own admissions; they could, and did, ignore the LEA admissions principles and procedures in their pursuit of pupils and increased funding. The schools could also recruit their own teachers, consequently removing the LEA as sole employer. The influence exerted by the LEAs was thus closely related to the number of schools within their administrative boundaries that had achieved GM status. Those LEAs where a majority of schools had switched to GM status lost a considerable amount of control and were left with the task of monitoring; while those authorities with only a limited number of such schools were able to persist with catchment area as a primary means of place allocation. Local admissions policies had the capacity to constrain parental choice and channel families towards particular schools (Fitz et al. 1993, 2001). As the policy of opting-out has continued under successive governments up to the present day, the number of direct government-funded schools has soared, resulting in a continuous decrease of local authority power and union influence.

Abolishing Collective Bargaining

At this time (the late 1980s), the majority of schools were still run by the local authorities, which were the employers of teachers and had strong links to the teacher unions. Formal negotiations which supplemented national bargaining over pay (in the Burnham Committee) and conditions of service (in the Council of Local Education Authorities/Schoolteachers' Committee, CLE/ST), as well as concerning job regulation including many aspects of teacher employment, were held in standing joint committees between local authorities and the teacher unions. Although the LEAs' role as employer had already eroded as schools became relatively free-standing management units that were able to hire and fire their own teachers, this formal negotiating arrangement was brought to an abrupt end when teachers' national collective bargaining rights were abolished. The Burnham Committee was closed down and replaced by the 1987 Teachers' Pay and Conditions Act. The act was born out of a year-long strike – the worst and longest period of industrial conflict in education in England (Seifert 1987).

[25] Only 15 CTCs had opened in 1993, and these were abandoned and supplanted by technology colleges and specialist schools.
[26] Kenneth Baker had also proposed radical plans concerning accountability; that is, accountability to the market via a voucher scheme. Such a voucher scheme was discussed, but rejected because it would result in huge subsidies to the private sector. Instead, as part of the 1988 reforms, the government opted for formula funding, delegated budgets and open enrolment.

The complexity of the situation can best be understood from two angles: a powerful government seeking to curb union power, and an inter- and intra-union rivalry which constantly hampered teachers' efforts to gain power and influence. For the first time the NUT was threatened by the vastly expanded NASUWT. The NAS and UWT had merged in 1976 as a consequence of the Sex Discrimination Act in 1975, which prohibited the exclusion of members on the grounds of gender. The NASUWT, representing groups of teachers mainly in the secondary school sector, wanted to use its market strength for its own benefit – just like the NUT. Early on in the dispute, the unions formed a broad-based alliance, but divisions soon began to emerge, thus preventing them from presenting a united front on pay increases, pay structures and pay negotiations, something which the government exploited.

Despite the recession of the early 1980s, the NUT demanded higher salaries – 7.5 per cent more than was being offered by the employers – based on an argument that its members' pay had been falling behind other professional groups since the early 1970s. To reinforce its demand, the union had, in 1984, called for a series of one-day and three-day stoppages on a rotational basis, and linked these with various school-level actions such as providing no cover for absent colleagues. The claim went through an arbitration process under Burnham, but collapsed as the NUT refused to accept the offer of a 5.1 per cent increase. More strikes and militant actions immediately followed. The NUT, lobbying local authorities, was backed by more than half of them (a number of them with New Labour majorities after the 1984 May elections) over its salary claim. This resulted in a new offer of 6.9 per cent, which the NASUWT and the smaller unions were now prepared to accept. But the increasingly militant NUT was adamantly opposed to this, arguing that 6.9 per cent would do nothing to help the erosion of teacher pay. It therefore used its teachers' panel majority on the Burnham Committee to reject the offer.[27] This provoked another series of strikes, for which 76 per cent of NUT members voted in favour in a ballot (Seifert 1987: 167–229).

By this time the unions were confronted by a secretary of state for education, Keith Joseph, who was more concerned with defeating the unions and weakening local government than the traditional approach of settling industrial disputes through arbitration. He altered the representational make-up of the various unions on the teachers' panel, resulting in the NUT losing the majority it had held on the Burnham Committee since its establishment in 1919. The NUT was outvoted for the first time when the other unions combined to vote in favour of an interim settlement. This settlement provided a 6.9 per cent increase with an additional 1.6 per cent the following year (1986). Under the auspices of a panel, the deal also comprised future talks on pay,

---

[27] Ideological and tactical rifts persisted within the upper echelons of the NUT. Since the early 1970s a 'Broad Left' alliance had controlled the union's National Executive, but this was constantly being challenged by a variety of Trotskyite factions, the STA being the most successful.

conditions of service and future negotiating machinery. This opened up a bitter and publicly fought row between the unions, and more strikes soon followed all over the country.

In response to all of this, the government abolished the Burnham Committee, thereby putting a definitive end to teachers' negotiating rights. In its place, Kenneth Baker, the new secretary of state, enacted the 1987 Teachers' Pay and Conditions Act, which gave him the power to impose a settlement. The pay dispute was brought to a close with this piece of legislation – a settlement worth 16.4 per cent over two years (far in excess of the sums Sir Keith Joseph had proposed), a payscale of five levels, and a detailed list of duties – including an obligation to work 1,265 hours of directed time. Subsequently, a government-appointed advisory board – later called the Pay Review Body – was established to advise the secretary of state on pay and conditions. The review body was not applicable to the 'opted out' GM schools and CTC colleges, which instead would issue individual contracts. In any case, the GMs and CTCs had a policy of non-recognition of the unions. This 1987 act provoked an outburst of unity among the unions and yet another wave of strikes ensued (Ironside and Seifert 1995; Seifert 1987: 167–229).

The abolition of the Burnham Committee dealt a massive blow to the unions, who had now lost their most important arena of influence. Once again they failed to hold together a broadly based alliance of teachers committed to a national labour market strategy, resulting in a debacle that left the unions defeated and even more divided. For the NUT there had been an alarming drop in membership as teachers left for smaller and less militant unions. This caused the NUT considerable financial difficulty.[28] In the run-up to the General Election, the government took full advantage of the teachers' weaknesses to announce a radical reform package – the 1988 Education Reform Act. (See Dolton 1996; Dolton *et al.* 2003, 2010 on teacher pay after the abolishment of collective bargaining.)

Central Regulation of Teachers' Working Conditions

Central government took over functions formerly carried out by or shared with local government and teacher unions, as well as devolving many powers once vested in local authorities to greatly empower governing bodies in individual schools. Central government gained a tighter control on curriculum and examinations as well as teachers' practice and training. The 1988 Education Reform Act gave the government substantial and unprecedented control of the curriculum and its assessment. It was a highly prescriptive curriculum, focusing on 'back to basics' for all pupils aged 5–16, who were to be assessed at four key stages (age 7, 11 and 14), with Key Stage 4 (KS4) at age 16 being the GCE

---

[28] Not all members were left-leaning – far from it. For example, in 1983 a larger proportion of teachers voted Conservative than for any other party (Barber 1992; Ironside and Seifert 1995; Tomlinson 2005).

examination.[29] The performance of schools in these tests and exams, except for KS1 (age 7), were to be published in 'league tables'. The curriculum was to be overseen by a newly established National Curriculum Council (NCC) and the School Exam and Assessment Council (SEAC, replacing the School Council), but the secretary of state was granted the ultimate power of decision over actual curriculum content. Inspection, on a four-year cycle, and carried out by semi-privatised inspectorates according to published criteria by Ofsted, was introduced in 1993. In addition, the performance of schools and teachers at all levels was to be assessed on an annual basis.

The government also proceeded to reform teacher training, an action that served to curb teachers' autonomy, and, ultimately, the unions' opportunity to develop a strong platform for teacher professionalism. Prior to 1984, initial teacher training in England was the exclusive province of higher education. The government automatically recognised university-validated qualifications for the formal award of 'Qualified Teacher Status'. The next ten years was a period of intense struggle and confrontation between the government and higher education, a battle that higher education eventually lost. Training was seen by the government as suffering from 'producer capture', with courses primarily being operated in the interest of the universities themselves rather than their 'customers' – schools, parents and children. Hence, attempts were made to open up the teacher training market and make it more accountable to its consumers. Following the foundation of the TTA in 1994 – which marked the formal end to university autonomy – there has been a growth in new routes into teaching that sidestep higher education altogether, such as employment based routes (Furlong et al. 2008). At the same time, training became closely regulated. In 1986, the government established the Council for the Accreditation of Teacher Education (CATE), whose task was to provide national priority areas or criteria for the training of teachers. In 1989, a new government circular took this a stage further by linking the CATE criteria to the National Curriculum. The LEAs in their turn were required to take these into account when submitting plans for the in-service education of teachers to the secretary of state for approval.

The teacher unions saw their longstanding efforts to raise teachers' professional status through a university-based education diminished. The teacher unions had been successful in setting up a committee in 1972 for 'all graduate professions', which was instrumental in the integration of initial teacher training into the higher education sector. This was now being eroded by government intervention, which provided detailed prescription of training courses based on skills development rather than academic knowledge.[30] All of these new polices

---

[29] Subject working groups, appointed by the secretary of state, were to devise the programmes of study and attainment targets for each subject. Children were to sit Standard Assessment Tasks (SATs) in four key stages at ages 7, 11, 14 and 16.

[30] It also effectively removed higher education institutions from developing new teacher training courses.

were met with fierce union opposition, but the unions now lacked the necessary power to obstruct them.

New Labour: New Policies

New Labour continued much of the Thatcher reform agenda, but they also broke away from it in some respects. The 'traditional' Labour policy of substantial increases in funding for education, stricter control of school admissions, and the targeting of low-performing schools in deprived areas, were strongly pursued under New Labour (Bara 2001; Bara and Budge 2001; Wiborg 2015). However, there is one crucial issue on which the Conservative and Labour governments shared a common stance, an issue whose analytical importance seems to be overlooked; namely, both governments excluded the teacher unions and other interests in the policy-making process. This enabled the Labour government, just like its predecessors, to push through a raft of far-reaching education policies without serious constraint. Policy decisions under the Labour government remained central, since it neither wished for a return to a decentralised education system nor to reinstitute the traditional 'iron triangle'. However, Labour did, on occasions, seek consultation with the teaching profession through non-union bodies such as the Teacher Training Agency (later the Training and Development Agency for Schools) and the newly formed National College for School Leadership and General Teaching Council. This, however, was still a far cry from the pre-Thatcherite practice of putting reform proposals through a process of consultation with vested interests.

In contrast to the Conservatives, the Labour government did not seek to undermine the local authorities, but instead developed a tighter fit between central and local government when it came to policy implementation. The government required LEAs to set targets for their own improvement and draw up education plans under guidance from the newly established Standards and Effectiveness Unit of the Department for Education and Employment (DfEE), which set national strategies for literacy and numeracy.[31] On the basis of these strategies, schools were, in their turn, required to set targets for raising standards. The levers of monitoring and target-setting allowed the government to manage the strategies more closely than had been possible under earlier government initiatives. As such, the New Labour period witnessed stronger centralised control of education.

Raising Standards
The overarching policy agenda of the Labour government was to launch an 'attack on low standards' in schools. There would be, as the White Paper

---

[31] Finance regulations stipulated that central government was to decide how local authorities allocated funds to education, and, from 1998, the LEAs' own performance was scrutinised by Ofsted.

Excellence in Schools (1997) stated, 'unrelenting pressure on schools and teachers for improvement'. In 1998 the School Standards and Framework Act was introduced, which outlined an array of initiatives and programmes to raise standards in schools, particularly in relation to literacy and numeracy. Baseline assessment would be made at entry to primary school, as well as the rate of progress pupils had made and their absolute level of achievement. A new set of tests were developed for this purpose. Furthermore, it was ordered that in primary schools at least one hour should be spent on English and one hour on maths, and after-school homework clubs were established. Disadvantaged children were enrolled in 'Education Action Zones' and later 'Excellence in Cities' programmes (Moss 2004; Whitty 2008).

Successful schools that performed well against government targets, and during school inspections, were rewarded with new freedoms; since 2003 these have included the opportunity to expand pupil numbers. In contrast, failing schools, usually in deprived areas, were subjected to special measures and targeted support. Schools not making a sufficient improvement (as identified by Ofsted) could either be closed and reopened with a new programme developed for this purpose – Fresh Start – or taken over by a private education company.[32] Another measure to target low-performing schools was the introduction of the City Academy in 2000 (Gorard 2005). These bear a close resemblance to Thatcher's City Technology Colleges, CTCs, in that they exist outside local authority control and are sponsored by private sponsors (West and Bailey 2013). However, they differ in that a fixed number of them were established (around 400 in all) to replace poorly performing schools in deprived urban areas.

Teachers

Teachers were also targeted with an array of policies aimed at enhancing their standards, reinforced by a programme of performance management based on private sector models. With regard to teacher training, further moves were undertaken to make teaching a skills-based occupation rather than a university-based profession. This development – which had begun in the 1980s – was in part designed to undermine universities' hold over initial teacher training. An initiative called the National Partnership Project (2001–05) was launched to support providers of teacher training – including universities, schools and LEAs – by increasing the training capacity in schools through the creation of 'partnerships' between groups of schools.

At the same time, teacher training was subjected to increasing regulation. National regulations specified the structure, curriculum and standards of all courses, including courses that were once provided by a university; as well as dictating the requirement to work in 'partnership' with schools. As part

---

[32] In 1999 the DfEE had named ten consortia willing to take a lead in partially privatising state education.

of this regulation, all students are required to spend a large part of their programme – up to two-thirds of it for trainee secondary school teachers – working in schools. All programmes are inspected by Ofsted to ensure provision conforms to national requirements (Beck 2009; Furlong *et al.* 2008).

Performance Management, Pay and Working Conditions
Teachers' salaries continued to be determined by national wage arrangements by the School Teachers' Review Body. But in 1998, a Green Paper set out a new career and pay structure for teachers. It also contained plans for improved management and leadership for head teachers, and the dismissal of incompetent teachers.[33] The paper proposed two payscales for classroom teachers with a performance threshold to be passed via a new appraisal system. Teachers would be reviewed annually against agreed objectives and those exceeding the threshold would receive higher pay. The programme was implemented on a nationwide level the following year and fiercely resisted and undermined by all interests opposing it. In a random survey of 1,000 schools, Wragg (2004) found that 88 per cent of eligible staff had applied, but school managers had used their discretionary powers to award bonuses to 97 per cent. The entire principle of attaching pay to performance floundered. However, in July 2000, and as a result of action by the NUT, the High Court ruled that the 'standards' teachers should meet for the threshold pay increase were invalid since they should have been formally referred to the Review Body. It further ruled that the consultation period on the draft duties had been too short.

Individual appraisals, a statutory requirement in 1992, was used to identify ways of improving skills and performance, situations where a change of job might be appropriate, candidates for promotion, training needs, and poor performance. In 1994–95, some 5,000 redundancies were made (Ironside and Seifert 1995: 123). Under intense political pressure to deliver results, school leaders were also fired. The figure increased fivefold between 2004–05 and 2007–08, from 30 to 150 (West *et al.* 2011: 55). However, in spite of this, teacher job security was, and still is, very high in the UK.

The teacher unions initiated a campaign of industrial action against the increasing workloads that New Labour's brand of public management was ushering in – particularly the increased administration of accountability procedures. The NUT, along with two other unions, passed identical motions at their 2001 conferences in support of a 35-hour week. This represented a rare show of unity among the unions, and one which resulted in a government response (Stevenson and Carter 2009). For the first time since the abolition of the Burnham Committee in 1987, the government opened formal discussions with the teacher unions at a national level. This resulted in a collective agreement, in

---

[33] The Chief Inspector of Schools, Chris Woodhead, had claimed there were some 13,000 teachers in this 'incompetent' category, as well as some 3,000 head teachers who were guilty of offering poor leadership.

2005, between the teacher unions and employers (the Department of Children, Schools and Families, the Local Government Employers and the Welsh Assembly), an agreement that was inked in the form of the *Raising Standards and Tackling Workload* document.[34] It was agreed that teachers should be allowed more time for planning, preparation and assessment (PPA), and that classroom assistants should take over more administrative and clerical tasks. However, the adversarial NUT refused to sign the national agreement. It was opposed to the notion of staff without Qualified Teacher Status having responsibility for whole classes.[35] New Labour did not restore teachers' negotiating rights, and the government maintained the Review Body – but it did include unions in negotiations over workloads, although the NUT refused to take part.

The Coalition: A Nation of American-Style Charter Schools?

The Conservative Party and the Liberal Democrats, who formed a Coalition government in 2010, developed an effective policy to further undermine union power: the Academy and Free School programme. Almost immediately after the Coalition assumed power, it introduced an Education Act that provided a framework for rolling out these schools nationwide. Scholars frequently point to the strong affinity between the New Labour and Coalition governments' Academy programmes, whereas in fact the two governments have fundamentally different scopes for, and rationales behind, them (Avis 2011; Hatcher 2011; West 2014; West and Bailey 2013). Whereas New Labour restricted the number of Academies – as a way of offering a fresh start for failing schools in areas of high deprivation and historically low achievement – the Coalition regarded the Academies as a model applicable to all schools.

There are no clear conceptual differences between the Academies and Free Schools in the act, but in reality Academies are already-established schools converting to Academy status, whereas Free Schools are entirely new schools established mainly by groups of parents, charities, religious organisations and academy chains. Non-state providers wishing to set up a Free School must (usually after receiving free advice from the partly government-funded Schools Network) submit an application to the Department of Education for approval. To enforce quick implementation, the government removed the local authorities' power to veto a school becoming an Academy, dispensed with parents' and teachers' legal rights to oppose such plans, and allowed schools categorised by inspectors as 'outstanding' to 'fast-track' the process of becoming

---

[34] *Raising Standards and Tackling Workload* had many features of a traditional collective agreement, but it cannot be regarded as the product of traditional Burnham-style collective bargaining.

[35] This suspicion appeared to be vindicated when at the end of 2003 a 'blue skies' paper circulating in the DfES suggested fewer qualified teachers and the employment of unqualified private-agency staff in schools.

Academies. After four years, more than half of secondary schools and about one in ten primary schools have changed to Academy status; and about 175 Free Schools have opened. Many more schools are in the pipeline to be established in the coming years (Hatcher 2011, Higham 2013; Wiborg 2015).

It is important to point out here that all these schools – and many more schools on their way – are outside the realms of local authority control and funded directly by the government, which has contributed even further to the erosion of the local authorities' responsibility for providing education. The Academies and Free Schools have more autonomy than local authority-maintained schools – for instance in the way in which they use the national curriculum and set their own terms and conditions for staff, including permission to hire unqualified teachers. They do not have to abide by School Teachers' Pay and Conditions, the Conditions of Service for School Teachers in England and Wales (also called *The Burgundy Book*, 76 pages), which are incorporated into teachers' contracts, and other terms and conditions negotiated nationally for school teachers and support staff. The Academies are constrained by the protection of employment law of 2006 (also called TUPE) as it limits the new employers' ability to vary contractual terms and conditions. However, it does not prevent an employer from deciding on dismissals, something which has occurred increasingly over the last few years.

All the teacher unions have retaliated by pumping large amounts of money into an anti-Academy, anti-Free School campaign. The unions, affiliated with the Trade Union Congress, and in association with the anti-Academy Alliance, warn governors, head teachers and parents who are considering converting their status. They warn teachers against taking a job in an Academy, arguing that they will not be protected against their managers or employers. They also provide a large package of information to aid members, representatives and parents in the campaign against Academy status. If their campaign fails – and they often do – they will then try to lobby head teachers or the academy chains (such as Oasis, ARK, EACT and ULT) to keep to the national agreements, arguing that a national framework must be provided for all teachers' contracts so as to avoid all the 'dangers and complications associated with the developments of a two-tier system' (NUT 2014). The new teachers in the Academies will put at risk, so the warning goes, much that the unions have negotiated in recent years: guaranteed planning, preparation time and assessment time, removal of administrative tasks from teacher duties, limits on working time, continuing professional development entitlements, etc. Many of these came as the result of the school workforce remodelling agenda agreed with the unions in the early 2000s.

The NUT, along with other unions, offers help in negotiating pay and conditions for members who are already working in the Academies (transferred teachers retain their previous contracts). In these negotiations, the NUT, as its overriding priority, seeks to secure the application of the national provisions on pay structure, pay levels and working time, or approximate to comparable arrangements. The NUT will also, like the other unions, stand in the way of a head teacher trying to dismiss teachers. Heads are aware that this is very difficult in a local authority school, but in an Academy this may prove easier.

The resistance against the Academies programme was exacerbated when the education secretary, Michael Gove, called for an introduction of regional pay differentials, less generous teacher pensions, and the reintroduction of performance-related pay. As part of funding cutbacks, the Coalition has also tried to remove school union representatives who are given time off from teaching and paid by local authorities. In 2010, 52 per cent of all days lost as a result of industrial action were attributed to those working in the education sector. This was the highest ever proportion; even during the height of their power, teacher unions only accounted for a small percentage of the total days lost to industrial action. Regardless of this, the Coalition government continued implementing its policies.

In 2013, legislation ruled that all schools in the country be made subject to performance-related pay, following recommendations from the School Teachers' Review Body. From September 2014 schools would need to have revised their pay and appraisal policies and set out how pay progression will be linked to teacher performance as opposed to an annual salary increment structure. The issues determining pay settlement are: its impact on pupils' progress, its impact on wider outcomes for pupils, its contribution to improvement in other areas (e.g., pupil behaviour), professional and career development, and the wider contribution to the work of the school. Heads and school leaders are responsible for developing arrangements for performance-linked pay, and each school can decide how it wishes to do so. It is too early to say how this is being implemented, but there is good reason to expect greater variation between schools in terms of remuneration levels, and the role the teacher unions will play in this. The unions will still be consulted in the local authority-controlled schools, but the Academies and Free Schools might be more inclined to adopt non-union recognition – although the majority of them at present have an agreement with the unions.

Teachers on the whole appear positive about the principle of linking pay to performance (a 2014 YouGov poll found that 89 per cent of teachers supported it). The unions, on the other hand, have been vehemently against it. They claim the new system is lacking in transparency and clear expectations, and that it is based on excessive managerial discretion. They also mistrust the government's assertion that the system is designed to pay good teachers more, arguing that it serves rather to pay everybody less as the government reduces funding for education. They want to maintain the national payscale, which secures teachers a salary above the OECD average (for instance, primary school teachers with at least 15 years' experience average a pay of $44,145, well above the OECD average of $37,603) (OECD 2010). The NUT called a national strike on the 26 March 2014, in which about 10,000 schools took part. More strikes are planned for the future (NUT 2014).

The move towards schools becoming single-employer institutions will radically alter the ways in which pay is determined. Once employers are exempt from a single wage bargaining process then competition for labour can develop on a salary basis, allowing the better-off schools to bid higher. The single-employer bargainer will be forced, as encouraged by the government, to be more competitive. It is not clear to what extent the teacher unions, if at all, will be recognised for bargaining purposes. At the time of writing, the NUT is driving a campaign which demands a rate which is applicable in every school and for all teachers. In the past this demand was met by a national rate that applied to all local authorities, since their individual budgets, political disposition and labour markets varied. Now, the national pay settlement will become much less important, and will effectively set a low minimum rate that will be the rate in schools with tight budgets where teachers' bargaining power is much reduced.

Conclusion

The history of teacher unions in England is one of rise and fall. Much of the NUT's influence in the post-war period until the late 1970s was enabled by and exerted through the close relations it had gained through the 'iron triangle'. This manifested itself in exhaustive consultations which proposed policy changes via various consultation forums – particularly the Burnham Committee and the Schools Council – and often as part of close relations between officials of the various organisations involved. The growing rancour of the 1960s and 1970s put this partnership under strain, and government policy in the 1980s tore it asunder. The centralisation and control of education – together with the emergence of managerial and market models – underpinned by a neo-liberal or New Public Management ideology, removed the historic partnership between government, local authorities and teachers. Teacher autonomy was eroded by the introduction of the National Curriculum and the national literacy and numeracy strategies, and by the enforcement of their contractual duties codified under the 1987 Teachers' Pay and Conditions Act. Reduced funding and increased control of public expenditure, the implementation of private sector management practices in schools, the abolition of national collective bargaining institutions, and, finally, the increased powers of central government at the expense of the local authorities, had a strong impact for the teachers and their unions.

For the NUT the picture is one of long-term decline. It ended in a vacuum that affected it more than any other union. Defending the basic rate of pay has been the NUT's key organising principle, but the continuing existence of the Review Body has eroded its campaign focus. To overcome this hurdle, the NUT has recently turned to professionalism, aiming to influence education policy through building school-level alliances between teachers, parents and governors. During the Coalition government, the union experienced a revival, not in terms of achieving influence over education policy, but rather as part of a focused attempt to protest against it. There has been a recent resurgence of the left in the NUT, which has prompted stronger activism. The campaign is strongly focused on its dislike of Academies and Free Schools and the perceived worsening and unprotected working conditions of teachers. The opposition from the NUT intensified when plans by Michael Gove were announced to have a more rigid application of appraisal and performance-related pay.

Teacher unions are defeated, but not destroyed. They have maintained their overall membership and have demonstrated a sustained capacity to persist. In searching for a new role, the unions will not allow themselves to be reduced to mere watchdogs holding head teachers to account. The question is whether the union would even maintain that role if Academies were to start a policy of non-union recognition or were to be run by the ever-increasing number of voluntary sponsors, and, if given the green light by government, for-profit businesses. Moreover, teachers are increasingly seeking advice from recently established legal firms specialising in teachers' pay and working conditions. These new developments simply add to the unions' reduced ability to negotiate pay and conditions, both at national and local levels.

References

Avis, J. (2011) More of the same? New Labour, the Coalition and education: Markets, localism and social justice. *Educational Review* 63(4), pp. 421–38.
Ball, S.J. (1990) *Politics and Policy Making in Education: Explorations in Policy Sociology*. London: Routledge.
 (2008) *The Education Debate*. Bristol: Policy Press.
Bara, J., and Budge, I. (2001) Party policy and ideology: Still New Labour? *Parliamentary Affairs* 67(2), pp. 590–606.
Barber, M. (1992) *Education and the Teacher Unions*. London: Cassell.
Beck, J. (2009) Appropriating professionalism: Restructuring the knowledge base of England's 'modernised' teaching profession. *British Journal of Sociology of Education* 30(1), pp. 3–14.
 (2010) Governmental professionalism: Re-professionalising or de-professionalising teachers in England? *British Journal of Educational Studies* 56(2), pp. 119–43.
Benn, C., and Chitty, C. (1997) *Thirty Years On: Is Comprehensive Education Alive and Well or Struggling to Survive*, 2nd ed. Harmondsworth: Penguin Books.
Benn, C., and Simon, B. (1972) *Half Way There: Report on the British Comprehensive School Reform*, 2nd ed. Harmondsworth: Penguin.
Budge, I. (2001) *Mapping Policy Preferences. Estimates for Parties, Electors, and Governments 1945–1998*. Oxford: Oxford University Press.
Chitty, C. (2004) *Education Policy in Britain*. New York: Palgrave Macmillan.
Coates, R.D. (1972) *Teachers' Unions and Interest Group Politics: A Study in the Behaviour of Organised Teachers in England and Wales*. Cambridge: Cambridge University Press.
Cooper, B., ed. (1992) *Labor Relations in Education: An International Perspective*. Westport: Greenwood Press.

Dolton, P., and Robson, M. (1996) Trade union concentration and the determination of wages: The case of teachers in England and Wales. *British Journal of Industrial Relations* 34(4), pp. 539–55.
Dolton, P., Makepeace, G., and Marcenaro-Gutierrez, O. (2010) *Public Sector Pay in the UK: Quantifying the Impact of the Review Bodies.* Mimeo.
Dolton, P., McIntosh, S., and Chevalier, A. (2003) Teacher pay and performance, Institute of Education, Bedford Way Papers.
Fitz, J., Halpin, D., and Whitty, G. (1993) *Education in the Market Place: Grant Maintained Schools.* London: Kogan Page.
Fitz, J., Taylor, S., Gorard, S., and White, P. (2001) *Local Education Authorities and the regulation of educational markets: Four case studies.* Occasional Paper, Cardiff University.
Furlong, J., McNamara, O., Campbell, A., Howson, J., and Lewis, S. (2008) Partnership, policy and politics: Initial teacher education in England under New Labour. *Teachers and Teaching: Theory and Practice* 14(4), pp. 307–18.
Gorard, S. (2005) Academies as the 'future of schooling': Is this an evidence-based policy? *Journal of Educational Policy* 20(3), pp. 369–77.
Gosden, P. (1972) *The Evolution of a Professional Union.* London: Basil Blackwell.
Green, A. (1990, 2013) *Education and State Formation. Europe, East Asia and the USA.* New York: Palgrave Macmillan.
Hatcher, R. (2011) The Conservative-Liberal Democrat Coalition government's 'free schools' in England. *Education Review* 63(4), pp. 485–503.
Higham, R. (2013) Free schools in the Big Society: The motivations, aims and demography of free school proposers. *Journal of Education Policy* 29(1), pp. 122–39.
Hinton, J. (1983) *Labour and Socialism. A History of the British Labour Movement 1867–1974.* Norfolk: Wheatsheaf Books Ltd.
Ironside, M., and Seifert, R. (1995). *Industrial Relations in Schools.* London: Routledge.
Jones, K. (1985) The National Union of Teachers (England and Wales). In Lawn, M, ed., *The Politics of Teacher Unionism. International Perspectives.* London: Croom Helm.
Moss, G. (2004) Changing practice: The National Literacy Strategy and the politics of literacy policy. *Literacy* 38(3), pp. 126–33.
NUT (2014) www.teachers.org.uk
OECD (2010) *Education at a glance 2010. OECD indicators.* OECD.
Rhodes, R.A.W. (1992) Local Government Finance. In D. Marsh and R.A.W. Rhodes, eds, *Implementing Thatcherite Policies.* Buckingham: Open University Press.
 (1997) *Understanding Governance. Policy Networks, Governance, Reflexibility and Accountability.* Buckingham: Open University Press.
Robinson, W. (2002) Historical reflections on the 1902 Education Act. *Oxford Review of Education* 28(2,3), pp. 159–72.
Salter, B., and Tapper, T. (1981) *Education Politics and the State: The Theory and Practice of Educational Change.* London: Grant McIntyre.
Saran, R. (1992) The History of Teachers' Pay Negotiations. In H. Tomlinson, ed., *Performance-Related Pay in Education.* London: Routledge.
Seifert, R.V. (1987) *Teacher Militancy: A History of Teacher Strikes 1896–1987.* London: Falmer Press.

Simon, B. (1965) *Education and the Labour Movement, 1870–1920*. London: Lawrence & Wishart.
—— (1974) *The Politics of Educational Reform, 1920–1940*. London: Lawrence & Wishart.
—— (1991) *Education and the Social Order, 1940–1990*. London: Lawrence & Wishart.
Stevenson, H. (2007) Restructuring teachers' work and trade union responses in England: Bargaining for change? *American Educational Research Journal* 44, pp. 224–39.
Stevenson, H., and B. Carter (2009) Teachers and the state: Forming and re-forming 'partnership'. *Journal of Educational Administration and History* 41(4), pp. 311–26.
Thompson, D. (1927) *Professional Solidarity Among Teachers of England*. New York: Columbia University Press.
Tomlinson, S. (2005) *Education in a Post-Welfare Society*. Berkshire: Open University Press.
Tropp, A. (1957) *The School Teachers*. London: Heinemann.
Vlaeminke, M. (2000) *The Higher Grade Schools: A lost opportunity*. London: Woburn.
West, A. (2014) Academies in England and independent schools (fritstående skolor) in Sweden: Policy privatization, access and segregation. *Research Papers in Education*.
West, A., and Bailey, E. (2013) The development of the Academies programme: 'Privatising' school-based education in England 1986–2013. *British Journal of Educational Studies* 61(2), pp. 137–59.
West, A., Mattei, P., and J. Roberts (2011) Accountability and sanctions in English schools. *British Journal of Educational Studies* 59(1), pp. 41–62.
Whitty, G. (1989) The New Right and the National Curriculum: State control or market forces? *Journal of Educational Policy* 4(4), pp. 329–34.
—— (2008) Twenty years of progress? English education policy 1988 to the present. *Educational Management Administration & Leadership* 36(2), pp. 165–84.
Wiborg, S. (2015) Privatising Education: Free School policy in Sweden and England. *Comparative Education Review* 59(3), pp. 473–97.
Wragg, E. (2004) *Performance Pay for Teachers. The Views and Experiences of Heads and Teachers*. London: Routledge Falmer.

4

Teacher Unionism in France
Making Fundamental Reform an Impossible Quest?

Michael Dobbins

Introduction

This chapter examines teacher unionism in France. Contrary to most other cases highlighted in this book, France stands out with its highly centralized education system (Cole 2001) and longstanding (but never fully realized) attachment to the principle of educational egalitarianism (Baudelot and Establet 2009; Dobbins and Martens 2012). By exploring the structural foundations of French teacher unions and their strategies vis-à-vis the state, this chapter shows how teacher unionism has stymied government reform proposals time and time again. Through concerted action and the exploitation of their internal differences, teachers unions have played a crucial role in upholding central pillars of French secondary education such as low institutional autonomy, centralization, and high expenditure. Thus, French teacher unionism presents a fascinating case for analysts of interest group power.

I first discuss the historical rise of teacher unionism in France, before addressing the striking diversity of the teacher union landscape. The bulk of the analysis focuses on how teachers unions interact not only with the state bureaucracy, but also with each other, labour unions and other educational stakeholders. I also elaborate on the strategies of French teachers unions in public sector strikes, which have served to frustrate government reform efforts for decades. As shown below, French teachers unions have applied inward pressure, i.e. through educational "co-management" within the ministerial bureaucracy; and outward pressure, i.e. through concerted strikes, to assert their vested interests. Altogether, the analysis shows that educational policy-making distinguishes itself substantially from other policy areas in France, in which policy-making tends to be of a more hierarchical nature.

Historical Development

Teacher unions emerged simultaneously with the construction of the centralized school system during the Third Republic (1870–1940) (Ambler 1985: 28), thus earlier than many other countries discussed in this book. The strong centralization of education essentially was the result of a power struggle between the central government and religious interests at the local level, a struggle in which the central government asserted itself. The argument prevailed that a centralized school system would ensure nationwide equality and fend off local religious influences and "territorial solidarities" (Ambler 1994; Cole 2001; Lelièvre 2000: 8). The central state came to be seen as a progressive, rational force (van Zanten 2002: 294), while schools were regarded as secular, neutral venues in order to ensure justice and equal opportunity (Cole 2001: 709–10). Thus local diversity has historically been viewed as subordinate to national concerns, while the centralized bureaucracy is supposed to defend the public interest against private interests.

French education has historically been regarded as a vehicle for nation-building and social leveling. Elite (secondary) schools are largely absent, while – unlike in Germany – there is no stratification of secondary pupils into different school types based on academic ability. Moreover, education is regarded as intrinsically intertwined with the welfare state, which has resulted in a legacy of policies from the center. These guiding principles are reflected in the institutional set-up in which teachers unions operate. French schools are almost exclusively publicly financed and all primary and secondary teachers are employed by the central government, making the Ministère de l'Éducation Nationale (MEN) the country's largest employer (MEN 2010) and one of the largest bureaucratic structures in the world. The influence of the state goes to the extent that even private schools, which are largely Catholic, increasingly came under state control after the Second World War. Most private institutions are under contracts of association with the state and are also primarily state-funded. In fact, one main priority of French teachers unions has been to fully integrate the private sector into the public education system.

Not least due to teachers unions, the central government has historically exerted and continues to exert extensive control over curricula, teacher training and personnel matters. Against this background, the story of French teacher unionism is a story of strategic mobilization around the centralized Parisian bureaucracy (Athanasiades and Patramanis 2002: 22). The first federated union of primary school teachers – the Fédération nationale des syndicats d'instituteurs – was created in 1905 and allied with the CGT labour union (Confédération générale du travail). In 1930, the so-called Fédération Générale de l'Enseignement (FGE) was established within the CGT, while the primary school teachers joined the federation as the SNI (Syndicat National des Instituteurs). Secondary-level teachers then grouped to form the Union of Secondary Teaching Personnel (Syndicat des personnels de l'enseignment secondaire). Even then, the union landscape was characterized by its strong leftist thrust, as essentially all groups allied with socialist and communist political forces.

However, the Vichy regime dealt a major blow to teacher unionism by banning all union activities. After liberation, the FGE became the Fédération de l'éducation nationale (FEN), while several secondary school unions regrouped to form the SNES (Syndicat national des enseignements de second degré) within the FEN. Besides the SNES, the most notable group operating within the FEN was the anti-clerical Syndicat National des Instituteurs (SNI) (see Bourdoncle and Robert 2000: 75). The post-war phase heralded a new union strategy, as the main teachers unions severed formal ties with national labor unions. As an autonomous federation, the FEN consisted of approximately 45 teachers' groups from different segments of the education system (primary *écoles*, lower secondary *collèges*, upper secondary *lycées*, and higher education), of which an overwhelming majority were of a leftist persuasion (Fowler 1992; Gaziel and Taub 1992; Mouriaux 1996).

Essentially, the FEN came to reflect the entire diversity of French leftism. The Federation comprised three major ideological streams (so-called "tendencies"), which shared different political alignments and competing visions of school organization: (1) a majority group called *autonomes*, which later increasingly aligned with the Socialist Party and after 1971 called itself "Unité, Indépendence et Démocratie"; (2) the Unité et Action group, which was strongly affiliated with the Communist Party, but also included several non-communist factions; and (3) the extreme leftist École émancipée (emancipated school) (Ferhat 2011). The aim of the emancipated school movement was to make schools more cooperative, egalitarian and solidarity-based, by ensuring that all young people benefited from the same quality of education in highly uniform schools. In the late 1960s, Unité et Action took control of two major unions within the Federation, the SNES and SNEP (Syndicat national de l'éducation physique and National Union of Physical Education).

Instead of joining the federated structure, the Syndicat Général de l'Éducation Nationale (SGEN) aligned itself with the CFDT labour union (Confédération française démocratique du travail) after its foundation in 1937. Initially left-leaning, the SGEN has increasingly viewed itself as a reformer and pedagogical innovator (Geay 2005). It expressly promotes educational democratization – e.g. a longer integrated track (*tronc commun*) – and played a critical role in creating so-called Educational Priority Zones.[1] Like the FEN, its political home is generally the Socialist Party. Thus, all French teachers unions have traditionally competed to become the primary "consultant" for education policy for French socialists (Ferhat 2011).

---

[1] *Zones d'éducation prioritaires* (ZEPs) were established in disadvantaged socioeconomic areas and received additional government funding.

After profoundly shaping the French union landscape and education policy (see below), the FEN was dismantled during the 1990s. The SNES and SNEP were excluded from the Federation for not adhering to the so-called "federal pact." At the same time, activists from the Unité et Action groups also left the FEN to found the Fédération Syndicale Unitaire (FSU), which was joined by the SNES and an array of other groups. The remaining factions within the FEN then established the UNSA (Union nationale des syndicats autonomes), which became a more general union without exclusive teacher membership. However, the leftist clout of the union landscape was by no means weakened during this period of reshuffling. In the mid-1990s a conglomeration of ardent leftists abandoned their respective unions to form SUD Éducation (*Solitaires, Unitaires, Démocratiques*), which consists of adamantly leftist teachers and students who vehemently oppose educational deregulation and privatization.

Despite the organizational shifts in the 1990s, the level of teacher unionization in France remains comparatively high and the previous policy-making logic from the FEN era continues to apply (Geay 2005; Moriaux 1996). While teacher union membership surpassed 70 percent in the 1970s, it decreased to approximately 50 percent in the 1990s. Ever since, membership has continued to decline and currently amounts to approximately 30 percent (Andolfatto and Labbé 2007: 120). Nevertheless, the level of teacher unionism is still significantly higher than the level of overall public sector unionism in France (approximately 15 per cent, EPSU 2008). Like the FEN, the FSU remains the dominant teacher union federation and accounts for about 50 percent of union membership with approximately 163,000 adherents (FSU website 2013). The UNSA is the second largest teacher union, although teachers do not constitute the majority within this primarily public sector union (teacher membership approximately 100,000, UNSA Éducation website 2013). The reform-oriented SGEN accounts for about 10 percent of teacher union membership despite a gradual decline. There is also a union representing private education (Fédération de l'enseignement privé – FEP), in which approximately 40,000 private education employees are organized. This amounts to a unionization rate of approximately 7.5 percent, which is much lower than in public education, and on a par with the overall level of unionization in France (Andolfatto and Labbé 2007: 120). Despite declining membership levels, the strong presence of public teachers unions is also accompanied by the active interest of labor unions (e.g., CFDT, Force Ouvrière) in education, who engage in fluctuating alliances with education-specific unions. Particularly noticeable in recent years are the strong synergy effects between teachers unions and anti-globalization movements such as Attac, which in turn reinforces the broader leftist orientation.

Internal Union Structures and Relationships to the State and Partisan Actors

The question arises as to how teachers unions interact with the state and other actors. I first briefly address the relationship between teacher organizations and the Socialist Party (Parti socialiste), before turning to the crucial patterns of interaction between teachers and the executive. Like in the United States, where teachers unions generally have aligned with the Democratic Party, French teachers unions are also very politically active. Ferhat (2011), for example, speaks of an "overrepresentation" of teachers unions in the Socialist Party. In the 1970s, the Socialist Party initially aimed to fend off the communist movement by reinforcing its ties with the FEN. This opened numerous new avenues for teachers unions to assert their clout. However, precisely when French socialists were the governing party under François Mitterrand, the FEN was rapidly losing membership. Thus, the FEN lost its influence over the Socialist Party, which did not intervene to sustain the FEN when it collapsed in the 1990s. Nevertheless, we can still speak of a broader ideological proximity between the major teachers unions (FSU, UNSA, SGEN) and French socialists, who have historically pushed for greater state investment in, and the expansion of, public education. In fact, the efforts of the center-right Sarkozy government to downsize the teacher corps and decentralize educational governance (see below) served to revitalize union ties with the Socialist Party.

What is more important, however, for understanding the influence of French teachers unions is their relationship to the executive, regardless of the governing party. There is a predominant view in the social sciences that the French executive has a strong capacity for action and can easily assert its preferred policies through its relatively homogenous bureaucratic structures. The fact that French labour unions tend to be weak and fragmented (Quittkat 2006; van Waarden 1993) plays into this conventional perception of central government as omnipotent. Along these lines, France is seldom classified as a corporatist country (Siaroff 1999; Schmidt 2000) since the main policy-making mode is generally "top-down" and hierarchical. This image is compounded by large societal divisions along religious, ideological and socioeconomic lines, which would intuitively bolster the position of the state over fragmented interests. Thus, it is plausible to assume that education policy – in particular in view of its highly centralized character – falls in line with this general pattern of decision-making.

However, upon closer examination, French (primary and secondary) education policy-making is a highly "sectoral-corporatist" affair that follows its own logic. Instead of an almighty assertive state, education unions have created a system of institutionalized interchanges with the ministry, which could best be defined as "competitive union co-management" of education policy. In its efforts to "democratize" education and be seen as closely collaborating and winning consent (Duclaud-Williams 1985: 91), the education ministry has enabled teachers unions to become heavily entangled within its decision-making apparatus. This falls in line with the general French mode of governance which encourages the growth and incorporation of powerful interest groups (Baumgartner and Walker 1989). For example, the French government subsidizes interest groups which it regards as its current political allies and therefore as crucial for policy implementation. Precisely, this applies to education policy, where a system of institutionalized co-administration between the state and education unions has emerged. For example, van Zanten speaks of an "alliance between the educational state and the republic of teachers" (2002: 295) to the extent that education policy is never made without union input (Fowler 1992: 29). This interweaving with the ministry is reinforced by a system of personnel and financial interchanges, as many interest groups receive monetary and non-monetary resources (e.g., office space) from the government (Wilsford 2001). Thus, the MEN has proved to be an astoundingly open and penetrable institution, through which teachers have wielded remarkable veto power.

Yet how exactly do teachers unions penetrate the policy-making process? Two particularly important channels of access are the so-called Commissions administratives paritaires (CAP) and Commissions techniques paritaires (CTP), which are essentially ministerial venues for collective public sector bargaining. Membership in these committees is generally based on the parity of representatives from public administration and elected teacher organizations (Cole 2001: 713; Duclaud-Williams 1985: 82). Unlike in the United States (see Moe's chapter in this book), where teachers unions tend to use their power in political elections to gain influence within parties and policy-making, French teachers unions focus their efforts primarily on so-called "professional elections" (*élections professionelles*). These elections determine which union representatives participate in the CAP and CTP, within which all matters concerning the functioning of the public teaching service are collectively negotiated. This includes the opening and closing of positions, transfers, further education and training, discipline, and scheduling (Geay 2005: 22). Most importantly, the committees decide on personnel issues such as staff transfers and the maintenance of schools (Cole 2001: 713). This enables teachers unions to exert significant leverage over career and resource management. Thus, the ministry essentially provides teachers unions a platform for professional self-regulation.

However, these arrangements are not necessarily as favorable to teachers as may initially seem. Teacher wages are linked to the national public service system and the government has engaged in regular consultations with public sector unions since the end of the 1960s. While talks were generally conducted on an annual basis until the early 1980s, they have become much less frequent in the past 30 years. As a result, salary scales have not been revised since 1990 and annual increases remain well below inflation levels. At the same time, numerous previous French governments have focused their efforts on downsizing the national public sector (EPSU 2013). Hence, the government's steadfastness regarding salary levels has prompted teachers unions to focus their efforts on other vested interests such as securing benefits and, most importantly, upholding and expanding the public teaching service (see below).

Although unable to secure higher wages, teacher unions still strongly regulate their own profession in France, which often leads to a blurring of the boundaries between the civil service and teachers interest groups. For example, civil servants dealing with education are frequently temporarily transferred to work full-time in education unions (Baumgartner and Walker 1989), while teacher union representatives are often temporarily employed within the ministry. These "revolving door" politics enable teacher interest groups to intertwine their personal interests with the public interest. As Cole and John argue (2001: 116), as soon as a new and ambitious education minister takes office, he/she is confronted by an alliance of officials and unionists who insist on upholding the existing (teacher-dominated) corporatist structures and associated consultative privileges.

However, the term "corporatism" comes with several caveats. First, French educational corporatism should not be understood as an institutionalized balancing of interests. Instead, skeptics may be inclined to speak of an institutionalized platform for "teacher rent-seeking," often to the detriment of other actors. For example, organizational rivals to teachers unions – e.g., parent and pupil organizations – have been slow to organize in France. Historically, parents have only played a very small role in the education system compared to the United States and the United Kingdom. For example, the largest parent organization (*Fédération des Conseils de Parents d'Élèves* – FCPE) essentially was created by the SNI teacher union in 1951 to bolster its own position by allying with parents. Thus, the FCPE has historically been strongly linked to teacher unionism, as the main actors generally hold key functions within both the FCPE and SNI, which, as noted above, is incorporated into the Federation structure (Gombert 2008). In fact, parents were only formally recognized as "partners" with the Education Act of 1989. What is noticeable is the strong alignment of objectives and discourse of the parent council and the FSU, which both strongly advocate the national character of education, secularism and centralism (Gombert 2008).

The main institutional addressee for parent and pupil interests – the *Conseil national de l'éducation* (since 2005, the *Haut Conseil de l'éducation*) – is also characterized by a strong teacher union presence. These configurations leave little room for independent parent initiatives. Thus, instead of multilateral and multi-stakeholder policy-making, one could speak of teacher-dominated corporatism, as teachers unions can steer policy towards their preferences both from within the ministerial apparatus as well as through other consultative bodies.

Second, the institutionalized interchanges between the ministry and teachers unions by no means imply that policy-making is predominantly consensual. As shown above, the teacher union landscape is highly fragmented and reflects deeply entrenched cleavages between moderate and far-left, reformist, secular and religious groups (Baumgartner and Walker 1989). Although the FEN has historically aligned itself with the Parti Socialiste (Ferhat 2011), numerous authors highlight the strong ideological and structural divisions within the Federation. In addition to socialist, communist and emancipatory tendencies, the FEN consists of so-called anarcho-syndicalists (Fowler 1992; Gaziel and

Taub 1992: 75). Such groups advocate a takeover of the means of production through union self-organization as a counter-force to the state and to capital. This organizational plurality has to do with the fact that the preferred strategy of the Federation leadership has been to keep far-left forces *within* the federated structure rather than outside of it (see Mouriaux 1996). Due to the strong leftist thrust, there are powerful forces within French teachers unions which advocate the "doubling-down" of existing policies. This pertains, in particular, to further centralization and the integration of private (mainly Catholic) schools into the public education system (FSU 2010). Furthermore, the FSU (previously FEN) consists of different unions representing different educational sectors. This has resulted in divisions between upper-secondary *école* teachers (*instituteurs*), who are primarily of a working-class background, and secondary *collège* and *lycée* teachers (*professeurs*) (Geay 2005: 16).[2] The upcoming section focuses on how French teachers unions strategically pursue their interests vis-à-vis the state and broader society, and how they exploit these internal divisions to foil government reform projects.

Vested Interests, Guiding Principles, and Strategies of French Teacher Unionism

Despite the high density of teacher unions and their close proximity to the state, one might intuitively assume that their inter- and inner-union fragmentation would ultimately weaken their collective clout and enable central government to "divide and rule." However, I argue that the strength of French teachers unions lies precisely in their capacity to strategically manage their own divisions.

What one can frequently observe in France is a strategy of "concerted policy blocking." Specifically, union factions often strive to undermine government proposals which cater for the interests of rival internal groups or other teacher unions (Interview SGEN, Syndicat Général de l'Éducation Nationale, November 16, 2011). For example, the FSU (previously FEN) and its leftist factions often rally against policy proposals which are favorable to more reform-oriented unions such as the SGEN. Along these lines, Mouriaux (1996) argues that this strategy is applied all the more when the government is run by the center-right: in order to counteract the weakness of center-left parties, left-leaning unions tend to overcome their differences and form a common front against government policy. Thus, the political dynamics of teacher unionism are largely driven by fears over the dominance of other union groups. Factions operating within the FSU often fear that other groups will conspire to control the reigns of the entire Federation, which – due to its size – is a key player in opinion formation and policy-making. Along these lines, rival groups often

---

[2] See Fowler (1992) with regard to additional age and gender gaps within the FEN and the SNI-PEGC.

seek to "poach" members from one another in order to increase their clout within the Federation. This logic of internal competition and mistrust also applies to inter-union politics. Rival unions see themselves in a constant struggle for presence and visibility vis-à-vis the government, since this facilitates access to the above-mentioned administrative committees. According to the same logic, *professeurs* and *instituteurs* organized within the FSU (and other unions) seek to steer government resources towards their own educational sector (see Duclaud-Williams 1985: 78–9).

As a result of these dynamics, there are manifold incentives for teachers unions to block government policy. First, union factions often reflexively oppose policies that threaten their professional privileges and ideological convictions. Regardless of their ideological *couleur*, French teachers tend to rally around the principle that education is a protected public space (*espace publique*) constructed around the principles of the "one indivisible republic" (*l'une et indivisible république*) (FSU 2011; 2003). Therefore, efforts to shift decision-making authority to the local level or to school management have frequently been thwarted by teachers unions, which – for strategic reasons discussed below – collectively fear the "denationalization" of education (SNES 2012) and the potential loss of their public service status. In fact, any general overview of position papers from French teachers unions would reveal that upholding the national character of education and national teacher corps is the main recurring theme, and not salary increases (see below). In other words, much of their activity is centered around preventing job losses and the closure of schools (in contrast to the pursuit of higher wages).

Second, due to their close proximity to the ministerial apparatus, teachers unions are in a position to resist policy proposals which might benefit rival inner-union and inter-union interest groups. Interestingly, they frequently use their veto position to thwart government plans – which they may in fact support ideologically – because they are in competition with each other for members and resources (Baumgartner and Walker 1989; Interview SGEN, November 16, 2011).

Third, centralization itself is an additional power resource for unions, since it has the effect of politicizing all issues (see Archer 1979). Specifically, teachers unions target partisan political actors and the central state to assert their demands. This makes education policy-making a highly mediatized affair. In decentralized systems school headmasters or principals are usually not partisan political actors. French teachers unions, by contrast, use the national political arena to gain greater media exposure and garner sympathy for their demands.

However, if centrally operating teachers unions are so intertwined with the governmental bureaucracy and can easily "swat down" reforms from within, why do they strike so frequently? Due to the strong fragmentation and diversity of French teachers unions, it is indeed difficult to obtain consistent reliable data on the frequency and magnitude of teachers' strikes. This problem is compounded by the frequent "contagion effects" of general union strikes or university strikes, which teachers' organizations often join. Based on data from the Education Ministry, there has been an average of eight strike actions per year since 2009, with a great deal of inconsistency in terms of actors and participation rates. While most teacher strikes are one-day events, France has experienced an average of one to two school closures per year, which have lasted more than several days (MEN 2013).

Why are teacher strikes so common in France? Aside from relatively low teacher salaries as a motivational factor (OECD 2011, see below), I argue that their frequency and intensity can again be traced back to institutionalized patterns of conflictual cooperation between the state and teachers. As each group strives for privileged access to the state apparatus and administrative committees (CAP and CTP, see above), fierce competition exists between the education unions. This competition is compounded by the ideological cleavages within the federated unions, as centerist, leftist and far-left forces compete for control of the overarching Federation. Along these lines, strikes frequently serve to increase their presence and visibility vis-à-vis other unions, with whom they are in a state of permanent competition for government resources. This explains why French teacher unions frequently strike when reform proposals do not go far enough. This applies, in particular, to the reformist SGEN (Interview, SGEN, November 16, 2011): if it refused to participate in a strike involving leftist unions, the leftist forces would likely be able to pull the reform outcome in their desired direction.

Moreover, internal union dynamics are also a crucial factor. Union leaders often draw their legitimacy from their previous successes in organizing and carrying out strikes and demonstrations. Against this background, the organizational precision, breadth and impact of strikes can be seen as important reputational criteria among union leaders. For example, Frajerman (2008: 546) argues that teachers unions aim for a strike participation rate of between 50 and 80 percent of members (ibid: 546). Hence, they often strive to outperform each other with regard to the overall participation rate. Strikes also have a strong component of social desirability about them (Interview, SGEN, November 16, 2011), with union members frequently "shaming" fellow non-striking members by publishing lists of non-participants (Frajerman 2008: 545).

Unlike classic labour unions, which generally strike *ex post* – i.e. after a government proposal – French education unions also frequently employ a concerted mid-negotiation tactic. Once the ministry puts forward a proposal, the otherwise ideologically and politically divided teacher unions opt to organize strikes as a means to mitigate dissent and form a common front vis-à-vis the ministry. Hence, strikes often serve to reinforce social ties with other unions (Frajerman 2008: 544–5) to increase their bargaining position. Along these lines, different unions and internal Federation factions often engage in coordinated "rotating strikes" to put pressure on the government. The segmented structure of French teacher unionism, combined with broader ideological proximity and shared policy goals, enables individual teacher unions to strategically coordinate their protest activities. This makes it difficult for the government to strategically exploit divisions between rival factions (Cole and John 2001) and places strong limits on its capacity for policy change.

The Impact of Teacher Unionism on French Education Policy

What has been the concrete impact of teacher unionism on policy-making? I argue that the strong clout of French teacher unionism is reflected in several key dimensions. First, unions have consistently exerted their preference for institutional uniformity over institutional diversity. In other words, a main *leitmotiv* of their actions has been the push for policies aimed at the expansion and preservation of the highly centralized governance model and educational bureaucracy, and, conversely, the rejection of any efforts at decentralization and school autonomy. Second, union power has resulted in the preservation of relatively favorable working and institutional conditions for French teachers within an ever-expanding educational bureaucracy. As shown further below though, French teachers have arguably promoted policy goals which have ultimately undermined their own interest in higher salaries due to the resulting administrative inefficiencies. In the following, I briefly discuss their role in the introduction of comprehensive schools (*collèges*), before focusing in greater detail on their more recent vehement efforts to prevent administrative decentralization and school closures.

Teachers Unions and Comprehensive Schools

No analysis of the politics of education in France should neglect the expansion of post-primary comprehensive schools. In line with several other countries discussed in this book, French policy-makers also aimed to expand educational access by creating a common lower secondary school for all pupils. In line with egalitarian traditions, the *collège* (or *école unique*) was broadly seen as a means of upholding the historically ingrained principles of educational justice and equal opportunity by enabling a shift from stratification by cycle, to stratification by level (Derouet 1991: 120).

The so-called Plan Langevin-Wallon (1947) served as an initial blueprint for the structural design of the *collèges* and a basis for long-term negotiations with the union front, in particular the SNI and SNES (representing primary and secondary teachers within the FEN respectively). In the post-war era, so-called *collèges d'enseignement général* and *collèges d'enseignement technique* offered supplementary instruction for pupils who had completed primary school, and served as a point of orientation before entry to the secondary *lycées*. These initially heterogeneous and locally diverse schools were further institutionalized as *collèges secondaires* after 1963 and began offering additional courses to a larger proportion of pupils based on merit. The Plan Langevin-Wallon aimed to facilitate structural convergence with the comprehensive school system of the UK and USA (Frajerman 2007) and enable free, compulsory and public schooling up to university age by institutionalizing the *collèges* as a common lower secondary school nationwide.

The measures were broadly favored by the unions, as they were ideologically consistent with their core ideals of educational justice and educational uniformity based on centralized standards (Derouet 1991; Frajerman 2007). However, there were several matters of contention. First, it was unclear whether the *collège* would be a mere structural extension of primary schools or be conceived as the first stage of secondary school, whereby the SNI and SNES favored structural integration into their own respective form of school. Moreover, there were disputes over the extent to which pupils would be selected for different learning tracks within the *collège* based on aptitude; and what assessments of aptitude should be applied. While the Plan Langevin-Wallon rejected the idea of aptitude-based selection, both the SNI and SNES unions initially were favorable towards some form of selection. Yet the merger of the SNES with the more technically oriented and less elitist Syndicat national de l'enseignement technique (SNET) in 1967 compelled the SNES to accept the government's highly egalitarian plans for the comprehensive schools (Frajerman 2007).

The 1975 Haby law ultimately introduced uniform instruction at the *collège* for all French adolescents up to the age of 16. By then, the unions had given up any resistance which they initially had towards the introduction of the *collèges,* since this new type of school constituted an additional step towards the centralization of previously locally heterogeneous forms of lower secondary schooling. Perhaps more importantly though, this structural modification played perfectly into the hands of primary teachers, since the *collèges* enabled all pupils from primary school to progress into lower secondary school and keep the same teachers, the same programs, and the same pedagogical methods (Chartier 1999). Thus, they provided opportunities for upward mobility for primary teachers as well as additional job opportunities for upper secondary teachers (*professeurs*) (Frajerman 2007), because both primary and secondary teachers could be employed in the *collèges* after brief additional training at the Instituts pédagogiques de l'enseignement secondaire (IPES). In other words, the *collèges* were viewed as a job-creating measure for teachers from both levels without requiring any major additional effort on the part of the teaching corps. While there was disharmony regarding which union factions would have the most to gain (Donegani and Sagoun 1976), they were – and remain – much more concerned with the prospects of a decentralized education system.

Teachers Unions and Educational Centralization
As noted above, France operates one of the world's most centralized education systems, which was again reinforced by the introduction of the structurally homogenous *collèges* in the 1970s. In many countries though, there has been a manifest trend towards educational decentralization (see Wiborg in this book for Scandinavia). Generally, decentralization can be understood as the "transfer

of power from the state to elected bodies of regions and departments" and the "devolution of power [...] to appointed rectors, elected local authorities and/ or head teachers" (Menéndez-Weidman 2001). While decentralized decision-making has been standard practice in most English-speaking countries for decades now (for New Zealand see Dobbins 2009; for Great Britain see Cole and John 2001), most Western European systems have only recently begun to decentralize educational decision-making (for Sweden see Lundahl 2002; for Germany see Rürup 2007) with the aim of improving educational outputs and quality.

In France though, government efforts to decentralize educational governance actually date back much earlier than in most other European countries. One main impetus for decentralization was Pierre Bourdieu's study *Les Héritiers* (1964), which revealed that the highly centralized education system significantly (re)-produced social inequality. Thus, while the government was reinforcing the centralist character of education with the expansion of the *collèges*, the state – somewhat paradoxically – simultaneously began to promote the notion of educational decentralization. This was seen as a means to facilitate greater pedagogical, administrative and structural diversity in order to deal with the heterogeneity of pupils, their needs and skills at the local level.

For example, the 1975 Haby law not only institutionalized the *collèges*, but also aimed to shift the (financial) burden of education to local authorities by requiring them to participate in the financing of school operations. The decentralization laws of 1982 and 1983 reinforced this trend by granting schools the status of local public teaching establishments (*établissements publics locaux d'enseignement*) (see Mallet 2006). This enabled them to allocate a small part of their budgets to non-core curricular activities and draw up strategic plans (*projets d'établissement*). The regions in turn obtained responsibility for the construction, extension and repair of upper secondary *lycées*, while the *départements* assumed responsibility for the lower secondary *collèges*. The principle of decentralization was then fortified by the Savary law of 1984, which recognized the administrative, financial and pedagogical autonomy of education providers.

However, the precise competences of local authorities remained limited to those outlined in the 1982 and 1983 decentralization laws. Here, the teacher unions refused to cede to the local authorities control over any policy aspects which they regarded as essential to their national public servant status (Mallet 2006: 105). The union front insisted that the state maintain responsibility for the content, organization and monitoring of educational activities as well as personnel management. Thus, elected bodies at the lower level (departments and regions) were only granted responsibilities for the material functioning and investment – i.e. construction and repair – of school facilities. The state effectively continued to control core policy decisions such as the course curriculum, recruitment and management of teachers, while regional partners were obliged to participate in the funding and administration of schools (with the help of central government subsidies) (Cole and John 2001).

Thus, one could speak of "pseudo-decentralization," even with regard to planning and administration. Although heads of schools gained more extensive decision-making authority and – together with regional councils – can theoretically operate their budgets as they choose, their de facto autonomy remained significantly restricted because planning and structural autonomy is inherently intertwined with personnel autonomy. Against a backdrop of union resistance, schools obtained little leeway for autonomous budgetary planning because the main expenditure – the recruitment and wages of teachers – remained the responsibility of the national government (Daun 2004: 333).

In line with an increasingly global trend, the French government further persisted with its efforts to transfer authority to local providers. Decentralization was touted by the socialist government as a means of relieving the strain on the national budget, facilitating improved resource utilization, and promoting educational diversification through local innovations (Allègre 1998; see also Chubb and Moe 1990). The ministry's decentralization plans were further bolstered by the OECD, which vehemently criticized the high degree of centralization in its 1994 review of French education. Particular points of criticism concerned the lack of individuality in teaching and pedagogical methods (OECD 1994; Corbett 1996), and the inflexible governance of the system. As a result the government put forward several proposals to weaken the ministry's influence, including the creation of independent agencies to administer staff recruitment, school examinations and civil service issues.

Once again though, teachers unions functioned as a "decentralization gatekeeper," as the plans to decentralize staffing procedures and everyday school management met particularly bitter resistance (see Cole 2001). In January 1991 the teaching unions mobilized, nationwide, in defence of the "principle of *laïcité*" (secularism). In doing so, they strategically drew on one of the guiding principles of French education – i.e., that education is a secular national public sphere – to convey the impression that they were acting in the public interest by upholding the centralized governance structures.

Another particularly interesting case of union power was the reaction to the decentralization measures of August 2004 initiated by Prime Minister François Fillon. The reform originally intended to transfer matters governing all public workers to local authorities, including teachers. However, the proposals again incited widespread public protests among the teaching corps, who interpreted them as an attack on public service and as a means of back-door privatization (Bronner 2004). Amid coordinated, rotating union strikes, Fillon was forced to retract the planned measures. Consequently, only the management of technical and service staff employed in education was transferred to the local authorities.

The French education community again mobilized to water down reforms proposed in 2004 (*loi Fillon d'orientation scolaire*) (see Mons and Pons 2009). One crucial reform component involved the decentralization of the *baccalauréat*, a centralized national graduation examination that entitles graduates to attend a university or *grande école*. The proposal would have enabled schools to administer the examination themselves. However, concerns were expressed that teachers would not be able to objectively and neutrally judge student performance without reference to their social background. Student representatives, in particular, argued that only the central government was capable of guaranteeing objectivity, anonymity, and thus, educational equality. As a result, students bitterly opposed the notion that the final exam result be partially based on school performance during the past three years, and not exclusively on central and nationally defined examination standards. Importantly, the teachers unions also joined in the nationwide strikes; they too saw their core interest in a centralized, national education system at stake. They viewed the decentralization of the examination procedure as a "slippery slope" towards the "denationalization" of the entire education system and as a broader plot to downsize and decentralize the public service (Bronner 2004; SNES 2009; SUD Education 2009). Thus, the reform proposals were swatted down after intensive and enduring teacher and student strikes.

Altogether, through their strong internal position within the ministry, teachers unions have succeeded in preventing proposals that would increase schools' autonomous administrative capacities. This pertains in particular to the above-mentioned dimensions of decentralization that would threaten their privileged public service status – i.e., personnel and resource management, planning and structures. Moreover, they have employed the above-described strike tactic to prevent or significantly water down all other indirectly related policy measures which could be remotely interpreted as a step towards decentralization.

The incentives for teachers unions to uphold the existing centralized structures, and resulting opportunity structures, can be traced back to the above-described corporatist policy-making structures. Not only are they directly involved in policy-making and can thereby secure numerous privileges (e.g., tenure, and seniority-based promotions) (Fowler 1992), they are also shielded from school headmasters and local authorities (see below). To avoid conveying the perception that they are acting in self-interest, they often legitimize strong centralization as a precondition for upholding the historical guiding principle of education as a protected national space. In other words, the vested interest of teachers unions in preserving the centralist, sectoral-corporatist structures coincides well with the traditional understanding of French schools as neutral venues, isolated from their socioeconomic environment (Cole 2001: 709–10). This has the effect that French academics frequently protest *against* local institutional autonomy, since such measures would likely undermine their bargaining power vis-à-vis the centralized decision-making apparatus. Here, the central state – via co-management with teachers unions – purportedly functions as a guardian of the public interest and as a buffer against local (i.e., religious and economic) interests (FSU 2011; 2003). To date the fluctuating alliances of teachers unions, labour unions and students have succeeded in preserving these organizational structures (Geay 2005).

Favorable Working and Institutional Conditions

What other benefits and privileges have French teachers unions achieved through their concerted actions? Despite low pay by international standards (see below), they enjoy an array of fringe benefits such as subsidized car insurance, retirement supplements, and psychiatric care (Ambler 1994: 54; Fowler 1992: 29). Most notably though, French teachers have considerably fewer teaching obligations compared to their colleagues abroad. For example, French upper secondary teachers had 628 hours of teaching in 2009 (OECD average 656 hours), while their American counterparts taught an average of 1,051 hours. This also applies to lower secondary education: while American teachers taught 1,068 hours a year, French teachers only spent 642 hours in the classroom, and again were below the OECD average of 701 hours. However, these favorable conditions do not apply to French primary teachers, whose teaching hours (2009) were above the OECD average of 779, yet still below those of their American colleagues (1,097 hours) (OECD 2011; Pech 2012).

The disparity both between primary and secondary teachers, as well as between France and other OECD countries, is also reflected in the teacher-student ratio. While French primary school classes are relatively large by OECD standards (approximately 19 pupils per teacher), upper secondary classes are among the smallest by international comparison. In France, the average class size amounts to ten pupils, compared to 16 in the United States and 18 in Finland (OECD 2011). These favorable institutional framework conditions leave French (secondary) teachers considerably more time for class preparation, administrative tasks and educational self-management through teachers unions.[3]

Importantly, French teachers unions have vehemently resisted the introduction of evaluations and performance criteria. For example, following up on the weak French results in the PISA study (Programme for International Student Assessment, see below), the previous center-right government aimed to introduce teacher evaluations by school headmasters/principals (*chefs d'établissements*). Up to now, French teachers are only assessed once every seven years by means of a so-called *double notation* inspection procedure

---

[3] Although my core argument is that these favorable conditions for teachers as public sector employees are largely the result of union power, they need not be viewed entirely negatively and solely as the result of self-interested policy-making. In scientific analyses, high public sector employment is positively correlated with high birth rates (Adsera 2011). Maintaining a large public sector with favorable employment conditions for women (particularly in the primarily female teaching profession) has perhaps been an instrument of French family and fertility policy and an additional reason for the high birth rate, though this argument has not been explicitly put forward by the main teacher unions. This aspect of "cross-fertilization" of education and family policy through public sector employment warrants attention in future analyses.

consisting of an administrative grade from the *chef d'établissement* (based on criteria such as punctuality, initiative) and a regional pedagogical inspector. However, the process lacks any follow-up or sanction mechanisms and has no impact on remuneration. In other words, salary increases are based entirely on seniority. The Sarkozy government and the then education minister, Luc Chatel, lamented the "overprotection of teachers as part of the public service" and the fact that teachers are shielded from school headmasters (*Le Monde* 2011). With the so-called *Nouveau statut pour les enseignants* (new status for teachers), the Sarkozy/Fillon government proposed that each teacher conducts an interview with the *chef d'établissement* every three years to evaluate his/her ability to foster student progress (*Libération* 2011). The result of the evaluation would in turn be calculated, on a formula-basis, into annual salaries.

However, the teacher unions argued that the measures would "devalue the profession" and that competition over salaries would infringe on "teamwork between teachers" (Peiron 2011). This resulted in a nationwide "Day of Action" and strikes in December 2011, in which all major unions except SGEN participated. SNES-FSU decried the proposed measures as a "declaration of war" and warned of abuses of power, favoritism and a return to the feudalist structures of the nineteenth century (*Le Monde* 2011). These events again reflect the same conflict lines as before regarding centralization and decentralization. French teachers unions once again rejected any efforts that would reinforce the autonomy of schools and powers of school management, or enable the differential treatment of teachers, since this would potentially undermine their protected national status and expose them to a new array of local actors. Following intense strike activity, the teachers unions then postponed further negotiations due to internal union elections. Instead of risking further conflict with its political allies, the incumbent Hollande government buried the reform and proposed an alternative evaluation method (Vousnousils 2012); namely, the evaluation of entire schools instead of teachers. However, this brings us back to the recurring theme of decentralization: conducting institutional evaluations would require a significant increase in the autonomy and managerial capacity of individual schools, a practice that is again vehemently opposed by most of the teacher union landscape. Thus, French educational authorities and individual schools still lack the means to reward or sanction teachers for their performance.

Nevertheless, there are still limitations to the widespread perception of French teachers being part of a privileged profession (*Libération* 2001). Compared to their OECD counterparts, French teachers lag behind in one crucial indicator – salaries (OECD 2009). For example, French upper secondary teachers with 15 years of experience earn the equivalent of $36,145 per year, while the salaries of their American counterparts with the same experience is nearly $48,000 (OECD 2011). At the same time, French secondary teacher salaries also lag behind those of not only Finnish teachers ($49,237 after 15 years of experience) and German teachers ($68,619), but also the OECD average of $43,711) (OECD 2011; *Le Monde* 2013)

This may come as a surprise in view of the immense power resources at the disposal of the French teachers unions. As I argue below though, these lower teacher salaries can again be traced back to two (perhaps unintended) effects of teacher unionism: (1) the extreme centralization of education and the resulting administrative inefficiencies, and, (2) the preferred strategy of teachers unions to combat public sector downsizing (instead of pressing for higher salaries).

Educational Decentralization, Administrative Efficiency, and Educational Performance in France

Historically, the main strategic aim of French teachers unions has been to acquire, preserve and expand the national civil service (see also footnote 3 for an additional aspect). This approach and the national guiding principles of republicanism and egalitarianism have mutually fed into one another and have been further reinforced by the state-centered, Keynesian institutional structures of French policy-making (Athanasiades and Patramanis 2002). Combined with internal and inter-union politics – which offer multiple incentives to block reforms – these factors have foiled any efforts by the state to decentralize the education system. Seen from this angle it is safe to say that French teacher unionism has had a substantial negative impact on the government's pursuit of reforms intended to improve schools – and arguably come back to haunt French teachers in terms of salaries (see below).

On the whole, research has revealed a positive relationship between educational decentralization and/or deregulation, and performance (Chubb and Moe 1990; Schlicht-Schmälzle *et al.* 2011). However, by sustaining the centralized structures, French schools largely forego the opportunity to experiment with new governance approaches. This became particularly apparent after several rounds of poor French results in the OECD's Programme for International Student Assessment (PISA). PISA is the largest cross-national standardized evaluation scheme, which provides comparative data on the skills of 15-year-olds in reading, mathematics and scientific literacy. Conducted every three years, the scheme focuses on educational output and how students are capable of applying knowledge and skills learned in school for their future working life. As the largest comprehensive set of comparative data on school performance ever, PISA has taken on an almost authoritative character in much of Europe and become the centerpiece of the European Union's peer-learning activities (Grek 2009: 25). Thus, PISA has significantly affected the education reform discourse in France (Aghion and Cohen 2004) and pressured policy-makers to improve education systems by adapting to "winning models" (Martens *et al.* 2010).

After the deterioration of the French PISA results, French policy-makers and media dedicated increased attention to PISA "winners" such as Finland, New Zealand and Canada (Bruneel 2008; Dobbins and Martens 2012; Jacob 2008; Robert 2008). These three top-performing countries operate education systems with high levels of institutional autonomy and diversity and do not carry out centralized testing procedures. In fact, the French Education Ministry under the Sarkozy government developed a sort of "PISA hypothesis" that high educational performance correlates directly with extensive school autonomy and targeted measures to assist weak performers. This view is also underscored by French educational researchers who link the sub-optimal French performance to the lack of school autonomy and pedagogical freedom (Meuret 2003). The uniform, centralized system purportedly provides insufficient leeway for individualized and tailor-made teaching and learning methods (Rémond 2006: 79). For example, Meuret (2003) traces the poor French performance back to the attitude of teachers towards students, and the large degree of homogeneity among them with regard to values and teaching practices (see also Dubet and Martucelli 1996). Along these lines, Meuret (2003) argues that teachers who pay strong consideration and attention to all students are less common in France than in English-speaking countries.

Thus, numerous policy-makers and researchers have called for tangible measures to increase the flexibility, adaptability and diversity of French education (Robert 2008). However, the inability to decentralize governance structures due to union resistance has essentially translated into France's inability to follow the "PISA leaders" – i.e., school systems with high institutional and pedagogical flexibility, which dedicate particular attention to poorly performing pupils. Numerous recent reform attempts aimed at empowering schools to pursue their own educational strategies have been thwarted by teachers unions. For example, the so-called *lycée à la carte* reforms under Education Minister Xavier Darcos were strongly inspired by "PISA winners" in terms of the pedagogical and structural flexibility they aimed to grant schools (Dobbins and Martens 2012). In addition, the reform package intended to partially deregulate the *carte scolaire* so that students from outside a school district may also be admitted to schools. These deregulatory measures were foreseen to promote inter-institutional competition and the principle of *mixité sociale* (social diversity), which is increasingly regarded as a recipe for success in view of the Canadian and Finnish PISA results (Bruneel 2008; Duru-Bellat and Marin 2010). Moreover, additional teaching staff were to be deployed to "problem schools" in order to develop innovative projects to alleviate social conflicts and overcome performance disparities, while three hours of special lessons were envisioned for slow learners.[4]

However, mass strikes that included students as well as teachers and labour unions, once again caused the reform package to fail on two grounds. First, the argument was put forward that the flexibility- and autonomy-promoting measures would be a slippery slope towards the denationalization of the

---

[4] The measures were also aimed at limiting *redoublements* – i.e., repeating classes – which had a particularly negative impact on France's PISA performance (Duru-Bellat and Suchaut 2005: 190; Baudelot and Establet 2009).

education system (Pech and Sérès 2008; Chayet and Court 2005). Second, and importantly, the teaching corps' attachment to the principle of educational equality proved to be a major obstacle. Amid simultaneous plans to abolish 15,000 teacher jobs as part of an overarching reform of the pubic sector, teachers argued that additional special lessons for poorly performing students would place a too large burden upon them and undermine the ideal of equal educational opportunities – understood here as equal attention to all pupils (Cody 2009).[5]

Against this background, one can justifiably argue that teacher unionism has put the French education system in an *inefficiency trap*. The fervent resistance to decentralization, and attachment to the (never fully realized) principle of educational equality, has impeded French government attempts to transfer policies from better-performing systems (e.g., institutional evaluations, school autonomy, targeted support for poor performers) to France. Recent research has also shown that the centralized educational bureaucracy, which teachers unions assiduously seek to uphold, has brought about multiple inefficiencies – arguably to their own detriment. Despite the weak performance of French secondary education by international comparison, diverse indicators show that France is among the OECD forerunners when it comes to public education expenditure. For example, in 2007 the expenditure per secondary-level student in France amounted to $9,303 and was higher than the OECD average of $8,006 (OECD 2009). In other words, the French government spends more (and more) money on education (MEN 2003), yet at the same time achieves below-average results by international comparison.

For example, educational expenses are nearly €20 billion higher in France than in Germany – despite a similar teacher-to-pupil ratio, similar educational performance, and much higher teacher pay in Germany (OECD 2011). While in Germany half of educational expenditure is dedicated to teacher salaries, less than a third is spent on teacher salaries in France. Besides the high expenditure on teacher benefits (i.e., pensions and retirement supplements, subsidized car insurance, etc.), this can be traced back to the high administrative costs of the French educational infrastructure (Institut Thomas More 2012). While nearly 50,000 educational establishments operate in France, only 28,000 establishments are maintained in Germany – despite its significantly higher population. This leads to substantially higher infrastructural and administrative costs in France. Or, by way of comparison, a German pupil costs the government €6,000 per year (despite higher teacher salaries), while a French

---

[5] The reform package that was ultimately passed (*lycée pour tous*) (Sérès 2008) was a watered down version of the Darcos proposals. Specifically, all initially foreseen efforts to decentralize or "denationalize" education (e.g., the *baccalauréat* procedure, abolition of the *carte scolaire*, greater financial autonomy for schools) were dropped following intense strike activity. As a result, the *lycée pour tous* measures are entirely restricted to pedagogical aspects – e.g., flexibility regarding teaching content.

France: The Impossibility of Reform?

pupil costs €7,000 Euros annually (ibid.; Rabreau 2012). Even more striking is the number of secondary school teachers in both countries compared to the ratio of secondary pupils. In Germany approximately 8.5 million secondary students are taught by 580,000 teachers; but the number of secondary school teachers in France is nearly as high (500,546) despite there being a significantly lower number of secondary school pupils (5.95 million) (Institut Thomas More 2012).

To put it simply, French teachers unions have traditionally pushed to prevent school closures and to maintain a large teaching corps, not least due to the ministry's unwillingness to substantially raise wages in the past 20 years. The effect has been a larger workforce than necessary to cater for (declining) student numbers (see footnote 3). The French Court of Auditors reported in 2005, for example, that there are nearly 100,000 teachers in France who do not teach (*L'Express* 2005). The fact that this has resulted in lower pay by international standards has done little to prevent them from further pressing to uphold and expand the national public teaching service. Besides the abovementioned Fillon reform, prominent recent examples of this are the protests of late January 2012, during which teachers unions successfully rallied to prevent the loss of 12,000 teaching jobs (RFI 2012). And, importantly, after a highly antagonistic relationship with the Sarkozy government, teachers unions have pressured the Hollande government to create 60,000 more teacher jobs, of which 40,000 were recruited in 2013 alone (Serraf 2012).

These administrative efficiencies are thus a direct result of both the highly centralized French education system and teachers unions' persistent efforts to expand the public teaching corps. Decentralized systems such as Germany, the United States, New Zealand or Sweden have enabled a funding mix from national, local and regional sources, and empowered individual school districts, municipalities or individual schools to administer their own budgets based on demand and financial capacity. Centralized systems, however, prevent local educational establishments from adapting solutions and financial means to local needs. In France, for example, less than a third of the expenses are covered by the municipalities, departments and regions (Institut Thomas More 2012). All in all, the concerted actions of teachers unions to uphold the centralized structures, expand the national public teaching service, and combat the closure of excessive numbers of school establishments, have resulted in a one-sided educational funding system, an oversized educational bureaucracy, and severe administrative inefficiencies. Much to their own detriment, the high administrative expenses leave little leeway for higher teacher salaries.

Conclusions

What are the prospects for French teachers unions in the future, and what role will they play in the nation's education system? As shown above, French teachers unions – despite their being strongly interweaved with the governmental decision-making apparatus – have found themselves in a particularly antagonistic relationship with the state due to their conflicting interests. In view of enormous budgetary constraints, a broader international trend towards educational decentralization, the regionalization of French public administration, and demographic developments, the French government has a vested interest in downsizing the public education bureaucracy. Teachers unions, by contrast, have chosen a strategy of expansion of the public teaching service and wielded their collective clout on every occasion to stymie any plans to downsize and decentralize education. Despite a significantly smaller membership than just a few decades ago, teachers unions continue to act as a formidable veto player against any reforms that would undermine their public sector status. This was brought to bear, in particular, during the reforms of the previous center-right government, which aimed to increase school autonomy and decentralize numerous aspects of education.

As for the future, there are very few indications that French teachers will soon moderate their tactics or resort to a more collaborative strategy towards the ministry, even under a socialist government. During the last presidential and parliamentary elections, teachers unions vociferously supported the Socialist Party and President Hollande, who promised to further expand the teacher corps and thus double down on existing policies (i.e., centralism, heavy state investment for education). The resulting 60,000 new teaching jobs can thus be regarded as a major triumph for the unions. This victory is all the more remarkable when one considers the widespread phenomenon of teachers without students (*profs sans élèves*) in France. However, initial union enthusiasm once again turned into antagonism when the Hollande government proposed adding an additional half-day of primary school classes to the present four days a week (the free day is usually dedicated to extra-curricular activities). Once again, the reform proposals resulted in school closures and strikes in the capital (France24 2013). In view of the unions' steadfast resistance to any type of education reform other than reinforcing the status quo, fundamental change to French education policy is likely to remain a nearly impossible endeavor in the foreseeable future, regardless of the government's ideological orientation.

References

Adsera, Alicia. 2011. Where are the babies? Labor market conditions and fertility in Europe. *European Journal of Population* 27(1): 1–32.

Aghion, Philippe, and Cohen, Élie. 2004. *Education et Croissance*. Paris: La documentation française.

Allègre, Claude. 1998. "La rénovation et la réforme du service publique de l'éducation." Letter in *Le Monde*, December 15.

Ambler, John. 1985. Neocorporatism and the politics of French education. *West European Politics* 8(3): 23–42.

1994. Why French education policy is so often made on the streets. *French Politics & Society* 12(2&3): 41–64.
Andolfatto, Dominique, and Labbé, Dominique. 2007. Les syndiqués en France 1990–2006. Nancy – Grenoble: Institut d'études politiques de Grenoble-PACTE.
Archer, Margret. 1979. *Social Origins of Educational Systems*. London: Sage.
Athanasiades, Harris, and Patramanis, Alexandros. 2002. *Globalization, Education Restructuring and Teacher Unions in France and Greece: Decentralization Policies or Disciplinary Parochialism?* Paper presented to the European Science Foundation, Barcelona, October 3–5, 2002.
Baudelot, Christian, and Establet, Roger. 2009. *L'Elitisme Républicain. L'école française à l'épreuves des comparaisons internationales*. Paris: Seuil.
Baumgardner, Frank and Walker, Jack. 1989. Education policymaking and interest group structure in France and the United States. *Comparative Politics* 21(3):273–88.
Bourdieu, Pierre. 1964. *Les Héritiers: les étudiants et la culture*. Paris: Minuit.
Bourdoncle, Raymond, and Robert, André. 2000. Primary and secondary school teachers in France: Changes in identities and professionalization. *Journal of Education Policy* 15(1): 71–81.
Bronner, Luc. 2004. Le SNES appelle seul à la grève dans le second dégrée, *Le Monde*, December 7.
Bruneel, Lisa. 2008. Organisation et politique de l'enseignementfinlandais, L'école démocratique. Available at: www.skolo.org/spip.php?article478&lang=fr [accessed 30 August 2013].
Chartier, Claire. 1999. Collège unique: La fin d'une utopie?, *L'Express*, 13 May. Available at: www.lexpress.fr/informations/college-unique-la-fin-d-une-utopie_633642.html
Chayet, Delphine, and Court, Marielle. 2005. La démonstration de force des enseignants. *Le Figaro*, January 21.
Chubb, J.E. and T.M. Moe. 1990. *Politics, Markets and America's Schools*. Washington, DC: Brookings Institution.
Cody, Edward. 2009. French Teachers Resist Neo-Liberal Reform. *Washington Post Foreign Service*, July 11. Available at: www.teachersolidarity.com/blog/french-teachers-resist-neo-liberal-reform
Cole, Alistair. 2001. The new governance of French education. *Public Administration* 79(3): 707–24.
Cole, Alistair, and John, Peter. 2001. Governing education in England and France. *Public Policy and Administration* 16(4).
Corbett, A. 1996. Secular, Free and Compulsory: Republican Values in French Education. In A. Corbett and B. Moon, eds, *Education in France, Continuity, Change in the Mitterrand Years 1981–1995*. London: Routledge.
Daun, Holger. 2004. Privatisation, decentralisation and governance in education in the Czech Republic, England, France, Germany and Sweden. *International Review of Education* 50: 325–46.
Derouet, Jean-Louis. 1991. Lower secondary education in France: From uniformity to institutional autonomy. *European Journal of Education* 26(2): 119–32.
Dobbins, Michael. 2009. *Transforming Education Policy in New Zealand*. TranState Working Papers, 97. Universität Bremen.

Dobbins, Michael, and Martens, Kerstin. 2012. Towards an education approach à la finlandaise? French education policy after PISA, *Journal of Education Policy* 27(1): 23–43.
Donegani, Jean-Marie, and Sadoun, Marc. 1976. La reforme de l'enseignement en France après 1945. Analyse d'une non-decision. *Revue française de sciences politiques* 26(6): 1125–46.
Dubet, François, and Danilo Martuccelli. 1996. *A l'école: Sociologie de l'expérience scolaire*. Paris: Seuil.
Duclaud-Williams, Roger. 1985. Local politics in centralized systems: The case of French education. *European Journal of Political Research* 13: 167–86.
Duru-Bellat, M., and B. Suchaut. 2005. Organization and context, efficiency and equity of educational systems: What PISA tells us. *European Educational Research Journal* 4(3): 181.
Duru-Bellat, M., and B. Marin. 2010. La mixité scolaire, une thématique (encore) d'actualité? *Revue française de pédagogie* 171: 5–8.
EPSU (European Federation of Public Service Unions). 2008. Collective bargaining in the public services: Country profile France. Available at: www.epsu.org/IMG/pdf/France_EN.pdf
EPSU (European Federation of Public Service Unions). 2013. France. www.epsu.org/r/476
Ferhat, Ismail. 2011. Le syndical et le politique. Le cas du parti socialiste et de la FEN, des années 1970 au début des années 1990. *Histoire et Politique* 13: 125–45.
Fowler, Francis. 1992. Teacher unionism as mission and battle: Success and crisis in French teacher unions. American Educational Research Association, San Francisco, California, April 1992.
Frajerman, Laurent. 2007. La Fédération de l'Éducation nationale face aux enjeux de l'école moyenne sous la Quatrième République: Cartographie d'un débat. *Revue française de pédagogie* 159: 69–79.
2008. Le syndicalisme enseignant français et la grève: Normes et normalisation d'une pratique (1948–1959). *Paedagogica Historica* 44(5): 543–54.
France24. 2013. "Paris teachers rebel against Socialists' school reform," TV program, 13 January. Available at: www.france24.com/en/20130122-paris-teachers-strike-school-day-socialists
FSU. 2003. Concernant le projet de loi sur la décentralisation: Analyse de la FSU. Available at: www.snuasfp-fsu.org/Concernant-le-projet-de-loi-sur-la [accessed November 8, 2012].
2010. Appel national pour l'école publique. Available at: www.snetap-fsu.fr/APPEL-NATIONAL-POUR-L-ECOLE.html [accessed November 8, 2012].
2011. Pacte du service public 2011. Available at: www.fsu.fr/IMG/pdf/actu_110201_Pacte_du_Service_Public_20110130.pdf [accessed October 25, 2012].
Gaziel, Haim, and Taub, David. 1992. Teachers unions and educational reform: A comparative perspective. *Educational Policy* 6: 72–86.
Geay, Bertrand. 2005. *Le syndicalisme enseignant*. Paris: Editions La Découverte.
Gombert, Philippe. 2008. Les associations de parents d'élèves en France: Approche socio-historique et mutations idéologiques. *Revue française de pédagogie – Recherches en éducation* 162 (January–March): 59–66.

Grek, Sotira. 2009. Governing by numbers: The PISA effect in Europe. *Journal of Education Policy* 24(1): 23–37.
Institut Thomas More. 2012. *Éducation Analyse comparée de la dépense publique en France et en Allemagne*. Note de Benchmarking No. 8. Available at: www.institut-thomas-more.org/upload/media/notebenchmarckingitm-8.pdf
Jacob, Antoine. 2008. Le lycée finlandais, un modèle qui inspire Xavier Darcos. *Le Figaro*, June. Available at: www.lefigaro.fr/actualites/2008/02/06/01001-20080206artFIG00304-le-lycee-finlandaisun-modele-qui-inspire-xavier-darcos-.php
L'Express. 2005. Le nombre d'enseignants qui n'enseignent pas selon la cour des comptes. Available at: www.lexpansion.lexpress.fr/economie/le-nombre-d-enseignants-qui-n-enseignent-pas-selon-la-cour-des-comptes_108530.html
Lelièvre, Claude. 2000. The French model of the educator state. *Journal of Education Policy* 15(1): 5–10.
Le Monde. 2011. Les enseignants mobilisés contre le projet de réforme de l'évaluation, December 15.
Le Monde. 2013. Le salaire des enseignants français à la loupe, January 24.
Libération. 2001. Les privilèges illusoire des enseignants. Available at: www.liberation.fr/tribune/0101397899-les-privileges-illusoires-des-enseignants
Liberation. 2011. Un nouveau statu de l'enseignant version UMP inquiète les syndicats, November 8.
Lundahl, L. 2002. From centralisation to decentralisation: Governance of education in Sweden. *European Educational Research Journal* 1(4): 625–36.
Mallet, L. 2006. Décentralisation de l'éducation et de la formation professionnelle: compétences sans moyens, moyens sans compétences, Formation emploi. Available at: www.formationemploi.revues.org/index2466.html [accessed June 2012].
Martens, Kerstin, Nagel, Alexander-Kenneth, Windzio, Michael, Weymann, Ansgar (Hg.). 2010. *Transformation of Education Policy*. Basingstoke: Palgrave Macmillan.
MEN (Ministère de l'Éducation Nationale). 2003. Quels moyens sont consacrés à l'éducation et comment sont-ils repartis. *Education & Formations* 66. Available at: www.media.education.gouv.fr/file/17/8/5178.pdf
MEN. 2010. La maîtrise des dépenses publiques à Éducation Nationale. Available at: www.educa tion.gouv.fr/cid52031/la-maitrise-des-depenses-publiques-a-l-education-nation ale.html [accessed November 2011].
2013. Modalités de la négociation préalable à un préavis de grève dans l'enseignement du premier degré. Available at: www.education.gouv.fr/cid57800/preavis-de-greve-negociation-prealable.html
Menéndez-Weidman, L. 2001. Policy trends and structural divergence in educational governance. *Oxford Review of Education* 27(1): 75–84.
Meuret, Denis. 2003. Pourquoi des jeunes Français ont-ils à 15 ans des compétences inférieures à celles de jeunes d'autres pays? *Revue Française de Pédagogie* 142: 89-104.
Mons, Nathalie, and Xavier Pons (2009) *La réception de PISA en France: Connaissances et régulation du système éducatif*, Knowledge and Policy in Education and Health Sectors Working Paper 12.
Mouriaux, René. 1996. *Le syndicalisme enseignant en France*. Paris: PUF.

OECD. 1994. *Reviews of National Policies for Education*: France, Paris.
2009. *Education at a Glance*. Paris: OECD.
2011. *Education at a Glance*. Paris. OECD.
Pech, Marie-Estelle, and Sérès, Aude. 2008. La réforme Darcos renvoyée à des jours meilleurs. *Le Figaro*, December 13.
Pech, Marie-Estelle. 2012. Les profs français travaillent moins que les autres. *Le Figaro*, February 29. Available at: www.elections.lefigaro.fr/presidentielle-2012/2012/02/29/01039-20120229ARTFIG00651-les-profs-francais-travaillent-moins-que-les-autres.php [accessed July 21, 2013].
Peiron, Denis. 2011. Enseignants, comment passer de l'inspection à l'évaluation La Croix, December 14. Available at: www.la-croix.com/Actualite/France/Enseignants-comment-passer-de-l-inspection-a-l-evaluation-_EP_-2011-12-14-746999 [accessed July 29, 2013].
Quittkat, Christine. 2006. *Europäisierung der Interessenvermittlung: Französische Wirtschaftsverbände zwischen Beständigkeit und Wandel*. Wiesbaden: VS Verlag.
Rabreau, Marine. 2012. Les dépenses d'éducation sont mieux gérées en Allemagne. *Le Figaro*, 3 September.
Rémond, M. 2006. Eclairages des évaluations internationales PIRLS et PISA sur les élèves français. *Revue française de pédagogie* 157: 71–84.
RFI – Radio France Internationale (2012) "Grève des enseignants contre les suppressions des postes," February 1. Available at: www.rfi.fr/france/20120131-france-enseignants-greve-contre-le-projet-evaluation-suppressions-postes
Robert, Paul. 2008. *La Finlande: un modèle éducatif pour la France – les secrets d'une réussite*. Paris: ESF.
Rürup, Matthias. 2007. *Innovationswege im deutschen Bildungssystem. Die Verbreitung der Idee "Schulautonomie" im Ländervergleich*. Wiesbaden: VS-Verlag.
Schlicht-Schmälzle, Raphaela, Teltemann, Janna, and Windzio, Michael. 2011. *Deregulation of Education – What Does it Mean for Efficiency and Equality?* TransState Working Paper 157. Universität Bremen.
Schmidt, Vivien. 2000. The Changing Dynamics of State-Society Relations in the Fifth Republic. In *The Changing French Political System*, ed. R. Elgie. London: Frank Cass.
Sérès, Aude. 2008. L'OCDE critique les rythmes scolaires français. *Le Figaro*, September 10. Available at: www.lefigaro.fr/actualite-france/2008/09/10/01016-20080910artfig00046-l-ocde-critique-les-rythmes-scolaires-francais-.php [accessed July 2011].
Serraf, Hugues. 2012. Profs sans élèves: mais combien sont-ils au juste? September 26. Available at: www.slate.fr/story/62319/60.000-recrutements-enseignants-detaches
Siaroff, Alan. 1999. Corporatism in 24 industrial democracies. *European Journal of Political Research* 36: 175–205.
SNES. 2009. Depuis la loi Fillon: Un collège à plusieurs vitesses. Available at: http://www.snes.edu/IMG/pdf/College_vitesse-2.pdf [accessed September 18, 2012].
2012. La laïcité, une vieille idée neuve. Available at: www.irhses.snes.edu/IMG/pdf/Laicite_une_vieille_idee_neuve.pdf [accessed October 29, 2012].
SUD Education. 2009. Lycées: Analyse détaillée de la réforme Chatel. Available at: www.sudeducation35.fr/spip.php?article63 [accessed July 2012].

van Zanten, Agnès. 2002. Educational change and new cleavages between head teachers, teachers and parents: Global and local perspectives on the French case. *Journal of Education Policy* 17(3): 289–304.

Vousnousils. 2012. Le décre sur l'évaluation des enseignants sera abrogé par Hollande. Available at: www.vousnousils.fr/2012/05/10/le-decret-sur-levaluation-des-enseignants-sera-abroge-par-hollande-526716

Waarden, Frans van. 1993. Über die Beständigkeit nationaler Politikstile und Politiknetzwerke. Eine Studie über die Genese ihrer institutionellen Verankerung. In R. Czada, and M. Schmidt, eds, *Verhandlungsdemokratie, Interessenvermittlung, Regierbarkeit*. Opladen: Westdeutscher Verlag.

Wilsford, David. 2001. Running the Bureaucratic State: Administration in France. In Ali Farazmand, ed., *Handbook of Comparative and Development Public Administration*. New York: Marcel Dekker.

5

Teacher Unionism in Germany
Fragmented Competitors

Rita Nikolai, Kendra Briken, and Dennis Niemann

Introduction

This chapter underscores the historically significant role that teachers unions have played in German education policy. As we will show, German teaching unionism is highly fragmented. In comparative social stratification research, Germany is considered a prototype of a stratified school system with distinct educational tracks and early academic selection (Schneider and Thieben, 2011). In contrast to most Western democracies, Germany has not yet introduced comprehensive schooling as a nationwide standard in secondary education (Wiborg, 2010). After the Second World War the Federal Republic of Germany reinstated the traditional tripartite school system comprising the *Gymnasium*, *Realschule*, and *Hauptschule*.[1] After four[2] years of elementary schooling, students were traditionally referred to distinct secondary educational tracks, each associated with a different curriculum and certificate. The academic track (*Gymnasium*) prepared pupils for the university entrance qualification (*Abitur*); the two other tracks prepared them for vocational training – with the shortest track (*Hauptschule*) primarily directed at crafts and manual occupations, and the middle track (*Realschule*) at technical and service occupations (Nikolai and West, 2013). Based on this tripartite school system, German teacher education is also highly stratified (Blömeke, 2002), and teachers unions have emerged around each school type of the German secondary school system. Accordingly, German teaching unionism is highly fragmented. However, two unions stand out as the leading lobby groups for teachers: the Trade Union of Education and Science (GEW, Gewerkschaft

---

[1] For the period between 1949–90 this chapter mainly follows developments in the Federal Republic of Germany, and does not address the situation in the German Democratic Republic.
[2] In two *Länder*, Berlin and Brandenburg, elementary schooling lasts six years.

Erziehung und Wissenschaft) and the German Philological Association (DPhV, Deutscher Philologenverband). Together, they represent 23 percent (GEW) and 12 percent (DPhV) of the teaching workforce. They rely on different kinds of members and face each other as political counterparts. Since they are the leading collective actors in the realm of teaching unionism and vested interests, the remainder of this chapter will focus on the two.

Following this introduction, we discuss the historical developments of teacher unionism since the nineteenth century by outlining how certain legacies constituted paths in education policy and politics that have influenced Germany's teachers unions until today. We elaborate on the political agenda of teachers unions in the light of their vested interests (Moe, 2015) and their various opportunities for exerting influence in collective bargaining and in determining the duration of elementary schooling, school structures, and in influencing encompassing education reforms after the so-called 'PISA shock' of 2001.

Historical Development

Teaching unionism in Germany is rooted in the historical development path of the tripartite school system, teachers' employment status as civil servants, and teacher training – the origins of these three defining characteristics go back far beyond the foundation of the Federal Republic of Germany in 1949.

Discovering the potential of education for the shaping of national identity, German state authorities gradually began to set up a public education system in the eighteenth century (Luhmann, 2002). Prussia, first and foremost, set out to establish a state-run and state-supervised education apparatus in 1794. At that time the education system, which had been mainly in the hands of the clergy, came under the authority of the state. Just as with the military, teachers were defined as inherently obligated to the state and thus the teaching profession was integrated as a state-employed civil service. As civil servants, teachers were (and still are) directly subordinate to state authorities and, taking an official oath, bound to principles of political neutrality. Historically, teaching was a typical civil service profession, with the appointment of teachers as civil servants being the general rule in Germany until the end of the 1980s (Gehrke and Latocha, 2013). German civil servant status is entwined with the person – meaning that even after work hours public servants still have to act in support of the state. The right to strike and other collective actions do not apply to them. In return for their loyalty, civil servants were offered comprehensive assurances following the so-called principle of alimentation – which in practical terms means a secure, lifelong income. This system of remuneration was designed to guarantee civil servants and their families a standard of living appropriate to their position in society. However, significant income differences existed across the teaching profession, reflecting the tripartite structure of the German school system: the higher the school level, the better the work and employment conditions. This class-stabilizing divide is one of the three pillars underpinning German teachers' unionism.

The second important pillar is the German school system itself. In the nineteenth century, a class-based, segmented school system emerged with the institutional segregation of elementary schools (*Volksschule*) and secondary schools (*Gymnasium, Realgymnasium, Oberrealschule*). The eight-year-long elementary school was reserved for the lower social strata and provided a basic education. Secondary schools (including their special pre-schools) were accessible to the upper classes and the emerging middle classes.

Across Germany, the *Gymnasium* played a significant role as it was the only school form that granted access to higher education. Unlike in England, the United States, or at the *Grand Ecoles* in France, the entry requirement for higher education did not consist of an entrance examination. Instead, the successful completion of a higher education entrance qualification, which could only be acquired at the *Gymnasium* (Trautwein and Neumann, 2008), provided the necessary requirement in Prussia from 1834 onwards.[3] This strengthened the *Gymnasium*'s dominant position.

The exclusive role of the *Gymnasium* was, furthermore, sustained by the educated elite (*Bildungsbürgertum*) which emerged as part of the process of monarchical state-building and the strong bureaucratization that was occurring across the German states during the nineteenth century (Wiborg, 2010). The educated elite consisted of officials, priests, university professors and *Gymnasium* teachers. This broad social group was united by the classical ideal of *Bildung*. Based on an education in the humanities, they emphasized romantic and idealist literature, the classics, and philosophy (Ringer, 1969). Separated from the rest of society by their exclusive educational institutions, this educated elite formed a bulwark against any attempts to democratize schooling.

Following the establishment of the elitist *Gymnasium*, different teaching professions evolved in the nineteenth century. Only teachers with a university degree were entitled to teach at secondary schools (Jeismann, 1999). Teachers at elementary schools attended so-called state seminars and were not university-educated (Geißler, 2011a: 124–6, 130). Both groups held a specific civil servant status. Whereas elementary school teachers were local officials, secondary school teachers were state officials (Bölling, 1978: 24).[4] These differences in

---

[3] The developments in Prussian school policy provided the guidelines for developments in the other federal states during the period of the German Empire (1871–1918) and the Weimar Republic (1919–33).

[4] This changed with the Weimar Constitution (*Weimarer Reichsverfassung*) of 1919, which subordinated most of the teachers to the *Länder* authorities. Only in Bavaria and Bremen have teachers remained local officials (Füssel, 2011).

training and civil servant status led to differences in remuneration, career prospects and social status. Even though school teachers' qualifications and training became harmonized over time, remuneration, career prospects and social status were not in turn adjusted (Blömeke, 2002; Herrlitz *et al.*, 2009: 124).

These developments impacted significantly on the emergence of teachers unions in Germany. It was during the course of the German revolution of 1848 that a nationwide teachers' union[5] was established: the General German Teacher Association (ADLV, Allgemeiner Deutscher Lehrerverein), which was closely aligned to Political Liberalism and was involved in the revolution itself. The majority of teachers at the *Gymnasium* did not join the ADLV since the association was regarded as too radical and was threatening to abolish status privileges. Hence, the ADLV did not succeed in forming a common organization for all teachers and was abolished shortly afterwards (Bölling, 1978).

The ADLV's legacy was revived by the German Teacher League (DLV, Deutscher Lehrerverein). Founded in 1871, it understood itself as a nondenominational teachers' union. The teacher associations from all federal states of the German Empire joined the DLV before the First World War (Bölling, 1978; Kopitzsch, 1983). Members of the DLV were mainly male elementary school teachers (*Volksschule*)[6] (Morell, 1973). The precursors of modern teachers unions were not allowed to act collectively due to civil servants' obligation to neutrality. However, they played an important role in the establishment of the teaching profession, teacher education, and knowledge transfer within the profession itself (Kemnitz, 1999). It was after the First World War that civil servants in general, and hence teachers, obtained the right to organize – but still they had no right to strike (Ebbinghaus *et al.*, 2000: 292). In 1918, the German Association of Civil Servants (DBB, Deutscher Beamtenbund) was founded as an independent umbrella federation representing the interests of all German civil servants, including teachers.

Teachers at secondary schools unionized comparatively late. Local secondary school teachers joined for the first time in the Union of Academically Educated Teachers in Germany (Vereinsband akademisch gebildeter Lehrer Deutschlands) in 1903. In 1921, the union was renamed the German Philological Association (DPhV, Deutscher Philologenverband), the name it is still known by. Soon the DPhV became the leading professional association of male teachers at secondary schools.[7] At a political level, it became influential

---

[5] All organizations representing teachers' interests in Germany before the Second World War should be seen more as associations rather than as employee union representations.
[6] Female teachers organized themselves in their own unions (Bölling, 1978).
[7] In Prussia, female students were only admitted to the *Abitur*, and university, in 1908. University training became compulsory for female teachers in upper secondary schools in 1909 (Gass-Bolm, 2005; Kraul, 1991).

since many *Gymnasium* teachers were also members of conservative parties and held political offices (Bölling, 1977: 26; Kopitzsch, 1983).

The establishment of a union expressly for secondary school teachers can be regarded as a critical juncture (Mahoney, 2000; Pierson, 2000) because it was at this time that a new dynamic of teachers' representation emerged. The institutional divide between elementary and secondary schooling led to the evolution of two distinct teaching professions and two 'opposing' teachers unions (Herrlitz *et al.*, 2009: 40). Following the dissolution of teachers unions during the period of National Socialism (1933–45) (Feiten, 1981), the dichotomy between elementary school and secondary school teachers was re-established after the Second World War and remains to this date a constitutive element of German teaching unionism.

The ADLV, for elementary school teachers, was revitalized in the British occupation zone in 1947[8] under the name of the 'General German Union of Male and Female Teachers' (ADLLV, Allgemeiner Deutscher Lehrer- und Lehrerinnenverband), and for the first time included women (Morell, 1973). The ADLLV merged a year later with the Trade Union of Education and Science (GEW, Gewerkschaft Erziehung und Wissenschaft). The GEW united members and interests in all education-related subfields, such as higher and further education and pre-school. Most of the latter were employed as salaried workers and were in full possession of the right to strike.[9] The DPhV, as the organization for *Gymnasium* teachers, was also quickly re-established in 1947. As we will see, the restoration of the vertically structured school system in all German *Länder* (Geißler, 2011b; Herrlitz *et al.*, 2009) was backed by the country's social and political elites, and organized and mobilized specifically by the DPhV. Despite this rapid re-establishment of teachers unions after the Second World War, the unification of all of them under a single umbrella institution did not take place.

On the contrary, the dualism of German teachers unions became more strongly institutionalized with the post-war re-establishment of both the German Association of Civil Servants (DBB, Deutscher Beamtenbund) and the German Trade Union Association (DGB, Deutscher Gewerkschaftsbund) as umbrella groups. Both the DGB and the DBB basically targeted the same constituency – teachers – but had different political positions, interests, and mindsets regarding the organization of schooling and the employment status of teachers, to name but two examples. While the DGB would soon pursue the vested interest of the traditional working class by targeting a more social democratic political agenda, the rationale for the DBB lay in forming

---

[8] The American and French occupation zones were integrated in 1949 (Fuhrig, 1969).
[9] Only the Bavarian Association for Elementary Teachers, which in 1951 was renamed the Bavarian Teacher Union (BLLV, Bayrischer Lehrer- und Lehrerinnenverein), has remained independent until today.

an exclusive representation for civil servants 'given their lack of bargaining and strike rights and the uneasiness with the DGB's left political leaning' (Ebbinghaus et al., 2000: 292). Consequently, the GEW joined forces with the DGB,[10] while the DPhV continued to be a member of the DBB (Kopitzsch, 1983).

The GEW policy during the 1950s and 1960s was dominated by the specific interests of teachers from elementary schools (Heidenheimer, 1974; Ratzke, 1981). Over the decades, the education system became further differentiated and stratified. The once homogenous composition of union membership was challenged with the separation of the elementary schools into a four-year elementary school (*Grundschule*) and the *Hauptschule*, as well as the establishment of comprehensive schools as pilot schools in the 1960s. Additionally, the expansion of the German welfare state was accompanied by a strong focus on education (*Bildungsexpansion*) (Gottschall, 2009: 469), and the GEW successfully unionized new and growing groups within the teaching profession – including research associates at universities and university teachers, nursery school teachers, teachers from comprehensive schools and the *Hauptschule*, and even students – leading to a considerable increase in membership. The GEW became an all-encompassing education union with various departments; the determination of school policy was only one its many concerns.

Despite this widening remit, GEW membership nevertheless failed to become attractive for most *Gymnasium* teachers.[11] Following its obvious social democratic bias, the GEW aimed for equal pay for all teachers and the right to strike for civil servant teachers. The GEW questioned the traditional and conservative vested interests of privileged civil servant teachers to perpetuate the status quo of different payment schemes and the general prohibition to go on strike. For the DBB and the DPhV, this meant a move to the political left and deepened the already-existing rifts between the GEW and the DPhV.

To counterbalance the large membership of the GEW, the DPhV joined forces with other like-minded secondary schools teachers unions such as the *Realschule*, as well as vocational schools and commercial schools. In 1969 this led to the creation of the German Teachers' Union (DLV, Deutscher Lehrerverband) as an umbrella organization, a process that consolidated the fragmentation of German teacher unionism.

German reunification in 1990 hardly changed the landscape for the teachers unions. Many members of teachers unions in the German Democratic Republic

---

[10] However, this was only on the condition that the DGB supported civil servant status for all teachers (Morell, 1973). Only since the end of the 1960s has the GEW questioned the civil servant status of teachers (Brinkmann, 1977).
[11] In 2012 the GEW had around 31,000 members employed in the *Gymnasium*. Compared to the DPhV, the GEW is the weaker teachers union when it comes to membership numbers in the German *Gymnasium*.

joined the GEW. The number of members, including non-teachers, nearly doubled from 190,000 to 360,000. The GEW immediately moved into East Germany by setting up headquarters and cooperating with key representatives of the teaching profession in East Germany even before the fall of the Berlin Wall in 1989 (Hildebrand, 1993). In parallel to this, the DPhV also launched regional associations in the new German *Länder* but could not increase its membership by as much as the GEW was able to (Ballauf, 2009). For most of the teachers in the East, joining the GEW was more attractive: the GEW was traditionally perceived as much less of an elite organization of the West than the DPhV was (Hildebrand, 1993). Furthermore, the GEW offered collective action and was even in favor of the right to strike, making it even more attractive to teachers from the East.

German reunification created a division in teacher employment status between *Länder* in the East and those in the West. Teachers who were redeployed in the East *Länder* became salaried workers (employees). With this action, the East *Länder* broke with the former principle of employing teachers as civil servants.[12] This led to a diversification of teachers' employment status – with some employed as civil servants, and others as salaried workers. However, in recent years some of the East *Länder* have begun to assign teachers the status of civil servant. In contrast to the West *Länder*, teachers at the *Gymnasium* in most of the East *Länder* were not employed as civil servants, and teachers at the *Gymnasium* in the East *Länder* even became members of the GEW rather than the DPhV. Today the GEW is the largest German education union, and 170,000 of its members were school teachers in 2012. Taking into consideration the total number of German teachers (about 730,000 in 2011 (KMK, 2012)), the GEW represents about 23 percent of the German teaching workforce.[13] The DPhV with its 90,000 members (about 12 percent of the teaching workforce) represents the largest section of teachers in higher secondary education (primarily those of the *Gymnasium*). In sum, teaching unionism is characterized by a monopoly of representation: the DPhV is still the main advocating body for the teachers of the *Gymnasium*.

This section has highlighted the fact that teaching unionism in Germany is divided, but monopolized by two strong collective bodies that reflect the vested interests of their class-based constituencies. The DPhV is regarded as the representative of the bourgeois coalition of interests in education policy (Kuhlmann, 1970: 170). As we will see in the following section, the GEW often faced difficulty in mobilizing the educated elite behind its policy goals.

---

[12] Before 1990, in the West *Länder* teachers were employed only as salaried workers if they did not reach the requirements for civil servants, or because of illness, or because they exceeded the age limit for civil servants (Gehrke and Bruno-Latocha, 2013).

[13] This number represents full-time teaching positions in Germany. Taking the number of part-time teachers into consideration, the total number of teachers is higher and therefore the degree of representation of the GEW is lower.

Teachers Unions' Interests and Influence

Teachers unions' interests are strongly affected by the employment status of their members. Since 1990 an increasing number of teachers have not been employed solely as civil servants. Of the GEW's membership, only around 27 percent (2014) are civil servants (DGB, 2016), compared to the DPhV representing 81 percent of the civil servant members.[14]

One of the priorities of the GEW in education is the abolition of a status-related system that structurally disadvantages not only schoolchildren but also their members in terms of wages and working hours. In line with their social democratic convictions, the GEW promotes a 'school for everyone' and battles for a unified school system in which all children study together over an extended period and in which all teachers teach at the same type of school. The GEW aims for a public education system that offers a variety of learning opportunities and guarantees equal educational opportunities for all children, as well as calling for a larger teaching workforce. The GEW criticizes the early segregation of students and the tripartite school system on the grounds that it hampers equality of condition (Brinkmann, 1977; DGB, 2009; Fuhrig, 1969; GEW, 2006). According to the GEW, a comprehensive school system is able to compensate for disadvantages caused by pupils' socioeconomic backgrounds. Based on the principles of social justice and an egalitarian society, the GEW emphasizes the support and promotion of children's individual needs instead of advocating a selection policy that follows ability levels. The GEW calls for the implementation of an inclusive education system and the abolition of special schools, in accordance with the UN Convention on the Rights of Persons with Disabilities (GEW, 2013b). It also objects to differentiation according to type of school, and therefore calls for standardized teacher training as well as the equalization of salaries and status. The status of teachers as civil servants is not considered mandatory by the GEW, but as long as teachers remain civil servants the GEW argues that they are entitled to strike according to the provisions of the European Declaration of Human Rights as well as European case law.

The call for a right to strike ultimately serves the GEW's vested interests. Its membership structure is oriented more towards the political left and GEW members are considered to be politically active. The GEW is also experienced in organizing strikes and is supported by the resources and the apparatus of the larger and well organized unions of the DGB (Briken et al., 2014). In this regard the most recent decision of the Federal Administrative Court, once again confirming the absence of a right to strike for teachers, is of relevance with regard to the GEW's resources and influence. The court emphasized that Parliament should decide the status of civil servants in Germany, given that their public service holds a political dimension.[15] As we will see in the following sections,

---

[14] These figures were kindly provided to us by the DPhV.
[15] See the decision of the Federal Administrative Court of February 17, 2014.

the GEW's power in the political arena is weak compared to its counterpart, the DPhV.

Through its membership in the DBB, the DPhV pursues the continuation of civil servant status for teachers as essential to securing its members' privileges. Thus, the DPhV opposes the right to strike for teachers and favors the Federal Administrative Court's decision. For the DPhV, as well as for the DBB, civil servant status symbolizes the register of their members' interests. In contrast to the GEW, the DPhV aims to secure the vested interests of its core members, the *Gymnasium* teachers; and to perpetuate their privileged work and employment conditions over and above their colleagues in other types of school. This requires the maintenance of a multi-tiered school system with a four-year-long elementary school system (DPhV, 2010a). The DLV, as the umbrella organization, and other teachers unions organized in the DLV, also support this demand. The DPhV legitimizes its profound belief in the need for a multi-tiered school system through an ideological conviction and theoretical underpinning that education be based on individual ability. According to these premises, learning outcomes will always be better in same-ability groups than in mixed-ability ones. Students, therefore, are to be assigned to different types of schools, with varying degrees of academic rigor, according to their 'talent' – and to teachers with varying qualifications. Thus, the DPhV was for decades the main advocate for a tripartite school system and the early selection of students (DPhV, 2004b, 2006; Ried 1955). In some German *Länder* it resisted the establishment of comprehensive schools as an additional school track in the 1960s and 1970s, considering it as an attack on the 'approved' tripartite school system and the exclusive role of the *Gymnasium* (as well as its teaching staff). The DPhV fights to preserve the *Gymnasium* as an independent school type, and therefore opposes a uniform teacher education. In contrast to the GEW, the DPhV does not call for an overall inclusive education system. It favors a mixture of joint teaching of disabled and non-disabled children, but without abandoning special needs schools (DPhV, 2010b). In the 2000s, a change in teachers' union policy could be recognized: the DPhV no longer blocked attempts for partial school integration and is now ready to accept the introduction of models that consist of an academic and a combined vocational track, with *Hauptschule* and *Realschule* partially integrated (DPhV, 2010a). This slight shift is the result of strategic requirements rather than a change in overall conviction. As long as the *Gymnasium* is not affected by the integration of schools, their members' interests are not jeopardized.

Although the GEW and DPhV emphasize in their statutes and publications their independence from political parties, strong relationships between teachers unions and the main political dispositions exist. Close ties can be found between the GEW and the center-left Social Democratic Party (SPD), and a large proportion of GEW members are also members of the SPD (Ebbinghaus, 2003: 184). In contrast, members of the DPhV are seen as closer to the conservative Christian Democratic Union (CDU). Whereas in most other cases discussed in this book teacher unions were historically allied with the leftist parties, there is a strong political fragmentation in the German teacher union landscape. An analysis of party political manifestos reveals that significant differences in education policy can be found between the left and the conservative parties in Germany. The SPD still votes for an 'equality of condition' whereas the CDU emphasizes an 'equality of opportunity' (Nikolai and Rothe, 2013). In line with the GEW, the SPD argues for comprehensive schools and is against the early selection of students. But in view of several unsuccessful attempts to extend primary schooling, and following a number of electoral defeats, the SPD abstains from abolishing the *Gymnasium* (Helbig and Nikolai, 2015; Nikolai and Rothe, 2013). The CDU gives priority to a multi-tiered school system and the early selection of children in accordance with the principle of schooling children according to their level of performance (Hepp, 2011; Hüfner et al. 1977; Kuhlmann, 1970; Nikolai and Rothe, 2013). Like the DPhV, the CDU is committed to a specific teacher education for teachers at the *Gymnasium*. Any attempts at establishing a uniform teacher education is interpreted as the introduction of an overall comprehensive school 'by the back door' (Die Welt, 2013; FAZ, 2013; Hüfner and Naumann, 1977: 49–51; Reuter, 1980). According to German teachers unions the classic political cleavages apply: the DPhV forms a close bond with the conservative CDU while the GEW is associated with the SPD.

Even though teachers unions cannot make use of collective bargaining privileges, the opportunities teachers unions have to influence school policy are manifold in Germany. Due to *Länder* sovereignty in the field of education the regional associations of the teachers unions are the main actors in school policy at the subnational level.[16] The German Constitution refers the regulation, planning, design and supervision of the school system to the Parliaments of the *Länder* – the main arenas of political decision-making in relation to education issues (Wolf, 2008).[17] In the past the *Länder* Parliaments made abundant use of their exclusive legislative competencies, one outcome being that the educational systems of the *Länder* differ in the length of elementary schooling, secondary school types and their pedagogical orientations, as well as the organization and curricula of teacher education.

Teachers unions are consulted by the ministerial bureaucracy in decision-making processes, such as during the preparation of school laws or legislative changes, and are asked for their written expertise on the given subject (Schröder, 1999: 441). With regard to the Christian Social Union (CSU) in Bavaria – the sister party of the CDU – Kral (1984: 427) shows how, in the past, it adopted its

---

[16] Germany has a strong tradition of regional government. Since unification in 1990, the Federal Republic has consisted of 16 *Länder*: the ten of the former West Germany, five new *Länder* of the former East Germany, and Berlin.
[17] Since the Federalism Reform of 2006 the *Länder* have exclusive responsibility for education policy (Burkhart, 2008).

reasoning and programs from the DPhV. Furthermore, civil servants are over-represented in the *Länder* Parliaments and therefore are more likely to express empathy and understanding for the positions of the DPhV. Teachers unions are able to influence details, and even partly govern changes, by submitting their own proposals. Consultation is possible, for example at parliamentary evenings, official hearings of parliamentary school committees and consultative bodies – namely, councils at school, regional and *Land* levels where teachers unions are represented. Even though these are only consultation rights, without any formal veto power, the strong corporatist tradition in decision-making processes in Germany (Abromeit, 1993; Weßels, 2000) also holds true for the public sector (Briken *et al.*, 2014). This is why German public sector unions in general, and teachers unions in particular, have a central role to play for the ministerial bureaucracy.

Teachers unions hold a huge 'threat potential' as far as elections and referenda are concerned (Keller, 1983: 172). Hence, and so as not to risk defeat at the ballot box, the ministerial bureaucracy very much takes into account teaching union positions during decision-making processes. As we will see in the next section, teachers unions mobilize both teachers and parents during election campaigns. Here, the DPhV is very successful in mobilizing the educated elite and in exerting pressure on the *Länder* governments. Over the past half century the higher tracks of early secondary education (*Gymnasium* and *Realschule*) have expanded considerably, leading to substantial changes in the distribution of students in Germany's secondary school system (Nikolai and West, 2013). The once so elite *Gymnasium* has become accessible for an increasing number of students from all socioeconomic backgrounds. In the wake of educational expansion, the educated strata of society has also increased considerably. Thus, between 1970 and 2009, the proportion of parents with a *Hauptschule* education as their highest level of attainment fell by nearly 57 percentage points (from 83 percent to 26 percent). The proportion of parents with at least a higher education entrance qualification (*Abitur*) increased by 24 percentage points (from 9 nine percent to 38 percent) and the proportion with at least a tertiary-level education increased by 17 percentage points (from 7 percent to 24 percent) (Helbig and Nikolai, 2015). As an important part of the German electorate, this educated sector of the population consists of a significant proportion of parents who themselves reaped the largest benefits from the status-(re-)producing effects of the German school structure, and who therefore broadly support a multi-tiered school structure (Blanck *et al.*, 2013; Edelstein and Nikolai, 2013; Kuhlmann, 1970: 170–1).

Furthermore, the unions' right of co-determination strengthens their influence at school level, where an elected staff council represents all employees. Due to their co-determination rights, staff councils have a huge influence in teachers' working life. Staff councils' rights are threefold. The strongest co-determination rights are assigned to decisions regarding appointments, shift working time and work schedules, as well as applications for part-time work.

At the school level, staff councils have further veto powers over the organization of day-to-day work and related social aspects. Additionally, all measures undertaken by school management to increase teachers' performance (such as the integration of Information Technology), and to changes in the organization of teaching (such as changing job descriptions), preventative healthcare, as well as the introduction of new forms of control (visits during class hours, exams, etc.), are subject to co-determination. Co-determination means approval by the staff council is required. If the staff council does not consent, the case will be submitted to arbitration at the school board. If arbitration fails, the dispute is referred to the main staff council in the education ministry. Last but not least, the school management has to inform the staff council of every planned project, e.g., the introduction of student assessments. The council also has the right to request information. Even though this does not imply any veto powers (for example, redundancies are legally void without the staff council's comment), staff councils are formally involved in every decision made at the school level. For the unions they become an important part in supporting their members' interests. Although the elected members of the staff council do not need to be union members, most of them are. Unions make use of this double structure to mobilize parents and teachers, and they offer training opportunities to the school-level representatives.

In sum, German teachers unions can use multiple veto points at the parliamentary level, at the ministerial bureaucracy level, and at the school level, to protect and promote the vested interests of their members. In the arena of employment conditions and collective bargaining, reforms of payscales or civil servant law are discussed with teachers unions beforehand. In other educational policy fields like the employment condition, school structure, or PISA reforms, teachers unions have the potential to influence or even block reforms by threatening the withdrawal of public support and votes during elections and referenda. Even though their institutionalized powers in traditional trade union terms are rather weak, the overall administration structure allows teachers unions to play a strong role in education policies.

In line with these observations, the DPhV as a professional association has proven to be more influential than the GEW. Focusing on lobbying more than on protesting in the streets, the DPhV has successfully defended its members' vested interests. With the *Gymnasium* still seen as the most prestigious of all the school types, and with an increase in attendance at such institutions (36 percent of pupils in grade 8 attended a *Gymnasium* in 2013, see Allmendinger et al., Forthcoming),[18] the DPhV could even strengthen its position. Across the German population, parents from middle and upper classes have a preference to send their children to the *Gymnasium* and are strongly opposed to the abolition of the tripartite system. And even the SPD is no longer a natural ally since

---

[18] In 1955, only 16 percent of pupils in grade 8 attended the *Gymnasium* and 69 percent the *Hauptschule*.

it increasingly also represents a clientele advocating for the maintenance of the *Gymnasium* (Nikolai and Rothe, 2013). The DPhV successfully mobilizes support for the maintenance of the stratified school system during elections and referenda. This ability to activate broad public support to maintain the *Gymnasium* (including its privileges) explains why the DPhV has the potential to block reforms that could alter the stratified school system. In contrast, the GEW is less capable of mobilizing support for the comprehensive schools and the abrogation of early tracking of students. Compared to the DPhV, the GEW represents a plethora of different subgroups. In addition, general public opinion regarding teachers impedes the GEW from forming an alliance with the broader public. In the German context, the public image of non-*Gymnasium* teachers is rather poor. The common stereotype is that they are lazy (having lots of holidays), and that they do not have a challenging job profile (see Ricken, 2007). In consequence, political and public support for teachers' demands for the further improvement of their employment conditions is rather weak, and even the SPD is no longer a reliable ally in this regard.

The Impact of Teachers Unions in German Education Policy

Teachers unions play an important role in formulating educational policy and they have a strong impact on ministerial bureaucracy and the *Länder* governments – as the next section will show. Although comprehensive analysis of teachers' union influences after 1945 is still rare, a few studies on individual reform processes in the German *Länder* exist. These enable us to examine the role of teachers unions in the politics of education. Our analysis refers to four arenas of teachers' union activities, all of them central to school politics: employment conditions and collective bargaining, the duration of elementary schooling, school form integration, and governance reforms after the 'PISA shock' of 2001.

Employment Conditions and Collective Bargaining

Despite the differences in status and the varying union impact mentioned earlier, teacher salaries in Germany are among the highest in the OECD – albeit with stark differences between the different levels of education taught. For instance, in 2011, upper secondary teachers with 15 years of experience earned 20 percent more than elementary teachers, and 11 percent more than lower secondary teachers.[19] On average across OECD countries, upper secondary teachers earned only 9 percent more than elementary teachers and 4 percent more than lower secondary teachers. The disparity between elementary and secondary

---

[19] In comparison to other states the salaries of teachers in Germany are above average. After 15 years of service a teacher's average annual salary in elementary education is $59,000, in lower secondary education $64,000, and in upper secondary education $70,000; while the OECD averages are $38,000, $40,000, and $43,000 respectively (OECD, 2013: 388–9).

Germany: Fragmented Competitors

teachers in Germany is also reflected in their teaching hours. Whereas in 2011, elementary school teachers spent 804 hours a year teaching, teachers in lower secondary education spent 757 hours, and in upper secondary education 715 hours. In international comparison, however, these differences in teaching hours are equivalent to other OECD member states (OECD, 2013).

Teachers are employed directly by one of the 16 *Länder*.[20] Due to the regional fragmentation of education policy in Germany, the labor market of teachers is segregated and can be characterized as pluralist (Causarano, 2012). Even though the majority of teachers in Germany are employed as civil servants (approximately 75 percent (StBa, 2013: 58)), there are substantial differences between the German *Länder* with regard to the share of teachers being civil servants.[21] An important consequence of this diversification of teachers' employment status for the influence of teachers unions is that the ability for collective action (including strikes) varies between *Länder*. Hence, the formal capacities for the influence of teachers unions are unevenly distributed across Germany.

With the Federalism Reforms of 2006 and 2009, the jurisdiction and political competences were reorganized between the *Länder* and the federal government. The now 17 employers of civil servants (the federal government plus the 16 *Länder*) are independent with respect to the employment conditions of the public service. The legislators made use of these newly acquired competencies, particularly in the fields of pay and career structure (Briken et al., 2014; Tondorf, 2008).[22]

Collective bargaining now takes place at the *Länder* level, and teachers unions in general are challenged on two levels. First, they need to build up the resources (human resources, knowledge transfer, money) to follow and intervene in 17 bargaining arenas. Second, austerity as a new factual constraint becomes a strong argument against any payrise, especially in the public sector, and so interest representation requires new arguments. By now it seems obvious that with a more and more diversified bargaining process the unions have to face additional expenses to support their members. Having said that, teachers unions, as a collective, possess relatively little formal power to pursue their interests within the system of collective bargaining.[23] For the group

---

[20] Except for Bavaria and Bremen: in both of these *Länder* teachers are employed directly by the municipalities (Füssel, 2011).

[21] In most West German *Länder* around 90 percent of teachers are civil servants, but in some East German *Länder* this quota is well below 20 percent (Behörden Spiegel, 2012: 6).

[22] According to the latest figures published by the DGB, the pay gap between Bavaria and Bremen amounted to €5,000 (net) per annum in 2012 at the most common pay grade for teachers (GEW, 2013c).

[23] It is important to recall that collective bargaining in Germany involves only the issues of wages and working hours. Any other organizational, educational, or pedagogical issues are part of political negotiations. It is here where the teachers unions in Germany can make use of their power.

of the public service workforce employed as civil servants, neither collective bargaining nor negotiations for each profession take place. In contrast, as the employer the central state (and since 2009 also the *Länder*) unilaterally decides upon the salary levels and other job-related regulations of *all* civil servants, including teachers. During the formal law-making procedure, the unions have the right to be heard and to take advantage of so-called consultation with the state representative. However, the informal modes of influence are manifold. In the German corporate system, union representatives are approved as informal lobbying partners for the state representatives at the local, the *Länder*, and the federal level, as well as during all phases of law-making.

While the teachers unions are barely visible during the salary-setting process, they are highly influential when it comes to group-specific improvements to pay. The DPhV in particular, was able to achieve substantial improvements in salaries and promotion for *Gymnasium* teachers following petitions made to state parliaments and as a result of negotiations with ministries of education (Kral, 1984; Schröder, 1999). In contrast, a uniform salary system for all teachers as a central goal of the GEW has not yet been achieved.

In Berlin, where newly recruited teachers can only become employees, a lively debate is taking place. In 2013, the GEW called on employed teachers to strike as part of a fight for the removal of income differentials between employed teachers and teachers with civil servant status. There is some evidence that political action is taking place more and more frequently; members appear ready to rally against austerity measures, and media coverage remains at a high level (Briken *et al.*, 2014). In sum, the strike action that was taken was successful to the extent that parent associations began to complain about the number of lessons lost and about how their children were being instrumentalized (GEW, 2013a; TSP, 2013a, 2013b). It became clear that in pursuing their members' interests the GEW still struggles to form reliable alliances with parent organizations. Unlike the DPhV, the GEW was not able to articulate its interest as being conducive to the perceived needs of good (or, to be precise, more equal) education.

The Duration of Elementary Schooling

The duration of elementary schooling, and thus the time shared with all students in a non-stratified school form, is a highly controversial and ideologically laden discussion in Germany (Helbig and Nikolai, 2015). The governing SPD of some German *Länder* established a six-year elementary school (Bremen, Hamburg, Schleswig-Holstein) or even an eight-year elementary school (in Berlin, as part of the 12-year comprehensive school) after 1945. In all these *Länder* the prolonged elementary schooling was criticized by conservative parties, churches, and conservative teachers unions and associations in the DPhV. The DPhV mobilized parents, teachers and professors in numerous events and publications against the six-year elementary school, because it threatened the *Gymnasium*'s existence (Gass-Bolm, 2005: 131). The parliamentary elections in the 1950s saw a fierce controversy developing over the future course of school policy. The SPD lost their majority in Hamburg, Schleswig-Holstein and Berlin, and the victorious CDU returned to the four-year elementary school in Hamburg and Schleswig-Holstein, and in Berlin to the six-year elementary school. The SPD were able to win the election in Bremen, but, facing electoral defeat in other *Länder*, withdrew the obligatory six-year elementary school[24] and allowed children to switch to the *Gymnasium* after Year 4 (Helbig and Nikolai, 2015).

The controversy about the duration of elementary schooling is still evident. In Hamburg, the CDU decided in their coalition treaty with the Greens in 2008 to extend primary education from four to six years, and to integrate *Hauptschule, Realschule* and the comprehensive *Gesamtschule* into one school form. This reform was supported by a unanimous vote of all parties represented in the Hamburg state parliament. A grassroots initiative was formed with the goal of stopping the introduction of 'primary schools as comprehensive schools until Year 6 as a compulsory model for all' (Edelstein and Nikolai, 2013; Töller *et al.* 2011).[25] In close cooperation with the DPhV the initiative was highly effective in mobilizing the *Gymnasium* clientele in a political campaign for a referendum in July 2010 in which the opponents of a six-year elementary school prevailed. This recent example from Hamburg emphasizes how the *Gymnasium* clientele form a powerful coalition of resistance against any reform attempts to extend the four-year elementary school, even today. By working together with the parents' associations, the DPhV has a powerful partner. The success of the grassroots initiative in Hamburg also shows a new development in school policy: the increased importance of parents associations, which are deeply embedded in the *Gymnasium* clientele and have initiated several popular initiatives in the last few years. However, parents' initiatives have only a realistic chance of success when they form alliances with teachers unions and/or opposition parties (Hepp, 2011: 76). On the other hand, German teachers unions can compensate the loss of party allies by building extra-parliamentary coalitions with parents' associations or other actors to pursue their interests.

School Form Integration

In stark contrast to other Western European nations that converged towards models of comprehensive schooling (Wiborg, 2009), Germany has for decades retained a traditional tripartite school system which tracks students into hierarchically structured and spatially segregated school types.

---

[24] In Bremen, the six-year elementary school was officially abolished in the school year 1977–78.
[25] In comparison to the other *Länder*, Hamburg's population has the highest education level with 49 percent of parents with at least a higher education entrance qualification (Helbig and Nikolai, 2015).

Some *Länder*, governed by the SPD, established the comprehensive *Gesamtschule* in the 1970s, catering for all ability levels and preparing students for the leaving certificates of the other three main school types within one institutional setting (Köller, 2008). This school form did not significantly alter the basic school structure since it was established as an additional fourth track and remained a marginal school type in most of the *Länder*. In 2010, only 10 percent of students nationwide attended the *Gesamtschule* (Nikolai and West, 2013).

The rigorous tracking system has been repeatedly challenged and criticized for being socially selective and more recently for being incompatible with the skills requirements of an increasingly knowledge-based economy (Allmendinger *et al.*, Forthcoming; Nikolai and West, 2013; Schneider and Thieben, 2011). Despite this criticism, the school structure has remained largely unchanged for decades. In the *Länder* with a clear conservative majority and with strong regional associations to the DPhV (Bavaria, Baden-Wurttemberg) the comprehensive *Gesamtschule* was not established as a regular school type at all (Kral, 1984). Only in those *Länder* where the SPD have long held a majority, and where there are strong regional associations with the GEW, has the comprehensive school become increasingly important, growing to be the most popular school type besides the *Gymnasium*. However, by the end of the 1970s, the Social Democrat-led *Länder* had refrained from implementing the comprehensive school as the only school type when faced with electoral defeat (Herrlitz *et al.*, 2009: 178). The *Gymnasium* is firmly anchored in society as a 'lead institution' (Tenorth, 2008) and it is strongly supported by its growing educated clientele.

In recent years, though, many *Länder* have implemented reforms that enforce a partial integration of school types (Edelstein and Nikolai, 2013). While some of the East *Länder* adopted the basic idea of a multi-tiered school system, they refrained from introducing the *Hauptschule* as an independent school form in the aftermath of reunification. After decades of polarizing controversies and failed attempts at reform, most West German *Länder* started to change their traditional school structures and abolished the *Hauptschule*.[26] In some of these *Länder*, the integrated school forms are conceived as a 'second pillar,' integrating all tracks and offering the full range of secondary school certificates, including the *Abitur*. Bavaria is the only German state that has not made any changes to its school structure so far. It is crucial to note though that despite the extensive school reforms implemented over the last two decades, none of the *Länder* replaced the *Gymnasium*.

In contrast, and something that in part explains this stubborn stability, over the past half century the higher tracks of lower secondary education (*Gymnasium* and *Realschule*) have expanded considerably. Today, 36 percent

---

[26] Such as the city states of Bremen, Hamburg and Berlin, Rhineland-Palatinate, Saarland, and Schleswig-Holstein.

(2013) of all pupils in grade 8 attend the *Gymnasium* compared to 16 percent in 1955. Thus, between 1955 and 2013, the proportion of students in the *Hauptschule* fell by nearly 60 percentage points (from 69 percent to 14 percent) (Allmendinger et al., Forthcoming). The associated decline in enrolments at the *Hauptschule*, and the degeneration of the *Hauptschule* into a 'school for leftovers' (Rösner, 2007), has made the preservation of the *Hauptschule* as an independent school type increasingly difficult.

For decades the DPhV was the main advocate for the maintenance of the tripartite school system. Its position was challenged by the establishment of two-tiered school structures in most of the *Länder* and the reorientation of the CDU, its traditional ally. Since 2011, the federal CDU has called for a two-tiered school structure in all *Länder* (CDU, 2011). It was strongly criticized for this turn by the DPhV as evidence of furthering the 'social democratization of the CDU' (Kraus, 2007, own translation); and for abandoning its principles concerning education policy (DPhV, 2001; Kraus, 2010). In order to avoid a more and more defensive position, the DPhV is now prepared to accept a two-tiered school structure so long as it does not endanger the existence of a multi-tiered school system in which the *Gymnasium* retains its distinctive position (DPhV, 2010a). With this demand, the DPhV did not abandon its core tenet that homogenous learning groups lead to better achievement. Its acceptance of a two-tiered school structure is more a strategic position than a change in ideology. In sum, the distinctive position of the *Gymnasium* as an elite educational institution was never endangered, but is in fact further strengthened. In contrast to the DPhV, the GEW considers the integration of the *Hauptschule* and the *Realschule* (and in some *Länder* with the comprehensive *Gesamtschule*) in one institutional setting only as an interim step towards a comprehensive school for all students (Lohmann, 2011; Ratzki, 2009).

In sum, both GEW and DPhV tried to influence the political decision process by addressing parents, politicians and partisans. In this case, the DPhV could clearly profit from the strong support that the *Gymnasium* has both in terms of the teachers working there and the politically overrepresented middle and upper classes.

Teachers Unions and the PISA Reforms

Between the mid-1970s and the early 2000s the German education system was comparatively resistant to reform, and no fundamental changes took place to substantially challenge conservative teachers unions and their vested interests. As illustrated above, the DPhV played its part in supporting educational conservatism regarding school structures and the length of elementary schooling.

The situation of the educational reform deadlock eventually changed with the publication of the first PISA study in 2001.[27] PISA showed that the

[27] See www.oecd.org/pisa/ [accessed January 2016].

performance of students in Germany was below the OECD average and it highlighted significant weaknesses of the German education system from an internationally comparative perspective. This result was in stark contrast to what the country generally perceived about its own position (Martens and Niemann, 2013). An extensive public reaction was generated in the aftermath of PISA – often referred to as the 'PISA shock' – and almost all areas of the German secondary education system were reformed, referring to best practice examples from other countries as provided by PISA (Niemann, 2010). This PISA shock explains why the governments in the *Länder* were more committed to education reform than were other countries discussed in this book (Martens et al., 2014). Overall, the reforms comprised measures intended to directly improve the academic performance of students in Germany, the expansion of quality assurance, the extension of all-day services, and improvements in the methodological and diagnostic skills of teachers (KMK and BMBF, 2008; Tillmann et al., 2008). Additionally, strong emphasis was placed on the introduction and monitoring of binding educational standards that defined what skills students should have at certain points in their academic career (Ertl, 2006; Klieme et al., 2003; KMK, 2011). This reflects a paradigmatic change towards output-oriented education governance. Previously, education governance relied on ex-ante budget allocations and structured education plans, which were set up centrally. A shift occurred from a system driven by bureaucratic supervision towards practices of continuous performance evaluation (Herrmann, 2009), and, hence, more accountability was introduced into the German school debate (Gruber, 2006).

The comprehensive post-PISA reforms affected the work of teachers, and, hence, deeply challenged teachers unions' vested interests. Accordingly, teachers unions were alert to saving their clientele from unwelcome change. At the same time, the unions (GEW and DPhV) widely acknowledged that education reforms were overdue and tried to seize the opportunity offered by reformist momentum to further their own interests and preferences. In this, some interests and preferences of the DPhV and the GEW were identical, such as more funding (also for teacher education) and better employment conditions (more preparation time, more assistance from social workers). However, both teachers unions pursued different positions regarding other issues. While the GEW used PISA to call for the establishment of more comprehensive schools to counteract the diagnosed performance variation between students from different school types and from different socioeconomic backgrounds (GEW, 2001, 2013d), the DPhV vehemently defended the tripartite school structure by also making references to PISA. The DPhV argued that those *Länder* with the strictest tripartite school structures (e.g., Bavaria, Baden-Wurttemberg) achieved the best test scores in PISA (DPhV, 2004a, 2005). Thus, according to the DPhV, the tripartite structure was crucial for good education performance outcomes. In contrast, the GEW's line of reasoning was fueled by PISA's best practice examples from Scandinavian countries such as Finland. These countries were characterized by very good PISA test scores, low performance variations between social strata, and also by comprehensive school systems (OECD, 2001, 2004).

In general, however, the teachers unions did not evaluate the reforms as a chance to further their own interests and to improve teachers' working conditions; first and foremost they regarded them as a potential threat to their vested interests. In contrast to neoliberal reforms (as discussed in this book using the examples of Sweden and England), German teachers unions were able to block reforms that aimed at the further introduction of performance management, accountability or privatization. These measures would have undermined the autonomy of teachers by establishing instruments to monitor and evaluate their work. Their resistance was strongly driven by defending the job interests of their members in regard to salaries, careers and job security – which would all have been jeopardized if mechanisms of external review and evaluation were introduced.

The teachers unions focused on criticizing some reforms as going too far, and being counterproductive to improving students' performances. Controversy was provoked from the unions regarding the introduction of accountability through empirical tests. It is important to note that the turn to output-oriented governance entailed two main consequences for teachers in Germany. First, the introduced education standards defined goals; while the way to achieve these was not regulated in detail. Thus, teachers were more autonomous in applying strategies to achieve the goals, and they had to 'fill the vacuum caused by the absence of curricular guidance' (Ertl, 2006: 626). Second, teachers were now increasingly faced with evaluations and PISA-like testing. Schools and school districts were externally monitored through national and international comparative assessments, while internal evaluations (on the level of individual schools) were also standardized and expanded.

Generally, the GEW claimed that the implementation of reforms was rather poorly done and that a lack of human and financial resources made effective implementation at school level difficult (GEW, 2010). First and foremost, the GEW argued strongly against the overemphasis of testing measures. Constant evaluations led to a teaching-to-the-test mentality whereby teachers just concentrate on achieving good test results instead of good education (GEW, 2012, 2014). Instead of extensive testing and performance evaluations, teachers and schools needed more assistance and better infrastructure to produce better outcomes (GEW, 2010: 3).

Furthermore, the GEW supported a series of protest events in 2009 in which students, parents, university employees, and teachers called for the cutting back of some of the more controversial education reforms. However, the protests did not exclusively address the interests of teachers but can be understood as a broad alliance against too many education reforms within a short period of time. Furthermore, the GEW refused any future attempts at more market orientation in school policy (Avenarius, 2011; GEW, 2007) since these threatened the employment position of their members, who are mainly public school teachers. Here the GEW position is in line with the DPhV, who see the civil servant status of their members threatened by the increasing number of privatized schools. Incidentally, it should be noted for Germany, in contrast to many other countries, market-based reforms play a marginal role in school policy. Although the private school sector has increased in size over the last few years (Koinzer and Leschinsky, 2009), the share of private schools is rather small compared to other OECD countries (OECD, 2013: 272). Also, unlike in other countries, parental school choice is not a prominent topic in teacher unions policy because of the existence of school districts.[28]

In the context of recent education reforms, the DPhV was not particularly skeptical towards education tests and performance evaluations. Instead, the DPhV claimed to use evaluations for monitoring compliance with education standards across all *Länder* in order to mitigate performance variations across Germany (DPhV, 2004b). The DPhV also emphasized that the implementation of reforms, and their positive effect on educational performances, depended heavily on more efforts and more assistance in teacher training (DPhV, 2005). The greatest concern of the DPhV was that the debate regarding school structures was going to be revived in the context of PISA reforms. The arguments of some interest groups (e.g., the GEW) who called for the introduction of comprehensive schools in the light of the PISA results were met with great concern (DPhV, 2004a, 2011: 8). Consequently, the DPhV put great effort into the preservation of the traditional German school structure.

Overall, during the course of PISA reforms the German teachers unions, particularly the DPhV, were not able to activate their usual alliances to stave off pending reforms. This was for two reasons. First, necessity and impulses for reform were initiated outside the usual political processes; an external, international initiative was exerting pressure for reform. Reforms were not discussed behind closed doors, but rather came under the focus of the public-political discourse. Second, teachers unions (especially the DPhV) were almost always successful in preventing disadvantageous reforms by forming alliances with parents' organizations interested in keeping the school system separate and to conserve the status of the elite *Gymnasium*. In the case of PISA, this alliance was split because all parents were interested in improving the education system. However, the DPhV was successful in preventing an extensive debate over school structures by constantly referring to the satisfactory performances of the *Gymnasium*.

---

[28] Only North Rhine-Westphalia and Lower Saxony allow free school choice for public denominational schools (Riedel *et al.*, 2010). Since 2010, Berlin is the only federal state which introduced free school choice for all public secondary schools.

Conclusion

In Germany, there exists a highly fragmented teaching unionism that represents teachers according to different school types. As a political legacy, the historical distinction between teachers at the *Gymnasium* (represented by the DPhV) and the elementary school teachers (represented by the GEW) is still evident today. Despite the fragmented structure, teachers unions had a strong impact on school policy in the past. The strength of the teachers unions in Germany becomes apparent when they are able to mobilize the educated elite. Several failed attempts for a longer duration of elementary schooling and a uniform teacher education from the 1950s, through until today, demonstrate an important point: the DPhV is a 'powerful interest group' (Wiborg, 2009: 199) able to block reforms for extended elementary schooling as a result of its ability to mobilize the *Gymnasium* clientele.

As noted above, in Germany the highly educated middle class (*Bildungsbürgertum*) forms a strongly pro-*Gymnasium* interest group that reaps the biggest benefits from the status-(re-)producing effects of the German school structure. In the wake of educational expansion, the once-so-elite *Gymnasium* has become accessible for an increasing number of students from all socioeconomic backgrounds. The *Gymnasium* clientele constitutes an important part of the German electorate, not only in quantitative terms but also in terms of its ability to engage in advocacy and wield considerable political clout. It shares the DPhV's view that learning outcomes will always be better in same-ability groups than in mixed-ability ones, and the view that to sort students into different types of school is inevitable. Strongly embodied in middle-class parents' associations, the *Gymnasium* clientele forms – together with the DPhV and other secondary school teachers' associations – a powerful coalition of resistance to comprehensive schooling (Blanck et al., 2013; Edelstein and Nikolai, 2013; Kral, 1984: 419; Wiborg, 2009: 199). In contrast to the DPhV, the more diversified GEW has encountered difficulties in mobilizing the educated elite and forming a competitive counterforce against the conservative coalition. Thus, its ability to exert pressure is considerably lower than that of the DPhV.

The DPhV not only shapes the school structure, it also pursues the employment-related interests of its members. With its commitment to a multi-tiered school system with early student selection and a divided teacher education, along different school forms, the DPhV also fights for the maintenance of the pay and working conditions of their teaching members at the *Gymnasium*. The GEW stands for a unified school system and the equalization of teachers' salaries and status, but unlike the DPhV it has failed to form a decisive alliance with parents' organizations in the past. Just as in the United States or France, teacher unions in Germany have been able to block profound changes to their education systems in the *Länder*. In comparison to other countries discussed in this book, German teachers unions, especially the DPhV, are powerful. Because of their informal participation in pre-parliamentary debates and parliamentary hearings, as well as their capacity to mobilize the highly educated middle class in elections and referenda, teachers unions in Germany have been able to defend their vested interests. Some of the political positions the DPhV pursues (e.g., the preservation of the *Gymnasium*) are deeply rooted in large parts of German society and allow for strong leverage by the DPhV. Nevertheless, so long as the interests of their members regarding job security, careers and salaries are not affected, teacher unions are able and willing to contribute more constructively to reforms (e.g., integration of refugee children in the school systems) (DPhV, 2015a, 2015b; GEW, 2015).

Future research will need to consider how far teachers unions in Germany will still be able to influence school policy and defend their vested interests in the light of a reconfiguration of school governance. Over the past two decades schools in Germany have obtained a greater scope to determine their own profile as well as greater decision-making powers (Nikolai and Helbig, 2013). In contrast to the cases of Sweden and England presented in this book, Germany has experienced more decentralization in education policy. In the realm of the Federalism Reforms of 2006 and 2009, jurisdiction and political competencies between the *Länder* and the Federal Government were reorganized. The now-17 employers of civil servants (the federal government and the 16 *Länder*) are independent with respect to the employment conditions of civil servants but are still confined to special, traditional principles. The former close connection between the two status groups (civil servants and employees) has been undermined, and decentralization and fragmentation of employment regulation, the Federalism Reform for the civil servants, and the break-up of the bargaining alliance of public employers, has set into motion a growing divergence of the terms and conditions of employment (Gottschall *et al.*, 2015; Tondorf, 2008). The unsettling effect of the two reforms – brought about by PISA in 2001 and the Federalism Reform process that started in 2003 – hit German teachers' unions almost simultaneously. It remains an open question as to how far these processes will lead to the decline of teachers unions' power in education policy and how strong this decline will be in comparison to other countries. The implementation of the UN Convention on the Rights of Persons with Disabilities constitutes a further challenge for teacher unionism, and it remains to be seen to what extent teachers unions in Germany facilitate or hinder inclusive education. Further research is needed into whether the outlined reforms will weaken the unions' political bargaining and veto powers.

References

Abromeit, H. (1993). *Interessenvermittlung zwischen Konkurrenz und Konkordanz. Studienbuch zur Vergleichenden Lehre politischer Systeme*. Opladen: Leske + Budrich.

Allmendinger, J., Ebner, C., and Nikolai, R. (Forthcoming). Soziologische Bildungsforschung. In R. Tippelt and B. Schmidt, eds, *Handbuch Bildungsforschung*. Wiesbaden: Springer VS.
Avenarius, H. (2011). *Die Herausforderung des öffentlichen Schulwesens durch private Schulen. Aktuelle Rechtsfragen in einer angespannten Beziehung*. Frankfurt a.M.: Gewerkschaft Erziehung und Wissenschaft.
Ballauf, H. (2009). 60 Jahre GEW: Ein Kapitel GEW-Geschichte: Ost-West-Integration nach 1989. *Erziehung & Wissenschaft* 61(12): 20–2.
Behörden Spiegel (2012). Es bleibt dabei. Länder wollen Einstellungspraxis bei Lehrern nicht ändern. Behörden Spiegel No. 1, January 2012. Online: www.genios.de/document/BSPI__20120101285401935761225458128054953 [accessed July 2016].
Blanck, J.M., Edelstein, B., and Powell, J.J.W. (2013). Persistente schulische Segregation oder Wandel zur inklusiven Bildung? Die UN-Behindertenrechtskonvention und Reformmechanismen in den deutschen Bundesländern. *Schweizerische Zeitschrift für Soziologie* 39(2): 267–92.
Blömeke, S. (2002). *Universität und Lehrerausbildung*. Bad Heilbrunn: Klinkhardt.
Bölling, R. (1977). Zur Entwicklung und Typologie der Lehrerorganisationen in Deutschland. In M. Heinemann, ed., *Der Lehrer und seine Organisation*: 23–37. Stuttgart: Ernst Klett.
(1978). *Volksschullehrer und Politik: der Deutsche Lehrerverein 1918–1933*. Göttingen: Vandenhock & Ruprecht.
Briken, K., Gottschall, K., Hils, S., and Kittel, B. (2014). Wandel von Beschäftigung und Arbeitsbeziehungen im öffentlichen Dienst in Deutschland – zur Erosion einer sozialstaatlichen Vorbildrolle. *Zeitschrift für Sozialreform* 60(2): 123–48.
Brinkmann, W. (1977). Die Berufsorganisation der Lehrer und die "pädagogische Selbstrolle". Zur Professionalisierungs- und Deutungsfunktion der Gewerkschaft Erziehung und Wissenschaft und des Deutschen Philologenverbandes 1949–1974. In M. Heinemann, ed., *Der Lehrer und seine Organisation*: 393–408. Stuttgart: Ernst Klett Verlag.
Burkhart, S. (2008). Reforming federalism in Germany: Incremental changes instead of the big deal. *Publius: The Journal of Federalism* 39(2): 1–25.
Causarano, P. (2012). Teachers and trade unions: Between corporate tradition, professional associations and collective representation. *Transfer: European Review of Labour and Research* 18(2): 157–70.
CDU, Christlich Demokratische Union Deutschlands (2011). Beschluss Bildungsrepublik Deutschland. 24. Parteitag der CDU Deutschlands vom 14.-15.11.2011. Online: www.leipzig2011.cdu.de/images/stories/docs/111115-beschluss-bildungsrepublik-deutschland.pdf [accessed January 2016].
DGB, Deutscher Gewerkschaftsbund (2009). *Konsequent: Eine gute Schule für alle. Gewerkschaften zur Schule der Zukunft*. Berlin: DGB.
(2016). Mitglieder in den DGB-Gewerkschaften 2013. Online: www.dgb.de/uber-uns/dgb-heute/mitgliederzahlen/2010/?tab=tab_0_0#tabnav [accessed January 2016].
Die Welt (2013). Opposition kritisiert Konzept des "Einheitslehrers. *Die Welt* Online, 10 April. Online: www.welt.de/regionales/stuttgart/article115187343/Opposition-kritisiert-Konzept-des-Einheitslehrers.html [accessed January 2016].
DPhV, Deutscher Philologenverband (2001). Droht ein Etikettenschwindel? *PROFIL*, July/August, 3.

(2004a). DPhV zu PISA 2003: Fortschritte bei Förderung leistungsschwächerer Schüler. Gegliedertes Schulwesen ist konkurrenzfähig. Online: www.dphv.de/fileadmin/user_upload/presse/material/Pressemitteilungen_DPhv_2004.pdf [accessed January 2016].

(2004b). Resolution der Vertreterversammlung 2004 des Deutschen Philologenverbandes zur Bildungspolitik. Online: www.dphv.de/fileadmin/user_upload/positionen/bildungspolitik/standpunkte/ResolutionBildungspolitik.pdf [accessed January 2016].

(2005). PISA und die Konsequenzen für das Gymnasium. Online: www.dphv.de/fileadmin/user_upload/positionen/bildungspolitik/PISAAktuell0205.pdf [accessed January 2016].

(2006). Philologenverband befürchtet neuen Schulkampf in Deutschland. Online: www.dphv.de/aktuell/archiv/news-archiv-liste/article/philologenverband-befuerchtet-neuen-schulkampf-in-deutschland.html [accessed January 2016].

(2010a). DPhV-Positionspapier zur Schulstrukturfrage. Online: www.dphv.de/fileadmin/user_upload/positionen/bildungspolitik/PositionspapierSchulstruktur.pdf [accessed January 2016].

(2010b). Position des Deutschen Philologenverbands zum Thema "Inklusion." Online: www.dphv.de/fileadmin/user_upload/positionen/bildungspolitik/Positionspapier_Inklusion.pdf [accessed January 2016].

(2011). 8 Thesen des DPhV zur Struktur und Qualität von Schulen und Abschlüssen. Online: www.dphv.de/fileadmin/user_upload/positionen/bildungspolitik/Schule_und_Schulstruktur__2_.pdf [accessed January 2016].

(2015a). Zusatzmilliarden des Bundes müssen auch Schulen zugutekommen! Online: www.dphv.de/aktuell/nachrichten/details/article/philologenverband-zusatzmilliarden-des-bundes-muessen-auch-schulen-zugutekommen.html [accessed January 2016].

(2015b). DPhV bekennt sich uneingeschränkt zur Willkommenskultur. Online: www.dphv.de/aktuell/nachrichten/details/article/dphv-bekennt-sich-uneingeschraenkt-zur-willkommenskultur.html [accessed January 2016].

Ebbinghaus, B. (2003). Die Mitgliederentwicklung deutscher Gewerkschaften im historischen und internationalen Vergleich. In W. Schroeder and B. Weßels, eds, *Die Gewerkschaften in Politik und Gesellschaft der Bundesrepublik Deutschland*: 174–203. Wiesbaden: Westdeutscher Verlag.

Ebbinghaus, B., Armingeon, K., and Hassel, A. (2000). Germany. In B. Ebbinghaus and J. Visser, eds, *Trade Unions in Western Europe since 1945*: 279–337. London: Palgrave Macmillan.

Edelstein, B., and Nikolai, R. (2013). Strukturwandel im Sekundarbereich. Determinanten schulpolitischer Reformprozesse in Sachsen und Hamburg. *Zeitschrift für Pädagogik* 59(4): 482–94.

Ertl, H. (2006). Educational standards and the changing discourse on education: The reception and consequences of the PISA study in Germany. *Oxford Review of Education* 32(5): 619–34.

FAZ, Frankfurter Allgemeine Zeitung (2013). Für alle Schulformen. Der Einheitslehrer ist wieder da. FAZ Online, June 7. Online: www.faz.net/aktuell/beruf-chance/campus/fuer-alle-schulformen-der-einheitslehrer-ist-wieder-da-12200875.html [accessed January 2016].

Feiten, W. (1981). *Der Nationalsozialistische Lehrerbund. Entwicklung und Organisation*. Basel: Böhlau.
Fuhrig, W.D. (1969). West Germany. In A.A. Blum, ed., *Teacher Unions and Associations. A Comparative Study*: 83–118. Urbana/Chicago/London: University of Illinois Press.
Füssel, H.-P. (2011). Rechtsstellung, Laufbahnen und Besoldung der Lehrkräfte. In E. Terhart, H. Bennewitz, and M. Rothland, eds, *Handbuch der Forschung zum Lehrerberuf*: 79–97. Münster: Waxmann.
Gass-Bolm, T. (2005). *Das Gymnasium 1945–1980*. Göttingen: Wallstein Verlag.
Gehrke, A., and Bruno-Latocha, G. (2013). Die Verbeamtungspraxis der Bundesländer bei Lehrkräften. *Recht der Jugend und des Bildungswesens* 61(3): 306–16.
Geißler, G. (2011a). *Schulgeschichte in Deutschland. Von den Anfängen bis in die Gegenwart*. Frankfurt a.M.: Peter Lang.
Geißler, R. (2011b). Bildungsexpansion und Wandel der Bildungschancen. Veränderungen im Zusammenhang von Bildungssystem und Sozialstruktur. In R. Geißler, ed., *Die Sozialstruktur Deutschlands*: 274–99. Wiesbaden: VS Verlag für Sozialwissenschaften.
GEW, Gewerkschaft Erziehung und Wissenchaft (2001). PISA ... und was in Deutschland anders ist. Online: www.gew.de/Binaries/Binary34599/pisa_broschuere.pdf [accessed February 2014].
(2006). *Eine Schule für alle. Argumente, Informationen und GEW-Beschluss*. Frankurt a.M.: GEW.
(2007). *Privatisierungsreport 5. Bildung als Privatsache: Privatschulen und Nachhilfeanbieter auf dem Vormarsch*. Frankfurt a.M.: GEW.
(2010). PISA-Bilanz – PISA verstehen – Was hat sich seit dem PISA-Schock getan? Online: www.gew.de/index.php?eID=dumpFile&t=f&f=23924&token=50d825f385066461554fdd3524da889fec6b6b2a&sdownload= [accessed January 2016].
(2012). Vom PISA-Test zur VERA-Hitparade. *Erziehung & Wissenschaft* 58(7–8): 14–17.
(2013a). 2.300 Angestellte Lehrkräfte streiken auf dem Gendarmenmarkt. Online: www.gew.de/tarif/aktuelles/detailseite/neuigkeiten/2300-angestellte-lehrkraefte-streiken-auf-dem-gendarmenmarkt/ [accessed January 2016].
(2013b). Auf dem Weg zu einem inklusiven Schulsystem. Beschluss 3.12. auf dem Gewerkschaftstag 2013. Online: www.gew.de/index.php?eID=dumpFile&t=f&f=24138&token=dbe4bd246e1e36bb33b88aa5786fdb3a617680e-5&sdownload= [accessed January 2016].
(2013c). Jahresbruttobesoldung 2012 in der BesGr. A13. Online: www.gew.de/Binaries/Binary92332/Besoldungsvergleich_A13_2012_DGB.pdf [accessed March 2014].
(2013d). Soziale Auslese ist Bremsklotz des deutschen Bildungssystems. Online: www.gew.de/aktuelles/detailseite/neuigkeiten/soziale-auslese-ist-bremsklotz-des-deutschen-bildungssystems/ [accessed January 2016].
(2014). 10 Jahre VerA – das Ziel ist verfehlt. Schulen brauchen Unterstützung statt Testeritis. Online: www.gew-nds.de/gs/images/GEW_PDF/Manifest_Gemeinsam_fuer_Bildung.pdf [accessed January 2016].

(2015). Bildung für Flüchtlinge kann nicht warten! Online: www.gew.de/presse/pressemitteilungen/detailseite/neuigkeiten/gew-bildung-fuer-fluechtlinge-kann-nicht-warten/ [accessed January 2016].

Gottschall, K. (2009). Der Staat und seine Diener. Metamorphosen eines wohlfahrtsstaatlichen Beschäftigungsmodells. In H. Obinger and E. Rieger, eds, *Wohlfahrtsstaatlichkeit in entwickelten Demokratien, Herausforderungen, Reformen und Perspektiven, Schriften des Zentrums für Sozialpolitik/20*: 461–91. Frankfurt a.M.: Campus.

Gottschall, K., Kittel, B., Briken, K., Heuer, J.-O., Hils, S., Streb, S., and Tepe, M. (2015). *Public Sector Employment Regimes. Transformations of the State as an Employer.* Basingstoke: Palgrave MacMillan.

Gruber, K.H. (2006). The German 'Pisa-Shock': Some Aspects of the Extraordinary Impact of the OECD's Pisa Study on the German Education System. In H. Ertl, ed., *Cross-National Attraction: Accounts from England and Germany*: 195–208. Didcot: Symposium Books.

Heidenheimer, A.J. (1974). The politics of educational reform: Explaining different outcomes of school comprehensivization attempts in Sweden and West Germany. *Comparative Education Review* 18(3): 388–410.

Helbig, M., and Nikolai, R. (2015). *Die Unvergleichbaren. Der Wandel der Schulsysteme in den deutschen Bundesländern seit 1949.* Bad Heilbrunn: Julius Klinkhardt.

Hepp, G.F. (2011). *Bildungspolitik in Deutschland: Eine Einführung.* Wiesbaden: Verlag für Sozialwissenschaften.

Herrlitz, H.-G., Hopf, W., and Titze, H. (2009). *Deutsche Schulgeschichte von 1800 bis zur Gegenwart: Eine Einführung.* Weinheim/München: Juventa.

Herrmann, U.G. (2009). "Alte" und "neue" Steuerung im Bildungssystem. Anmerkungen zu einem bildungshistorisch problematischen Dualismus. In U. Lange, S. Rahn, W. Seitter, and R. Körzel, eds, *Steuerungsprobleme im Bildungswesen*: 57–77. Wiesbaden: VS Verlag für Sozialwissenschaften.

Hildebrand, R.F. (1993). Teacher union blitz in the former East Germany. *European Journal of Education* 28(1): 99–104.

Hüfner, K., and Naumann, J. (1977). *Konjunkturen der Bildungspolitik in der Bundesrepublik Deutschland, Band 1: Der Aufschwung (1960–1967).* Stuttgart: Klett-Cotta.

Hüfner, K., Naumann, J., Köhler, H., and Pfeffer, G. (1977). *Hochkonjunktur und Flaute: Bildungspolitik in der Bundesrepublik Deutschland 1967–1980.* Stuttgart: Klett-Cotta.

Jeismann, K.-E. (1999). Zur Professionalisierung der Gymnasiallehrer im 19. Jahrhundert. In H.J. Apel, K.-P. Horn, P. Lundgreen, and U. Sandfuchs, eds, *Professionalisierung pädagogischer Berufe im historischen Prozess*: 59–79. Bad Heilbrunn: Klinkhardt.

Keller, B. (1983). *Arbeitsbeziehungen im Öffentlichen Dienst. Tarifpolitik der Gewerkschaften und Interessenpolitik der Beamtenverbände.* Frankfurt a.M./New York: Campus.

Kemnitz, H. (1999). *Lehrerverein und Lehrerberuf im 19. Jahrhundert. Eine Studie zum Verberuflichungsprozeß der Lehrertätigkeit am Beispiel der Berlinischen Schullehrergesellschaft (1813–1892).* Weinheim: Deutscher Studienverlag.

Klieme, E., Avenarius, H., Blum, W., Döbrich, P., Gruber, H., Prenzel, M., Reiss, K., Riquarts, K., Rost, J., Tenorth, H.-E., and Vollmer, H.J. (2003). *Zur Entwicklung Nationaler Bildungsstandards. Expertise*. Berlin: Bundesministerium für Bildung und Forschung.

KMK and BMBF, Kultusministerkonferenz and Bundesministerium für Bildung und Forschung (2008). Ergebnisse von PIRLS/IGLU 2006-I und PISA 2006-I: Gemeinsame Empfehlungen der Kultusministerkonferenz und des Bundesministeriums für Bildung und Forschung. Online: www.kmk.org/fileadmin/veroeffentlichungen_beschluesse/2008/2008_03_06-PISA-PIRLS-IGLU-2006-1.pdf [accessed January 2016].

KMK, Kultusministerkonferenz (2011). *The Education System in the Federal Republic of Germany 2010/2011. A Description of the Responsibilities, Structures and Developments in Education Policy for the Exchange of Information in Europe*. Bonn: KMK.

(2012). *Schüler, Klassen, Lehrer und Absolventen der Schulen 2002 bis 2011*. Berlin: KMK.

Koinzer, T., and Leschinsky, A. (2009). Privatschulen in Deutschland. *Zeitschrift für Pädagogik* 55(5): 669–85.

Köller, O. (2008). Gesamtschule – Erweiterung statt Alternative. In K.S. Cortina, J. Baumert, A. Leschinsky, K.U. Mayer, and L. Trommer, eds, *Das Bildungswesen in der Bundesrepublik Deutschland*: 437–64. Reinbek bei Hamburg: Rowohlt.

Kopitzsch, W. (1983). *Gewerkschaft Erziehung und Wissenschaft (GEW) 1947–1975: Gründzüge ihrer Geschichte*. Heidelberg: Carl Winter.

Kral, G. (1984). *Struktur und Politik des Bayrischen Philologenverbandes 1949–1982*. Köln, Wien: Böhlau.

Kraul, M. (1991). Höhere Mädchenschulen. In C. Berg, ed., *Handbuch der deutschen Bildungsgeschichte Bd. IV, 1870–1918: Von der Reichsgründung bis zum Ende des Ersten Weltkriegs*: 279–303. München: C.H. Beck.

Kraus, J. (2007). Sozialdemokratisierung der CDU-Schulpolitik. *Die Tagespost*, January 18. Online: www.lehrerverband.de/cduschul.htm [accessed January 2016].

(2010). Schulpolitik als offene Flanke der CDU. *Frankfurter Allgemeine Zeitung*, January 21. Online: www.lehrerverband.de/schulpol.htm [accessed January 2016].

Kuhlmann, C.J. (1970). Schulreform und Gesellschaft in der Bundesrepublik Deutschland. Die Differenzierung der Bildungswege als Problem der westdeutschen Schulpolitik. In S.B. Robinsohn, K.-D. Mende, and D.R. Glowka, eds, *Schulreform im gesellschaftlichen Prozess*: 1–206. Stuttgart: Ernst Klett.

Lohmann, J. (2011). Die Zweigliedrigkeit ist Ausgangspunkt für die gemeinsame Schule für alle. Forum Kritische Pädagogik. Online: www.forum-kritische-paedagogik.de/start/wp-content/plugins/download-monitor/download.php?id=53 [accessed January 2014].

Luhmann, N. (2002). *Das Erziehungssystem der Gesellschaft*. Frankfurt am Main: Suhrkamp.

Mahoney, J. (2000). Path dependence in historical sociology. *Theory and Society* 29(4): 507–548.

Martens, K., and Niemann, D. (2013). When do numbers count? The differential impact of the PISA rating and ranking on education policy in Germany and the US. *German Politics* 22(3): 314–32.

Martens, K., Knodel, P., and Windzio, M., eds (2014). *Internationalization of Education Policy*. Basingstoke: Palgrave Macmillan.
Moe, T.M. (2015). Vested interests and political institutions. *Political Science Quarterly* 130(2): 277–318.
Morell, R. (1973). Die Anfänge der westdeutschen Lehrerbewegung nach 1945. *Das Argument: Zeitschrift für Philosophie und Sozialwissenschaften* 15(80), 208–34.
Niemann, D. (2010). Turn of the Tide – New Horizons in German Education Policymaking through IO Influence. In K. Martens, A.-K. Nagel, M. Windzio, and A. Weymann, eds, *Transformation of Education Policy*: 77–104. Houndmills: Palgrave Macmillan.
Nikolai, R., and Helbig, M. (2013). Schulautonomie als Allheilmittel? Über den Zusammenhang von Schulautonomie und schulischen Kompetenzen der Schüler. *Zeitschrift für Erziehungswissenschaft* 16(2): 381–403.
Nikolai, R., and Rothe, K. (2013). Konvergenz in der Schulpolitik? Programmatik von CDU und SPD im Vergleich. *Zeitschrift für Politikwissenschaft* 23(4): 545–73.
Nikolai, R., and West, A. (2013). School Type and Educational Inequalities. In R. Brooks, M. McCormack, and K. Bhopal, eds, *Contemporary Debates in the Sociology of Education*: 57–75. Houndmills, Basingstoke/New York: Palgrave Macmillan.
OECD. (2001). *Knowledge and Skills for Life: First Results from PISA 2000*. Paris: OECD.
(2004). *What Makes School Systems Perform? Seeing School Systems Through the Prism of PISA*. Paris: OECD.
(2013). *Education at a Glance*. Paris: OECD.
Pierson, P. (2000). Increasing returns, path dependence, and the study of politics. *American Political Science Review* 94(2): 251–67.
Ratzke, E. (1981). *Die Stellung des Lehrerverbandes Niedersachsen (Gewerkschaft Erziehung und Wissenschaft) in der niedersächsischen Schulpolitik 1946–1954*. Frankfurt a.M./Bern: Peter Lang.
Ratzki, A. (2009). Verlockende Zweigliedrigkeit. Kritische Nachfragen und Anmerkungen zum Hamburger Schulkonzept. *Pädagogik* 61(9): 46–9.
Reuter, L.R. (1980). Bildungspolitik im Parteienvergleich. Die bildungspolitischen Konzepte von CDU/CSU, SPD und FDP. *Aus Politik und Zeitgeschichte* B35: 3–40.
Ricken, N. (2007). Über die Verachtung der Pädagogik. In N. Ricken, ed., *Über die Verachtung der Pädagogik* : 15–40. Wiesbaden: Verlag für Sozialwissenschaften.
Ried, G., ed. (1955). *Dokumente zur Schulpolitik. Stellungnahmen des Deutschen Philologenverbands und anderer Verbände und Einrichtungen 1949–1953*. Frankfurt/Berlin/Bonn: Moritz Diesterweg.
Riedel, A., Schneider, K., Schuchart, C., and Weishaupt, H. (2010). School choice in German primary schools: How binding are school districts? *Journal for Educational Research Online* 2(1): 94–120.
Ringer, F.K. (1969). *The Decline of the German Mandarins: The German Academic Community, 1890–1933*. Cambridge, MA: Harvard University Press.
Rösner, E. (2007). *Hauptschule am Ende: Ein Nachruf*. Münster: Waxmann.
Schneider, S.L., and Thieben, N. (2011). A healthy sorting machine? Social inequality in the transition to upper secondary education in Germany. *Oxford Review of Education* 37(2): 139–66.

Schröder, H. (1999). *Zwischen Schulreform und Bildungsexpansion. Niedersächsische Schulgeschichte von 1945 bis 1990 am Beispiel des Philologenverbandes Niedersachsen*. Hamburg: Krämer.
StBa, Statistisches Bundesamt (2013). *Finanzen und Steuern. Personal des öffentlichen Dienstes 2012*. Wiesbaden: Statistisches Bundesamt.
Tenorth, H.-E. (2008). Das Gymnasium – Leitinstitution des deutschen Bildungswesens. *Engagement* 3: 252–63.
Tillmann, K.-J., Dedering, K., Kneuper, D., Kuhlmann, C., and Nessel, I. (2008). *PISA als bildungspolitisches Ereignis. Fallstudien in vier Bundesländern*. Wiesbaden: Verlag für Sozialwissenschaften.
Töller, A.E., Pannowitsch, S., Kuscheck, C., and Mennrich, C. (2011). Direkte Demokratie und Schulpolitik. Lehren aus einer politikfeldanalytischen Betrachtung des Scheiterns der Hamburger Schulreform. *Zeitschrift für Parlamentsfragen* 42(3): 503–23.
Tondorf, K. (2008). Neue Entgeltordnung und Leistungsentgelt. In R. Bispinck, ed., *Verteilungskämpfe und Modernisierung. Aktuelle Entwicklungen in der Tarifpolitik*: 123–38. Hamburg: VSA.
Trautwein, U., and Neumann, M. (2008). Das Gymnasium. In K.S. Cortina, J. Baumert, A. Leschinsky, K.U. Mayer, and L. Trommer, eds, *Das Bildungswesen in der Bundesrepublik Deutschland: Strukturen und Entwicklungen im Überblick*: 467–501. Reinbek bei Hamburg: Rowohlt.
TSP, *Der Tagesspiegel*. (2013a). Die Lehrer streiken, die Eltern streiten, *Der Tagesspiegel*, 12 November.
   (2013b). Eltern wollen sich nicht instrumentalisieren lassen. *Der Tagesspiegel*, November 9. Online: www.tagesspiegel.de/berlin/schulstreiks-eltern-wollen-sich-nicht-instrumentalisieren-lassen/9051424.html [accessed January 2016].
Weßels, B. (2000). Die Entwicklung des deutschen Korporatismus. *Aus Politik und Zeitgeschichte* B26–B27: 16–21.
Wiborg, S. (2009). *Education and Social Integration: Comprehensive Schooling in Europe*. New York: Palgrave Macmillan.
   (2010). Why is there no comprehensive education in Germany? A historical explanation. *History of Education* 39(4): 539–56.
Wolf, F. (2008). Die Schulpolitik – Kernbestand der Kulturhoheit. In F. Wolf, and A. Hildebrandt, eds, *Politik der Bundesländer. Staatstätigkeit und Institutionenpolitik im Vergleich*: 21–41. Wiesbaden: Verlag für Sozialwissenschaften.

6

Teachers Unions in the Nordic Countries
Solidarity and the Politics of Self-Interest

Susanne Wiborg

Introduction

Teacher unions in the Scandinavian countries (Denmark, Norway and Sweden) were once exceptionally powerful, a situation facilitated by the corporatist political system and the social democrats – the largest political party. However, corporatist governance and social democracy have weakened over the last three decades, which has reduced teacher unions' influence on *national* policy formulation and diminished their bargaining power. Nevertheless, teacher unions have proved resilient as they have found new allies and avenues, especially at *local* level, to exercise their power. The diminution of teacher union power across the Scandinavian states has varied considerably – the Swedish teacher unions have experienced greater reduction of power than their counterparts in Norway and Denmark. In striking contrast to Scandinavia, the single teacher union in Finland has remained immensely influential and therefore is a bit of an outlier.

Research on teacher unions in the Nordic countries is sparse, particularly in Finland, and tends to be conducted by researchers commissioned by teacher unions.[1] There are no studies on how the teacher unions as *political actors* have exercised power through a corporatist tradition that makes the unions part of the political system and the civil administration. The close involvement of organised interests in public policy-making – which makes such interests an integral part of the political structure of the Nordic countries – is evidenced in numerous studies that place Scandinavia, but not Finland, at the upper end of scales measuring the degree of interest integration (Lijphart and Crepaz 1991; Rommetvedt 2003: 134). The corporate system affords teacher unions

---

[1] A special thank you is due to Semi Ritvi, OAJ, Nina Parssinen, Association of Finnish Independent Education Employers, and Reijo Laukkanen, NBE, who have provided information about the Finnish teacher union.

a number of opportunities to exercise influence over policy initiatives, legislative decision-making and policy implementation. In order to understand the extent to which teacher unions are enabled to influence policy, it is crucial to investigate this system of corporatism and how it has changed in recent years. Corporatism can be understood as an 'institutional arrangement whereby important political-economic decisions are reached via negotiations between or in consultation with peak-level representation of employees and employers (or other interest groups and the state)' (Kenworthy 2003: 11).

The first part of the chapter will analyse how and why corporatism and social democracy were propitious for the rise of teacher union power, and in which ways the unions' interests played out in education politics and collective bargaining from the interwar period until the 1980s. The second part of the chapter discusses the subsequent weakening of teacher unions that came about mainly as a result of a decline in the governmental power of the social democratic parties, these parties' move toward the Right, and the dismantling of corporate structures. We demonstrate how the links between the teacher union, the government and the civil administration in Finland diverges from the Scandinavian trajectory. An analysis of this situation receives special attention in the latter part of the chapter.

The Nordic Teacher Unions: Early Beginnings

Scandinavia

Teacher unions in Scandinavia were established in the last quarter of the nineteenth century, and in Finland a little later, with the explicit aim of advancing their professional positions through higher salaries and improved working conditions while concomitantly seeking to influence school policy. The union landscape was highly fragmented. Teacher unions represented a variety of teachers working in different types of school, and were divided into those representing pre-school teachers, women teachers, elementary school teachers, subject teachers, free-school and private school teachers, religious teachers, university-educated teachers, etc.

The teacher unions in Scandinavia became increasingly unified as a coherent system of public education was established during the period of 1869–1905. Private schools and various other alternative school types were either gradually phased out or integrated into the public system (Wiborg 2009). Consequently, teacher unions were either closed down or merged with each other, resulting in fewer, but larger, unions.

The most significant union became the union for elementary school teachers. It recruited primarily from rural areas or from the ranks of the artisans and clerks in towns as well as fishing communities; the latter situation was particularly the case for Norway. Elementary school teachers have historically played an important and highly visible part in the public life of small towns and rural communities, and have often been at the forefront of political and social reform movements. They often became members of parliament or local councillors, or were active in interest groups and trade unionism (Kvavik 1976). In Scandinavia the industrialisation process began in the 1850s, producing a significant labour movement in which the teacher unions became increasingly involved; later this process also involved the social democratic parties after they were established in the 1870s[2] (Esping-Andersen 1985). The other large, but less significant, teacher union was the academic teacher union, which represented university-educated secondary school teachers from the cities and urban areas. They formed an association based on their subject areas, for instance as linguists, classicists, historians, etc. The academic secondary teachers, fewer in number and concentrated in larger towns, have been less politically noticeable than the elementary school teachers, and were associated primarily with the conservative parties – parties which rarely obtained power.

Finland

In stark contrast, Finnish teacher union mobilisation not only began later, it produced a more influential teacher union for secondary school teachers (established in 1917) than it did for elementary school teachers (established in 1893). Additionally, neither of these unions became associated with the labour movement. The industrialisation process began later in Finland, and was more limited than in the rest of Scandinavia, a fact that resulted in a numerically insignificant and politically weak labour movement (Kirby 2006).

Instead, the teachers were involved in a 'nationalist project' – the *Fennomen* movement – which aimed at separating Finland from its Swedish past. Swedish rule had ended in the Finnish war in 1809, but the Swedish elite continued to dominate throughout the century. The movement, which later turned political – albeit without clearly defined parties – was rooted in the class of wealthy farmers and the clergy, who fought for political power against the ruling Swedish-speaking upper class; it was also a channel for Finnish-speaking people to reach the upper levels of the civil service, which recruited from the Swedish-speaking population. The aim of the pro-Swedish education policy was to give Finnish-speaking people a lower level of education while reserving upper-level education – the secondary schools and universities – for the Swedish-speaking population. Since Swedish was the official language, Finnish had, as a result, been excluded or neglected from the educational institutions. The central goal of the *Fennoman* movement was therefore to establish Finnish-speaking secondary schools which would lead to the same outcome for universities, and, ultimately, the civil service (Kirby 2006: 96; Elovaino 1983).

So, in striking contrast to the rest of Scandinavia – where the land-owning peasantry (from which the school teachers were mainly recruited) held a negative attitude towards secondary schools and supported elementary school

---

[2] Rural teachers tended to be associated with the liberal parties, which were led by land-owning farmers.

reforms – the Finnish population, bolstered by the clergy, promoted secondary education at the expense of primary schools as part of a wider struggle for linguistic, cultural and political power. In consequence, elementary education was slow to develop and was only made compulsory in 1921. Secondary school teachers therefore gained dominance via their union due to its historical role in expanding the secondary schools. Between the years 1880 and 1910 the number of students in secondary education, particularly in Finnish-language secondary schools, grew rapidly.[3] The proportion of children in secondary schools in Finland was twice as high as in was in Sweden (Elovaino 1983: 8; Kirby 2006: 96). This trend could be seen all the way up the 1960s. For example, in 1960, 24 per cent of 10–19 year olds in Finland attended secondary schools, compared to 15 per cent in Sweden, and only 12 per cent Norway (Elovainio 1983: 12).

Separating Finland from its Swedish past was a long and complex process, and one in which Finnish-speaking secondary schools became one of the most important aspects. The nationalist stance of teachers was fortified by the Finnish Civil War, which broke out in 1918 during the transition from Grand Duchy of the Russian Empire to independent state. The teachers, mainly residing in rural areas, generally took the side of the conservative 'Whites', who were dominated by peasants, middle- and upper-class factions who successfully fought against the 'Reds', and the labour movement, led by the social democrats with support from the Russian Soviet Republic (Simola 2005). This event galvanised the nationalist and rightist stance among teachers, and, as we shall see later, this political leaning has proved to be enduring (Kettunen 2001: 225; Kirby 2006).

The Political Integration of Teacher Unions: The Interwar Period

Scandinavia

The corporate system – the integration of organised interests into political and administrative decision-making – was developed in the first decades of the twentieth century. The economic crisis of the 1930s, heavy public regulation of the private sector, and the development of the welfare system following two World Wars, aided the process in a large number of policy areas. The corporate system – which can be seen as a by-product of the welfare system – featured substantial state intervention, and multiple political parties and interest organisations. Interest organisations became increasingly institutionalised through their participation in boards, councils, committees, and hearings. This went hand-in-hand with the practice of collective negotiations and agreements that cut across across political coalitions of workers including social democrats, farmers and liberals. Despite the impeding factor of Scandinavia being

---

[3] Moreover, Finnish was adopted as the language of instruction in the new elementary school system designed by Cygnaeus in the 1850s.

a predominantly rural society well into the 1950s, the exceptional power of the social democrats was made possible by their moderate political stance and their readiness to forge alliances with the dominant liberal parties who were rooted in the land-owning agricultural class. Cross-party collaboration over parliamentarianism, votes for women and various social policies brought them out of 'isolation' and gave them a firm foothold in politics (Esping-Andersen 1985).

Class compromise and interest corporatism strongly impacted upon education policy and inspired a concerted attempt to create a comprehensive education system. A moderate form of comprehensive education was introduced at the turn of the twentieth century, with the governing liberal parties as the main driver. Liberal governments in Scandinavia set on creating 'class circulation' broke down the old class-biased, parallel system of education by creating a new school – the middle school – which would bridge the gap between elementary and upper secondary school. In order to create this three-step school system, the nine-year secondary school was cut down to three years. National differences aside, the three-step system consisted, basically, of the primary school, the middle school, and the academic-oriented upper secondary school (for those aged 15–18). This system – which would allow children to progress all the way through the system according to their academic ability and aptitude, regardless of their social class – was introduced in Norway in 1869, in Denmark in 1903, and Sweden in 1905. The academic union fought hard but unsuccessfully to maintain 'their' nine-year secondary school system – the failure being caused mainly by its association with the politically weak conservative parties and a corporatist system that was still in its infancy (Wiborg 2009).

During the interwar period the social democrats held power for the first time and sought to integrate the school system even more strongly along comprehensive lines. The situation the parties were trying to deal with was this: those children who did not pass the entry exam to the middle school at the age of 11 (Latin was required) would normally complete their education in two extra classes in the elementary school, then subsequently enrol in a vocational programme or, more typically, enter the labour market. By creaming off the best-performing students to the middle school system, the two extra top classes in the primary school – so the social democrats claimed – had become a 'dumping ground' for children, usually those from working-class families.

The social democrats saw this as an obstacle to social equality throughout the school system; and despite the growing popularity of the middle school, they abolished this system in favour of a seven-year comprehensive school, which was followed by two additional classes: Year 8 and Year 9. The seven-year comprehensive system was introduced in Norway in 1920 and in Sweden in 1927, at a time *prior* to teacher unions having much of a foothold in politics. In Denmark the system was introduced much later, in 1958. This 'delay' was partly caused by a deep split in the Social Democratic Party concerning comprehensive education – in start contrast to their political counterparts in Sweden and Norway. Additionally, the teacher unions there – who by this time were starting to benefit from the corporatist structures that developed immediately after the Second World War – succeeded in *delaying* the development of the system. They argued that it was not the school system itself that needed improvement, but rather individual schools within that system. Ultimately, they did not manage to block the comprehensive school system, but by exploiting corporatist structures in the way that they did they were able to delay its introduction for many years (Bregnsbo 1971; Wiborg 2009: 184–90).

Finland
But in Finland the organised interests of labour, industry and farming were poorly developed as a result of the Civil War of 1917, and these interests remained relatively weak throughout the interwar (1918–39) period. International statistics analysing the extent of unionisation in individual countries, often list Finland near the bottom (Kettunen 2001: 230). It was only after the Second World War that public policy – particularly with regard to wage agreements – started to be handled in a corporatist fashion. Finland, in comparison to Scandinavia, was a late developer – industrialisation occurred late, and its social structure remained predominantly agrarian and rural. It is true that there was a coalition government between social democrats and the Agrarian Party – beginning in 1937 – and that the position of the social democrats within the Finnish political system of the late 1930s began to resemble the situation in Scandinavia, even in terms of its electoral support. However, this situation did not result in early interest corporatism or the development of a coherent school system and Finland remained highly divided. The secondary school system continued to expand throughout the interwar period, but remained private and therefore separate from the public elementary schools. The teacher unions were largely operating outside the political system, and anyway were focused mainly on providing a 'nationalist' education in rural areas.

Social Democracy, Corporatism, and the Political Integration of Teacher Unions in the Postwar Period

Scandinavia
During the first couple of decades of the postwar period, the Scandinavian teacher unions underwent extensive reorganisation and expansion, and became even more strongly involved in policy-making in education.[4] This was

[4] The teacher unions in Scandinavia embarked on intensive union organisation, building internal structures and developing external channels for participating in national politics and collective bargaining. The teacher unions expanded their leadership, centralised their administration, established an extensive network of local union branches, and organised workplace representation throughout regional counties and municipalities. A central committee was established in each of these unions to ensure a tight connection with union representatives in the counties and municipalities. The teacher unions grew considerably in size through mergers with other

facilitated by social democratic governments, who by developing the welfare state had expanded corporatist governance. The power of the social democrats increased as they abandoned the rural liberals and instead joined forces with the urban middle classes, primarily those employed in the quickly expanding public sector. By renouncing narrow working-class agendas in favour of universal welfare policies, the social democrats managed to become the leading middle-class party for most of the postwar period (Arter 2007; Esping-Andersen 1985). They reached the peak of their power during the 1960s and 1970s – a period also known as the one of the 'social democratic order.'

The teacher unions had close ties to the social democrats, a 'symbiosis' that was probably stronger in Sweden and Norway than it was in Denmark because in the former the social democrats had achieved governmental power much earlier in their history, and without the need for parliamentary alliances. In Denmark, the social democrats were the weakest party and, although they led minority governments, they often had to share their power with the centre and centre-left parties. The centre party, the Liberal Left, has been particularly powerful in Danish education policy – so the union has formed strong ties with this party (Brøcher 1974).

The Scandinavian social democrats actively involved interest groups in public politics as a way of gaining control over them. It was believed at the time that if organised interests were to be given an active role in societal development, their narrow self-interests would be minimsed. Numerous institutional bodies were established for negotiating between politicians, civil servants and interest organisations. Within education, governments established boards, commissions and councils, etc. – an activity that peaked around 1980 – to effect solutions to various problems, and as a way of enabling unions, through advisory or administrative roles and hearing processes, to become a part of the political system. There was a particularly close interaction with government departments responsible for the provision of welfare and other public services. Legislation prepared using this process was therefore endorsed by corporate interests, and had a comparatively easy journey through Parliament.[5]

---

smaller teacher unions (except for the academic teacher unions) and through recruitment of new members.
[5] Corporatist governance was further extended to the civil service in Scandinavia; in education, this included the education ministries. In his major study on interest organisations in Sweden, Bo Rothstein stated that the *Skolöverstyrelsen* (Board of Education) was an example of such a corporative forum (Rothstein 1992). Until 1981 its board represented a wide array of educational interests including the teacher unions, parents, employers, pupils, MPs and officials. After 1981 the board became political, and educational interests were represented only through an advisory committee. The *Skolöverstyrelsen* assumed formal responsibility for the implementation of government decisions, but because it was an independent body with decision-making power of its own, it initiated reforms, or what have been called 'rolling' reforms, in which the teacher union played an essential role (Rommetvedt 2003: 138; Rothstein 1992: 59–65; Persson 2008: 113, 337).

Collective Bargaining

The corporatist system was also extended to wage bargaining in the public sector through the triangular relationship between government, trade unions and employer associations (Åmark 1989; Blom-Hansen 2000: 165; Due and Madsen 1987: 373–81). The basis of the Scandinavian bargaining model was, and still is, that the framework for negotiations is principally determined by agreements between federations on the labour market, as opposed to through legislation. Based on the long tradition of extensive participation of the organisations of employers and employees, the unions, in the interest of minimising legislation, have been actively seeking to determine the setting of salaries and employment terms through collective agreements.[6] Bargaining is not conducted by individual unions, but by union 'cartels', and the bargaining structure is based on extensive labour law or basic agreements. Unions for public sector workers, including teachers, are thus organised in separate confederations (Elvander 2002; Stokke 2002).

In all four countries, these public sector bargaining cartels at the national level have been, and still are, very strong – although to a lesser degree at the local level – in negotiating salaries, and, crucially, individual unions within these 'cartels' are restrained from pursuing their own salary campaigns. Moreover, the moderation institutions[7], which are established in all of the Nordic countries curb the unions from taking strike action; hence strikes have been relatively rare. Union 'cartelism' and the mediation institutions have removed powers from the individual unions to act independently and aggressively in pursuing their own narrow self-interests. Although collective bargaining provides the teacher unions, as elsewhere, with a platform to seek influence during negotiations, this is somewhat restricted in the Nordic countries by these special institutional features within the collective bargaining process.

---

[6] The coverage rates for collective bargaining in the public sector in Scandinavia have remained high for decades. In 2008, Scandinavia was ranking among the highest of the OECD countries: Sweden 91 per cent, Denmark 83 per cent, and Norway 73 per cent (USA 14 per cent). The collective bargaining coverage for teachers' employment since the 1960s has been extremely high. In 2008 it was at 100 per cent in all of Scandinavia, and it is even high for the private school sector, at, for instance, 90 per cent in Sweden (Galgóczi and Glassner 2008).

[7] Although these mediation institutions vary across the Nordic countries, mediation is based on two basic principles: the legal requirement of the parties to notify the mediation institution about industrial action, and to take part in mediation when called upon. The mediation institutions are conferred with power to force the parties to mediate, and it is considered unlawful if they refuse to do so. Unique to the Nordic countries is the rule on notice and postponement (to reserve at least two weeks of industrial peace to allow mediation to take place), the aim of which is to facilitate the mediation process by allowing a 'cooling' period for parties stuck in negotiations. Compulsory mediation is a recurring element in preventing labour conflicts that are threatening essential public services, curbing the activities of militant unions and suppressing competing unionism.

Education Politics

Scandinavia: Radical Comprehensive Education

The teacher unions in Scandinavia have been more powerful in education politics than in collective bargaining, especially between the 1950s and the early 1990s. Through the corporate system and their close ties to the social democrats, the teacher unions have been very influential in shaping the further development of the comprehensive school system. Being originally opposed to comprehensive education, the general teacher union changed its tune and tactics as the change looked more and more inevitable. Instead it set out to capitalise from the change. In fact, the union pushed for an expanded comprehensive education since this would increase the scope for employing more primary teachers in the upper phases (grades 6–9/10), something that had already started to happen during the interwar period.

During the period of the 1950s until the late 1980s and early 1990s, social democratic governments in Scandinavia initiated major reforms to expand and integrate the comprehensive school system. The seven-year comprehensive schools had been maintained since the interwar period (Denmark from 1958) and were followed by two extra years, grades 8 and 9, and then the three-year upper secondary schools. The plan was to integrate the two years, grades 8 and 9, into a nine-year comprehensive school with mixed ability classes throughout. From the late 1950s, large, long-serving education commissions were established in Scandinavia, which comprised a wide spectrum of education interests, the general teacher unions being most dominant. The negotiations in these commissions were critical to the outcome, since once the agreements were put forward to the government, they were ratified usually with only a few amendments following a hearing process. The nine-year comprehensive schools were introduced in Norway in 1962, in Sweden in 1969, and in Denmark in 1975 (Wiborg 2009).

The smaller academic teacher unions fought bitterly against comprehensive education; they had already experienced their teaching jurisdiction decrease and reasoned that this would continue with the introduction of the nine-year comprehensive schools. In support of their demand, the general teacher unions framed college-educated primary school teachers and secondary school teachers with university degrees as two irreconcilable professions – the former having pedagogical expertise, the latter specialising in academic subjects. The argument about the shape of the school structure was fundamentally related to the question of what kind of teacher should be employed in the lower secondary phase. The teachers educated at the teacher training colleges (for a period of three or four years) were employed in the primary schools, whereas the university-educated teachers would teach in the upper secondary schools. Both teacher categories taught 'side-by-side' in the middle schools. When the middle schools were abolished in the interwar period (Denmark 1958) and the seven-year, now nine-year, comprehensive schools were introduced, the elementary teachers increasingly taught at the lower secondary level, grades 6–9/10.

School teachers with a university education who had traditionally taught at the lower secondary level were now gradually phased out, with the result that the vast majority of teaching positions at all grades in the comprehensive schools came to be held by primary school teachers with teacher training college backgrounds. University-educated teachers saw their jurisdiction restricted to the three-year upper secondary schools (age group 15–18). This development was most profound in Denmark and Norway, whilst in Sweden, university-educated teachers remained for longer at the lower secondary level. The two main teacher categories of the old system, the class teacher (teaching all subjects for grades 1–6), and the subject teachers (some of whom were university-educated, and teaching a few subjects for grades 7–9), were maintained until 1988. Following an act on teacher training, the teacher categories within the comprehensive schools were abolished, and the subject teachers here lost dominance as a result.

The Construction of the Comprehensive School Teacher

Having secured a near-monopoly of non-academic teachers in the comprehensive schools, teacher training reform was now the key objective of the teacher unions to bridge the skills gap created by their teachers' lack of a university education; and to form a strong, unified teaching profession (Christensen 1966; Rovde 2004; Persson 2008: 315, 337). During the preparation of these reforms, which also took place in large government commissions, the teacher unions had an even bigger say than they did in the planning of comprehensive schools. In his detailed analysis of the Danish teacher training reform of 1966, Dan Ch. Christensen (1966: 100) concludes:

The teacher training reform [...] is a product of the teacher unions' exploitation of their peculiar position as advisor within the state apparatus. This position has until now – in spite of attacks from different administrative and political sides – been defended with incredible success.

The unions' agenda was to develop a type of teacher training that would correspond closely to the comprehensive school system so as to consolidate the profession with comprehensive school teachers who would be strongly demarcated from the upper secondary school teachers. National differences aside, the Scandinavian countries introduced a four-year integrated training programme that would prepare primary school teachers to teach at all grades, including the newly acquired lower secondary grades, 7–9/10. The guiding principle underpinning the training was broad subject orientation with a strong focus on pedagogy, didactics and educational psychology. Progressive pedagogy, particularly John Dewey's theory of pragmatism and the German *Reformpädagogik* – focusing on child-centred and experimental learning – strongly underpinned this approach to teacher training reform and, as such, went hand-in-hand with the principle of comprehensive education. This pedagogy, for example, was and still is practically organised in the form of what is called the 'class-teacher system'; that is, one teacher, usually the mother-tongue instructor, who teaches the same class in one or two core subjects at grades 9–10.

This holistic approach to education was planned to equip teachers to teach – as the motto went – at 'all grades and in all subjects' in the nine-year comprehensive school. Consequently, narrow subject specialisation and age-group expertise were drastically minimised (Christensen 1966; Rovde 2004; Persson 2008: 338). The one teacher/one class arrangement, intended to create coherence in children's social and intellectual development, was also used to legitimise primary school teachers working across all nine grades. The teaching profession became more uniform through a socialisation process across the whole teacher training programme; and by drawing upon a limited and highly selective range of educational theories, the teacher unions were successful in helping construct a new teaching professionalism. The need to preserve this structure has been used ever since as an argument for erecting barriers to prevent university-educated teachers from entering the comprehensive schools.

More Money, Less Work
As mentioned earlier, the teacher unions in Scandinavia were not as successful in collective bargaining as they were in politics, but during this period they were effective in exploiting the 'social equality' trend in Scandinavian societies to justify demands for the same salary to be paid to all comprehensive school teachers. Teachers were divided into categories of primary, lower secondary and secondary, the higher levels receiving higher salaries. Teachers were placed on a centralised salary scale based on qualifications, experience, and the type of school in which they were employed. As time passed they would gradually move up within this system, receiving a salary corresponding to their seniority. While the teacher unions generally endorsed this system because it ensured uniform treatment of all teachers, they nevertheless campaigned for an equalisation of salaries across the different teacher categories: 'equal pay for same qualification and same work'. The teacher unions in the previously mentioned union 'cartels' negotiated the abolition of the different teacher categories in favour of just one single category that would pay the same. In Sweden, this equalisation of salaries went even further by giving the primary school teachers the same ending salary as the university-educated upper secondary school teachers. The teacher unions also demanded more time to implement any new requirements that new education legislation might stipulate. In particular they negotiated, with some success, for the allocation of increased time for non-teaching activities such as pastoral care, morning assembly, parents' consultations, etc. – at the expense of classroom teaching.

In summary, during this period the unions were highly successful in getting what they strived for: a nine-year comprehensive school in which the lower secondary level was integrated into the primary schools rather than into the secondary schools; allowing primary school teachers to secure promotion into the secondary schools; an overhaul of teacher training to match more closely the comprehensive schooling system; and the unification of the teacher corps. This was helped by constructing 'comprehensive school professionalism' based upon a progressive pedagogy rather than on academic subjects, something that was used to strongly demarcate the comprehensives from the upper secondary schools. Finally, unification of the teaching profession was consolidated by the equalisation of pay and improved working conditions; i.e., less time actually teaching pupils. By ensuring that primary school teachers held the monopoly to teach in the nine-year comprehensive schools, and by pushing out university-educated teachers, teacher unions demonstrated perhaps the most astonishing example of power in Scandinavian educational history.

Finland – A Deviation

Weak Social Democracy and the Late Development of Corporatism

A rather different trajectory unfolded in Finland because the political situation varied from that in Scandinavia in several important ways. Most crucially for this study, social democracy was weaker than in Scandinavia and corporatism developed late – two factors that, as we have seen, impacted strongly upon the political integration of teacher unions. Political scientists point to Finland's slower economic development, agrarian social structures and the relative weakness of social democracy to explain why the rural class of independent small-scale farmers persisted until a very late stage (1950s). As a result, the Agrarian Party, (renamed the Centre Party, AKA, in 1965) – a typically Nordic phenomenon – continued to play a crucial role in the political system for much longer in Finland than in Scandinavia. But the electoral strength of the party does not, in itself, explain its durability.[8] Its status as the 'presidential' party and its 'special relationship' with the Kremlin leadership also played their part (Kirby 2006: 245–5). The prolongation of the Agrarian Party was also facilitated by a very divided left that comprised the radical leftist, communist-dominated, SKDL; and the social democrats. From the early 1950s to the early 1960s the social democrats were notably riven by internal divisions, which kept the party from power for a decade, until 1966 (Kettunen 2001; Arter 2009).

As a result of all the above, corporatism was 'underdeveloped', at least in comparison to Scandinavia. It was not until the 1970s and 1980s that a corporate mode of governance prevailed, with the exception of a temporary decline in the early 1990s. Finnish trade unions and public sector unions experienced sharp growth, giving the country one of the highest rates of union membership in Europe. In 1973, the National Union of Elementary School Teachers and the National Union for Secondary School Teachers were unified into one

---

[8] At best, it commanded just over a quarter of the parliamentary seats.

general teacher union (OAJ), providing a striking contrast to Scandinavia, where the two unions remained separate. This united Finnish teaching union, backed by a total of 97 per cent of teachers, was in a position to vastly increase its collective clout in its dealings with the state.

From the mid-1960s the social democrats started to gain influence in Finnish politics, which was in part caused by the 'Moscow link'. The Soviet Union intervened in Finnish domestic affairs, and the long-serving president Kekkonen (1956–81) negotiated with Moscow to nominate governments that were acceptable to Soviet leaders. Consequently, coalitions tended to the centre-left and included representatives of the reformist wing of the Communist SKDL for 12 of the 16 years between 1966 and 1982. The centre-left parties worked together to promote an extensive social welfare system along Swedish lines, but the party can hardly be said to have generated the kind of socialist thinking or activity that was holding sway in neighbouring Sweden.

During these social democratic decades, the teacher union remained on the right. Radical labour union politics, not to mention the members and ideas of the far left, continued to be virtually non-existent among Finnish teachers. Teachers on the left joined the small Democratic School Workers Association, Demko, which existed only from 1973 to 1989 (Räisänen 2014). Finnish teachers continued to legitimise their elitist status by basing their role around the notion of defending the Finnish cultural and linguistic legacy. This ideology was fortified by the emergence of a new external threat to Finland: the Soviet Union. According to Kirby (2006: 271–2)

The inward-looking and obsessive concern with Finland and Finnishness was shaken, but in all its essentials, remained untouched by the radicalism of the sixties and seventies [...] it was actually reinforced by the frequently reiterated call [particularly by President Kekkonen] to preserve good relations with the Soviet Union.

The unions, permeated with a 'nationalist education spirit', were set on a collision course with government when they introduced a comprehensive school system modelled on the Swedish system (Räisänen 2014; Simola 1998, 2005; Simola et al. 1997). In 1968, the social democrat-led government – imbued with Eastern authoritarianism – rapidly and systematically abolished the selective system, and, to some observers, did so in a totalitarian manner. The school system that was abolished consisted of four years of common schooling, after which children were selected into two tracks (two extra years in the elementary school or the grammar/secondary school) that differed both in their educational content and in their eligibility for and access to further and higher education (Pekkarinen et al. 2006: 3). The teacher unions fought against comprehensive education on the grounds that it would break up their 'own' institutions and that it challenged the private ownership of secondary schools. The majority of secondary schools were privately owned (but nearly all state-funded), a situation that afforded secondary teachers substantial autonomy and a high-ranking status (Ahonen 2002: 176).

The Grand Compromise

To get the non-cooperative union for primary school teachers to 'support' comprehensive school reform, the government gave concessions in the form of university-based teacher training and salaries that would follow the university payscale (Simola 2005: 458). Since the 1950s, the union had demanded – with increasing force – that the training of elementary school teachers be at the same level as that of secondary school teachers; that is, at university level. This demand should probably be interpreted in recognition of the fact that, even before the Second World War, more Finnish elementary school teachers had received upper secondary school certificates than in any other European country, and thus had themselves received more education (Simola 2005: 460).

A grand teacher training reform was implemented during 1973–79, and this impacted the teacher training for elementary school teachers (grades 1–6) most radically. Their training was moved from teachers' colleges and small-town 'seminaries' to the newly established university faculties of education created by the new reform. With an additional reform in 1979, the training of elementary teachers was raised to a master's degree level (bachelor degrees were abolished, but reintroduced in the 1990s) (Kansanen 2003).

The reform had little impact on the training of secondary school teachers, an area of education that remained separate. In striking contrast to Scandinavia, where teacher training was developed to match comprehensive schools by breaking down the teacher categories, subject specialisation and age-group expertise were maintained and even strengthened in Finland. Secondary school teachers used their influence through the corporate system to continue to demarcate themselves from elementary school teachers. Following the 1979 reform, the distinction between primary school teachers, grades 1–6, and secondary teachers, now called subject teachers, grades 7–12, was maintained and consolidated by a requirement that stipulated teachers in every category must complete a master's degree. The subject teachers were required to major in just one subject. Compare this with, for example, a Danish teaching student, who would at this time have been obliged to study at tertiary college-level *four* different subjects – each at grade 1–9/10 – in order to teach in all subjects and at all levels in a comprehensive school.

The teaching profession was bolstered by a sharp increase in the number of teacher professors who were heavily involved in developing a 'scientific' base for teacher training and teaching methods in schools (Simola *et al.* 2002).[9] In contrast to Scandinavia, where progressive pedagogy and child-oriented

---

[9] Psychology had long dominated the field of education in Finland due to the enduring influence of the centuries'-old educator, Johan Friedrich Herbart (1776–1841). Although Herbartian didactics was outdated elsewhere in Europe in the 1920s, it continued to play a dominant role in Finnish textbooks on didactics until the 1960s. Herbartian didactics had indeed started to wane by then, but its emphasis on psychology continued to strongly define the field of pedagogy and teacher professionalism.

didactics were used to underpin the professionalism of the comprehensive school teacher, educational psychology and intelligence testing were employed for this purpose in Finland (Kansanen 1990; Kivinen and Rinne 1990, 1994; Rinne 1988; Simola 1993, 1998: 327; Simola et al. 1997: 884). According to Simola (1997: 883): 'The psychology-based background of Finnish didactics has strongly bound the whole legitimisation of Finnish teacher training with psycho-metric theory and statistical testing, which have been the core contents in educational methodology.' This tradition, he claims, continued – albeit with minor changes – until the 1990s.

The teacher union for elementary school teachers benefited most from the comprehensive school reform, and consequently little criticism from this quarter was voiced. Jaakko Numminen, director general of the Ministry of Education, attacked teacher reform as an abject failure. In a public statement in 1987, he claimed:

A university training offers no better guarantee of good teaching than the one provided by the old seminaries [...] The benefits which have been obtained are essentially for members of the educational profession, namely, improved salaries and status for teachers in the schools, inclusion on university pay scales for teaching staffs from the old teachers' seminaries, and a fivefold increase in the education profession within two decades.[10]

Decline of Teacher Union Power: 1980–2015

Scandinavia: Lost Battles but a Few Gains

From around the 1980s until the present day, the power of the teacher unions in Denmark, Norway and Sweden has weakened. The great victories of the 1960s and 1970s were not repeated in the following decades, indeed major defeats were suffered. Teacher unions and governments started to collide more often over national education policy as a greater divide emerged between them (Anthonsen and Lindvall 2009; Anthonsen et al. 2010). During the 1960s and 1970s the political situation was conducive to teacher union mobilisation; they did not, according to Rovde (2004), have to do much to advance their cause. But now the teacher unions saw themselves increasingly excluded from the political decision-making process, and instead their opinions were sought as part of government consultation processes only, and even then inconsistently. The reasons behind the prolonged decline of teacher union power at a national level are complex and not yet sufficiently explored, but explanatory factors are likely to be identified within the wider political changes that have taken place over the last 20–30 years.

---

[10] Another criticism came from two professors, Kivinen and Rinne, who claimed that for teacher trainees whose work in primary schools would be essentially of a practical nature, to do a scientific master's thesis would inevitably produce 'pseudo-scientific thesis-imitations [which] contribute little to their development as teachers, [giving] them a grotesque conception of science' (quoted in Simola 1993: 192).

First of all, a reduction of and changes in the practice of corporatist governance meant less power to the teacher unions in national politics. This was part of an overall change in which a number of commissions across a wide range of public policy areas were abolished during the 1980s and onwards. This was more significant in Scandinavia than in Finland, where corporatism during this time had in fact reached its peak. In the case of Denmark, corporatism was in crisis in the 1970s and early 1980s, but it experienced a resurgence in the late 1980s and 1990s before falling back into a continuous decline. In the late 1980s, Sweden's previously strong corporatist system within the area of public policy-making – except in the area of wage bargaining – disintegrated gradually.[11] As part of the process of dismantling corporatist interests, right-wing governments abolished a number of permanent education committees in order to cut union influence – and instead sought consultative expertise elsewhere.[12] Corporatism did not entirely disappear as a result of these actions, but the use of commissions, boards and other institutionalised corporatist structures was significantly less frequent than before (Blom-Hansen 2000; Christiansen and Rommetvedt 1999; Christiansen and Togeby 2006). Interest organisations continue to gain some influence through these, but increasingly they achieve this via lobbying efforts and political pressure – as is also the case for interest organisations in non-corporatist political systems (Anthonsen and Lindvall 2009; Öberg et al. 2011; Rommetvedt 2005).

Second, in contrast to their almost unchallenged power in the 1960s and 1970s, the social democratic parties have lost their position of superiority and given way to increasingly frequent right-of-centre governments. From 1982 to 1989 and again from 2001 to 2011 – a total of 19 years – right-wing governments ruled in Denmark. In Sweden, by the mid-1980s, two centrist parties, the People's Party and the Centre Party, had joined the Conservatives in creating, for the first time in Swedish post-war history, a concerted bulwark against social democratic policy. In Norway in 1981, after many years of social democratic dominance, governments started to alternate between minority Labour governments and Conservative-led centre-right governments (Arter 1999; Wiborg 2013). Although teacher unions were also active in pursuing their interests through these governments, they were met with greater unwillingness.

[11] The crucial change occurred in Sweden in 1991, when the Confederation of Swedish Employers (SAF) left the governing boards of all government agencies. Active labour market policy was the centrepiece of the Swedish model, and interest organisations used to be heavily involved in the preparation of legislation and the implementation of policy in this area. Since the 1980s and 1990s institutionalised negotiations and attempts to reach agreement among labour market organisations have been gradually phased out (Svensson and Öberg, 2002: 295–315),

[12] In Denmark, the Liberal education minister, Bertel Haarder, eliminated a long-standing education committee for experimental learning, and, in Norway, his counterpart, the education minister, Tore Austad, closed down the Council for Experimental Schooling (Forsøksrådet) because it was regarded as a mouthpiece for the Labour Party. Other education committees such as the Council for Schools (Grunnskolrådet), and the Council for Further Education and Teacher Training (Rådet for videregående opplæring og lærarutdanningsrådet) were also shut down (Rommetvedt 2005: 138–9; Telhaug et al. 2004: 33).

Third, and perhaps more importantly, the social democrats, still being the largest party, began in all Scandinavian countries from the early 1990s to move towards the right and thus embrace market-oriented education policies. Although it was usually right-wing governments that introduced reforms such as decentralisation, school choice, voucher schemes, etc., the social democrats endorsed many of these, and, indeed, even initiated some of them (Klitgaard 2007; Wiborg 2013, 2015). The move to the right promoted a near-consensus between the social democrats and centre-right parties with regard to some market-oriented reforms of education, a situation that created a bulwark against teacher union interests. The teacher unions not only lost influence when right-wing governments were in power, they now also did so when social democratic governments were formed.

In Sweden, where market-oriented education policies were pursued earlier and more vigorously than in Norway and Denmark, the power of teacher unions at a *national* level declined more rapidly. Norwegian teacher unions remained influential for longer, certainly throughout the 1980s and 1990s, and, most paradoxically, the same held true in Denmark during the long-serving liberal governments of the 1980s. It was not until the 2000s that a significant lull in teacher union power occurred in Denmark. The political alignment between the teacher unions and the social democrats weakened considerably as a result, prompting the unions to garner new support further to the left, mainly within the socialist parties. Historically, the socialist parties have been small, rarely in government, and therefore have enjoyed little political clout. But having lost power at national level, the unions *gained* power at local level. After major decentralisation reforms in Scandinavia, which we will turn to below, the unions succeeded in creating corporatist-like practices at the municipality level, giving them a new platform from which to influence policy formulation and implementation.

Sweden

The decentralisation process in Sweden brought about perhaps the most fundamental changes to the school system in the post-war period. It completely altered the governance of education and working conditions for teachers, and had devastating effects for the teacher unions. Sweden went from a highly centralised system in which municipalities and schools had very limited influence over teachers and work-related issues, to one of the most decentralised systems in Europe – and all in a relatively short period of time. The education policy research (Lindblad *et al.* 2002; Lundahl 2002, 2006; Lundahl *et al.* 2010), explaining this apparent about-face, points to economic globalisation, budgetary constraints, and the rise of right-wing politics. However, the social democrats 'acting' right, and teacher union activism, is conspicuously absent from these standard explanations. The near-exclusion of the teacher unions from policy-making, explains, according to Dobbins (2014), the speed and extent to which the decentralisation of education was implemented in Sweden.

In the 1980s, the right-wing bloc, consisting of the Conservatives, the Peoples Party and the Centre Party, mustered for the first time in post-war Sweden an effective opposition to the social democrats, and delivered a severe attack on the welfare state. They blamed efficiencies in market mechanisms for the financial crisis of the time, a crisis that was characterised by declining long-term growth in productivity, rising unemployment, and a record-high budget deficit and national debt. To combat these problems they called for deregulation and decentralisation to enhance local responsibility in the public sector and to provide services that were more efficient, cheaper to run, and closer to users. Additionally, the association of municipalities lobbied for greater responsibility in implementing government policies (Bäck 2003).

During the period 1976–82, a Conservative government initiated a decentralisation process in education that, at the time, only involved the method by which state subsidies were transferred from the state to the municipalities. This new system of resource allocation, introduced in 1978, was intended to ensure that the municipality education departments gained greater influence over how to use such resources to meet nationally decided objectives.

When the social democrats assumed power in 1982, it was acknowledged within the party that their devastating electoral defeats of 1976 and 1979 were linked to increasing public dissatisfaction with the heavily centralised and bureaucratic public sector. However, there was also growing dissatisfaction from within the party itself that government actions had been insufficient in reforming the public sector and enhancing local participation. The consequence was that – especially from the late 1980s – the social democrats started to move away from their previous rejection of deregulation and decentralisation. They were not united in this stance, but the views of the fractious pro-market wing of the party – which revolved around the minister of finance, Kjell-Oluf Feldt – came to represent the official party line (Andersen 2006; Wiborg 2013).

Back in government from 1986–91, the social democrats enacted further decentralisation reforms that were intended to make public service more efficient and closer to users. Within education, control and administration of education was transferred from the state to the municipalities. The role of the state was restricted to 'management by objectives', whereby government was responsible for formulating broad aims for education, providing general funding and controlling outcomes through an inspection regime. In 1989 a parliamentary bill was introduced which stipulated that the municipalities should assume responsibility for teachers' employment conditions and salaries.

Within the framework stipulated by government, the municipalities were now furnished with more decision-making power regarding the organisation and provision of education, and the allocation of resources to it. The municipalities were now the employers of teachers, not the counties – or in the case of the upper secondary school teachers, central government. The basic terms of those appointments were still, however, to be governed by national agreements with the teacher union. In addition, the longstanding practice of guaranteeing aprroximately 80 per cent of all teaching appointments under permanent tenure was abolished, although job security has since remained relatively high. Prior to this it was virtually impossible to remove teachers or to transfer them to other posts elsewhere (Lakomaa 2009; Persson 2008: 446; Rothstein 1997: 30).

The teacher unions were, for the first time in their history, entirely circumvented during this reform process. The previous tradition of long-serving commissions on which education interests were well represented was replaced with a system of fast-acting working groups on which it was mainly civil servants and education experts who served (Lindvall and Sebring 2005). Despite a historic cleavage between the general teacher union and the academic teacher union, these joined forces in opposing the new reforms via a campaign of intensive lobbying and public protest. They argued that the reforms would undermine their centralised power in the state bureaucracy and claimed that the municipalities lacked the capacity to govern schools. They also feared their members' employment conditions would worsen since, unlike the centrally regulated employment conditions that had previously ensured the uniform treatment of teachers, local governments would inevitably adopt a new approach. Furthermore, they viewed their status as civil service teachers as being higher than that of a 'mere' municipal employee.

In order to get the unions on board, the social democratic education minister, Göran Persson (1989–91), tied the ongoing salary negotiations with the decentralisation reforms. The teacher unions, realising that their anti-decentralisation campaign had failed, entered into direct negotiations with the education minister and representatives from the Swedish Confederation for Professional Employers, TCO-S. The TCO-S had been won over by Persson and thus supported the idea of placing schools under the control of the municipalities. In return for the unions accepting decentralisation, teachers would receive a salary increase (these had fallen to below the OECD average (OECD 1994)), a fixed final salary and a reduction in teaching hours. The union had long been fighting for further equalisation of salaries and workloads between comprehensive school teachers and upper secondary school teachers. According to Lakomaa (2009: 37), the fact that the salary increase came in conjunction with the decision about decentralisation took the heat out of a confrontation that had involved strike action.

The state 'monopoly' of education was further broken down by the following Conservative-led coalition government under Carl Bildt from 1991 to 1994. As the country's first 'neo-liberal' government, it set out to transform the Swedish public sector to an even greater extent. In addition to welfare cuts and tax reforms, it deregulated, privatised, and introduced a variety of other measures to encourage competition and 'restore' the market.[13] Many of

---

[13] For example, telecommunications and broadcasting monopolies, the national telephone company, postal services, and state alcohol authorities and retail companies have been subject to

these changes were hastened by the prospect of European Union membership, which encouraged such developments. In education, the government allowed for private ownership of profit-making schools, an idea that was supported through a newly established tax-funded voucher scheme. As a result there was a rapid expansion of the free schools (Lidström 1999). About 10 per cent of pupils are enrolled in free schools at lower secondary level and 25 per cent at upper secondary level (Arreman 2011; Vlachos 2011). The voucher scheme ensured that the free schools could compete against state schools for students on an almost equal financial basis. The unions were again bypassed when these reforms were introduced; and the reform had the knock-on effect of them losing less politicised members as they drifted to the free schools where they were paid 2 per cent more than their colleagues in the state schools. Additionally, the free schools were able to employ uncertified teachers outside the pay and conditions arrangements.

When the social democrats took back governmental control in 1994–98, they did not attempt to reverse these developments. Having now moved even further to the centre-right, and with the Centre Party as their primary ally during the reform period, the social democrats supported a voucher scheme that allowed parents and pupils to choose between public and public-financed private schools. They even increased the coverage of the operational cost of the schools from 15 percent, set by the previous right-wing government, to 100 percent in order for the schools to be free of charge. New forms of state control were enacted, including national tests at various grades. School inspections were decentralised to the municipalities, but national evaluations were conducted by the National Agency of Education every third year (Daun and Siminou 2005: 32). This cross-party consensus concerning market-oriented educational provision remains largely intact today, despite the fact that the social democrats have lost three elections in succession – an unprecedented series of defeats (Wiborg 2015).

As part of the decentralisation process an individual pay scheme was introduced in 1995. This new scheme was to provide the local municipalities with the necessary tools for recruiting and rewarding teachers, and enhancing their performance, productivity and the quality of education they could offer. Collective bargaining was no longer to be conducted only at a central level, as described earlier in this chapter, but also at sector level and in the municipalities. The sectoral agreements define the average pay levels and general working time provisions that serve as a framework for procedural rules for negotiations at municipality level. Within the framework of the agreement, the local municipalities and schools have the right to choose one of two procedures for wage-setting. The first option, called the 'dialogue' procedure, is a conversation between the teacher and the line manager, usually the school principal,

---

deregulation, while municipal cleaning services and parts of the public transportation system have been contracted out.

about determining the salary.¹⁴ The other option is through ordinary negotiations, which implies that the local union branch can be actively involved in the negotiating process for its members. This also often implies that the local parties agree on the total share of the municipality budget that should be allocated to teacher salaries, and sometimes how it should be distributed across different schools and individuals. When the 'dialog' procedure is chosen – and it has increased in popularity over the years – the local union branch has less influence since the main responsibility lies with the school manager (Strath 2004).

Part of the rationale behind the new individual pay scheme was that teacher salaries could be linked to clearly defined performance objectives, and would serve as an instrument for retaining effective teachers. It was also believed that the process would encourage higher levels of productivity and efficiency in achieving these objectives. Most crucial of all was the decision that pay should be based on pupil results. The teacher unions, who were unable to block the individual pay scheme reform, set out to influence the implementation of performance-related pay, which they judged highly controversial. They were instrumental in having remuneration levels determined by vaguely defined criteria other than pupil results – such as degrees of effort, and commitment to school development. A whole catalogue of criteria were developed to this end: behaviour towards children, contribution to a positive learning environment, instilling democratic values and tolerance, motivating pupils and boosting their self-esteem, cooperation with other teachers, a desire to pursue professional development, and so on. The unions have, as a result, shifted the focus of salary negotiations away from a link with pupil performance and more towards teachers' own accomplishments – these to be measured by imprecise standards rather than by specific objectives, as the agreement had originally required. The unions have capitalised on an array of incentives and bonuses tied to what is regarded as favourable school development. For example, many schools now pay bonuses to teachers who assume management responsibilities, teach more subjects and classes than required, and teach special needs children or teach in rural or disadvantaged areas (Strath 2004: 17; Lundahl 2006: 68; Mausethagen and Granlund 2012).¹⁵

---

¹⁴ The employer presents the rationale behind the planned pay review before presenting a pay proposal to the individual employee. The employee, thereafter, passes it on to the local trade union of which the employee is a member. If the union does not call for local negotiations, the employer's proposal is accepted.

¹⁵ It was expected that an individualised pay system would lead to an increased differentiation in the wage structure as teachers were remunerated differently according to their performance. But Söderström (2010) has shown that the effect of this reform has in fact been a reduction in the steepness of the 'age-earnings profile', such that younger teachers received wages closer to those of older teachers. More competent teachers are thus rewarded earlier in their careers than was previously the case; 'seniority' is now less of a determining factor in wage levels. Additionally, the demand for teachers has exceeded supply, thus forcing many municipalities to raise entry-level salaries. Consequently, the salary gap between teachers has decreased in the country as a whole.

Norway

In Norway, the teacher union has been influential in national politics for longer than in Sweden, primarily because the Labour Party has been much more reluctant in endorsing a market-oriented agenda. Since the right-wing parties, until recent years, never posed any major threat to Labour, the teacher union could thus maintain its close links to the country's largest party. The Labour Party even pursued welfare expansion in the late 1990s, when the Swedish social democrats had already started to deregulate and outsource public services. 'As for school policy,' Francis Sejersted (2006: 426) writes in his major study on social democracy, "the political left [in Norway], including the Labour Party, is at least as radical and mindful of the traditional Social Democratic goals as it was earlier in the Post War period." The 'iron triangle' between the teacher union, Labour politicians and civil servants in the Department of Education was still operative throughout the 1980s and into the early 1990s, and hence school development continued to proceed largely along Labour policy lines, much supported by the union. The teacher union maintained the channels through which it influenced policy decisions within the representative political system – actual teachers were still well represented in Parliament – as well as within the corporative system (Rovde 2004: 113). While that decade witnessed increasingly difficult circumstances for the teacher union, it did not produce the dramatic consequences that it did in Sweden – at least until 2001, perhaps.

During the 1980s a neo-liberal agenda was also advanced by the rightwing in Norway, but it lacked the Swedish potency. The right and centre-right governments of 1981–83 and 1989–90 hardly advanced their cause due to their short period in office, but also because they did not entirely embrace the agenda. The two largest right-wing parties, the Liberal Party (Venstre) and the Conservative Party (Höjre) focused on quality, efficacy and standards within the public school system rather than creating a 'quasi-market' of education.[16] The latter, interestingly, was only pushed forward by the far-right Populist Party (Fremskridtspartiet).[17] However, that party is small and only entered government for the first time in 2013. Despite the fact that marketisation of education was still in its infancy in Norway, the teacher union attacked it severely anyway, and, accustomed to setting the agenda, the union launched several public campaigns during the 1980s which revolved around expanding the comprehensive school system[18] (Rovde 2004: 235).

---

[16] In fact, the Conservatives were directly against privatisation until recently, and the Liberals supported, as they had done for many years, Labour's comprehensive school policy.

[17] The Populist Party pronounced that it would make a radical break with the Norwegian egalitarian school tradition by introducing market forces into it. This entailed, among other things, school choice and a voucher scheme, ability grouping, and performance-based teacher pay.

[18] They demanded an 'all day school', which involved the creation of stronger links between the pre-school, comprehensive school and after-school activities for pupils, and employing only qualified teachers (Rovde 2004: 235).

Unexpectedly, it was not the right wing which curbed teacher union power, but rather the Labour Party itself. And this was not because the party had moved to the right and incorporated neo-liberal ideas into its education policies, as was the case in Sweden. The OECD education expert, Gudmund Hernes, who became education minister in Gro Harlem Brundtlands' third government (1990–95), was determined to break the power of educational corporatism in order to bring about major reforms aimed at enhancing the standards of the entire education system. In fact, he could be characterised as a 'typical' Scandinavian social democrat in that he wanted to retain central state control over education – that is, the comprehensive school system – and to restrict private education. However, his major study on power distribution in Norwegian society a decade earlier had convinced him that corporatism had deprived the state of too much power. The commissions and hearing procedures had integrated educational interest organisations, particularly the large teacher unions, so closely with government and the civil administration that they 'blocked policy reforms and killed new ideas'. He argued that they were a major threat to democracy, and wanted to 'bring back the state' and 'recapture education policy' (Rovde 2004; Telhaug 1993; Volckmar 2008).

During his entire time in office, Hernes circumvented consultation processes with the teacher unions. Rather than establishing long-serving commissions representing a broad spectrum of educational interests and politicians – as had been the case in the past – he hand-picked a few advisory experts to take part in small and short-lived parliamentary committees. Furthermore, the Ministry of Education received greater leverage in the implementation of reforms by excluding the representational function of the teacher union within various working groups. Other consequences included shorter deadlines for hearings and the acceleration of the reform-passing procedure.

The exclusion of the teacher union resulted in the government passing an array of reforms in a relatively short period of time, these aimed at enhancing the academic standards and efficiency of the education system, from pre-primary education through to higher education. The teacher union was 'shocked and angry' at the changes made to the corporatist system, which had left them completely excluded from it for the first time in its history. The union was vehemently opposed to Reform 97 – which strengthened the core subjects in the national curriculum – because this was essentially an attack on teaching professionalism that the union had helped to construct on the basis of child-oriented pedagogy. The union claimed that the national curriculum was overly controlled and standardised by the state, leaving teachers without sufficient room for professional judgement. It also claimed that teachers' pedagogical skills in educating the 'whole child' would be of little use in an 'intellectualised' school that focused mainly on academic subjects[19] (Helgøy and Homme 2007; Rovde 2004; Telhaug 1993).

---

[19] The teacher union received a good deal of support from education experts in the country's largest universities in Oslo, Bergen and Trondheim. The curriculum was also a 'veiled' threat to

The issue came to a head during the reform of teacher education, as pedagogy was no longer a *leitmotif* of reform. The government, with Hernes' strong imprint, passed an act in 1992 which extended teacher training by one year, to four years, and strengthened the academic component by enhancing specialisation in core subjects and practical teaching skills at the expense of pedagogy and didactics.[20] Once again shut out of the decision-making process, the teacher union, along with large parts of the education research community, was fiercely opposed to this new direction in teacher training. During the hearings the union found allies in the Socialist Party (SV), and sections of the Labour Party, but, still unable to block this reform, it changed strategy and sought concessions in return for acceptance. The union's former demand of extending the fast-track teacher training course for those with non-teaching qualifications was thus granted. The union therefore succeeded in raising barriers to 'outsiders' wanting to enter the teaching profession; it would now take a full year (as opposed to the previous six months) to gain this diploma, and at increased cost to the individual. By making it more difficult for people to become teachers, the union sought to safeguard jobs in schools for those with initial teacher training (Rovde 2004: 241–2).

Throughout the 1990s reform period, the teacher union, in shifting alliances with other trade unions and education interests, retaliated by launching several campaigns in support of the survival of comprehensive schools and pedagogical-oriented teacher training and professionalism – using catch-phrases such as 'equality', 'community' and 'cohesion' – as well as severely criticising the municipalisation process.[21] These largely unsuccessful campaigns and diminished Labour support forced the teacher union further to the left. The teacher union has since received its strongest support from parties left of the Labour Party, most notably the Socialist Party, SV, nicknamed 'the teachers' party' (Rovde 2004: 300).

This move to the left brought the union into stronger opposition to the more frequent centre-right governments of the 2000s. The teacher union suffered an unprecedented loss of power, most notably during the tenure of the right-wing government of 2001–05. Kristin Clement, the education minister, not only sought to increase academic standards and accountability but also create a quasi-market through the mechanisms of competition and school choice. During her ministry a new national curriculum, coined 'Knowledge Promotion', was introduced (Telhaug 2005). This emphasised 'core' skills and

---

their departments' strong interest in theoretical pedagogy and school-related research, which lent legitimacy to the teaching profession.

[20] In 1998, another act on teacher education was passed that strengthened subject specialisation even further, at the expense of pedagogy and didactics.

[21] These were the union for manual workers, LO, The National Association for Schools (Skolernes Landsforbund), the Organisation for Teacher Trainers (Organisajonen til lærarstudentane) and the Association for Parents in the Public School (Foreldrerådet for grunnskolen). The campaigns culminated in a 1997 nationwide petition that resulted in 450,000 signatures.

'basic' knowledge in each subject. This was followed by national tests, the results of which were made publicly available to parents. Swedish-style free schools were also allowed to thrive in the country – with state support – as a way of boosting the private school sector (albeit on a small scale). Even subsequent left-wing governments did not alter many of these reforms, having themselves started to move towards the centre of politics. But there was one notable exception, and in 2005 the Labour-led coalition prohibited the free schools from operating in the country.

Most damaging for the teacher union, however, were the decentralisation reforms passed during Clement's ministry. They were built on the Municipalisation Act of 1992, which gave local government greater authority over public service provision, including education. The Association of Municipalities (Komunernes sentralforbund, KS) had been lobbying to acquire bargaining responsibility, arguing that responsibility for such a large group of municipal employers should be vested in the same body that exercised employers' responsibility. The teachers were transferred from the state sector bargaining area to the municipalities. Pay, working time, teaching schedules and other duties were now also partly handled at a local level, a change that had happened in Sweden around ten years earlier (Rovde 2004: 250).

The teacher union in Norway, as in Sweden, also reacted strongly against these decisions, which it branded 'the worst kind of betrayal and breach of trust'. It had pleaded for national standards with regard to class size, rules for the ability grouping of pupils, the allocation of teaching hours per class, and the teacher-pupil ratio. But it was now left to the municipalities to issue guidelines on such matters. The discontent felt by teachers resulted in a one-day strike, and the union cancelled, for a period of two weeks, all participation in meetings and seminars organised by the Ministry of Education and Research. To settle the dispute, the teachers – along with other public sector employees – managed to win higher salaries both in real terms and at the same increased percentage as employees in the private sector. To fund this increase, revenues from the oil industry were channelled into public salaries. In 1998, and again in 2000–02, the starting salary for teachers was raised considerably, although this was done in an attempt to attract more applications from teachers – which had fallen dramatically. Teachers now received a higher salary increase compared to other public sector employees. Between 2000 and 2004, when the wage agreement was up for renewal, teachers' salaries increased by 23.5 per cent (Rovde 2004).

By the early 2000s, national wage bargaining was supplemented with local negotiations, and by 2002 the majority of municipalities had introduced meritpay for teachers. The government argued that the peculiar tradition within education of 'equal pay for all teachers with the same qualification' had to be replaced by individual pay just as in all other public sectors. As in Sweden, the teacher union was staunchly against this pay policy, but later accepted it. This was probably due to the fact that only a small percentage, 6.65 per cent of the total budget for teacher salaries, was allocated to differential pay.

This allocation was simply not sufficient to create a great wage differentiation between teachers. Furthermore, individual pay was determined by criteria that were acceptable to the union; for instance, working time was assessed in relation to specific tasks, not teachers' performance. However, this gradually changed when the central state salary commission decided, against the teacher unions' recommendations, that the remuneration of school principals and teachers should be based on performance-based criteria relating to teachers' proficiency and motivation in their work with pupils.[22] However, these are still generalised criteria, and the union is determined to keep it that way.

Denmark
The Danish case is remarkable in that even though the country was ruled by long-serving right-wing governments (1982–93; 2001–11), for a total of 19 years, the general teacher union remained powerful. Indeed, almost no reforms aimed at privatisation of the public services were passed during that time.[23] When the social democrats returned to power in 1993, after being in opposition for ten years, the Danish welfare state was in even better shape than it had been in 1982; it had been further developed by expanding universal, flat-rate, and tax-financed benefits. Its economic foundations were much improved, and public support remained strong (Green-Pedersen 1999, 2002; Green-Pedersen and Thomsen 2005). The comprehensive school system was even further expanded when an act in 1993 did away with the last vestiges of academic streaming in favour of mixed-ability classes at all 9/10 grades (Wiborg 2009). Only during the last few years or so did the unions face similar obstacles as their counterparts in Norway and Sweden had. How could the teacher union still remain influential during all these 'liberal' years?

The long-serving education minister, Bertel Haarder (1982–93), vigorously sought to reform the school system along neo-liberal lines, advocating a policy of devolution that would give schools managerial autonomy, introduce greater parental influence on the school boards of individual schools, improve school choice, and foster in quasi-market regulation of resource allocation to the schools. However, his power to enforce these policies was heavily restricted because the governments of the 1980s were coalition affairs without majority support in Parliament (Christensen 2000: 400). Furthermore, the decentralisation process that had begun earlier, in the 1970s, made the National

---

[22] The criteria were stated as follows: 'Contribution in the school development through experimental and development work, project work or work in groups. A will to undertake difficult and challenging tasks beyond what is normally expected in relation to the work regulations and the curriculum.' Translated from Telhaug *et al.* (2004): 76.

[23] The government succeeded in shifting economic policies from demand management to supply-side economics, to further integrate the Danish economy into that of the European Union and to weaken the role of the central state institutions. However, their attempts to cut public social expenditure and reform the basic structure of the social democratic welfare state failed completely (Nygård 2006).

Association of Municipalities a much more significant player in corporate politics. When it allied itself with the union against the government, reforms were usually blocked or watered down during the implementation period.

The proposals of Haarder were met with fierce opposition from the teacher union, which was against 'outsourcing' power to principals and parents. Haarder's strategy was to bypass the union to form an alliance with the National Association of Municipalities. In order to gain its support, the deal was to give local governments increased authority over the comprehensive schools if they in turn would accept that the school boards change from advisory school boards into directly elected boards with some decision-making powers. The National Association of Municipalities wouldn't agree to this proposal, and instead formed an alliance with the teacher union. Based on their common dislike of devolution of power to the school boards, they forced the minister into a diluted compromise.

The compromise was the Act on School Boards of 1989 – called the 'little school act' – and it was the only act introduced during Haarder's ministry. The act made the school boards (one for each school) responsible for developing policies and approving the school budget. The school boards were to be elected by parents and students but had to include staff and teacher union representatives (with no voting power). The act was almost completely watered down – mainly by the municipalities, but with the help of the local union branches – in that it transferred responsibilities to school principals rather than to the school boards, as originally intended[24] (Christensen 2000).

Haarder also attempted to create quasi-market regulation of resource allocation to individual schools – i.e. funding schools on the basis of the number of students. While the government was successful in introducing a voucher scheme (called the 'taxi-meter system') within technical and vocational training institutions, Haarder was blocked by the Association of Municipalities and the teacher union when he made a similar attempt with the public schools. These establishments, as well as upper secondary schools, thus continued to receive funding through an annual budget. However, during the 1990s some municipalities gradually introduced more fine-tuned budgetary systems to enable them to respond better to changes in student numbers and teaching hours.[25] Although this has been a unilateral decision by the individual municipality

---

[24] Especially with regard to the financial management of schools, principals have seen an expansion of their authority (Christensen 2000: 209).

[25] According to Christensen (2000: 213), in cases where schools receive more teaching resources than required to cover the minimum number of lessons stipulated by law, and in local school plans, such schools show no inclination to offer more lessons to their students. Rather than expanding output, these extra resources are typically allocated to a de facto, but well disguised, reduction in the student/teacher ratio – for example, by having two teachers in the same classroom or by dividing a class for certain lessons. Interestingly, and although labour relations are regulated by the same collective agreements, private schools use the extra resources in ways that allow for more classroom teaching and for teachers to provide after-school and pastoral care for children.

councils concerned, such councils are heavily constrained by collective agreements negotiated by the Association of Municipalities, which represents teachers' interests as an employer. These agreements specify time allocated for classroom teaching and preparation. In addition, the councils have to negotiate a contract with the local branch of the teacher union that specifies the number of hours to be spent on other tasks, such as student counselling, supervision, post-entry education, and union-related work such as board membership duties. The size of these resources is decided locally, but according to national agreement it has to make up at least 50 per cent of the resources allocated to class teaching. However, this percentage is often higher – in some cases more than 60 per cent[26]. Consequently, only about a third of teachers' pay for working time was spent on classroom teaching. In spite of changes made to the collective agreements, this pattern has persisted (Christensen 1998; 2000: 207).

Haarder's proposal was that these teaching resources should be linked with student enrolments to improve school choice. It was left to the local governments to set up a policy for school choice and to define the authority of directly elected school boards. However, municipalities have been reluctant to do this. Typically, a municipality assigns children residing within a precisely defined geographical district to each school. Parents can apply for enrolment of their child in another local school within their municipality. However, local policy excludes any direct competition among schools for students as there must be excess capacity in a school class, and enrolment must not lead to the establishment of extra classes. Municipalities, with local union enforcement, have thus restricted choice (Wiborg and Larsen, 2017). However, parents increasingly use the private school option, so that since the mid-1980s the proportion of children attending these establishments has increased from 8.9 per cent to 10.3 per cent (and in Copenhagen about 24 per cent). Private schools are state-funded up to 85 per cent of their budget, and the fees are means-tested. In this way, state schools are subject to competition from alternative providers, even if they do not compete among themselves (Rangvid 2008).

The consequence of these alliance strategies between the unions and the municipalities was essentially that the minister could only win parliamentary support for devolution that did not challenge local democracy and public sector corporatism. The government achieved very little during the 1980s. The municipalities have experienced increased authority and decide how and to what extent management should be devolved to schools. Instead of focusing their efforts at a national level on policy-makers in government and in Parliament, the union have strengthened their organisational apparatus at the local level and instead directed their attentions towards the Association of Municipalities (Holm-Larsen 2006: 102).

[26] An analysis of the five biggest cities outside Copenhagen found that in the 1996–1997 school year, teachers' resources corresponding to about 60 percent of the resources allocated to teaching were tasks outside the classroom. (Christensen 2000, 207)

Collective bargaining was reformed in 1993. From being civil servants, teachers became employees of the municipalities and their working conditions subject to collective agreements. A new working time agreement was also introduced which detailed teachers' responsibilities. This new agreement was to give the employers increased control in determining the use of teachers' time. The teacher union was strongly opposed to these changes as they would lead to greater uncertainty – so the union argued – resulting in local disputes, some of which were resolved through central conciliation. During the following years' collective bargaining (every two or three years), the union sought to improve the working hours agreement by demanding fewer teaching hours and more time for other tasks – such as preparation time – but to no avail.

During the period 1993–2001, social democratic-led coalitions were in government. These years can perhaps be best described as a period of non-reform since efforts were concentrated instead on protecting the welfare state from privatisation. According to Green-Pedersen (2002), this period of low policy activity is largely linked to the success of the social democrats in opposition during the previous government. After having been being highly critical of the privatisation and outsourcing of public services to non-state providers, the social democrats, upon their return in government, were 'locked' in their own political rhetoric of the 1980s. The leadership of the party, inspired by Tony Blair's Third Way, tried in vain to push the party to the centre-right.

The social democratic-led government was defeated in the 2001 election and replaced by a series of Liberal-Conservative coalition governments that lasted until 2011. During this ten-year period, in which Bertil Haarder again acted as education minister (2005–10), the marketisation of education was pursued even more strongly, and this time the government was more successful in backing its policy with legislation. This was partly because the teacher union was now completely circumvented and unable to block national policies – it had by now been relegated to a position, along with other education interests, whereby it was only consulted during the hearing process; and partly because the tradition of broad consensus-oriented policy agreements, in which parts of the opposition were included, diminished in favour of narrow majority agreements (Holm-Larsen 2010: 106).

The social democrats, now in opposition, had started to move to the right. In 2005, the government, with crucial support from the social democrats, introduced an act on school choice, which was now extended so that parents could choose a different public school to the one allocated to them by the municipality – even across municipality boundaries. In spite of this legislation, the municipalities, with local union support, continue to assign children to schools based on precisely defined geographical boundaries. So in effect, school choice is hardly exercised within the public sector (fewer than 12 per cent of children attend schools other than the one allocated to them by the municipality (Wiborg and Larsen, 2017).

The primary efforts of the governments of this period concerned a revision of the curriculum with the intention of enhancing academic standards (2001, 2003 and 2009) – a direct result of the mediocre PISA results of 2001. Broad guidelines for each subject were replaced with mandatory national standards, and national testing was also introduced (2006, in force 2010) (Holm-Larsen 2010: 102). The liberal government's policies propelled it into confrontation with the teacher union, the latter believing these would undermine teachers' autonomy and lead to increased control of their activities and a heavier workload. Having previously enjoyed extensive autonomy in the classroom compared with many other countries, even Sweden, teachers now experienced a restriction of this freedom.

By the time of the social democratic-led coalition government of 2011, the social democrats had moved towards the right – just as we witnessed earlier in Sweden and Norway. The social democrats have, on the whole, endorsed the policies of previous governments, and so, during the preparation of a new school act (concerning plans to strengthen the academic component by requiring compulsory homework), the union was once again entirely circumvented. However, the preparations had to be shelved (until 2014–15) as an industrial dispute broke out between the Association of Municipalities and the teacher union. The teacher union had refused to sign up to a new collective agreement that was put forward by the Association of Municipalities, and, importantly, was fully backed by government. The agreement sought to change the conditions of the teachers' working week, specifically the amount of time they had for lesson planning. Prior to the dispute, teachers taught a maximum of 25 hours with the rest of the 37-hour week allocated to lesson preparation and other work-related duties.

The proposal of the Association of the Municipalities was to increase the authority of school principals in this matter so that they could decide on preparation and classroom time for individual teachers depending on the specific needs of the school and the class. At this time, teacher union representatives in schools still held much influence over the use of teachers' time, whereas the influence of school principals was somewhat limited. The Association of Municipalities wanted, furthermore, to extend the number of teaching hours per day (between two and three hours depending on age group), so that children who normally would finish school at 1p.m. would now receive further classes rather than be allowed play time in school clubs. The teacher union was furiously opposed to this suggestion and demanded that regulation of classroom teaching and preparation (a cap of 25 hours a week for teaching, so it would be clear what counted as overtime) be managed at national level and not under any circumstances be left to the authority of local school principals.

This dispute led the Association of Municipalities to bar teachers from their places of work, without pay, for a period of several weeks. More than 90,000 teachers were part of the lock-out, which was finally brought to an end by government intervention. The social democratic-led coalition government hastily passed an act that stipulated the terms and conditions of teachers' work, but without consulting the teacher union. The government had de facto changed the collective agreement for teachers by passing on the responsibility of school principals to decide individual work and preparation time. Importantly, this is extremely rare that a collective bargaining collapse should result in government intervention and legislation. The tradition of collective bargaining was, as described earlier, characterised by the absence of government legislation. The outcome of this dispute was that the teacher union lost further power at municipality level – more power was passed on to principals, resulting in less influence for the union representatives in the schools. The newly formed union for principals, which had tried to steer away from the two bodies that were in dispute, was clearly the 'winner' in this battle. During the dispute the teacher union's only real political ally from within the coalition was the socialists. This tie-up achieved little, but it does demonstrate that the teacher union now appears to be seeking support from a party even further to the left (Holm-Larsen 2013: 131–43).

The interaction between the three actors – central government, the municipalities and the teacher union – determined what it was possible to achieve politically in the education field in Denmark. However, the recent dispute appears to have created a new situation. School principals have gained much more power, to the extent that they have even established their own union, one which brings with it a new set of institutionalised interests.

Finland: A Pyrrhic Victory for the Teacher Union?
In striking contrast to Scandinavia, the only Finnish teacher union, the OAJ, backed by nearly all teachers (97 per cent), has remained closely interwoven into the political system both at national and local levels. However, corporatism experienced a temporary decline in the early 1990s due to a financial crisis brought about by the collapse of trade with the Soviet Union and a severe banking crisis. Corporatism subsequently revived and has remained extraordinarily strong to the present day.

During the recession, the government bypassed the union to hurry through sweeping decentralisation reforms and funding cuts. In 1987, for the first time since the Second World War, the Conservative Party held the post of prime minister in a right-left coalition government (followed by a centre-right coalition between the Centre Party and the National Coalition Party from 1991–95) with the education minister posts going to right-wing parties (Dunphy 2007; Laukkanen 2008; Paloheimo 2002; Simola *et al.* 2009). This right-turn in politics brought an end to the dominance of the social democrats and the Centre Party in the Ministry of Education and in the National Board of Education (the NBE, the body responsible for policy implementation). Even though the Conservatives in Finland are considered the 'teachers' party' (the union is right-leaning), the teacher union strongly opposed their decentralisations plans for the very same reasons as its Scandinavian counterparts: decentralisation undermines and disperses the unions' power.

The highly centralised, top-down orientation of the schools (in which the union had a lot of say) was abolished in favour of giving them more freedoms. The extremely detailed curriculum, centrally determined teaching materials, weekly timetables, and class diaries which recorded in detail the content of each lesson, were all abolished. The national curriculum, still determined at national level, became much less detailed and prescriptive, and allowed municipalities and schools to adjust it in order to meet local needs. Schools could now also choose their own textbooks and instruction methods (Rinne et al. 2002: 646–7).[27]

The decentralisation process was further enhanced by two acts, in 1992 and 1995, concerning local government. The increased autonomy of the municipalities, which the Association of Finnish Local and Regional Authorities, AFLRA, had long been lobbying for, included responsibility for providing social and healthcare services and education. The latter specifically included schools at both primary/lower secondary level and upper secondary schools (municipalities ended up providing two-thirds of all the public services). Municipalities also became responsible for school personnel, although teachers still maintained their civil service status and principals were given more leverage over financial and personnel matters. The greater authority of the municipalities was underpinned by changes to the funding system in which the old system of specifically 'ear-marked' subsidies was abolished in favour of a more flexible scheme.[28] The new scheme involved the allocation of lump-sum funding (based on pupil numbers, lessons, etc.) to the municipalities, which they could distribute within their jurisdiction – as they saw fit – for the planning of educational provision and the recruitment of teachers.

In striking contrast to the Scandinavian countries, teacher salaries and working conditions continued to be negotiated at a central level through the national collective bargaining process. Perhaps surprisingly, it was not on the political agenda in the 1990s to discuss whether local negotiations should supplement national agreements (whereby individual performance would be reflected in the salary package), or whether school principals should be given more influence in determining the use of teachers' time. It was these very issues that sparked fierce disputes between the government, municipality associations, and the teacher unions in Scandinavia. In contrast to Scandinavia (where part of the collective bargaining process was transferred to municipalities

---

[27] In 1994, following another curriculum reform, the National Board of Education was only to stipulate the broad aims and content of each subject (a 110-page document). The municipalities and, ultimately, the schools, set up their own curriculum on the basis of the national curriculum. However, in 2006–07 the national curriculum became yet more detailed (a 320-page document).

[28] On average, government subsidies are 57 per cent of costs while the municipalities' contributions are 43 per cent. However, the share of municipal funding has increased in recent years.

and schools), Finnish governments continued to adhere to the longstanding tradition of non-government intervention in the collective bargaining framework. However, perhaps just as importantly, AFLRA was and remains a less powerful political player than its Scandinavian counterparts. The teacher union, with its much stronger power base, would do anything in its power to block such plans, devoted as it is to equal pay. Any changes to teachers' salary and working time in Finland are therefore only achieved through the national collective bargaining framework, involving the employers' associations and the AKAVA to which the teacher union is affiliated.[29]

Corporatism was restored soon after the recession had come to an end. The teacher union was back in business. Having been sidetracked during the recession, the union did not remain passive. Like its Scandinavian counterparts, the union quickly built up its local capacities – backed by generous funding – trained its members to work hard and influence policy-makers, and fought for its interests in municipalities and schools. During the recession, the focus had been on minimising funding cuts to schools in the municipalities and preventing the loss of teachers' jobs. The local union branches also sought, and still seek, to eradicate differences across municipalities in teachers' working conditions (e.g., working hours)[30], especially between urban and rural areas.

It can reasonably be argued that the Finnish teacher union obtained even more power following the recession. Through mergers with other unions the membership base expanded considerably, and, in a single stroke, competition between unions was eliminated. In 1991 the Association of Kindergarten Teachers joined the OAJ, and, in 2006, the National Union of the Directors in the Educational and Cultural Sectors of the Municipalities followed suit. In addition, new groups of members joined – including college and university teachers, private school teachers, adult teachers, and teachers from the vocational and technical institutions. Headmasters, too, are members of the OAJ.

Having achieved a total monopoly, the Finnish teacher union strengthened its already-close proximity to the state apparatus and maintained an extensive system of institutionalised interchanges of both a formal and informal nature with Parliament, the ministries, the NBE, and the education sectors of the municipalities. The teacher union is, for instance, represented in every working group within the Ministry of Education and the NBE, and is in contact with them on an almost daily basis. The union is nearly always represented on parliamentary education committees, preparing new laws or budgets, and other commissions pertaining to its interests. It holds frequent meetings with all eight political groups in Parliament, particularly seeking out (former) teachers

---

[29] Although additional local bargaining is absent in the Finnish system, municipalities have some discretion in setting the level of teachers' salaries – for instance, by awarding extra to teachers responsible for pupils with special needs. Salaries have been maintained at a more or less equal level across the country.

[30] Some municipalities follow minimum requirements, while others require more.

who traditionally constitute a substantial but declining occupational group in Parliament; and it also meets the NBE on a regular basis. At regional and local levels, the union branches have close interrelationships with local decision-makers, especially as the municipalities' powers have grown stronger; and they have forged alliances with parents' associations.

Last but not least, the Finnish teacher union is very active in the media through its extensive network with local, regional and the only national newspaper in Finland: *Helsingin Sanomat*. The union feeds the media with data and a great amount of research that is either conducted by the union itself or delegated to specially commissioned researchers; it also makes use of many other resources to back up its policy advice, and promotes a public 'image' of itself. The strong association between the only teacher union and the media amounts, effectively, to having total authority over what is said and done in education in Finland. The union also drives a great number of campaigns, especially in the run-up to national and municipal elections and EU elections.

The release of the PISA results produced by the OECD in 2001 – which placed Finland as a top scorer in literacy, numeracy and science – came as a surprise, but was used effectively by the teacher union to promote its special interests. The union did this in two important ways: (1) to push for improved teacher conditions, and (2) to block or slow down the government reform process and so maintain the status quo in education. With regard to the former, the teacher union dominated the public debate by making effective use of its extensive media network. The union repeatedly attributed the outstanding results to the high professional expertise of the university-educated teachers, particularly evidenced by the fact that the resources used in education were 'only OECD average'. The relatively low cost of education, which the PISA researchers had used as a measure of the efficiency of the Finnish education system, was instead used as 'proof' by the union that Finland was lagging behind in investment in education and demanded increased resources. The government 'rewarded' teachers, at the request of the union, by increasing educational funding, much of this being channelled into higher salaries (Rautalin and Alasuutari 2009: 542).

In respect of the slowing down of government reforms, the union initiated large-scale public campaigns to upscale the 'historic collaboration between government and teachers' and to make government 'trust teachers'. The unions' campaign paid off, considering the far-reaching endorsement it has received from many education experts, politicians and civil servants. A statement made by the long-term director of the NBE, Reijo Laukannen, illustrates this succinctly: 'We trust our teachers [...] We don't have any evaluation of teachers [...] We trust they are competent, they know what to do'. The campaign managed to suppress the fact that teachers and their unions had historically constituted a blocking force. A study by Simola (Sahlgreen 2015: 12) – who analysed thousands of state documents between 1860 and the early 1990s – found only one instance since the introduction of the comprehensive school reforms where teachers were not viewed as roadblocks to education development. Teachers, it appeared, were in fact not trusted. The issue here is not whether the teaching profession should be trusted or not, but that the Finnish teacher union managed to persuade the public to have faith in teachers, which gave it a formidable platform from which to exert political influence. Referring frequently to catchphrases such as 'collaboration', 'consensus agreements', 'trust', etc., the union, utilising channels available to them as described above, set out to slow down education reform.

The unions' best weapon in arguing for the status quo – or, at least, no reform without union collaboration – was yet again the outstanding PISA results, which had 'demonstrated' that no major changes in education were necessary. Why change a system that was rated the best in the world? It is true that Finnish governments have been much less incentivised to reform education, at least in comparison to those countries that recorded poor PISA scores. However, the role of the union as a blocking force against unwanted reforms should not be underestimated. According to Simola (2005), the Finnish teacher union wields a certain amount of veto power in government, one which makes it difficult to get policies through Parliament. Politicians and policy-makers are reluctant to initiate changes if they know that the union will oppose them. As a result, the 'PISA period' from 2001 until the present day can largely be seen as a period of non-reform, resulting in a limited degree of actual change in the school system.

For example, privatisation of education has hardly made any headway in Finland (Ahonen 2002; Rinne 2000). The private sector is tiny – only 2 per cent of children are enrolled in private primary/lower secondary schools – and is barely growing.[31] The union is in total control of the private school sector and any agreements reached through the bargaining process are extended to private school teachers, whose working conditions and salaries are thus consistent with their colleagues in the public sector.

School choice was introduced by a social democratic-led coalition in 1998 as a result of several small policy changes. The old practice of allocating children to the schools closest to their homes, within a particular district, was abolished. Municipalities were now regarded as one large 'district' and parents could freely select a school of their choice within the municipality. However, in reality, school choice is extremely limited. The primary reason is not, as is often claimed by the union, a lack of parental interest. Municipalities, with strong union enforcement, continue to operate rigid catchment areas according to which students are allocated to their neighbourhood schools. The municipalities dictate that parental choice can only be taken into consideration if there are available places *after* local pupils have already been assigned to a particular school. Schools are not permitted to expand in case there is extra demand, and hence capacity remains constrained (Denessen *et al.* 2001; Rinne *et al.*

---

[31] Only eight new private schools have been given special permission by the government since 1999.

2002: 649; West and Ylönen 2010). However, larger cities, especially Helsinki, have more actively implemented choice within the public school sector, resulting in greater parental choice.[32] Being opposed to school choice, the local union branches lobby municipalities and parent groups to maintain these restrictive rules. We do not know exactly how successful the union branches have been in limiting choice – more research is needed in this regard – but given their considerable power to influence decisions made by the municipalities, especially the smaller ones, school choice is almost non-existent.

The decentralisation of education that took place prior to the 2001 PISA study was the last major piece of legislation in Finland in recent times, and brought about substantial changes to the Finnish school system (except for the collective bargaining process). Successive governments' zest for reform has since started to wane, exacerbated by the unions' resistance to change. No major reforms have therefore been introduced. This lack of change is largely a result of the widespread belief, or myth – forcefully communicated by the teacher union, but also by politicians and civil servants – that successful policy implementation depends on *union* consent.

Two recent and important events, however, goaded the government into prompt action. First, Finland plunged into a sharp recession following the financial crisis of 2009, which forced the Conservative-led coalition government to adopt austerity measures, including budget cuts to education and measures to increase productivity and efficiency through structural reform of public finances. This involved mergers between schools, closures of smaller schools, and, most importantly, increased class sizes in the municipalities. The teacher union strongly opposed these education measures but, unable to block the funding cuts, it is now fighting against job losses and has initiated mass public campaigns focused on the merits of smaller class sizes.[33] When municipalities lay off teachers or convert their contracts to part-time or temporary, the union will take their cases to court. The union supports approximately 200 such cases each year, around half of which they win. With regard to minimising budget cuts, the union forcefully lobbies members of Parliament, as well as the ministries and municipalities, to lower the student-teacher ratio. The average class size is around 20, which the union accepts as a maximum but wants lowered to 18 (Semi 2013: 37). Union lobbying has paid off: extra funding was given to the municipalities to lower class sizes (€60 million in 2013, reduced to €40 million in 2014).[34]

---

[32] In Helsinki, the Local Education Board decided in 2007 to begin per-capita funding of schools, with each pupil bringing a certain level of resources to a school. With funding following the pupil, a stronger school market has been developed, with schools incentivised to compete for children as a way of attracting more funding.

[33] During the 2000s, employment in the education sector has been relatively stable, but in recent years the recession has impacted on the sector and employment in it decreased by 4.3 per cent from 2007 to 2008.

[34] However, some municipalities have saved the money instead, thus allowing class sizes to increase, something which the union – in alliance with parents' associations – has appealed against.

The other event – perhaps the second PISA surprise for the Finns – was the release of the latest PISA results from 2012, which showed that Finland had slipped in two consecutive studies. The country had dropped slightly across all domains in PISA 2009, but to an even greater extent in PISA 2012. Between 2006 and 2012, Finland's performance declined by 18 points in scientific literacy, 23 points in reading literacy, and 29 points in mathematical literacy. On average, this was the largest fall of any Nordic country in this period (Sahlgreen 2015: 5). The teacher-centric views (in conjunction with an absence of standardised tests, accountability, and market reforms) – which the union had been instrumental in publicly promoting since 2001 – were brought into question. Alternative explanations came to the fore, which had long been downplayed since they were not considered relevant to policy changes, let alone to helping the union cause. These refer to the fact that after the Second World War, Finland was a resource-poor country that seized on education as its path out of poverty. A highly centralised education system was therefore developed, and controlled by the state. Education became academically oriented, and traditional class teaching became the norm – systematic and rigorous, using constant testing to monitor progress. Central government issued an extremely detailed curriculum, textbooks, and prescribed the teaching methods, affording little autonomy to teachers. Cognitive theory, rooted in psychology and intelligence testing, guided teachers in the instruction of children (Simola 2005).

But it is now argued that these historical factors, which accelerated under the old centralised system and contributed to the top scores in the first PISA tests, are now receding and explain to a large degree the recent PISA decline (Sahlgreen 2015). It is outside the scope of this chapter to explore the reasons behind this decline, but suffice it to say that the teacher union is likely to have played an instrumental role.

Every ten years the Finnish curriculum is revised. A new, revised curriculum has been developed over the last few years and will take effect in 2016. The union was represented in a working group that prepared its core content and will participate in municipality working groups where the curriculum will be further fleshed out. The teacher union (and progressive educators in the NBE) advocated for child-centred, individualised approaches to teaching. Progressive teaching styles are characterised by more pupil-driven instruction, including individual and group work. Such methods are related to various forms of 'constructivism', which, in short, holds that knowledge is constructed by pupils, not transmitted down from teachers, and that learning is the responsibility of pupils. These ideas have increasingly found their way into policy documents, but are most strongly emphasised in the recent curriculum reform that is about to take effect. What is more, constructivist ideas have grown even stronger in teacher education and professional development training. The Ministry of Education has recently established a working group on which the teacher union is represented, aiming – among other things – to develop teachers' education along these lines. Over the last ten years or so, there has already been a gradual, though uneven, shift from common curriculum-based teaching to a system based on individual learning paths (helped by an increased use of IT) and less authority in the classrooms.

These methods (facilitating unguided teaching that is associated with constructivist practices) may lead to further decline if we are to believe recent econometric research. This body of research (Bietenback 2014; Machin and McNally 2008; Schwerdt and Wuppermann 2011) suggests that these methods are less effective in raising test scores than structured teaching. If this research holds true for Finland – we don't know yet – the heavy involvement of the union in curriculum preparation and in advocating for less traditional methods in teacher training is a factor that will need to be considered in explaining future PISA outcomes. Given the power and position that the Finnish teacher union holds in politics, particularly in relation to teacher training at universities where these 'new' methods are developed, its role in shaping reforms should be scrutinised.

Teachers continue to enjoy a relatively high level of autonomy – largely negotiated by the union – which is increasingly being used to experiment with alternative methods in schools. By the same token, teachers are fighting against being held accountable for their performance. The unions' massive 'trust teachers' campaign over the last decade appears to have led to a culture – that has permeated deep into government institutions – that teachers need not be evaluated and that school inspections are unnecessary. The union has been relentless in communicating that there are no substandard teachers in Finland, as evidenced by the high PISA scores. It is most likely that Finland does indeed have less of a problem with poor teachers, given that they are university-educated; however, it is of course doubtful that having university-educated teachers automatically results in outstanding teaching in *all* schools and *all* classrooms. The absence of an accountability system (but also of a nationwide school inspection regime) – something the union would fight against if it were ever to be suggested by the government – makes it difficult, if not impossible, to identify and deal with poor teachers. The extent to which Finland is acknowledging and grappling with the problem of inadequate teachers is unknown. It does happen – but not often – that teachers are dismissed for poor performance; but since there is no formal evaluation of them that would provide evidence of poor conduct, the teacher union usually wins if the dismissal of a teacher is brought to court.

Performance evaluation may be introduced by other means, and there are currently plans being developed by the employers' association (Association of Finnish Independent Education Employers) to introduce performance-related pay for teachers along similar lines to the scheme already in place for civil servants – to also include universities and university training schools. Around 700 teacher educators in the training schools receive some performance-based pay in addition to their basic salary. The employers' association frequently involves the teacher union in the preparation of this proposal, completion of which is planned for 2016. Negotiations have begun and are currently focused on what percentage of salary should be allocated to basic pay, and what percentage should constitute performance-related remuneration. The teacher union, which mainly prefers equal pay for all teachers, is negotiating to have the performance-related allocation kept as small as possible. In the near future the issue of performance criteria will also need to be negotiated.[35]

The teacher union in Finland, with an immense power base that has been built up over the years, has gained immensely from PISA – using the results to push for higher salaries and as a way of dodging any performance assessment of teachers. At the same time it has been able to halt major reforms. Instead, only small-scale policy changes have been introduced, shaped to some extent by the union. Teachers are allowed substantial freedom, are increasingly encouraged to experiment with pupil-led instruction, and benefit from the lack of an accountability system. If the PISA results decline further, thus necessitating firm government action, education corporatism in Finland will be seriously challenged for the first time in the postwar period.

Concluding Remarks

The teacher unions in the Nordic countries have fared in strikingly similar ways, as well as in remarkably different ones. Their rise in Scandinavia was propelled by powerful social democratic parties that continued to build upon interwar corporate structures which were themselves further enhanced by a political left-turn in the first part of the postwar period. Boards and commissions prepared legislation in close cooperation with teacher unions and other educational organisations that represented the target groups of education policies. Teacher unions thus played an integral role in formal hearings concerning almost all proposals for legal and administrative legislation relating to their specific interests. The unions were also an integral part of the implementation process.

Teacher unions in Scandinavia were most sympathetic towards the political left, and brought their agendas to bear in large and long-serving government education commissions. Their power peaked during the 1960s and 1970s – a time of increased public spending – when party/union ties were at their strongest. Union members reaped great benefits in two general areas: (1) increased salary equalisation for comprehensive school teachers and upper secondary school teachers, as well as improved working conditions – meaning less time for instruction, and more time for non-teaching activities, and (2) the institutionalisation of comprehensive education, which conferred a near-monopoly on teachers over teaching and teacher training. The teacher unions won a

---

[35] In addition, a new working time system is being prepared. Instead of paying teachers based on the number of lessons they teach, the plan is to base salaries on the number of hours spent in the schools.

near-monopoly for the primary school teachers to teach in the nine-year comprehensive schools (for children aged 6–16 years), squeezing out university-educated secondary school teachers who belonged to the rival academic teacher union. The unions chose pedagogy and didactics, as opposed to academic subject specialisation, to inform teacher training methods, and to help demarcate comprehensive school teachers from university-educated teachers in the upper secondary schools. This monopoly still persists today, although governments have more recently tried to break down the barriers to entry for other professions. Teacher unions have erected other protectionist hurdles – with some success – but nevertheless, teachers with alternative qualification backgrounds have made inroads into the teaching profession.[36]

In Finland, the teacher union eschewed comprehensive education, but in political negotiations they relented on this position, gaining university-based teacher training in return, something they had lobbied for since the interwar period. University-based teacher training and the comparatively high number of professors of education with research obligations provided a strong political legitimacy for developing a 'science-based' teaching profession. The entry of primary school teachers into the ranks of the university-educated – which placed them on a university payscale – elevated primary schools teachers' status as a professional group. This was clearly conducive to the unification of multiple teacher unions into a single one, as the categories of primary and secondary teachers became more permeable (although clearly defined in the salary structure). Having just one teacher union, backed by the majority of teachers, gave the union unprecedented power in its dealings with the state. In Scandinavia some unification of teacher unions also occurred, but the union for primary school teachers, and later comprehensive school teachers, and the academic upper secondary school unions remained separate, and thus often found themselves in conflict with each other particularly when government policies involved the integration of the entire school system.

A significant decline in the position of organised interests in the policy-making process subsequently began (in the 1980s), and has endured to the present day – although to a much lesser extent in Finland. Neither the extent

---

[36] In the case of Denmark, for example, it was not until 2002 that this monopoly broke down, and even then only partially. The shortage of teachers in schools and a decline in applications to teacher colleges prompted the government to establish a new, fast-track (two-year, part-time) teacher training course for non-teachers (over 25 years of age) who wished to embark on a new career as a teacher. The teacher union was strongly opposed to this initiative, arguing that only college-educated teachers possessed the professionalism and required pedagogical skills to work in schools. However, the union was unable to block the introduction of this course (which was offered at teacher training colleges). It has since been lobbying strongly to extend the course's duration and increase its cost. The course provides an avenue for people with university degrees into schools, but the union is trying to undermine this by demanding the upscaling of college-based teacher training to university-based education (along Finnish lines). So far it has not been successful.

nor the consequences of this decline are fully understood; explanation requires further research. However, as evinced in this chapter, the very same factors that brought the Scandinavian unions to power – that is, social democracy and corporatism – serve to explain the subsequent decline of their influence. Since commissions are the main structural mechanism linking public bureaucracy to organised interests, it is evident that corporatism has come under strong pressure. Even though the use of corporatist practices is now less frequent, their utilisation as a linking mechanism with policy legislators is still a factor, seeing as commissions continue to include members from various educational interest organisations. However, these commissions tend to be smaller, work faster, and include experts and civil servants rather than representatives from the teacher unions. This shift in the balance of power implies that the influence of the teacher union at state level has been reduced, and lobbying has consequently become more widespread – mirroring the situation found in other non-corporatist countries.

The difference in the timing of the decline of teacher unions across the Scandinavian states can be related to the decline of social democratic power and its giving way to alternating centre-left and centre-right coalition governments. In Sweden, where the teacher union first went into decline (late 1980s and early 1990s), the Social Democratic Party lost its dominance and made a noticeable move to the right, endorsing and even initiating decentralisation and some market-oriented education reforms. This triggered an ideological struggle that proved to be incompatible with stable corporatism. In Norway and Denmark, corporatism started to decline during the period of the right-wing governments, but a far more profound rupture occurred in the 2000s when the social democrats started to move to the right and begin bypassing the unions. This forced the unions to build stronger allegiances with smaller parties further to the left of the social democrats. But these parties were in a poor position to safeguard the interests of the unions. These factors have led to a decline in the association between special interests and policy formulation.

In Finland, the teacher union has remained closely interwoven with the state system, thus continuing to wield extraordinary power. The consensus-making mode of government has been sustained for longer than in Scandinavia, partly due to oversized coalitions with a strong centre. Reflecting the general consensual pattern of politics, decision-making in public policy sectors is still broadly inclusive and based on extensive consultation with key interest groups. However, as in Scandinavia, the number of such committees has dwindled over recent times as a result of deep recession, to be replaced by non-partisan policy advisors or working groups consisting mainly of civil servants appointed by the ministries.

Reforms intending to deregulate and decentralise education have had – perhaps more than any other piece of legislation in recent years – the greatest impact on the teacher unions. Since the late 1970s, but especially during the 1990s, Nordic governments have transferred regulative decision-making powers to the municipalities and enhanced their autonomy as a way of fostering greater local participation. As a result, the municipalities have gained a high degree of autonomy and authority in implementing national policies compared to other European countries (Ibsen *et al.* 2011: 2296). This increased devolution of power has meant that the associations of local governments in Scandinavia (but less so in Finland) became powerful players in corporate politics both at the national and at the local level, often pursuing conflicting interests to those of the teacher unions. Municipalities seek to increase local power at the expense of central government intervention and by restricting the power of school boards and principals.

All the Nordic teacher unions fought a bitter but unsuccessful battle against this process. Instead, they changed tactics by seeking 'compensation' – for example, in the form of higher salaries – in return for accepting decentralisation and, importantly, reinforcing their local representation. It was a much more dramatic process in Sweden and Norway than in Denmark; the former countries went from highly centralised systems to extensive decentralised ones over the course of a relatively short time period. Municipalities became the employers of teachers, and schools decided upon curricula implementation, class size, and the number of lessons taught per year and per subject. The decentralisation of such decisions – which ran counter to the unions' interests in retaining national standards – made the unions quick to arrange corporate-like strategies on a local level. In Finland, the decentralisation process was also met with resistance by the teacher union; however, it never resulted in the same degree of controversy as it did in Scandinavia, because the most important issues for the union – salary and working time and conditions – continued to be decided centrally. National standards for these, including a national pay scheme that was negotiated centrally, have remained more or less intact until the present day. The decentralisation process primarily involved an increase in school autonomy and the freedom for teachers to plan instruction-related matters. The union, for obvious reasons, did not find these policies difficult to accept.

The decentralisation process, although it has played out differently across the Scandinavian countries, can nevertheless be seen as a critical period that has sent the teacher unions into decline as they lost access to policy-making mechanisms. The devolution of authority dispersed the power of the teacher unions. On a national level, it simply withered. What is happening to the unions on a local level, especially now that municipality associations have become powerful players in interest politics, is therefore crucial and remains to be researched in the Nordic countries. In Finland, the teacher union has likewise been undermined by the decentralisation process, but to a much lesser degree, and, crucially, it continues to carry considerable weight in national policy-making. In this regard it has been helped by the outstanding PISA results. The sole teacher union in Finland constitutes a major policy blocker and shaper, and is thus in a better position to resist profound changes to the education system.

References

Ahonen, S. (2002) From an industrial to a post-industrial society: Changing conceptions of equality in education. *Educational Review* 54(2): 173–81.

(2010) Bounded Rationality in Finnish Education Policy. In A.P. Jacobi, K. Martens, and K.D. Wolf, eds, *Education in Political Science. Discovering a Neglected Field*. New York: Routledge.

Åmark, K. (1989) Öppna karteller och sociale inhägnader. In S. Selander, ed., *Kampen om yrkesutövning, status och kunskap: professionaliseringens sociala grunder*. Lund: Studentlitteratu.

Andersen, J. (2006) *Between Growth and Security: Swedish Social Democracy From a Strong Society to a Third Way*. Manchester: Manchester University Press.

Anthonsen, M., and Lindvall, J. (2009) Party competition and the resilience of corporatism. *Government and Opposition* 44(2): 167–87.

Anthonsen, M., Lindvall, J., and Schmidt-Hansen, U. (2010) Social democrats, unions and corporatism: Denmark and Sweden compared. *Party Politics* 17(1): 118–34.

Arreman, I.E. (2011) Privatisation of public education? The emergence of independent upper secondary schools in Sweden. *Journal of Education Policy* 26(2): 225–43.

Arter, D. (1999) Party system change in Scandinavia since 1970: 'Restricted change' or 'general change'? *West European Politics* 22(3): 139–58.

(2007) The end of the social democratic hegemony? The March 2007 Finnish general election. *West European Politics* 30: 1148–57.

(2009) From a contingent party system to party system convergence? Mapping party system change in postwar Finland. *Scandinavian Political Studies* 32(2): 221–39.

Bäck, H. (2003) Party politics and the common good in Swedish local government. *Scandinavian Political Studies* 26(2): 93–123.

Bietenback, J. (2014) Teacher practices and cognitive skills. *Labour Economics* 30: 143–53.

Blom-Hansen, J. (2000) Still corporatism in Scandinavia? A survey of recent empirical findings. *Scandinavian Political Studies* 23(2): 157–81.

(2001) Organized interest and the state: A disintegrating relationship? Evidence from Denmark. *European Journal of Political Research* 39(3): 391–416.

Bregnsbo, H. (1971) *Kampen om skolelovene af 1958. En studie i interesseorganisationers politiske aktivitet*. Odense University Press.

Bröcher, K. et al. (1974) *Lærerne og folkeskolen gennem 100 år*. København: Danmarks Lærerforening.

Christensen, D.Ch. (1966) *Lærerinteresser of læreruddannelse*. Aarbog for dansk skolehistorie. Copenhagen: Selskabet for Skole- og Uddannelseshistorie.

Christensen, J.G. (1998) Institutioner, politikere og brugere. In Blom-Hansen, ed., *Offentligt og effektivt? Institutionelle valg i den offentlige sektor*. Copenhagen: Gyldendal.

(2000) Governance and Devolution in the Danish School System. In Arnott, M.A., and Raab, C.D., eds, *The Governance of Schooling: comparative studies of devolved management*. London: Routledge.

Christiansen, P.M., and Rommetvedt, H. (1999) From corporatism to lobbyism? Parliaments, executives, and organized interests in Denmark and Norway. *Scandinavian Political Studies* 22.

Christiansen, P.M., and Togeby, L. (2006) Power and democracy in Denmark: Still a viable democracy? *Scandinavian Political Studies* 29(1): 1–24.

Daun, H., and Siminou, P. (2005) State, market, and civil forces in the governance of education: The case of Sweden, France, Germany, the Czech Republic. *European Education* 37(1): 26–45.

Denessen, E., Sleegers, P., and Smit, P. (2001) *Reasons for school choice in the Netherlands and in Finland*. Occational Paper No. 24. National Center for the Study of Privatization in Education, Teachers College, Columbia University.

Dobbins, M. (2014) Explaining change and inertia in Swedish and French education: A tale of two corporatisms? *Policy Studies* 35(3): 282–302.

Due, J., and Madsen, J.S. (1987) *Fra Lokalkreds til fagforening. De lokale fagforeningers tilblivelsesproces i Danmarks lærerforening. Første rapport i forskningsprojektet fremtidens skole/fremtidens lærerforening*. København: Institut for Kultursociologi.

Dunphy, R. (2007) In search of an identity: Finland's Left Alliance and the experience of coalition government. *Contemporary Politics* 13(1): 37–55.

Elovaino, P. (1983) The nation-building process and the development of the secondary school system in Finland, Norway and Sweden at the end of the 19th century. *Scandinavian Journal of Educational Research* 27(1): 1–14.

Elvander, N. (2002) The new Swedish regime for collective bargaining and conflict resolution: A comparative perspective. *European Journal of Industrial Relations* 8(2): 197–216.

Esping-Andersen, G. (1985) *Politics Against Markets: The Social Democratic Road to Power*. Princeton: Princeton University Press.

Galgóczi, B. and Glassner, V. (2008) *Comparative Study of Teachers' Pay in Europe*. Brussels: EI/ETUCE joint research project.

Green-Pedersen, C. (1999) The Danish welfare state under bourgeois reign. The dilemma of popular entrenchment and economic constraints. *Scandinavian Political Studies* 22(3): 243–60.

(2002) New management reforms of the Danish and Swedish welfare states: The role of different social democratic responses. *Governance: An International Journal of Policy, Administration, and Institutions* 15(2): 271–94.

Green-Pedersen, C., and Thomsen, L.H. (2005) Bloc politics vs. broad cooperation? The functioning of Danish minority parliamentarism. *Journal of Legislative Studies* 11(2): 153–69.

Helgøy, I., and Homme, A. (2007) Towards a new professionalism in school? A comparative study of teacher autonomy in Norway and Sweden. *European Educational Research Journal* 6(3): 232–48.

Holm-Larsen, S. (2006) Uddannelserne i årets løb. Folketingsåret 2005–2006. *Uddannelseshistorie*. København: Selskabet for Skole-og Uddannelseshistorie.

(2010) Hvorfra – hvorhen? Tendenser og lovændringer mv. i dansk uddannelsespolitik 1998–2010. *Uddannelseshistorie*. København: Selskabet for Skole-og Uddannelseshistorie.

(2013) Lærerlockout, lektiecafeer og lavere SU – uddannelserne i folketingsåret 2012–2013. *Uddannelseshistorie*. København: Selskabet for Skole-og Uddannelseshistorie.

Ibsen, Ch.L., Larsen, T.P., Madsen, J.S., and J. Due (2011) Challenging Scandinavian employment relations: The effects of new public management reforms. *The International Journal of Human Resource Management* 22(11): 2295–310.

Kansanen, P. (1990) Education as a discipline in Finland. *Scandinavian Journal of Educational Research* 34(4): 271–84.

(2003) Teacher Education in Finland: Current Models and New Developments. In B. Moon, L. Vlasceanau, and L.C. Barrows, eds, *Institutional Approaches to Teacher Education within Higher Education in Europe*. Bucharest: UNESCO Studies on Higher Education.

Kenworthy, L. (2003) Quantitative indicators of corporatism. *International Journal of Sociology* 33(3): 10–44.

Kettunen, P. (2001) The Nordic welfare state in Finland. *Scandinavian Journal of History* 26(3): 225–47.

Kirby, D. (2006) *A Concise History of Finland*. Cambridge: Cambridge University Press.

Kivinen, O., and Rinne, R. (1990) The university, the state and the professional interest groups: A Finnish lesson in university development policy. *Higher Education Policy* 3(3): 15–18.

Kivinen, O., and Rinne, R. (1994) The thirst for learning, or protecting one's niche? The shaping of teacher training in Finland during the 19th and 20th centuries. *British Journal of Sociology of Education* 15(4): 515–27.

Kleven, T., Floris, T.S., Granberg, M., Montin, S, Rieper, O., and S.I. Valo (2000) Renewal of local government in Scandinavia: Effects for local politicians. *Local Government Studies* 26(2): 93–116.

Klitgaard, M.B. (2007) Why are they doing it? Social democracy and market-oriented welfare state reforms. *West European Politics* 30(1): 172–94.

Kvavik, R.B. (1976) *Interest Groups in Norwegian Politics*. Oslo: Universitetsforlaget.

Lakomaa, E. (2009) *The Municipal Takeover of the School System*. SSE/EFI Working Paper Series in Business Administration No. 2011: 2.

Laukkanen, R. (2008) Finnish Strategy for High-Level Education for All. In N.C. Soguel and P. Jaccard, eds, *Governance and Performance of Education Systems*: 305–24. Springer.

Lidström, A. (1999) Local school choice policies in Sweden. *Scandinavian Political Studies* 22: 137–156.

Lijphart, A., and M.M.L. Crepaz (1991) Corporatism and consensus democracy in eighteen countries. *British Journal of Political Science*. 21(1): 235–46.

Lindblad, S., Lundahl, L., Lindgren, and Z. Gunilla (2002) Educating for the New Sweden? *Scandinavian Journal of Educational Research* 46(3): 283–303.

Lindvall, J., and Sebring, J. (2005) Policy reform and the decline of corporatism in Sweden. *West European Politics* 28(5): 1057–74.

Lundahl, L. (2002) Sweden: Decentralization, deregulation, quasi-markets – and then what? *Journal of Education Policy* 17(6): 687–97.

(2006) Education politics and teachers: Sweden and some comparisons with Great Britain. *Hitotsubshi Journal of Social Studies* 38 (1): 63–78.

Lundahl, L., Arreman, I.E., Lundström, U., and L. Rönnberg (2010) Setting things right? Swedish upper secondary school reform in a 40-year perspective. *Journal of Education* 45(1): 46–59.

Machin, S., and McNally, S. (2008) The literacy hour. *Journal of Public Economics* 92(5–6): 1441–62.
Matilla, M., and Raunio, T. (2002) Government formation in the Nordic countries: The electoral connection. *Scandinavian Political Studies* 25(3): 259–80.
Mausethagen, S., and Granlund, L. (2012) Contested discourses of teacher professionalism: Current tensions between education policy and teachers unions. *Journal of Education Policy* 27(6): 815–33.
Nygård, M. (2006) Welfare-ideological change in Scandinavia: A comparative analysis of partisan welfare state positions in four Nordic countries, 1970–2003. *Scandinavian Political Studies* 29(4): 356–85.
Öberg, P.O., Svensson, T., Christiansen, P.M., Nørgaard, S., Rommetvedt, H., and Thesen, G. (2011) Disrupted exchange and declining corporatism: Government authority and interest group capability in Scandinavia. *Government and Opposition*. 46(3): 365–91.
OECD (1994) *Quality in Teaching*. OECD (Organization for Economic Co-operation and Development): Paris.
Paloheimo, H. (2002) Divided Government in Finland. From a Semi-Presidential to a Parliamentary Democracy. In Elgie, R., ed., *Divided Government in Comparative Perspective*. Oxford: Oxford University Press.
Pekkarinen, T., Uusitalo, R., and S. Pekkala (2006) *Education Policy and Intergenerational Income Mobility: Evidence from the Finnish Comprehensive School Reform*. IZA Discussion Paper No. 2204. http://ssrn.com/abstract=920645
Persson, S. (2008) *Lärayrkets uppkomst och förändring: en sociologisk studie av lärares villkor, organisering och yrkesprojekt inom den grunläggende utbildningen i Sverige ca. 1800-2000. Akademisk avhandling*. Göteborg: Sociologiska institutionen, universitetet.
Räisänen, M. (2014). Counter from the Catheda. Democratic School Workers Association redefining teachers' political agency in Finland, 1973–1989. *Pedagogica Historica* 50(4): 533–53.
Rangvid, B.S. (2008). Private school diversity in Denmark's national voucher system. *Scandinavian Journal of Educational Research* 52(4): 331–54.
Rautalin, M., and Alasuutari, P. (2007) The curse of success: The impact of the OECD's Programme for International Student Assessment on the discourses of the teaching profession in Finland. *European Educational Research Journal* 6: 438–63.
Rautalin, M., and Alasuutari, P. (2009) The uses of the national PISA results by Finnish officials in central government. *Journal of Education Policy*. 24(5): 539–56.
Rinne, R. (1988) The Formation and Professionalization of the Popular Teachers in Finland in the 20th Century. In Iisalo, T., and Rinne, R., eds, *Läraren i 1900-talets kultur och samhälle*. Turun yliopiston kasvatustieteiden tiedekunnan julkaisuja, B26: 106–48.
(2000) The globalisation of education: Finnish education at the doorstep of the new millennium. *Educational Review*. 52(2): 131–42.
Rinne, R., Kvirauma, J., and Simola, H. (2002) Shoots of revisionist education policy or just slow readjustment? The Finnish case of educational reconstruction. *Journal of educational policy* 17(6): 643–58.
Rommetvedt, H. (2003) *The Rise of the Norwegian Parliament*. London: Frank Cass.

(2005) Norway: Resources count, but votes decide? From neo-corporatist representation to neo-pluralist parliamentarism. *West European Politics.* 28(4): 740–63.
Rothstein, B. (1992a) *Den korporative staten: intresseorganisationer och statsförvaltning i svensk politik.* Stockholm: Nordstedts juridik: Allmänna förlaget.
— (1992b) Explaining Swedish corporatism: The formative moment. *Scandinavian Political Studies.* 15(3): 173–91.
— (1997) Den svenska modellens institutionella arv. In: A.L. Johansson, ed., *Fackliga organisationsstrategier.* Solna: Arbetslivsinstitutet. Stockholm: TCO.
Rovde, O. (2004) *Vegar til samling. Norsk lærarlags historie 1966–2006. [Roads to unification. The history of Norwegian teacher unions 1966–2006].* Oslo: Det Norske Samlaget.
Sahlgreen, G.H. (2011) Schooling for money: Swedish education reforms and the role of the profit motive. *Economic Affairs* (October). Oxford: Blackwell Publishing.
— (2015) *Real Finnish Lessons. The True Story of an Education Superpower.* Surrey: Centre for Policy Studies.
Schwerdt, G., and Wuppermann, A.C. (2011) Is traditional teaching all that bad? A within-student between-subject approach. *Economics of Education Review.* 30(2): 365–79.
Sejersted, F. (2006) *The Age of Social Democracy. Norway and Sweden in the Twentieth Century.* Princeton: Princeton University Press.
Semi, R. (2013) Common ground on class size. *American Educator.* Spring.
Simola, H. (1993) Educational Science, the State, and Teachers. Forming the Corporate Regulation of Teacher Education in Finland. In Popkewitz, T.S., ed., *Changing Pattern of Power, Self Regulation and Teacher Education Reform.* New York: State University of New York.
— (1998) Decontextulizing teachers' knowedge: Finnish didactics and teacher education curricula during the 1980s and 1990s. *Scandinavian Journal of Educational Research* 42(4): 325–38.
— (2005) The Finnish miracle of PISA: Historical and sociological remarks on teaching and teacher education. *Comparative Education* 41(4): 455–70.
Simola, H., Kivinen, O., and Rinne, R. (1997) Didactics closure: Professionalization and pedagogic knowledge in Finnish teacher education. *Teaching and Teacher Education* 13(8): 887–91.
Simola, H., Rinne, R., and Kivirauma, J. (2002) Abdication of the education state or just shifting responsibilities? The appearance of a new system of reason in constructing educational governance and social exclusion/inclusion in Finland. *Scandinavian Journal of Educational Research* 46(3): 247–64.
Simola, H., Rinne, R., Varjo, J., Pitkänen, H., and J. Kauko (2009) Quality assurance and evaluation (QAE) in Finnish compulsory schooling: A national model or just unintended effects of radical decentralisation? *Journal of Education Policy* 42(2): 163–78.
Söderström, M. (2010) Wage scales and centralized bargaining: A binding constraint on the wage-setting? *Applied Economics Letters* 17(3): 247–50.
Søreide, G.E. (2006) Teacher union and teacher identity. *Nordisk Pedagogik* 28: 193–203.
Stokke, T.A. (2002) Conflict resolution in the Nordic countries. *Transfer: European Review of Labour and Research* 8: 670–87.

Strath, A. (2004) *Teacher Policy Reforms in Sweden: The Case of Individualised Pay*. International Institute for Educational Planning, UNESCO.

Svensson, T., and Öberg, P.-O. (2002) Labour market organisations' participation in Swedish public policy-making. *Scandinavian Political Studies* 25(4): 295–315.

Telhaug, A.O. (1993) Et typisk Hernes-år. In *Skolen 1993–1994. Årbok for norsk utdanninghistorie*. Selskapet for norsk skolehistorie.

(2005) *Kunnskapsløftet – Ny eller gammel skole. Beskrivelse og analyse av Kristin Clemets reformer i grunnoplæringen*. Oslo: Cappelen Akademisk Forlag.

Telhaug, A.O., Mediås, O.A., and P. Aasen (2004) From collectivism to individualism? Education as nation building in a Scandinavian perspective. *Scandinavian Journal of Educational Research* 48(2): 141–58.

Vabo, S.I. (2000) New organisational solutions in Norwegian local councils: Leaving a puzzling role for local politicians? *Scandinavian Political Studies* 23(4): 343–72.

Vlachos, J. (2011) Friskölor i förandring. In J. Hartman, ed., *Konkurrencens konsekvenser. Vad händer med svensk velfärd*. Stockholm: SNS Förlag.

Volckmar, N. (2008). Knowledge and solidarity: The Norwegian social-democratic school project in a period of change, 1945–2000. *Scandinavian Journal of Educational Research* 52(1): 1–15.

West, A., and A. Ylönen (2010) Market-oriented school reform in England and Finland: School choice, finance and governance. *Educational Studies* 36(1): 1–12.

Wiborg, S. (2009) *Education and Social Integration. The Development of Comprehensive Schooling in Europe*. New York: Palgrave MacMillan.

(2013) Neo-liberalism and universal state education: The cases of Denmark, Norway and Sweden 1980–2011. *Comparative Education* 48(2): 407–23.

(2015) Privatizing education: Free school policy in Sweden and England. *Comparative Education Review* 59(3): 473–97.

Wiborg, S., and K.R. Larsen (2017) Why school choice reforms in Denmark fail: The blocking power of the teacher union. *European Journal of Education*.

7

Teachers' Unions in Japan

The Frustration of Permanent Opposition

Robert W. Aspinall

Introduction

The political history of educational development in Japan has much in common with Western nations, but it also has distinctive features of its own. Following the Meiji restoration of 1868, Japan's leaders embarked on a modernisation programme that consciously looked to the West for its inspiration and for practical models. A second period of Western-inspired reform followed Japan's defeat in World War II. This was a more democratic political settlement that allowed for real pluralism, including the formation of independent teacher unions.

In 1947, local unions came together to form a national organisation, the Japan Teachers Union (JTU). Although initially well supported by ordinary teachers, the JTU was frustrated in its efforts to have an influence on education policy by political and statutory constraints far more restrictive than those found in comparable advanced, democratic nations. Locked out of the central corridors of power, teachers' unions instead relied on the threat of disruption or non-compliance in schools to block education reforms they were opposed to. They had considerable success in pursuing this strategy until a chronic decline in membership sapped their power at the local level in most parts of the country. This decline was made worse by a major schism in the JTU that took place in 1989 and by the collapse of its main parliamentary ally, the Japan Socialist Party, in the 1990s.

Contemporary Japan's Government Structure and Education System

Japan is a parliamentary democracy with two elected chambers of its national legislature: the House of Representatives (or Lower House) and the House of Councillors (or Upper House). It is similar to the British parliamentary system in that the head of government, the prime minister, is always a member of the

Lower House. He is usually the leader of the majority party and his cabinet is also mostly drawn from the members of the two houses (Stockwin 2008). Japan is a centralised state with a national bureaucracy built on the nineteenth century French model. Japan's 47 prefectures are the heart of its local government system, but they have limited leeway in how they are allowed to interpret education policy in the course of its implementation. Large ('designated') cities like Osaka and Nagoya also have powers very similar to prefectures. Prefectures and designated cities are responsible for directly administrating senior high schools. Meanwhile, the day-to-day administration of elementary and junior high schools is conducted by smaller local government units, cities in the case of prefectures, and wards in the case of large cities. The Ministry of Education sets and peridocially revises the curriculum that must be followed by all state schools in the elementary and secondary sectors. The ministry also approves the textbooks that can be used for delivering this curriculum (although local boards of education are allowed to choose from among the limited number of textbooks that are approved).

School teachers' unions in Japan are organised at three distinct levels. The most basic unit is formed at the level of the individual school. Today there are very few schools where all teachers are members of a union. Also, two or more unions may operate at the same school. This is a continuously shifting pattern, because teachers are regularly transferred from school to school within the same prefecture, usually moving every five years or so and never staying longer than ten. School-based groups are organised together in prefectural unions. The strength of unions varies greatly from prefecture to prefecture with a small number of prefectures having almost no union representation at all. One of the pecularities of the Japanese system is that unions are only legally recognised at the prefectural level. This legal conceit puts them in a weak position because the abilities of prefectures to determine or reform employment conditions is highly constrained by regulations decided in Tokyo; a level of administration where unions have no legal right to even be consulted. They also do not have the right to strike or the right to collective bargaining. Teachers' unions have compensated for this lack of access to central state power by a strategy of non-cooperation at the local level with policies they disagree with. Education bureacucrats at both the local and national levels are often reluctant to give their support to policies the unions do not like because of fear of the disruption that may be caused at the implementation stage. In this area the Japanese social norms of consensus-building and harmony play into the hands of those, unions and bureaucrats alike, who want to preserve the status quo.

Historical Development

The Formation of the Japan Teachers Union
The key event in the history of teachers' unions in Japan occurred in June 1947 with the formation of the Japan Teachers Union (usually refered to as the JTU

or its abbreviated Japanese name Nikkyoso). There had been earlier attempts to form independent teachers' associations before World War II, but they had been crushed by an ever-more coercive imperial state (see Marshall 1994: 105–17). Mass teacher-unionism only became possible after 1945 with the removal of coercive laws and the establishment of an American-inspired, liberal constitutional settlement. At the same time as the new constitution was established – which shifted sovereignty from the emperor to the people and made all citizens equal under the law – the Fundamental Law of Education was also passed, a document that stressed the goals of equality of opportunity, respect for the individual and the promotion of democratic citizenship. (In 2006 this law was repealed and replaced by one that placed an emphasis on teaching traditional Japanese values and love of country; see Takayama 2008b.)

The rapid growth of the new union took everyone by surprise. Within a few weeks of its inauguration in the summer of 1947, more than 80 per cent of all teachers had been enrolled. The first convention of the JTU adopted the defining goals of the new union (Duke 1973: 75). Some of these goals were concerned directly with the needs of teachers and their families as they emerged from a devastating war. The union called for the physical rebuilding of schools and houses destroyed in the bombing, combined with the establishment of living wages for all teachers. These were goals that were achieved remarkably quickly during the ensuing period of national reconstruction. Other goals that were decided upon in 1947 included anti-militarism, cooperation and solidarity with other labour unions, and the promotion of women's rights. From the start the JTU's leadership envisioned it as a 'radical political interest group exerting pressure on the government in regard not only to education but also to domestic and foreign policy problems' (Seraphim 2006: 88).

One of the most significant changes undergone by the Japanese educational workforce following the ending of World War II, was its transformation from a pro-militarist, pro-imperialist force to one that became overwhelmingly pacifist. The signature slogan of the new union that was subsequently put on prominent display at all national conferences was "Never send our children to the battlefield again!" Historian of education Benjamin Duke is very convincing in his analysis of some of the key leaders of the JTU in its early days (Duke 1973: Chapter 8). They were the product of pre-war normal schools (teacher-training colleges) that were run by the state in a highly disciplined and doctrainaire way, and when they became teachers they had all encouraged the boys in their classes to go off to war with enthusiasm and patriotism. When many of their former pupils failed to return from their overseas postings, and when Japan was defeated and occupied by a clearly much stronger enemy, these teachers experienced a combination of anger and guilt: anger that they had been decieved by their political and military leaders; and guilt that they had played a pivotal role in sending so many young people to their deaths. They therefore wholeheartedly welcomed the reforms of the Occupation period (1945–52) and the total abolition of the imperial army and navy, and applied themselves with determination to the task of building a teachers' organisation that would ensure the catastophic mistakes of the past could not be repeated in the future. Duke's analysis helps explain why so many ordinary teachers, who had been so obedient to government authority during the wartime and pre-war eras, so readily joined a union which adopted a confrontational stance to the post-war government.

Confrontation Between Government and Union Under the '1955 System'

Teachers' unions in all democratic states ally themselves with other unions and political parties in order to further their interests and to pursue shared goals (Cooper 1992: 6, Moe 2011: Chapter 9). In the case of Japan, unions found themselves exluded from influence in the corridors of power for much of the post-war period. Between 1955 and 1993, Japan was governed exclusively by one political party, the Liberal Democratic Party (LDP). The LDP is an ideologically conservatiave party which can be pragmatic and consensus-seeking in government. It is similar in many respects to the Conservative Party in the UK and the Republican Party in the USA. Like these parties, it has often followed policies that have led to confrontation with labour unions. During this period (which has been refered to as the '1955 system' after the year when the LDP was formed), the second largest party in Japan was the Japan Socialist Party (JSP), which was supported by labour unions. The Japan Teachers' Union was one of these, and in addition to campaigning for improved pay and job conditions for its members, was also deeply involved in the political struggle of the time. This occurred for two distinct reasons: first the JTU sought to protect the rights of all unions from attack by the LDP government; and second as a progressive educational force it sought to preserve the gains of the Occupation-era education reforms from government efforts to reverse some post-war changes and turn the clock back to a more ideologically conservative past. In the words of Okada 'the JTU found itself pushed into a defensive position as it struggled to guard the Occupation reforms' (Okada 2012: 56). In order to further its aims, it developed very strong ties with the JSP. Although the law forbade political activities by teachers, the JTU and JSP cooperated at the local level to work around the law by use of front organisations, informal contacts and the use of retired teachers (Aspinall 2001: 158–61). In fact the JTU was one of the most important vote-gathering organisations for the JSP. In return, the JTU virtually wrote the education policy position of the JSP, and relied on JSP Diet members to oppose legislation that the union did not like.

Even with the help of the Socialist Party, however, the JTU was very limited in its direct influence on national policy-making. This was due to two states of affairs: first, the JSP was kept firmly out of office by the dominant LDP until 1993; and second, the Ministry of Education refused to invite any representatives from the JTU to any of its policy-making or advisory bodies. The highly centralised nature of the education system made this a very frustrating time for the national union. The JTU, however, was able to indirectly block many reforms that it believed posed a threat to its interests. Leonard Schoppa describes its national strategy as a three-step process. First, the union sought to convince the public that education was a special, 'sensitive' issue requiring a higher standard of democracy than mere majority rule in the Diet. Second, it would then move to demonstrate that the government had failed to win a more-than-majority consensus on a particular issue. Finally, the JTU and its allies worked to persuade at least some members of the government or the governing party that if they pressed on with an 'unpopular' policy, it would damage the government's legitimacy (Schoppa 1991: 159–62). In the 1970s, a proposed probationary year for new teachers was dropped as a result of this kind of opposition. In addition to this, at the school level the threat of disruption by large, militant local unions put a break on some reforms during the 1950s and 1960s. One example of this was union resistance to the 'teachers' efficiency rating plan' that lasted from 1957 to 1959 (Thurston 1973: 207–8). The JTU was unable to prevent the plan from being brought into force, but they were successful in rendering it meaningless in almost all schools. In order to avoid disruption most principals simply gave all their teachers top grades for their performance (Marshall 1994: Chapter 7). The ability of the JTU to successfully block reform, but its inability to sponsor reforms of its own, brought about a situation of stalemate in Japanese educational policy in the period leading up to the 1980s.

Nakasone's Education Reform Proposals
Yaushiro Nakasone was prime minister from 1982 to 1987 and made education reform one of the main goals of his period of office. He believed that efforts to reform education in the 1970s had been hampered by the Ministry of Education's inertia and reluctance to sanction radical change, and he therefore decided to set up his own Ad Hoc Council for Education Reform (AHCE) that was separated from both the ministry and its official advisory organ, the Central Council on Education (CCE). The AHCE was established in 1984 and received extensive media coverage. Since Nakasone had fought and won the 1983 general election campaign on a platform of education reform, and since there was broad public support for many of his proposals, he was confident of success. What happened next, therefore, is an important case study of the difficulty of achieving substantial reform of the modern Japanese education system.

The main reforms proposed by Nakasone and endorsed by the AHCE can be categorised as falling under two headings: 'old issues' i.e. those that have been the subject of widespread debate since the Occupation era; and 'new issues' i.e. issues that came to prominence in the 1970s and 1980s. For Nakasone the two most important old issues were reform of the rigid '6-3-3' system of six-year elementary schools followed by three-year junior high schools and three-year senior high schools (he was especially interested in proposals to establish six-year secondary schools), and a return to moral education that would emphasise

Japanese values. The most important new issues were 'liberalisation' of the system (i.e. allowing more choice for parents and students, the deregulation of textbooks, and more variety within the curriculum) and 'internationalisation' (i.e. increasing the ability of the system to prepare Japanese young people for greater interaction with foreigners).

The best analysis of Nakasone's failure to achieve substantive education reform was written by political scientist Leonard Schoppa (Schoppa 1991). In his study, Schoppa clearly identifies the abililty of the JTU and its allies to block reform. Divisions within the ruling camp also hampered the development of an effective reform programme. The AHCE itself, as well as some of its key sub-committees, was divided over important issues. There was also a serious bureaucratic rivalry between the Ministry of Education – which wanted to retain its power and its budget – and the Ministry of Finance (and to a lesser extent the Ministry of Trade and Industry), which wanted a leaner, less centrally regulated and more economically responsive education system. Reformers called for prefectures and cities to be allowed to 'develop fully their diverse identities' (Schoppa 1991: 236), but they were unable to overcome the Ministry of Education's insistence that it would still be responsible for maintaining 'certain minimum standards' throughout the nation. In practice, the power to decide what counted as 'minimum standards' remained with the central ministry, which retained the power of veto over any educational innovations the localities might attempt.

Before it was dissolved, the AHCE issued four major reports which included about 500 different recommendations for education reform. Nakasone's supporters, however, were unable to control the implementation of these recommendations, and so the actual tangible change that was achieved in the day-to-day running of schools and colleges was minimal in the short term, and only slightly better in the medium term. The only three major accomplishments of this reform effort were the following: first, the enforcement of respect for the national flag and anthem; second, internationalisation policy (especially related to improving English language education by bringing foreign assistant teachers into the classroom); and finally, the privatisation of national universities (which was not implemented until 2004). The first and third of these reforms were opposed by teachers' unions, but their efforts to block implementation were eventually overcome. (The JTU only has a very small number of members in the tertiary sector but it opposed university privatisation in order to lend support to unions in that sector and in order to prevent the establishment of the precedent that public educational institutions can be privatised.) Political scientist Keith Nitta argues that the mixed results of Nakasone's reform efforts show the strength of Education Ministry bureaucrats and LDP nationalists, who were also able to block reforms that were aimed at deregulation and liberalisation and were put forward by business interests (Nitta 2008: 29–30). The Ministry of Education was always going to fight attempts to reduce the power it held over Japan's schools.

The JTU's Road to Division

At its peak, in 1958, 86 per cent of school teachers in Japan were members of the JTU. From then on there was a gradual but persistent decline until, in 1985, national newspaper headlines announced that the membership had dropped below 50 per cent for the first time. One of the main long-term causes of this decline was the unwillingness of new teachers to join the union. Union leaders have blamed this on government anti-union indoctrination during initial teacher training, but it was also clear to some of them that the JTU's image as a politicised organisation involved in long-running confrontation with the authorities was alienating upcoming generations of teachers who had no memory of the wartime excesses of a dictatorial and ultranationalist government (Thurston 1989). Moderate and pragmatic members of the union's national governing body, the Central Executive Council, realised that there were serious consequences of the history of confrontation with the government and so a search began for ways to end the conflict. The challenge facing the moderates was how to do this without opening themselves up to charges of betrayal from those who regarded any watering down of the union's traditional militancy as surrender to the enemy.

The news, in 1985, that membership had dropped below the 50 per cent mark came at the worst possible time for the JTU. It coincided with two more developments that were perceived as threats to the union's existence as a strong, independent organisation. First there was Prime Minister Yasuhiro Nakasone's Ad Hoc Council on Education (AHCE), discussed above, which many union leaders saw as another attack on the JTU and an attempt to impose right-wing values on the education system. Second, there was the process of labour unification, the aim of which was to unite all Japanese unions – those in the public sector as well as those in the private sector – into one giant labour confederation. The resulting organisation, the Japanese Trade Union Council (Rengo), would inevitably be to the right of the existing public sector federation, the General Council of Japanese Trade Unions (Sohyo), and therefore aroused the suspicion of left-wing trade unionists.

Although the JTU's national leadership regarded themselves as the national representatives of teachers throughout Japan, any decision about national policy made by the JTU's Central Executive Council in fact had no binding authority over the prefectural unions. When the national leadership decided to affiliate with the new labour confederation Rengo, they were opposed by about one third of the rank-and-file members. Instead of following their leaders and joining Rengo, they formed a rival national organisation, the All Japan Council of Teachers and Staff Unions, known as Zenkyo. This new national union at once affiliated itself with the National Labour Union Alliance (Zenroren), the new, militant, alternative confederation to Rengo that had links with the Japan Communist Party. Teachers' unions at the prefectural level were now faced with a clear choice. Throughout November and December 1989, local union conferences voted on their future. Some voted to stay with the JTU and thus affiliate with Rengo, while others voted to go the other way and side with the breakaway teachers' union Zenkyo and thus affiliate with Zenroren. A further, important development was the creation in many prefectures of new parallel organisations set up by the losers of the prefectural vote. After the schism, prefectural unions that supported the JTU claimed a membership of about 430,000, while Zenkyo affiliates claimed 210,000. These are national figures and it must be remembered that the effects of the schism were far from uniform across Japan – with some prefectures dominted by JTU, a smaller number by Zenkyo, and others evenly split between the two rival organisations.

Realignment of Unions and Political Parties After 1989

The JTU and its New Strategy of Compromise

The post-schism JTU, at the national level, has consciously abandoned its old policy of confrontation and has, since 1989, pursued a policy of compromise with the government and the ministry. The details of this change of direction can best be observed by an examination of two post-schism developments. One gives an insight into the JTU's strategic and long-term goals, while the other reveals its short-term change of tactics vis à vis the Ministry of Education. First, in 1994, the union commissioned a special committee to draw up and publish a far-reaching review of its entire structure and *raison d'être*. This committee was named the Twenty First Century Vision Committee, and it published its final report in April 1995. Second, and as a logical consequence of this report's recommendations, the union's national conference approved a list of major policy changes in September of the same year.

The Twenty First Century Vision Committee report called for a new national consensus on education. It declared that the existing system was over-centralised, and that therefore local autonomy should be developed, along with the creation of a local educational Ombudsman system. The weakness of the JTU's negotiating position at the national level made its support for increased local autonomy rational, from its point of view, since this would increase its influence in those prefectures and cities where it had a strong presence and/or the ear of sympathetic local politicians. Echoing the recommendations of Nakasone's AHCE, it also called for an increased emphasis on the independence and creativity of children, and on their role as 'global citizens'. Indeed, JTU moderates empahsised those areas of policy where the union position was not far removed from government proposals, and used this stance to criticise the Zenkyo stance of outright resistance to all reform. Completely absent from the JTU report was any of the left-wing political rhetoric that had characterised many of the comments of earlier union leaders and policy-makers, especially those of the 1940s and 1950s, when ideological warfare between government and union was at its height. This reflects a recognition by the leadership that the ideological rhetoric of the immediate post-war period was no longer resonating with new entrants to the profession who had been born long after the war was over. As Thurston notes in his 1989 paper, 'most [new teachers] do not have negative attitudes towards the educational policies of the Ministry of Education and therefore see little reason for [the JTU's] opposition to them' (Thurston 1989: 201). If teachers saw the JTU getting into fights with the government over ideological or political issues, rather than standing up for their interests as professionals, then they saw little incentive to join the union and pay its fees.

As soon as the Twenty First Century Vision Committee report was published, it became clear that its spirit of modernisation and compromise was out of step with existing union policy on many issues. It was therefore inevitable that there would have to be a major review of this policy at the next national conference. In spite of the absence of the many left-wing members who had gone to join Zenkyo, the JTU's 1995 conference was the scene of heated debate about the strategic and tactical consequences of the Twenty First Century Vision Committee's recommendations. Concerns were voiced that the union was abandoning its fundamental principles. In the end, the modernisers had their way and the union's position of opposition and non-cooperation with the government on five key issues was changed to one of compliance. The union dropped its opposition to the following: first, to the Ministry of Education course of study guidelines (which effectively made up a national curriculum for Japan's schools, usually renewed every ten years); second, to the role of the school principal as the teachers' manager; third, to the newly qualified teacher training system; fourth, to the new 'teacher responsibility' or *shunin* system (which allowed some teachers to receive extra pay for extra responsibility); and fifth, to the compulsory flying of the national flag and singing of the national anthem at school entrance and graduation ceremonies, which some saw as a throw-back to Japan's imperialist past (Aspinall 2001: 120–3). It is undeniable that the union's previous policy of non-compliance over the first four of the above issues had made it very difficult for school boards and local boards of education to adapt to the changing needs of the education system. Even taking into account the fact that opposition would have varied in intensity from school to school and prefecture to prefecture, there is no question that the union policy of obstruction would have slowed down any educational changes or initiatives that were being pursued by the government or local boards of education.

Before 1995, the intensity of the ideological struggle between government and the JTU at the national level meant that every new initiative that came from the Ministry of Education – whether it related to teacher training, school management or the reorganisation of teachers' responsibilities – was immediately distrusted by the union because of its potentially anti-union implications. New teacher training measures were distrusted because they were viewed as methods to indoctrinate new teachers. This suspicion has its origins in the pre-war and wartime Japan when normal schools (i.e. teacher training colleges) were run directly by the central government and were designed to instil militaristic and ultranationalist ideas into future teachers (Marshall 1994: 141). School management reform which gave more powers to the school principal was distrusted because it was seen as a threat to the democratic decision-making of the weekly teachers' meeting in which all full-time teachers participate and in which all the main business of the school is discussed. In schools with a strong unions presence, these meetings can be used to push union policy rather than government policy (Rohlen 1983: 230). School principals and vice-principals in Japan are not allowed to be members of a union, and although they are all former teachers, the JTU sees them as agents of the local government bureaucracy and does not want to see them granted extensive management powers. Finally, the 'teacher responsibility' system was distrusted because it was seen by the old JTU as a form of 'divide and rule'. The belief was that if some teachers were paid more for extra responsibilities (taking charge of career guidance for example) then these posts could be used by unscrupulous managers to promote non-union teachers and punish union members by not promoting them. The decision to end opposition to these measures by the largest techers' union in Japan, therefore, potentially opened the door for real reform to be implemented at the school level.

The continuation of anti-union rhetoric by many LDP politicians after 1995, however, was frustrating for modernising JTU leaders, as was the continued refusal of Ministry of Education bureaucrats to meet them to discuss reform. The sad consequence of this continued suspicion and lack of trust has been the failure of teachers and government-level bureaucrats to come together to share ideas about how schools could adapt to the changing needs of Japanese society and its children. In the post-war period, the refusal of government policy-makers to even meet with union teachers or their representatives drove discourse about how to improve Japanese schools into two parallel worlds. In one world, teachers consulted with other teachers as well as academics who specialise in educational issues – often at union-sponsored events. In the other, bureaucrats talked to a range of people, some of whom had expertise in education and others who did not. An example of the first of these worlds is the JTU's National Educational Research Conference which has been held every year since 1951. After the schism occurred in 1989, Zenkyo organised its own national conference to duplicate the existing arrangements. At these conferences, thousands of teachers come together for a three-day period to discuss every possible issue that could affect teachers as professionals and educators. From the present author's own experience attending some of these meetings and consulting the documentation that is produced, it can be noted that the vast majority of the sessions that occur during the three-day period are related to practical matters about how to improve teaching and about how to deal with serious problems like bullying and violence in schools (Aspinall 2001: 129–30). Although prefectures and cities arrange professional development sessions at the local level, the central government does not organise a similar national-level event. Thus the unions are the only organisations in Japan that sponsor regular events on this scale that allow teachers from different parts of the country to meet in order to improve educational performance. The missed opportunity here is that the participants in these meetings are not consulted by government-level policy-makers living in their own world. When Nakasone formed his AHCE in order to shake the bureaucrats out of their inertia, for example, he put together a team of 25 people that included only one (non-union) teacher (Schoppa 1991: 219–22). The clear risk that the JTU's leaders were taking in leading the union in the direction of compromise was that the ministry might refuse to enter into meaningful negotiations and continue to make education policy without discussing its implications with teachers or their representatives. In its critics' eyes this would render the union irrelevant.

Collapse of the Japan Socialist Party and the Realignment of Parties Following the 1994 Electoral System Reform

In the early to mid-1990s there were external developments taking place that undoubtedly hastened the JTU leadership's move towards a policy of compromise and made it more likely that the majority of the membership would acquiesce. Since its creation in 1947, the JTU's fortunes have always been closely tied to those of the Japan Socialist Party. Indeed, under the '1955 system', the JTU was the largest or the second largest public sector union, and the JSP was the largest opposition party in the Diet. Schoppa saw them as the two most dominant elements of what he termed 'the progressive camp' (Schoppa 1991). In the early 1990s, the rise of new parties and the disillusionment felt by many voters with established political parties led to an ending of the '1955 system' in Japanese politics (Stockwin 2008: Chapter 5). This was signified in 1994 by the controversial decision by the JSP to go into coalition government with their arch rivals, the LDP. To the great surprise of many observers, Socialist Party chairman Tomiichi Murayama became prime minister. The JSP leadership judged that joining with the LDP was the lesser of two evils when the alternative was an alliance with some of the new party leaders and their radical conservative views. Once in office, however, Murayama as head of government found it expedient in the space of a few days to pronounce complete reversals of JSP policy regarding the Self Defence Forces, the Japan-US security treaty, the sending of Japanese security forces beyond the shores of Japan, and official recognition of the national flag and anthem. It was difficult for JSP members and supporters to see what they were getting in return for these policy U-turns. By the time of the October 1996 House of Representatives election the situation had deteriorated to such an extent that the JSP only managed to win 15 seats. Six years earlier it had held 136 seats in that House.

The JSP-LDP coalition had a major impact on the JTU's policy of party support. During the period 1994–96, a series of overtures were made by the LDP towards the union, something that would have been unthinkable under the '1955 system'. Ryutaro Hashimoto became the first LDP prime minister ever to show open support to the union when he sent a congratulatory message to the JTU's annual Education Research Meeting in February 1996. JSP Diet members were suspicious that the LDP's motives were purely concerned with enlisting the cooperation of the JTU at election time. This was a natural concern given the introduction of a new election system for the House of Representatives in 1994. This replaced a system of large multi-member districts with a combination of 300 single-member districts and a series of regional proportional representation (PR) districts. Since the JSP was only fielding candidates in 80 out of the 300 single-seat constituencies in the 1996 election (the first one to be held under the new rules), it meant that the JTU would have the option of endorsing candidates from other parties in the remaining 220 constituencies. Since, at that time, the JSP was in a coalition government with the LDP, then it was a fairly logical step for the union to support candidates from that party. The very notion that the JTU could endorse an LDP candidate, however, showed how drastically things had changed in the brief period between 1989 and 1996.

The rapid collapse of the JSP after 1993 was accompanied by the emergence of new parties and a transformation of the Japanese party system (Schoppa 2012). This chaotic period in Japan's political history saw the birth and sudden demise of numerous new parties. However, the remorseless logic of the new election system – single member district systems always punish smaller parties – made it inevitable that two large parties would come to dominate the new system. In spite of some scares and many defections, the LDP was able to hold onto its position as the dominant party of the centre-right (Aspinall 2006: 76–7). On the centre left, a major new party eventually emerged, the Democratic Party of Japan (DPJ), which was founded in 1996 and gradually grew in power and influence until it captured the reins of power from the LDP in 2009. This party was clearly to the left of the LDP in its ideology and policies, but it carried none of the Cold War, socialist baggage of the JSP. It's programme had something in common with developments that were taking place in left-of-centre parties in other advanced democracies like the Democratic Party under Bill Clinton in the US or 'New Labour' under Tony Blair in the UK. Like them, it was less dependent on labour unions for support than its predecessors. Union support for individual DPJ candidates had to be negotiated locally on a case-by-case basis (Hyde 2006). Although there was a significant group of Diet members with strong links with public sector unions including the JTU, an inevitable tension arose between them and other DPJ politicians (some of whom were defectors from the LDP) who wanted to avoid the image of a party that was too close to the unions.

Zenkyo and the Continuation of the Strategy of Confrontation

Since the JTU's schism in 1989, Zenkyo has maintained its identity as a left-wing 'class conscious' union acting as the standard bearer of the traditions of post-war militant teacher unionism (Aspinall 2001: 127-9). It has therefore condemned the JTU for its 1995 policy U-turns, actions which it regards as surrender to the enemy. Zenkyo has also maintained the post-war tradition of involving teachers' unions in the broader struggles of the Japanese Left. Zenkyo set out its own positive policy proposals in a 'draft charter on essential rights of teachers and staff' published in 1995. It reaffirmed the right of teachers to get on with their jobs without interference from above. The charter re-emphasised the traditional concern of many Japanese teachers of the immediate post-war generation about the dangers of authoritarian control of education by the government. Opposing central control is also a policy that strengthens the hand of the union in prefectures, cities and individual schools where it has a large and active presence. Actually there is little in the wording of the charter that the post-schism JTU would disagree with. However, the JTU's decision to end its opposition to ministry course of study guidelines shows that it is not so absolute as Zenkyo in its resistance to 'directions from above'.

Zenkyo and Zenkyo-affiliated prefectural unions do not officially endorse the Japan Communist Party (JCP) or JCP candidates. The national federation to which Zenkyo is affiliated, Zenroren, also does not officially endorse the JCP. However, most observers of Japanese unionism can see that the alignment between party and unions is strong. Williamson, for example, comments as follows. 'Although it claims to observe "the principle of independence from political parties" Zenroren is aligned firmly with the JCP' (Williamson 1994: 86). Exactly the same comments have been made about Zenkyo and its affiliated unions. It was not surprising therefore that when Mitsuru Mikami, a former president of both Zenkyo and Zenroren, stood as a candidate for governor of Tokyo in 1999, the JCP adopted him as its recommended candidate. Although the JCP welcomes electoral support, it is at least as interested in ideological support and influence, especially with teachers' organisations. Therefore, at the same time as the JTU has become more concerned with professional and educational issues stripped of their political content, Zenkyo has continued the JTU's pre-schism tradition of involving itself in national campaigns, for example against American military bases in Okinawa.

Teachers' Interests and the Ambiguous Role of Unions in Japan

Comparative studies of teacher unions in various countries have found that they usually have similar functions to unions that represent other types of worker. In a pioneering study of 14 countries published in 1992, Bruce S. Cooper found that teachers join trade unions in order to 'compete for scarce resources' (Cooper 1992: 304). Most teachers work in the public sector and so they need unions to fight on their behalf for a share of public sector expenditure as well as favourable legislation. They therefore expect their leaders to represent their interests in negotiations with those in power at the national and at the local level. As Terry Moe puts it, the union leaders 'will be special interest advocates for their members' (Moe 2011: 21). In countries other than Japan they will typically promote these interests through a process of collective bargaining.

Teacher unions in Japan, however, do not have the same ability to negotiate basic pay and conditions enjoyed by their counterparts in other advanced democratic states. Teachers in Japan are mostly employed by the local board of education and are designated as being local public officials. Like other public officials they are denied the right to strike as well as the right to collective bargaining (Araki 2002: 10–11). These rights were taken away from public sector workers in 1948, only a few months after they had been granted under the process of post-war democratisation. Both the granting of rights and their taking away were direct results of supreme commander of the Occupation forces, General Douglas MacArthur's intervention. At first he wanted to encourage labour activism as a bulwark against a resurgence of a right-wing authoritarian government. By the end of 1948, however, he and his superiors in Washington were more worried about the dangers of disruption caused by militant unions, as well as the rise of communism in Japan and other parts of Asia (Marshall 1994: 160–1). Once the changes to the National Public Service Law had been made that took away the right to strike and the right to collective bargaining, the conservatives who ruled Japan after the departure of the American-led occupiers were more than happy to keep them on the books. Thurston argues that the 'paternatlistic' and 'traditional' attitudes of bureaucrats meant that they did not see the need for collective bargaining anyway (Thurston 1973: 71).

At the national level, the Ministry of Education has refused to have any direct negotiations with teachers' union leaders since 1948 (Duke 1973: 95). The ministry only recognises teacher unions at the local, prefectural level, because this is where they are employed. (A teacher will normallly spend his or her entire career within one prefecture and will have to sit a new qualifying exam if they want to move to a different one.) The national government of Japan, however, has a huge influence on local pay and conditions because it subsidises half of all teachers' salaries and decides the number of teachers each prefecture can employ. Teacher salaries, which are seniority-based, are also effectively set according to scales decided at the national level. The refusal of the Ministry of Education to negotiate or even meet with the JTU or any other national association representing teachers, means in practice they have no direct say over pay and conditions. Efforts to appeal to international organisations like the International Labour Organisation (ILO) in order to win redress regarding this denial of trade union rights have proved unsuccessful (Ota 1993: 246–7), as have efforts to use Japan's own legal system.

One reason for the chronic decline of union membership after its zenith in the 1950s is the perception, especially among new entrants to the profession, that unions are ineffective in standing up for their interests as employees. Just before the 1989 schism, Thurston wrote that 'most teachers are no longer convinced that the benefits they receive from the union are worth the high dues' (Thurston 1989: 201). New teachers who lacked sympathy with the political or ideological agenda of the union, did not perceive a pressing need to join a union for reasons of rational self-interest. This was true in the 1980s when there was only one national union to opt for. After the schism had taken place, new teachers were offered a stark choice about where to place their allegiance. Zenkyo, the breakaway union called for teachers to join its ranks for the traditional ideological reasons of the founders of the original JTU. In contrast the reformed, mainstream union promised the benefits of a more pragmatic approach in its dealings with the government. This meant, however, that if it failed to win tangible results from its policy of compromise and conciliation, its members and potential members might make an equally rational choice *not* to support it with deductions from their pay packets.

An inconvenient truth for teachers' unions in Japan is the fact that teachers' interests are mostly taken care of by factors that are unrelated – or only very slightly related – to the activities of those unions. Although at the time of the founding of the union, teachers were living in desperate, impoverished conditions, by the 1990s they were among the best paid teachers in the world, with salaries 2.4 times the national per capita income (Aspinall 2001: 48–9). Some politicians in the conservative camp supported more pay for teachers as a means of getting more support for reform (Marshall 1994: 244). Teachers also enjoyed security of employment, with sackings before the compulsory retirement age of 65 being extremely rare. These benefits accrued to teachers not due to union strength, but due to their status as permanent public employees. In rural Japan especially, teaching is an attractive profession for many young graduates.

It can also be noted here that security of lifetime employment in Japan is not confined to the public sector. During the period of economic success up to the 1980s, Japan's industrial relations were described as possesing 'three treasures'. These were lifetime employment, seniority wages and enterprise unions (Mouer and Kawanishi 2005: 48). In the private sector too, permanent employees enjoyed job security until retirement. Another factor is the health insurance and pension system in Japan. If a male worker is sacked then his entire family will lose their health and pension benefits. Also, the possibilities for re-employment mid-career are very poor in Japan. This means that managers are very reluctant to sack lifetime employees even when there are no unions present, or when those unions are 'collaborationist' (in the words of their left-wing critics) enterprise unions. Instead of laying off current workers, companies in dire economic straits cut down on the number of new hires. This feature of the employment system in Japan, which is backed up by long-established labour legislation, has been identified as a major cause of the lack of flexibility of Japanese corporations in international competition. It is a system that worked very well during the catch-up phase of Japan's post-war economic growth, but many now believe it is in serious need of an overhaul. An LDP-sponsored attempt in 2003 to ease restrictions on the ability of employers to dismiss permanent employees was defeated by the DPJ and its allies in Rengo (Miura 2012: 177).

Another important difference between Japan and advanced Western democracies is the nature of the employment contract. In the US, for example, employment contracts for teachers can be highly detailed documents that outline the conditions of work for the individual (Moe 2011: 174–7). In this kind of system, the abililty of the union to influence the drawing up of the contract is clearly a major source of power and influence. Employment contracts in Japan, by way of contrast, are much slimmer, more general documents. (This is true in the private sector as well as the public sector.) Scholars who have compared the professional lives of teachers in the US and Japan have noted the very open-ended nature of the responsibilities of the latter, which are not spelled out in clearly written legal documents. Okano and Tsuchiya, for example, note that 'the professional roles and responsibilities that Japanese teachers assume are much more extensive than those of their American counterparts' (Okano and Tsuchiya 1999: 172). Lifetime employees in Japan are assumed to have a strong relationship of trust between themselves, their employers and their colleagues. In this kind of workplace culture detailed documents spelling out the duties and responsibilties of each employee are not considered necessary.

The Influence of Teachers' Unions on Education Policy

Limits on the Influence of the JTU at Local and National Levels

As well as being denied the right to strike or to be involved in collective bargaining, there are also legal restrictions placed on the political activities of public sector teachers in Japan. They are forbidden from forming political organisations or participating in them as an executive or a canvasser; that is, canvassing for votes (or signatures or donations), or displaying written documents for the purpose of supporting/rejecting a particular candidate in an election (Okano and Tsuchiya 1999: 156–7). Because of these restricitons, the JTU maintained channels of communication with its political ally the Japan Socialist Party (JSP) via various front organisations, informal contacts and the use of retired teachers. The JSP was heavily reliant on the JTU for advice on its education policy. The failure of the JSP ever to win power by itself, however, meant that the JTU could never turn this influence into direct control over policy or law-making. While the LDP was in power, teacher unions had no say on national education policy and were never represented on government-sponsored advisory or deliberation councils formed to come up with new education policy. They were denied the kind of direct access to deliberations about education reform or the pay and conditions of educational employees, that is enjoyed by some teachers' respresentative organisations in other advanced democracies, for example France (see Dobbins, this volume).

As we have already seen, this did not mean that teachers' unions had no influence over policy. The threat of disruption at the local level by large, militant unions put a brake on some reforms during the 1950s, 1960s and 1970s. Schoppa has analysed the way the JTU used this kind of indirect influence to resist changes that might be a threat to the union's interests. 'As a force dedicated to maintaining the post-war system of "democratic" and egalitarian education its interest lies primarily in maintaining and "substantializing" the status quo' (Schoppa 1991: 163). He adds that the JTU used threats of non-cooperation and obstruction at the school level to put indirect pressure on politicians and bureaucrats not to introduce reforms that the union did not like. As the strength of the JTU declined, its ability to project this kind of pressure also declined (Aspinall 2001: 96–8).

Although union and government were at loggerheads at the national level, obstruction and conflict were not common at the school level, even when the union's power was at its height. In the vast majority of locations, union and non-union teachers were able to collaborate effectively for mutual benefit. In his research into high schools, anthropologist Thomas Rohlen found that for all concerned 'the school, rather than the administration or the union, becomes the main focus of loyalty' (Rohlen 1984: 145). School principals and vice-principals are not allowed to join a union in Japan, but their desire to preside over peaceful and cooperative centres of learning means they will also do anything they can to avoid conflict within the school (Rohlen 1983: 219). This helps explain how even with very bad relations between union and government at the national level, the important educational work done at the school level was usually uninterrupted by political conflict. Since much of the 'conflict' at the national level was rhetorical and symbolic it did not get in the way of the delivery of what was, by comparative standards, a high standard of education for the vast majority of the population. Few doubt that this contributed greatly to Japan's remarkable economic growth during much of the post-war period.

The JTU and its Strained Relationship with the DPJ

Following the victory of the Democratic Party of Japan (DPJ) in the 2009 general election, the JTU was able to gain at least some access to national-level policy-makers. Unfortunately for the union, Japan's first real experience with a government that was under the control of a major party other than the LDP proved to be very disappointing. Beset by the incompetence and inexperience of some of its key leaders, an extremely hostile media, an uncooperative bureaucracy, and the worst natural disaster to strike Japan for 1,000 years (the March 2011 earthquake and tsunami), the DPJ government lurched from crisis to crisis and was able to get very little done in terms of its reform agenda. In 2012 it suffered a major electoral defeat which brought the return of the LDP to power

(Pekkanen *et al.* 2013). The biggest disappointment from the point of view of the JTU was the failure of the DPJ during its brief time in office to reverse an earlier change in the law that required each school teacher to have their teaching licence renewed every ten years. The JTU argued that this was a means by which boards of education could put pressure on individual teachers who did not toe the line. Only time will tell if the JTU's fears here are well-founded or whether, as its proponents argue, the reform will result in an improvement in the quality of teachers in Japan. In August 2013 the JTU deleted its declared support for the DPJ from its official campaign literature. At a time of weakness and uncertainty for the DPJ, the JTU at the national level has clearly made the tactical decision to keep its options open.

Education Reform and the Lack of Union Influence Since 1990
Although it opposed changes to the teacher licence system, the JTU has supported many other proposals brought forward during the debate on education policy in the 1990s and 2000s. One of the main themes discussed during those years concerned the concept of *yutori* education (Tsuneyoshi 2004; Cave 2011). *Yutori* education can be translated as 'more relaxed education' or 'education with elbow room'. The concept is a response to the concerns that grew in the 1970s that there was too much stress, pressure and rigidity in the education system (Schoppa 1991: 49–50). The background to this was the growing sense that Japan needed to reassess its post-war emphasis on economic growth at all costs, and focus more on quality of life issues. Reforms were put in place to reduce the compulsory content of the curriculum and allow for more flexibility and choice for both teachers and students. One of the most visible manifestations of these reforms was the change from a six-day week (Monday to Saturday), to a five-day week that was introduced slowly in the years up to 2002. There was a wide consensus on this reform from all interested parties. Unions were naturally in favour because a two-day weekend would also reduce stress on teachers as well as on children, and the JTU subsequently claimed credit for this reform in its publicity literature.

In practice, the reforms involved slimming down the compulsory curriculum in order to give schools and individual teachers more choice and flexibility in how they taught. The volume of elementary and junior high school curricula was reduced by 30 per cent, with a corresponding reduction in size of the approved textbooks for all subjects. Many in the right-wing media characterised this as 'dumbing down', even though the ministry clearly stated that the new curricula were only intended to act as minimum standards, not a prescription for the entire content of school teaching. Criticism of the reforms seemed to be confirmed by the so-called 'PISA shock' of 2004 when a moral panic erupted in the media about supposed declining standards shown by Japan 'dropping' down several places in key global league tables of educational performance. A close look at the statistics revealed there was no such thing (Takayama 2008a; OECD 2012, 188–9), but the media and those who favoured a more 'back-to-basics' approach to education ignored the facts and promoted a narrative of decline and crisis. The result was a complete U-turn on the *yutori* reforms. The most recent curriculum reforms, introduced from 2010 onwards, have completely reversed the cuts in the compulsory curriculum that had been introduced ten years earlier. A rigid national curriculum with very little flexibility has been restored and official textbooks have returned to their pre-2002 size and weight.

Both the JTU and Zenkyo largely supported the initial draft of the *yutori* reforms in the 1990s. The thrust of this policy clearly benefited their members as well as being of educational value. In the 2000s they were opposed to the reversal of these reforms but their lack of access to either the Ministry of Education (which draws up the national curriculum) or the government of the day (which can issue directions to the ministry and draft education laws) meant they were reduced to watching from the sidelines. In contrast to the 'blocking power' they held during the years of the '1955 system', teachers' unions in Japan were now powerless to resist the reforms they did not like, or fight for the ones that they did. A Japanese education journalist quoted by Keith Nitta in 2008 estimated the Japan Teacher Union (JTU)'s influence over national policy as 'zero' (Nitta 2008: 42).

It should not be forgotten that some of the changes in education since 1990 have been driven by forces beyond the control of domestic actors, whether they be bureaucrats, teachers or union officials (DeCocker and Bjork 2013). One key issue is Japan's long-term demographic decline. Following the peak in 2008 of about 128 million people, Japan's population is expected to decline by about one million per year over the coming decades due to a drop in fertility rates. Japan's under-15 population fell from 35 per cent just after World War II to 13.3 per cent in 2011. On current trends, this is projected to decrease further to 8.6 per cent by 2050 (OECD 2012: 190). Unlike advanced nations with similar fertility rates in North America, Australasia and Western Europe, Japan has no large-scale immigration policies that could help rectify the imbalance between age groups. This trend has brought about an increase in the population of retirees and a decrease in the number of workers, and this in turn has confounded another serious, ongoing crisis, the gradual rise of Japan's national debt to 230% of gross domestic product by 2014, a fact that has put serious pressure on public finances. While there have been positive consequences of these changes (the most noticeable being reductions in class sizes) one clear, negative consequence has been a slight reduction in teacher pay in real terms and a lack of public investment in education compared to other OECD nations. Japanese schools in the public sector are still lacking in the kind of educational technology and sports facilities that most Western nations take for granted (OECD 2012: 201–2).

One reform initiative that failed to get off the ground in the 1980s but received a lot of attention during the 2000s was the establishment of six-year secondary schools in the public sector, i.e. the integration of three-year junior high and senior high schools. Some commentators have written about this as a major structural reform (for example, see OECD 2012: 189). However, official figures show that in 2011 there were only 32 such schools nationwide; a figure that must be compared to the 4,768 senior high schools and 10,057 junior high schools that continue separate existences within the public sector (Ministry of Education 2011). This therefore is a very limited increase in diversity within the system, with most of the country completely untouched. Both the JTU and Zenkyo are opposed to this reform because they see it as pushing selection down from the age of 15 to 12, but it is not their opposition that is key here. The obstacle that is most difficult to overcome is the administrative fact that junior high schools are organised on a city-wide basis while senior high schools are usually administered at the level of the prefecture. The amalgamation of an existing senior high school with two or more junior high schools requires the cooperation of two completely different sets of local government officials, a task which has proved extremely difficult to perform.

School choice is another area where much has been debated but little delivered so far, although this could change in the future. In the post-war system, parents were required to send their children to the nearest elementary and junior high school, and if they did not like it their only other option was private education. In 1999 the law was changed to allow local boards of education to introduce some choice for one or both of these types of school. One year later, Shinagawa ward in Tokyo became the first local authority to introduce a quasi market system for elementary and junior high schools. This pilot project has attracted much attention both inside Japan and from foreign commentators (see for example OECD 2012: 190). By 2004 this experiment had expanded to 8.8 per cent of municipalities that introduced some choice for elementary schools and 11.1 per cent of municipalities that introduced it for junior high schools (Dierkes 2008: 234). The most recent estimate for participation in junior high schools that allow some form of choice is 11.5 per cent of the national public junior high school population (Peter Cave, private communication). One of the purposes of this policy is to encourage more diversity in educational provision. One scholar, however, has concluded that 'it is not diversity in teaching approaches that the education market produces [in Japan], but rather a minute differentiation of educational offerings to target populations that remain wedded to the overall educational philosophy represented by Japanese curricula and entrance exams' (Dierkes 2008: 246).

If more choice is introduced on a larger scale, parents will need to be able to see the results of student tests in order to judge which schools are better than others. In line with other OECD countries, Japan has recently introduced national testing of scholastic ability for sixth and ninth graders. The test results for individual schools, however, have not been published officially. This is due to the desire shared by many teachers and education bureaucrats to maintain the highly valued fiction that all elementary schools and junior high schools are the same. Of course people living in a particular locality will know where the 'good' schools and 'bad' schools are located, and advertisements for houses and condominiums are not shy about boasting that a certain property is within the catchment area of such-and-such 'popular' junior high or elementary school. However, to officially recognise that some schools are better than others would be a huge step that those responsible for administering education in Japan are unwilling to take. The weakening of union opposition has removed one barrier to this step, and the Ministry of Education has announced that from 2014 onwards city boards of education may make the results of individual schools public if they so wish. It remains to be seen how many cities decide to do this.

Conclusion: The Decline of Teacher Unionism in Japan

Okano and Tsuchiya predicted in 1999 that in Japan 'the future of the teacher union movement is not bright' (Okano and Tsuchiya 1999: 172). Since then, membership figures have borne out the truth of that gloomy prediction. By 2012, the membership of the JTU had declined to about 27 per cent of the nation's teaching workforce. The figure for Zenkyo was about 7 per cent. (There are also a small number of local unions that are not affiliated to either the JTU or Zenkyo.) This means that today, more than 60 per cent of Japan's school teachers choose not to join any union or staff association. This mirrors the national decline in overall union membership, with the total figure dropping below the ten million mark in 2012 for the first time in 47 years. The JTU after 1989 tried to adapt to changing times, but many would agree with the scholar Keith Nitta who concluded in 2008 that the JTU's policy of engagement with the Ministry of Education after 1995 was 'a failure' (Nitta 2008: 42). One JTU official interviewed by Nitta about his attitude to policy that the union did not like remarked with the Japanese phrase *shikata ga nai* – 'there is nothing that can be done' – a clear sign of defeatism in the top ranks of the union (Nitta 2008: 187). The fortunes of the union might have changed if the more union-friendly DPJ had been able to establish itself as a serious party of government after its election victory in 2009. Its failure to do so has cast the JTU and other unions back into the political wilderness. Today the blocking power of teachers' unions is a shadow of its former self. However, the blocking powers of bureaucrats at both the national and local level remain strong, along with other forces of inertia in the system (like the inherent conservatism of many parents and employers). Only time will tell if genuine reforms that further the educational interests of all children in Japan can finally be implemented.

References

Araki, Takashi, 2002, *Labor and Employment Law in Japan*. Tokyo: The Japan Institute of Labor.

Aspinall, Robert W., 2001, *Teachers Unions and the Politics of Education in Japan*. Albany: State University of New York Press.
  2006, The Rise and Fall of Nikkyoso: Classroom Idealism, Union Power and the Three Phases of Japanese Politics Since 1955. In R. Kersten, and D. Williams, eds, *The Left in the Shaping of Japanese Democracy, Essays in Honour of J.A.A. Stockwin*. London and New York: Routledge.
Cave, Peter, 2011, Explaining the impact of Japan's educational reform: Or, why are junior high schools so different from elementary schools? *Social Science Japan Journal* 14(2), July.
Cooper, Bruce S., 1992, *Labour Relations in Education: An International Perspective*. Westport, CT: Greenwood Press.
DeCocker, Gary, and Bjork, Christopher, eds, 2013, *Japanese Education in an Era of Globalization*. New York: Teachers College Press.
Dierkes, Julian, 2008, Japanese Shadow Education: The Consequences of School Choice. In M. Forsey, S. Davies, and G. Walford, eds, *The Globalisation of School Choice?* Oxford: Symposium Books.
Duke, Benjamin C., 1973, *Japan's Militant Teachers*. Honolulu: University Press of Hawaii.
Hyde, Sarah, 2006, The End-Game of Socialism: From the JSP to the DPJ. In R. Kersten, and D. Williams, eds, *The Left in the Shaping of Japanese Democracy, Essays in Honour of J.A.A. Stockwin*. London and New York: Routledge.
Marshall, Byron K., 1994, *Learning to be Modern: Japanese Political Discourse on Education*. Boulder: Westview Press.
Ministry of Education, 2011, *Statistical Abstract (Education, Culture, Sports, Science and Technology)*. Tokyo: Nikkei Printing Bureau.
Miura, Mari, 2012, The Impact of Two-Party Competition on Neoliberal reform and Labour Unions in Japan. In L.J. Schoppa, ed., *The Evolution of Japan's Party System: Politics and Policy in an Era of Institutional Change*. University of Toronto Press.
Moe, Terry M., 2011, *Special Interest: Teachers' Unions and America's Public Schools*. Washington DC: Brookings Institution Press.
Mouer, Ross, and Kawanishi, Hirosuke, 2005, *A Sociology of Work in Japan* Cambridge: Cambridge University Press.
Nitta, Keith A., 2008, *The Politics of Structural Education Reform*. London and New York: Routledge.
OECD, 2012, *Lessons from PISA for Japan, Strong Performers and Successful Reformers in Education*. OECD Publishing.
Okada, Akito, 2012, *Education and Equal Opportunity in Japan*. New York and Oxford: Berghahn Books.
Okano, Kaori, and Tsuchiya, Motonori. 1999. *Education in Contemporary Japan: Inequality and Diversity*. Cambridge University Press.
Ota, Haruo, 1993, Political Teacher Unionism in Japan. In J.J. Shields, ed., *Japanese Schooling: Patterns of Socialization, Equality and Political Control*. University Park: The Pennsylvania State University Press.
Pekkanen, Robert, Reed, Steven R., and Scheiner, Ethan, eds, 2013, *Japan Decides 2013: The Japanese General Election*. Basingstoke and New York: Palgrave MacMillan.
Rohlen, Thomas P., 1983, *Japan's High Schools*. Berkeley: University of California Press.

1984, Conflict in Institutional Environments: Conflict in Education. In Ellis S. Krauss, Thomas P. Rohlen, and Patricia G. Steinhoff, eds, *Conflict in Japan*. Honolulu: University of Hawaii Press.

Schoppa, L.J., 1991, *Education Reform in Japan: A Case of Immobilist Politics*. London and New York: Routledge.

ed., 2012, *The Evolution of Japan's Party System: Politics and Policy in an Era of Institutional Change*. University of Toronto Press.

Seraphim, Franziska, 2006, *War Memory and Social Politics in Japan, 1945–2005*. Cambridge (MA) and London: Harvard University Asia Center.

Stockwin, J.A.A., 2008, *Governing Japan: Divided Politics in a Resurgent Economy*. Oxford: Blackwell Publishing.

Takayama, Keita, 2008a, The politics of international league tables: PISA in Japan's achievement crisis debate. *Comparative Education*, 44(4): 387–407.

2008b, Japan's Ministry of Education 'becoming the right': Neoliberal restructuring and the Ministry's struggles for political legitimacy. *Globalisation, Societies and Education* 6(2): 131–46.

Thurston, Donald R., 1973, *Teachers and Politics in Japan*. Princeton, NJ: Princeton University Press.

1989, The decline of the Japan Teachers' Union. *Journal of Contemporary Asia* 19(2): 186–205.

Tsuneyoshi, Ryoko, 2004, The new Japanese educational reforms and the achievement 'crisis' debate. *Educational Policy* 18(2): 364–94.

Williamson, Hugh, 1994, *Coping with the Miracle: Japan's Unions Explore New International Relations*. London: Pluto Press.

8

Teachers' Unions in Mexico

The Politics of Patronage

Christopher Chambers-Ju and Leslie Finger

In Mexico there have been severe challenges to the modernization of the public school system and the implementation of much-needed reform. The backwardness of Mexico's education sector has persisted into the twenty-first century. Public education has exhibited a jarring lack of transparency as monitoring and evaluation systems have, at least until recently, been extremely weak. The sector has displayed major teacher payroll irregularities, chronic teacher absenteeism, and patronage-based practices in teacher hiring and management. In 2014, *The Economist* reported that 13 percent of the teacher payroll – or 298,000 teachers – did not show up for work. In the state of Nayarit, a local boss of the teachers' union and his family members simultaneously held positions as salaried classroom teachers, school principals, and district supervisors – and enjoyed a sizable income stream – without performing any of the duties that these positions entailed (del Valle 2014c).

These types of practices have contributed to the low quality of public schools. National and international standardized tests show that Mexican public school students have not learned basic skills in reading, math, and science. Mexico had the lowest average score of all OECD countries in those subjects on the 2012 Program for International Student Assessment (PISA). While socio-economic status heavily influenced these results (OECD 2013), the politicization of schools has surely also impacted achievement.

The political clout of the National Union of Education Workers (SNTE) helps to account for the backwardness of public education and the inability of governments to enact significant changes in policy. Since the union was founded in 1943, SNTE has incrementally expanded its patrimonial power over the public school system. According to Max Weber, patrimonial power is

---

The authors thank Jorge Domínguez, Douglas Hecock, Aldo Muñoz Armenta, and Carlos Ornelas for their extremely helpful comments on early drafts of this chapter.

a traditional form of domination in which a leader, who is not constrained by legal-rational rules, uses his or her official power to serve personal ends (Weber 1968). Embodying the concept of patrimonialism, union leaders exerted influence over the appointment of high-level officials in the education bureaucracy, placed union loyalists in significant administrative positions in schools, and influenced teacher hiring and promotion up the salary scale. Only in 2013, after the implementation of landmark education laws that reasserted the state's authority over the education sector, were there signs that the union's political power may have reached its limits.

This chapter addresses two central questions. First, what accounts for SNTE's patrimonial power, and how did this power shape education policy? Second, how should the recent set of education reforms, which marked a significant political setback for the union, be interpreted?

We argue that the union's patrimonial power originated with the resources it accumulated through its corporatist ties to the authoritarian ruling party, the Institutional Revolutionary Party (PRI), and were used strategically by the union under democracy to maintain its power and prevent education reform. Corporatism refers to the non-pluralistic system of interest representation[1] in which interest groups receive certain inducements – in the form of monopolies of representation and legal privileges – but are subject to certain constraints, such as the need to moderate demands. Corporatism in Mexico is a case of "state corporatism," in contrast to the "societal corporatism" of Western Europe (Collier and Collier 1979; Schmitter 1974). In Mexican-style corporatism, interest organizations were created by the state and operated under the political logic of the ruling party.

The PRI's corporatist relationship with SNTE allowed the union to accumulate resources, which it maintained even as Mexico moved towards democracy in the 1990s. We use the term "resources" to refer to the material, organizational, and legal tools the union had to discipline its member base. Like teachers' unions in India, the Mexican teachers' union projected its power into the electoral arena. It could do this because it could use its resources to discipline and mobilize its base, which reached 1.2 million members by 2012. The opportunities afforded by democratization and education decentralization made the union increasingly autonomous from the PRI and positioned the union to form instrumental alliances with all three major political parties. Multi-party competition made the union's political support a valuable commodity and it

---

[1] Schmitter (1974: 93–4) defines corporatism as "a system of interest representation in which the constituent units are organized into a limited number of singular, compulsory, noncompetitive, hierarchically ordered and functionally differentiated categories, recognized or licensed (if not created) by the state and granted a deliberate monopoly within their respective categories in exchange for observing certain controls on their selection of leaders and articulation of demands and supports."

enabled the union to seek rents and patronage in the public school system, in turn reinforcing the union's patrimonial power.

Yet the union faced a significant political setback. The union's success in lobbying for influence and resources began to attract negative media attention, and revelations of the union's excesses led to a broad-based political backlash. Governments faced increasing pressure to enact major education reforms. Over time, the ruling party in Mexico – like ruling parties in Sweden, Denmark, Norway, and England – demonstrated a new willingness to challenge the teachers' union and to pursue reforms that the union opposed. New education laws were passed in 2013 that, if fully implemented, could significantly undermine the union's patrimonial power and its control over teacher hiring and promotion. While the union has not lost control over all of its resources and is by no means broken, there are signs that it is becoming a victim of its own success. This recent political reversal is theoretically important; the Mexican case sheds light on the limits of the political influence of vested interests (Moe 2015).

This chapter is organized chronologically around the union's historical development and the recent episodes of education reform that pushed back against the union's power. The first section examines the historical roots of union power and the process by which SNTE accumulated resources through its corporatist relationship with the PRI. In the next section, we discuss education decentralization in a democratizing Mexico. The case of decentralization illustrates the union's ability to influence a policy that aimed to increase administrative efficiency and weaken the union, but which ended up granting the union more access to financial resources. In the third section, we consider how the union's political strategy developed in response to greater electoral competition. Last, we examine the recent political setbacks the union experienced in 2013, and their implications for the union's capacity to influence policy in the future. We conclude with a summary of our main findings and address theoretical questions about vested interests that come out of this analysis.

The Authoritarian Roots of Union Power

The patrimonial power of the Mexican teachers' union originated in the corporatist ties that formed between the PRI and SNTE. Unlike the majority of teachers' unions in Latin America, the Mexican teachers' union was a privileged insider. It was a product of an authoritarian regime, which granted it access to ample resources. It was responsible for maintaining labor peace and supporting the electoral campaigns of the PRI, and, in exchange, it was given material, organizational, and legal tools to discipline rank-and-file teachers.

Before SNTE's founding in 1943, Mexican teachers lacked a single labor organization. During the Mexican Revolution (1910–20) hundreds of regional and local teachers' unions sprang up. Throughout the 1930s, the PRI tried in vain to bring together more than 700 teachers' unions, including two national labor organizations, into a single pro-government union (Ornelas 2008b). The Federal Law of Workers at the Service of the Union of 1938 had established that there would be one union for each bureaucratic unit and obligatory membership. However, labor leaders, particularly those hailing from communist and socialist political parties, resisted the PRI's efforts (Espinosa 1982). Militant union leaders sought to maintain their autonomy from the regime and prevent rival leaders from usurping their power through union consolidation.

In 1943 the PRI succeeded in uniting the fragmented teacher labor movement within a single, centralized union called SNTE. President Ávila Camacho (1940–46) granted SNTE a monopoly of representation, declaring that SNTE would be the only recognized teachers' union, and he ordered the secretary of finance to transfer 1 percent of the salary of every teacher directly into the coffers of SNTE's national executive committee (Ornelas 2008a: 59). Teachers were automatically affiliated to SNTE – because Camacho applied the 1938 law – and the union was given the exclusive legal right to represent all public school teachers in collective bargaining. In 1960, the 1938 law was incorporated into the Mexican Constitution as Article 123, section B (Góngora Soberanes 1999). This legal framework served as the foundation for the corporatist relationship between the PRI and SNTE.

In the years that followed, the PRI promoted the concentration of power within a pro-PRI union leadership. When the union was initially formed, various communist and socialist union leaders remained active in the teacher labor movement. However, as factional conflicts between leftist and pro-government leaders intensified, the PRI sponsored efforts to put a group of party loyalists in the union's national executive committee and to purge leftist union leaders. In 1949, a new secretary general of SNTE, Jesús Robles Martínez, centralized power within the union and reduced the autonomy of state-level union sections (Cook 1996: 64). National union leaders supported the PRI while developing their own cults of personality and political organizations that monopolized leadership positions in the union.

Dissident, leftist teachers remained in the union, however. They periodically gained influence within state-level union sections. In 1956 the dissident Revolutionary Teacher Movement (MRM) emerged in the Federal District, but this movement was quickly stifled through government repression and cooptation (Loyo 1979). During the 1980s, dissident factions came together to form the National Coordinating Council of Education Workers (CNTE), which demanded better teacher wages and union democracy. Dissidents posed a direct challenge to national union leaders, but in some cases the disruptive capacity of the dissidents had the surprising effect of benefiting national union leaders by providing them with bargaining leverage. In such cases, SNTE leaders were uniquely positioned to demobilize dissident protests through cooptation and the withholding of union finances (Cook 1996: 80).

SNTE was responsible for both articulating and restraining teacher demands. The union was a partner in education policy making. New policies were negotiated and then formalized as national education pacts. The corporatist relationship involved a national system of collective bargaining that was established on July 15, 1944 with the Federal Tribunal of Conciliation and Arbitration (Loyo 1997: 209). Every year on the Day of the Teacher, May 15, national union leaders, education secretaries, and often the president himself, announced teacher salary increases and other fringe benefits. During good times, SNTE leaders negotiated significant improvements in teacher compensation. But during periods of economic downturn, union leaders were responsible for restraining teacher demands. Throughout the debt crisis of the 1980s, the PRI pressured union leaders to support austerity in education spending, which caused stagnation in teacher wages. When national SNTE leaders restrained teacher demands, dissident leaders mobilized teacher discontent and protests ratcheted up (Cook 1996: 268–9).

The union also organized electoral support for the PRI. Within the PRI's party machinery, the union became one of the largest and most powerful base organizations. Teachers were automatically affiliated to the PRI as party members, and the union formed "political brigades" that were in charge of organizing peasants and workers during elections (Loyo 2008: 25). In addition to working in schools, teachers were campaign activists, electoral brokers, and polling station workers. National SNTE boss Carlos Jonguitud (1973–89) described teachers as "electoral plumbers" who did the PRI's dirty work during elections (Ornelas 2012: 36). To carry out this work, teachers could be "commissioned" to the union. Commissioned teachers remained on the teacher payroll, maintaining their positions as salaried teachers while their classroom responsibilities were suspended – which allowed them to work full-time as electoral brokers. Union leaders were compensated for their electoral services with political careers in the PRI; union leaders regularly became national legislators, governors, state legislators, or mayors.

Union leaders were empowered with a dizzying array of carrots and sticks with which to deliver labor peace and political support for the PRI. The ruling party delegated key administrative functions to union leaders. This practice was formalized in what became known as "mixed commissions" – governing bodies within the education bureaucracy that had an equal number of representatives from the Secretariat of Public Education (SEP) and the teachers' union. Mixed commissions operated at both the federal and state levels, and they were in charge of teacher hiring, teacher transfers, teacher promotions, teacher training and evaluation, and the selection of principals and district supervisors (Santibáñez 2008: 434–8). These commissions gave union leaders direct control over entry into the teaching profession and career advancement.

In addition to serving on mixed commissions, union leaders were also appointed to high-level positions within the SEP. For the PRI, union representation within the education bureaucracy facilitated the acceptance and implementation of controversial education policies among teachers (Loyo 1979).

For the union, this representation enabled union leaders to selectively reward union loyalty: "administrative posts were regarded as one of the 'prizes' that the union could offer to its members; these positions were incorporated into the hierarchy of positions (*escalafón*) that teachers could aspire to by moving up through the system" (Cook 1996: 79). The boundary between the union and the education bureaucracy became increasingly porous. Union leaders had strong influence over teachers' daily lives, both in schools and in terms of advancing their economic interests.

The vertical concentration of power within the union had a dark, coercive side. The union used its administrative influence to crack down on teachers, especially those sympathetic to dissident groups. During the 1980s, administrators who owed their positions to SNTE punished teachers who supported dissidents by "transferring them to less desirable and distant schools, by denying their requests for transfers, by refusing to promote them, and by giving them heavy workloads, odious committee assignments, and little support" (Cook 1996: 79). There were also widely reported abuses of female teachers by male union leaders, who demanded sexual favors in exchange for help resolving work-related problems. The union developed a mafia-like reputation. Union leaders used violence to repress dissidents during internal union elections, which regularly spiraled into full-on brawls (Rodriguez 2014: 135). The Mexican teachers' union was even suspected of ordering the assassination of political opponents. For example, SNTE was suspected of orchestrating the assassination of Misael Núñez Acosta, a dissident union leader who was murdered in 1981.

In sum, through its corporatist relationship to the PRI, union leaders gained personal power over a resource-rich labor organization. The union developed a centralized, hierarchical infrastructure that included state-level union sections and representatives in schools. State-level union sections largely followed the national union leadership because national leaders controlled the purse strings. By the late 1970s, the union had over half a million members and 55 state-level union sections (Cortina 1989: 89). The union organized all workers employed by the SEP (Gindin 2006: 41). The union projected its patrimonial power over the entire education sector.

Political Transition and the Struggle for Education Reform

Mexico's political transition towards freer elections and greater electoral competition enabled the teachers' union to deploy its resources in new ways. The tainted presidential election of 1988, in which the PRI resorted to massive electoral fraud – and even then could only narrowly eke out an electoral victory – marked the end of undisputed PRI hegemony. The ruling party began to face serious electoral challenges from both the left and the right. As opposition parties won governorships in state elections, Mexico gradually moved towards democracy.

The union responded to increasing multi-party competition by operating as a standalone political machine. In 1992, SNTE formally ended the automatic affiliation of teachers to the PRI. The union began to establish instrumental political alliances with all three major parties, depending on which party seemed most likely to win. This strategy reached its height when the National Action Party (PAN) occupied the presidency from 2000 to 2012. Despite democratic changes, the union's patrimonial power over the public school system became stronger. This section examines SNTE's political influence during this period, specifically the union's capacity to shape a major decentralization reform, its shifting political strategy, and its influence over reforms to teacher hiring and evaluation.

Decentralization

The creation of the federal Secretariat of Public Education (SEP) in 1921 began a process of centralized education expansion, which aimed to deliver universal primary education. While some states, such as the State of Mexico, Chihuahua, Puebla, and Nuevo Leon, developed their own state-level public school systems, in poorer states the federal government stepped in to expand access to public schooling. The federal government came to play a prominent role in financing and administering the public school system. By the 1970s, the federal government took over the lion's share of teacher training, hiring, and promotion, in addition to curriculum, the teacher payroll, and the construction of schools. As late as 1992, the federal government enrolled the majority of primary (71 percent) and secondary school students (65 percent) (Ornelas 1995). Even though some state governments managed parallel public school systems, most of Mexico's public schools were administered by the federal government.

Over time, Mexico's federal public school system exhibited increasing signs of inefficiency. The system was bureaucratic and unresponsive: "Payroll mistakes could be rectified only by a costly and time-consuming trip to the capital" (Fiske 1996: 17). With a complicated infrastructure and a large number of employees, the SEP duplicated tasks, officials failed to communicate with each other, and political conflicts plagued the system (Ornelas 1988). Reformist bureaucrats sought to decentralize the federal public school system in order to make it more responsive to the needs of students (Cook 1996: 90).

Yet prior to 1992, decentralization reform efforts went nowhere. Early efforts in 1958 and 1969 aimed to wrest the appointment of school principals and district supervisors from the union, but these initiatives failed due to union opposition (Arnaut 1994: 244; Murillo 1999: 38). In 1978, the federal government transferred authority to newly created SEP offices run by officials without union loyalties, in an effort to reduce the union's influence over education governance. However, SNTE resisted the policies of these new SEP officials and demanded influence over bureaucratic appointments. By the early 1980s, the union had recovered its bureaucratic representation in 40 percent of states (Fernández 2012: 76–88).

The election of President Carlos Salinas de Gortari (1988–94) gave reformers reason to be optimistic about education decentralization. Salinas was a technocrat who had served as the secretary of planning and budgeting. Shortly after taking office as president, Salinas shook up SNTE's leadership. In 1989, as mobilizations led by dissident teachers reached new heights, Salinas ordered the resignation of SNTE's longstanding boss, Carlos Jonguitud Barrios, and replaced him with Elba Esther Gordillo, who appeared to be a more tractable leader. Gordillo seemed to be in a weak negotiating position because she owed her position to Salinas, and she faced internal challenges from both the dissidents and from the old guard that remained loyal to Jonguitud (Loyo and Muñoz 2003; Murillo 1999, 2001). Because of union leadership turnover, President Salinas seemed poised to push through a major education decentralization reform.

Yet Gordillo proved to be a shrewd negotiator who gained an unexpected level of political influence. Although Gordillo was loyal to Salinas, she faced a replacement threat from the dissident factions, who threatened to depose her and foment disorder. Because Salinas did not want to lose his ally in SNTE, he was willing to negotiate a more limited decentralization reform in exchange for Gordillo's help reining in the dissidents. Indeed, in 1991 as discussions on the decentralization project progressed, protests by the dissidents ramped up. These protests strengthened Gordillo's position to broker a weaker form of decentralization, because only she was positioned to demobilize the dissidents.

In addition, the PRI did not want to lose control over Mexico's largest labor union in an increasingly competitive electoral environment. Salinas's 1988 electoral victory had been the narrowest in the PRI's history. Worse, dissident teachers could strengthen the newly formed center-left party that had come close to beating Salinas, the Party of the Democratic Revolution (PRD). As Grindle (2004a: 66) notes: "SNTE was still formidable, its membership intact, and its capacity to corral votes and mobilize labor actions still largely in place. And, with congressional elections looming in 1991, the president was well-advised not to insist on a change that would further annoy the union. Its votes were needed." The PRI's declining political support led Salinas to offer SNTE concessions in exchange for the union's acceptance of the decentralization project (Murillo 1999, 2001).

The provisions of the decentralization project were detailed in an agreement signed by the SEP, SNTE, and state governors on May 18, 1992, called the National Agreement for the Modernization of Education (ANMEB) and passed as the General Education Law of 1993. With this agreement, teacher hiring and the teacher payroll were transferred to state governments. The federal government also handed over control of pre-K, primary, normal, and secondary schools to the states. States took on responsibility for "more than 14 million students, 513,000 teachers, 115,000 administrative employees, 100,000 schools and other buildings, and 22 million pieces of equipment" (Ornelas 2000: 426). In comparison to other education decentralization experiences in Latin America, ANMEB established a relatively clear division of responsibilities between levels of government. This policy substantially expanded the role of state governments in the delivery and administration of education (Falleti 2010: 205).

However, through the decentralization reform, SNTE achieved major compromises in the area of labor relations. The primary locus of collective bargaining remained at the federal level; this meant that the national secretary of education and SNTE's national leader negotiated teacher base salaries. But at the state level there were also separate negotiations between union sections and governors over fringe benefits; these negotiations added bonuses to salary base levels. In addition, states had to recognize teachers' labor rights. They could not change the labor contracts of the education workers who were transferred from the federal education system. Through this reform, the government failed to achieve one of the primary aims of the reform, which was to split the national teachers' union up into 31 separate state-level units.[2]

A merit-pay program, called *Carrera Magisterial,* was also included in the decentralization package. This program aimed to compensate the union by including seniority and other non performance factors in its definition of merit. Within the 100-point evaluation scale, tests of teacher expertise accounted for 28 points while student performance was worth 20 (Hecock 2014: 69). Mixed commissions that had at least 50 percent SNTE representation were responsible for managing this program (Santibáñez 2008). In many states the program became a "patronage tool to strengthen the position of union leaders" (Hecock 2014: 68–9). In the years that followed, SNTE used this merit-pay program to award salary raises to teachers who were loyal to the union (Fernández Marín 2012).

The case of decentralization, then, illustrates how SNTE modified a reform that it opposed and in the process extracted major policy concessions. The PRI could not afford to lose the union's support. As a result, rather than breaking up SNTE and evicting it from the education bureaucracy, decentralization reinforced the union's national collective bargaining power and increased its control over rank-and-file teachers via the Carrera Magisterial program (Ornelas 2000). Education decentralization, which was originally intended to roll back the teachers' union's political influence, ended up strengthening it.

---

[2] Other areas of policy making that remained in the hands of the federal government included curriculum, textbooks, and vocational education. In addition, teachers in Mexico City continued to be managed by the federal government (Fernández 2012: 99; Grindle 2004b: 300).

New Partisan Alliances

The 1988 presidential election signaled the end of undisputed PRI rule. As Mexico gradually transitioned from one-party rule to multi-party competition, the union adjusted its political strategy and asserted itself as an independent political force. In 1992, Gordillo modified the union's statutes and enabled teachers to freely affiliate to any party. The union established a National Political Action Committee that invited presidential candidates from all major parties to present their education programs to the union. This committee also provided campaign finance to teachers and union leaders who became political candidates, regardless of their partisan identity. As the union distanced itself from the PRI, it found new ways to exploit multi-party competition and redeploy its organizational resources.

SNTE began to forge state-level alliances with the center-right PAN and the center-left PRD. The union negotiated separately with all three political parties, and at the last minute decided which party to endorse, in order to maximize the compensation it received for its political support (Castañeda 2011: 5). State-level union sections put in place win-win agreements whereby governors received the union's political support, and in exchange the union was given subsidies, patronage, side payments, and the ability to name secretaries of education (Santibáñez 2008). The teachers' union developed a patchwork of political alliances with different parties across Mexico's 31 states and its federal district, depending on which party seemed most likely to win.

At the federal level, SNTE began to form political alliances beyond the PRI. Although the union reformed its statutes and ended the automatic affiliation of teachers to the PRI during the early 1990s, Gordillo and a large bloc of teachers remained PRI loyalists. Gordillo was even given a high-ranking leadership position; in 2003 she became the PRI's secretary general and headed the PRI's legislative caucus.

And yet, while holding these leadership positions, Gordillo simultaneously established her own, separate, political alliance with President Vicente Fox of the center-right PAN Party in 2000. This alliance sparked criticism from influential PRI party leaders, especially Gordillo's support for Fox's controversial fiscal reform, which sought to raise revenue through a regressive value-added tax (VAT) on medicine and food (Raphael 2007: Chapter 7). In 2005, tensions escalated between Gordillo and Roberto Madrazo, the PRI's presidential candidate, and Gordillo was ousted from the PRI.

Gordillo responded by forming New Alliance, a teacher-based political party. For this she relied on the union's organizational resources and in so doing was able to get the new party onto the 2006 ballot (Raphael 2007: Chapter 9). The party consummated the separation of the teachers' union from the PRI, and it became the institutionalized expression of the union's strategy. New Alliance aimed for a modern public image; it hired professional political consultants, launched slick campaign advertisements, and used catch-all, reformist rhetoric in order to appeal to disenchanted independent voters. The party also broadened its appeal by recruiting young politicians who did not have ties to the union, including student leaders from a leading private university (ITAM). New Alliance emphasized valence issues – such as women's rights and environmental protection – in an effort to hide its special interests. It avoided taking controversial positions on education, and updated its positions when they were no longer tenable – for example, it eventually came to publicly support teacher evaluation. The party was ideologically flexible and positioned itself to serve as an ally for all three major parties.

Following the formation of New Alliance, the union displayed striking levels of political influence. In 2006, Gordillo claimed credit for delivering a pivotal bloc of votes to PAN presidential candidate Felipe Calderón, who narrowly beat his leftist challenger Andres Manuel López Obrador by 243,934 votes (0.58 percent). Although New Alliance only received 1.7 million votes (4 percent), some analysts credited Gordillo with delivering more than a million votes to Calderón, although other analysts are skeptical of Gordillo's capacity to deliver her base support to the PAN (Raphael 2007: Chapter 9). Regardless, Calderon acted as though he owed Gordillo a huge favor. He ceded high-level cabinet positions to Gordillo's political allies, including the sub-secretary of basic education, which was given to Gordillo's son-in-law.[3] SNTE's increased influence was also apparent within the legislature. It had legislative allies in all three major parties, and in New Alliance's first election, it received a significant number of seats in the lower house (Bensusán and Middlebrook 2012).[4]

The union secured substantial benefits for teachers through these political alliances. Even though the PAN's party platform called for the dismantling of the PRI's corporatist system, Fox and Calderón were unwilling to confront the union because it was a key political ally. Union leaders secured resources for teachers. In 2004, a reform to Article 25 of the General Education Law set 8 percent of GDP as the national target for education spending (Cámara de Diputados, n.d.). In that same year, total public spending on education in Mexico was 23.1 percent of public expenditure, much higher than the OECD average, which was 13.4 percent (OECD 2009). From 2000 to 2007 teacher wages increased 45 percent, while fringe benefits increased 12 percent (Raphael 2007: 320). Teacher salaries increased faster than the salaries of other unionized workers in Mexico (Santibáñez 2008).

In addition, union leaders used their political influence to extract rents. Union leaders lobbied for government contracts for supplementary education programs, like the fund for affordable teacher housing (VIMA). This program

---

[3] High-level positions in the state Social Security Institute, National Lottery, and National System of Public Security were also given to politicians who worked closely with Gordillo.
[4] For example, from 2009 to 2012, SNTE's allies in the lower house of the legislature included six PRI deputies, two from the PAN, two from the PRD, one from the PT and seven from New Alliance.

was badly mismanaged and was tapped for rents (Raphael 2007: Chapter 8). Targeted benefits were distributed to union leaders to compensate them for their political support.

In sum, the union used the newly competitive electoral environment to its advantage, forming flexible alliances with all three major political parties and mobilizing its support base in the electoral arena. As a result, the union secured benefits for rank-and-file teachers alongside patronage and rents for union leaders.

Teacher Hiring and Evaluation

SNTE's political alliances allowed the union to maintain Mexico's bizarre system of teacher hiring and evaluation. Teacher hiring was historically governed by informal, union-brokered practices, and there was no coherent system for evaluating teachers. Presidents Fox and Calderón advanced policies to reform teacher hiring and establish a system of teacher evaluation, but this was done by forming pacts with the teachers' union, allowing the union to reduce the scope of these initiatives.

Prior to democratization – and well into the 2000s – teacher hiring in Mexico was marked by patrimonial practices. Instead of hiring teachers using a merit-based entrance exam, the union was a broker within a backward system whereby public school teaching positions could be bought, sold, and bequeathed to next of kin. For retirees selling their post, part of the logic behind this system may have been to provide teachers with an informal system of social insurance.[5] The union was embedded in normal schools, where teachers-in-training sought to "buy" teaching positions in order to enter the profession. Union leaders operated as brokers who helped to connect buyers and sellers, and took a cut (Ornelas 2012). Through this system, the union regulated entry into the profession.

Union control over teaching positions led to a disorganized teacher payroll and contributed to chronic teacher absenteeism. This system allowed teachers to simultaneously hold multiple salaried teaching positions, and these teaching positions could be held in someone else's name. As the teacher payroll became disorganized and politicized, there was an increase in the number of "ghost" teachers. These were teachers "commissioned" to work full-time for the union who continued to receive their salary as a classroom teacher. Ghost teachers, who never set foot in the classroom, were difficult to detect and almost impossible to fire. Through this system, teachers who had political connections could get hired and promoted, while more qualified professionals who lacked political connections had a difficult time entering the profession. This system was diametrically opposed to one in which new teachers were hired based on merit.

---

[5] Scholars have been unable to determine when this system began. Ornelas (2012: 129) suggests that it began in the 1980s in the state of Veracruz.

Formal institutions sustained union-brokered teacher hiring practices. In 1963 the Federal Law of Workers at the Service of the State made the union officially responsible for half of all new teacher hires (Gindin 2006: 43). Following decentralization, when teacher hiring shifted to the state level, the union established mechanisms to control hiring in the states. In some states, this was done with mixed commissions, which had at least 50 percent union representation (Santibáñez 2008: 434). In others, union control over teacher hiring was explicitly enshrined in state-level collective bargaining contracts (Fernández 2012: 131).

The lack of transparency in the public school system abetted the union's patrimonial hiring practices. The SEP could not identify which teachers simultaneously held multiple teaching positions. In order to avoid exposing these corrupt practices, state governments obscured data on the teacher payroll. Data that were collected by state education bureaucracies were disorganized and incomplete. State governments were unwilling to withhold teacher salaries for absenteeism or for days that teachers spent on strike. Moreover, state governments turned a blind eye when union sections commissioned a large number of teachers to do political work, because this political work benefited these very governments. While this patrimonial system of teacher hiring was well known, the lack of good data stymied documenting it and tracking its growth.

Another way in which these traditional practices were obscured was through a weak system of teacher evaluation. Since the 1970s, there had been various external evaluations of the education system, but these met SNTE's resistance and results were kept private. Under President Salinas, Mexico began participating in the Trends in International Mathematics and Sciences Study (TIMSS), but the government refused to publish the results and TIMSS itself withheld Mexico's scores, because they were dismal (Ornelas 2004). The closest thing to a teacher evaluation was the politicized merit-pay program, Carrera Magisterial, that the union had captured (Santibáñez et al. 2007). While states such as Aguascalientes experimented with evaluation as early as the 1980s, there was no systematic, national evaluation system.

After 2000, incremental progress was made in creating a system of evaluation. President Fox's signature policy agreement, the 2002 Social Compromise for Education Quality, marked a deviation from the exclusive mode of policy making that had occurred during the PRI-era; this pact included diverse groups from civil society. However, it set diffuse policy goals and lacked an actionable agenda; it was primarily symbolic (Loyo 2008 33–4). Fox also decreed the creation of the National Institute of Education Evaluation (INEE), which was tasked with developing evaluations and achievement indicators. INEE's purpose was to make information about the performance of the education system available to the public; INEE's creation was a response to the unwillingness of previous governments to publicize the TIMSS results. This institute was created as part of Fox's mandate to implement reforms aimed at increasing transparency and access to information.

If INEE's creation encroached upon the union's patrimonial power, why didn't the union actively oppose it? Some analysts speculated that the union did not oppose the creation of INEE either because it was but one piece in a broader agreement between the union and the federal government, or because the union did not want to publicly voice its opposition to a commonsense education reform (Mexicanos Primero 2007: 26). Union opposition may have also been subdued by the fact that INEE was not independent of the SEP when it was first created, and it included a SNTE representative (Santibáñez 2008). Initially INEE was politically weak and it made little progress in the implementation of universal teacher evaluations.

Nevertheless, over time this institute developed its technical capacity to evaluate and to disseminate information. Under the Fox administration, INEE carried out the first national standardized test, ENLACE, which measured the language and mathematics performance of primary and secondary school students (INEE 2012: 18–20). Despite being a technically sound instrument, ENLACE was marked by widespread cheating and implementation problems. In some states, union sections refused to participate and only half of all students took the test (Tapia Guerrero 2013). Still, while education reform was modest during Fox's administration, the creation of INEE and ENLACE marked an important step towards more technocratic governance of the education sector.

President Calderón made a more concerted effort to reform teacher hiring and evaluation. Recognizing the union's patrimonial power, Calderón sought to accommodate the union's interests in order to push through reforms to rationalize teacher hiring and evaluation (Ornelas 2012: 17–33). Calderón signed a pact with the union, the Alliance for Education Quality of 2008, which excluded other actors, in contrast to the Social Compromise of 2002. The Alliance called for a major overhaul of teacher hiring practices, including a national competition in which new teachers were selected through a merit-based exam. On May 31, 2011, the SEP and SNTE signed another pact, the Agreement for the Universal Evaluation of Teachers and School Principals of Basic Education, which set up universal – albeit non-compulsory – teacher evaluations. The president sought to work with the union to craft a comprehensive set of policies that accommodated the union's core interests.

However, Calderón's reforms achieved limited results. Not all new teaching posts were distributed through the national entrance exam; so this reform preserved the old system of buying and selling teaching positions (Barrera and Myers 2011). Moreover, the Alliance included other concessions to the union, such as social programs for students which were delegated to the union. The development and implementation of the Alliance's policy provisions fell to another mixed commission with equal SNTE-SEP representation (Amador 2009: 16). As for evaluations, these were voluntary and would not affect teachers' labor rights – that is, teachers who performed poorly on the evaluation could not be fired. One area of progress, however, was Calderón's decree to increase INEE's autonomy. INEE was freed from political interference, the areas that it evaluated were expanded, and it disseminated more information.

The union officially signed on to Calderón's hiring and evaluation reforms, but then staged a private campaign to delay and block them. Gordillo acknowledged that teaching positions were bought and sold and demanded an end to this practice. She also understood that her public resistance to teacher evaluations was no longer a tenable position and agreed to new evaluations. At the same time, the union used a number of tactics that included foot dragging and protracted negotiations over the details of teacher evaluations in order to obstruct implementation (Martínez 2010). National union leaders surreptitiously sabotaged Calderon's reforms. They recognized that state-level union leaders had a vested interest in the buying and selling of teaching positions, and strongly opposed teacher evaluations.

There were also other major implementation problems. The national teacher entrance exam was tainted by the lack of transparency in the naming of officials to the commission responsible for administering it. Despite President Calderon's rhetoric suggesting that technical experts would be appointed, union loyalists were suspected of obtaining significant representation (Ornelas 2012: 73–4). Moreover, there were concerns that teacher entrance exams were too easy, and in 2011 there were reports that these tests were available for purchase ahead of time. There were also reports that the provision of teaching positions did not follow exam results; some estimate that in 2008 only 18 percent of open teaching positions were filled through the teacher entrance exam (Barrera and Myers 2011). Many union sections refused to comply with the entrance exams and state governments also resisted them, since they also benefited from distributing teaching positions through patronage networks. Finally, without data on the number of teaching positions in the system, the buying and selling of teaching positions continued unabated.

Efforts to advance an obligatory, in-service teacher evaluation to measure teacher performance were also blocked in the implementation stage. The union had made it clear that punitive evaluations were unacceptable. While the national union leadership claimed to have signed off on evaluations, in three states dissident union sections simply refused to be evaluated and organized protests. Teacher participation in evaluations was voluntary, and as a result it was very low. While reforms were formally put in place, they were hardly drastic and even these generated sharp union resistance.

This section has shown how the teachers' union maintained its organizational, legal, and financial resources well into the twenty-first century. After decentralization, collective bargaining remained centralized at the national level and the union increased its influence within the education bureaucracy. By forming alliances with diverse political parties, the union captured new resources through programs such as Carrera Magisterial. In addition, the union weakened decentralization and new teacher hiring and evaluation policies. Yet over time the union's political power began to face mounting challenges.

Democratic Pressures and the Limits of Union Power

After the election of President Enrique Peña Nieto of the PRI in 2012, SNTE suffered a historic political setback. Instead of advancing new policies through pacts with the union, Peña Nieto made education policy unilaterally, and he did not appoint SNTE allies to high-level positions in the SEP. In February of 2013, Gordillo was arrested and indicted for embezzling more than US$156 million of the union's finances and hiding this money in offshore accounts. Gordillo's arrest effectively ended her control over the union. Her successor, Juan Díaz de la Torre, lacked Gordillo's political know-how and was unable to discipline state-level union sections. Díaz de la Torre was in a weak negotiating position vis à vis the federal government, and was forced to accept policies – namely, a new regime of teacher evaluations – that rank-and-file teachers firmly opposed. Peña Nieto directly confronted the union in order to reassert the state's control over the education sector.

Peña Nieto pushed forward an ambitious set of education reforms, building a multi-party coalition that brought together the PRI, the PAN, and the PRD. In 2013, this coalition passed the landmark General Law of Professional Teacher Service, which directly challenged the union's influence over the education sector. Congress also amended an article of the Mexican constitution to guarantee children a right to a high-quality education (Mejía Botero 2013). In addition, the Law of INEE authorized INEE to develop a teacher evaluation program and formally separated the institute from the SEP (Ornelas 2013).

These laws established a new entrance exam for the hiring of new teachers, which was to be held once a year. This competition loosened credentialing requirements and enabled professionals who did not attend teacher colleges to compete for teaching positions. This reform replaced patrimonial teacher hiring practices with legal-rational rules (Ornelas 2014).

These laws also set up teacher evaluations that governed teacher promotions and the appointment of school principals and district supervisors. In order to remain in the teaching profession, teachers had to pass an in-service examination. Teachers had three chances to pass this exam; upon failing for a third time, they were assigned to administrative positions, or encouraged to retire early. This law laid the groundwork for the termination of the corrupt Carrera Magisterial program, which was finally ended in 2015. Carrera Magisterial was replaced with a technically sound merit-pay program that was managed by INEE. A merit-based system for promoting teachers and selecting school principals was another blow to the union's control over teachers' careers.

According to the General Law of Professional Teacher Service, teachers who were commissioned to SNTE had to be paid with the union's own finances. The law forbade governments from strengthening the union's network of political activists by granting salaried, teaching positions – that were paid by the

SEP – to union leaders who never set foot in the classroom. To be sure, after this law was passed, local authorities continued to commission teachers to the union. Yet this practice was now illegal and easier to detect. States that had teacher payroll irregularities could face an external audit, and ghost teachers could be identified and publicly shamed. Whereas before 2013 the number of teachers who worked for the union but remained on the official payroll was unknown, new laws gave the government more information.

The newly empowered INEE conducted a full teacher census, bringing together the previously disparate and disorganized state-level teacher payrolls into a single, national database. In 2014 this census revealed considerable payroll irregularities; 13 percent of teachers never showed up for work (*The Economist* 2014). The teacher payroll had a large number of teachers on it who were taking a leave of absence – because they were commissioned to work for the union, were conducting work for the SEP as pedagogical advisers, or had quit, retired, or died. Armed with better data, INEE conducted a comprehensive report on teacher hiring, teacher compensation, and teacher training. With higher quality data on the public school system, identifying gross irregularities and correcting them became much easier.

Given the union's entrenched patrimonial power, how did this recent set of education reforms occur? While it is beyond the scope of this chapter to provide a complete explanation of this turnaround, we argue that democratic pressures played a central role in creating the conditions for the union's political setback.

First, an adversarial media challenged the patrimonial practices of SNTE. Investigative journalists, including Sonia del Valle, Nurit Martínez, Lilian Hernández, Arturo Cano, Alberto Aguirre, and Ricardo Raphael, shined light into the dark spaces in which the union operated and documented corruption scandals. Journalists began to swarm union events and document the union's practices. For example, in 2008, during the depths of the global financial crisis, Elba Esther Gordillo was found to be giving away luxury Humvee vehicles to her loyal cadres, a scandal that severely hurt the union's public standing. In the context of increasing education sector transparency, Gordillo became an icon of the widespread corruption within the Mexican political class. Her lavish consumption habits, expensive plastic surgery, and impunity from legal action became well known to the public (Ornelas 2012: 51). Increased reporting of the union's excesses made it a victim of its own political success; as the union became more powerful, it also became more closely scrutinized and criticized for engaging in patronage politics.

Second, new information about the state of education in Mexico prompted widespread outrage and spurred civil society groups to mobilize. As a result of Mexico's dismal PISA results, business leaders in particular became alarmed by how low levels of human capital might affect Mexico's economic competitiveness. Most notably, in 2005 a business magnate from the media company Televisa founded a think-tank and political advocacy organization called

Mexicanos Primero. During the 2012 election year, this organization launched a popular feature film, *De Panzazo* ("Barely Getting By!"), a scathing documentary about union corruption, negligent teachers, and dysfunction within public schools, a project similar to *Waiting for Superman*.[6] Mexicanos Primero also initiated publicity campaigns and lawsuits against the continued existence of ghost teachers. As early as 2010, Mexicanos Primero demanded that the government account for the lack of transparency in the teacher payroll. During Peña Nieto's presidential campaign, Mexicanos Primero lobbied for teacher evaluations to be a central component of national education policy.

Other civil society groups also began to influence education policy. The Mexican Institute for Competitiveness (IMCO), a think-tank, began focusing on education transparency, launching a website in 2013 that allowed users to search and compare school outcomes – including student performance on national standardized tests. Mexicanos Primero, IMCO, and another organization, México Evalúa, succeeded in pushing the government to increase the amount of data from the 2014 school census that was available to the public (Fernández 2014; Zapata n.d.). Political advocacy groups with close ties to business leaders established themselves as major political forces and mobilized in response to SNTE's growing political influence.

Third, efforts to politicize education successfully turned public opinion against the union. Attacks on the union in the media eventually convinced voters of SNTE's corruption. According to surveys, while 34 percent of Mexicans thought that SNTE had a negative effect on public education in February 2010, by January 2013 this number had increased to 55 percent (Parametria 2013). In addition to the short-term effect of negative media attention, this was also likely the result of the growth of Mexico's middle class, which likely was more concerned about quality of education issues. The union's efforts to counter negative publicity and to project an image of itself as a progressive education reformer fell on the deaf ears of an increasingly skeptical public.

SNTE's tarnished reputation made association with the union a political liability. In the 2012 election, the teachers' union was unable to form an alliance with any of the three major presidential candidates. When Gordillo attempted to form an alliance with Peña Nieto, Peña Nieto backed out at the last minute. He was far enough ahead in the polls to not need the union as an ally. This late decision also gave the union little time to seek out another political ally. Eventually the union supported the New Alliance presidential candidate, who was not a significant contender. Unlike Calderón, Peña Nieto claimed a popular mandate to challenge SNTE and retake control of the education sector. Over the course of six years, the union went from being valuable coalitional partner to political pariah.

---

[6] *Waiting for Superman* is a documentary feature film from 2010, which offered a controversial critique of the US public school system, and attributed many problems to teachers' unions. *De Panzazo*, which was released in 2012, was directly influenced by *Waiting for Superman*.

But still, even at the time of this writing, questions remain regarding the extent to which the new reforms will eradicate patrimonial practices in the education sector. The federal government challenged the national union leadership, forcing it to accept teacher evaluations. But state-level union sections were only indirectly challenged, and still remained powerful. They continued to resist teacher evaluations and dissident sections mobilized significant protests (*Excélsior* 2013). State legislatures, particularly those in states where the dissidents were strong, pushed back against the federal government. State legislatures in Oaxaca, Chiapas, Michoacán, and Guerrero, passed laws to subvert INEE (Baranda 2014). More than 24,000 schools in those four states refused to allow school census officials to carry out their work (Fernández 2014: 13; SEP-INEGI 2014). While resistance died down somewhat after 2014, it has persisted in a handful of areas. In the state of Oaxaca teacher protests directed against the new teacher evaluations drew national attention in June and July of 2016 because they escalated into violent clashes with police and resulted in the deaths of at least eight teachers.

It is not only the teachers' union that has been deeply embedded within the old system of patronage politics. Other political actors – namely governors and local branches of the PRI – have also been loath to stop using teaching positions as patronage. Immediately prior to the implementation of the hiring reforms, there was a mass trading of teaching positions (Del Valle 2014a, 2014b). While the federal government signaled its commitment to a legal-rational set of education policies, parochial interests bore a high cost when they gave up patronage practices. Many state governments sought to maintain the status quo.

The extent to which these reforms will be sustained over time also remains an open question, especially since there is a protracted timeline of implementation. On May 29, 2015, an announcement to postpone teacher evaluations because of technical problems created a media ruckus and highlighted the vulnerability of these ambitious reforms – although subsequently the evaluations were said to be back on track. The political intentions of Peña Nieto and the PRI remain unclear. The PRI could seek to dismantle SNTE as an organization, in order to respond to business leaders who are an influential voice within the party. Or the PRI could simply have wanted to remove a disloyal union leader. Gordillo's arrest may have cleared the way for a new union boss to emerge, one who can rebuild the old, corporatist relationship between the PRI and SNTE. SNTE's resources remain a powerful bargaining chip during competitive elections. Moreover, the union remains uniquely positioned to contain the spread of dissident teacher protests, which continue to threaten governability.

The future of education reform will hinge on whether future governments continue to reject the union as a coalition partner. There are questions about the capacity of the federal government and the strength of the rule of law in Mexico. The federal government may have a difficult time punishing states for not complying with federal law. Moreover, the ability and willingness of state governments to crack down on teacher absenteeism and withhold the salaries of striking teachers is questionable. Given the major governance challenges that Mexico faces – narco-violence, corruption, poverty, and economic growth – education reform is likely to rank as a high, but not as a top priority. Governments may shortchange education in order to advance other, more pressing policy priorities.

Regardless of whether these reforms are sustained over time, SNTE will continue to be a resource-rich organization that is organized at the national level. The union still automatically deducts dues from teacher salaries, it has significant financial resources, and its electoral machinery is still intact. Various mechanisms of influence – like mixed commissions at the state and national levels, and centralized labor negotiations – persist. The union still controls a dizzying array of administrative functions and social welfare benefits. After the arrest of Gordillo, Peña Nieto was careful to say that he was not attacking the union, and reiterated his commitment to defending the labor rights of Mexican teachers. He continued to be mindful of the powerful dissident sections of the union that retained their ability to organize protests. The union's organizational structure is sticky, and it is likely to remain strong in the future.

Conclusion

In this chapter we traced the origins of the patrimonial power of the Mexican teachers' union and its endurance into the twenty-first century. SNTE's corporatist relationship with the authoritarian PRI allowed it to accumulate resources. These resources enabled the union to adapt to a democratic context. Once the PRI began to lose its electoral hegemony, SNTE took advantage of multi-party competition. As a coalition partner, SNTE maintained its patrimonial power and "colonized" the education bureaucracy, reproducing traditional practices that had been in place since the 1940s, while increasing its political influence (Ornelas 2012). The union blocked key aspects of education decentralization and delayed reforms to teacher hiring and evaluation.

The union's recent political setbacks give it central importance for building a theory of vested interests (Moe 2015). SNTE is an unlikely case of union decline; yet ultimately its political influence was at least temporarily exhausted. Our analysis suggests that vested interests may lose power when their excesses are exposed, and civil society groups mobilize against them. Vested interests are more secure when they pass under the radar, moderate their demands, and avoid excessive rent-seeking behavior. When they advance too quickly and push too hard, they face a political backlash. Under democratic governance, this backlash can give elected governments a popular mandate to challenge vested interests. In the Mexican case, pressure from an adversarial media and from business elites contributed to the union's political isolation and its inability to forge alliances with the major political parties. Vested interests may have an Achilles heel, in that the more their power is exposed, the easier it may be to correct the grossest policy distortions they generate.

However these conclusions are tentative and depend on whether SNTE has, in fact, been disrupted by the 2013 reforms. There are signs that these reforms only partially undermined the union's patrimonial power. If the union is able to bounce back, this would suggest that historical legacies are enduring and that, despite temporary setbacks, vested interests are resilient even in the face of democratic pressures. On the other hand, if the union has lost key resources, then perhaps vested interests are vulnerable to sudden and unexpected reversals. In this case the conditions under which these reversals are likely to occur would merit more analytic attention. Vested interests are not invincible, and a comprehensive theory calls for an explanation of both their stability over time and their decline.

References

Amador Hernández, Juan Carlos. 2009. La Alianza por la Calidad de la Educación: Modernización de los Centros Escolares y Profesionalización de los Maestros. *Centro de Estudios Sociales y de Opinión Pública*. Documento de Trabajo Núm. 74.
Arnaut, Alberto. 1994. La Federalización de la Educación Básica y Normal (1978–1994). *Política y Gobierno* 1(2): 237–74.
Baranda, Antonio. 2014. Acusan Alteración de la Ley Educativa. *Reforma*, April 16.
Barrera, Iván, and Robert Myers. 2011. Estándares y Evaluación Docente en México: El Estado del Debate. Serie Documentos No. 59. *Programa de Promoción de la Reforma Educativa en América Latina y el Caribe* (PREAL).
Bensusán, Graciela, and Kevin Middlebrook. 2012. El sindicalismo y la democratizacion en Mexico. *Foro Internacional* 52(4): 796–835.
Cámara de Diputados. n.d. Educacion. www.archivos.diputados.gob.mx/Centros_Estudio/Cesop/Eje_tematico/7_educacion.htm (accessed November 11, 2014).
Castañeda, Jorge. 2011. Amores y Desamores. *Reforma* 898, July 10. www.ipebc.org.mx/noticias/maestra_amores_desamores_castaneda.pdf
Collier, Ruth Berins, and David Collier. 1979. Inducements versus constrains: Disaggregating 'corporatism.' *The American Political Science Review* 73(4): 967–86.
Cook, Maria Lorena. 1996. *Organizing Dissent: Unions, the State, and the Democratic Teachers' Movement in Mexico*. University Park, PA: Pennsylvania State University Press.
Cortina, Regina. 1989. La Vida Profesional del Maestro Mexicano y su Sindicato. *Estudios Sociológicos* 7(19): 79–103.
Del Valle, Sonia. 2014a. Persiste Resistencia por Controlar Plazas. *Reforma*, September 4.
  2014b. Agandalla el SNTE Plazas Docentes. *Reforma*. May 11.
  2014c. Denuncian a Líder de SNTE-Nayarit. *Reforma*. November 30.
The Economist. 2014. Education in Mexico: Phantom Teachers. April 7.
Espinosa, José Antonio. 1982. Los Maestros de los Maestros: Los Dirigentes Sindicales en la Historial del SNTE. *Historias* 1, July–September: 67–101.

Excélsior. 2013. Primera Evaluación Docente se Realizará en 2015: INEE. April 11. www.excelsior.com.mx/nacional/2013/11/04/926931

Falleti, Tulia G. 2010. *Decentralization and Subnational Politics in Latin America.* New York, NY: Cambridge University Press.

Fernández, Marco. 2012. *From the Streets to the Classrooms: The Politics of Education Spending in Mexico.* Doctoral dissertation, Department of Political Science, Duke University.

———. 2014. *Censo Educativo. Radiografía del Dispendio Presupuestal.* México Evalúa: Centro de Análisis de Políticas Públicas, A.C.

Fernández Marín, S. Karla. 2012. Evaluación Docente. ¿Prueba Superada? *Perfiles Educativos* XXXIV: 57–69.

Fiske, Edward. 1996. *Decentralization of Education: Politics and Consensus.* Washington DC: World Bank.

Gindin, Julián. 2006. *Sindicalismo Docente e Estado. As Práticas Sindicais do Magistério no México, Brasil e Argentina.* Master's thesis in education, University of Río de Janeiro, Brazil.

Góngora Soberanes, Janette. 1999. Foro Libertad Sindical en México. In *El Futuro de la Libertad Sindical.* Mexico: Fundación Friedrich Ebert.

Grindle, Merilee. 2004a. *Despite the Odds: The Contentious Politics of Education Reform.* Princeton, NJ: Princeton University Press.

———. 2004b. Interests, Institutions, and Reformers: The Politics of Education Decentralization in Mexico. In Robert Kaufman, and Joan M. Nelson, eds, *Crucial Needs, Weak Incentives: Social Sector Reform, Democratization, and Globalization in Latin America.* Baltimore, MD: The Johns Hopkins University Press.

Hecock, Douglas. 2014. Democratization, education reform, and the Mexican Teachers' Union. *Latin American Research Review* 49(1): 62–82.

INEE. 2012. *INEE: Una Década de Evaluación.* México: Instituto Nacional para la Evaluación de la Educación.

Loyo, Aurora. 1979. *El Movimiento Magisterial de 1958 en México.* México: Era.

———. 1997. Sindicalismo y Educación en México: Las Voces de los Líderes. *Revista Mexicana de Sociología* 59(3): 207–35.

———. 2008. La Historia Reciente del Sindicato Nacional de Trabajadores de la Educación de México (SNTE). In *Sindicatos Dcoente y Refroma Educativa en America Latina* Konrad Adenauer Stiftung Foundation. www.kas.de/sopla/es/publications/16862/

Loyo, Aurora, and Aldo Muñoz Armenta. 2003. El Sindicato Nacional de Trabajadores de la Educación (SNTE). In *La Investigación Educativa en México 1992–2002: Sujetos, Actores y Procesos de Formación,* ed. Patricia Ducoing Watty. Mexico City: Consejo Mexicano de Investigación Educativa.

Martínez, Nurit. 2010. No Será Fácil Erradicar Venta de Plazas: SNTE. *El Universal,* June 22.

Mejía Botero, Fernando. 2013. Las Reformas al Artículo Tercero Constitucional: Hipótesis y Procedimientos Mejorables, Artículos Transitorios Pertinentes y Pendientes centrales. *Revista Latinoamericana de Estudios Educativos (México)* XLII(4): 5–13.

Mexicanos Primero. 2007. *La Creación del Instituto Nacional de Evaluación Educativa de México: Un Modelo de Institucionalidad Mixta como Experiencia*

de *Gobernabilidad en los Sistemas Educativos*. Centro de Estudios de Políticas Públicas.
Moe, Terry. 2015. Vested interests and political institutions. *Political Science Quarterly* 130(2): 277–318.
Murillo, Maria Victoria. 1999. Recovering political dynamics: Teachers' unions and the decentralization of education in Argentina and Mexico. *Journal of Interamerican Studies and World Affairs* 41(1): 31–57.
  2001. *Labor Unions, Partisan Coalitions, and Market Reforms in Latin America*. New York, NY: Cambridge University Press.
OECD. 2009. *Education at a Glance 2009*. OECD Publishing. www.oecd.org/education/skills-beyond-school/43636332.pdf
  2013. *PISA 2012 Results: Excellence Through Equity: Giving Every Student the Chance to Succeed (Volume II)*. PISA: OECD Publishing. http://dx.doi.org/10.1787/9789264201132-en
Ornelas, Carlos. 1988. The decentralization of education in Mexico. *Prospects* 18(1): 105–13.
  1995. *El Sistema Educativo Mexicano. La Transición de Fin de Siglo*. México: Fondo de Cultura Económica.
  2000. The politics of the educational decentralization in Mexico. *Journal of Educational Administration* 38(5): 426–41.
  2004. "The politics of privatisation, decentralisation and education reform in Mexico. *International Review of Education* 50: 397–418.
  2008a. *Política, Poder y Pupitres: Crítica al Nuevo Federalismo Educativo*. México: Siglo XXI.
  2008b. El SNTE, Elba Esther Gordillo y el Gobierno de Calderón. *Revista Mexicana de Investigación Educativa* 13(37): 445–69.
  2012. *Educación, Colonización y Rebeldía. La Herencia del Pacto Calderón-Gordillo*. México: Siglo XXI.
  2013. El Nuevo INEE. *Excelsior*, May 1. www.excelsior.com.mx/opinion/carlos-ornelas/2013/05/01/896827
  2014. *Mexican Educational Reform: Politics in the Frontline*. Working Paper.
Parametria. 2013. 55% de mexicanos: SNTE, negativo para la educación, February 14. www.animalpolitico.com/2013/02/72-de-mexicanos-cree-que-la-educacion-esta-estancada-parametria/
Raphael, Ricardo. 2007. *Los Socios de Elba Esther*. México: Planeta.
Rodriguez, Oscar. 2014. *La Configuración de las Relaciones de Poder: Legitimidad y Liderazgos en la Sección 20 del SNTE, Nayarit*. Masters Thesis, UNAM.
Santibáñez, Lucrecia. 2008. Reforma Educativa: El Papel del SNTE. *Revista Mexicana de Investigación Educativa* 13(37): 419–43.
Santibáñez, Lucrecia, José-Felipe Martínez, Ashlesha Data, Patrick J. McEwan, Claude Messan-Setodji, and Ricardo Basurto-Dávila. 2007. Haciendo Camino. Análisis del Sistema de Evaluación y del Impacto del Programa de Estímulos Docentes Carrera Magisterial en México. RAND Corporation.
Schmitter, Philippe C. 1974. Still the century of corporatism? *The Review of Politics* 36(1) (The New Corporatism: Social and Political Structures in the Iberian World (January)): 85–131.

SEP INEGI. 2014. Atlas Educativo. Secretaría de Educación Pública. Instituto Nactional de Estatística y Geografía. www.cemabe.inegi.org.mx/

Tapia Guerrero, Luis Arturo. 2013. *Sindicalismo Magisterial y Logro Educativo: La Sección 22 y las Secciones Institucionales del SNTE*. Doctoral Dissertation, Facultad Latinoamericana de Ciencias Sociales (FLACSO).

Weber, Max. 1968. *Economy and Society*. Berkeley, CA: University of California Press.

Zapata, Alejandra. n.d. Datos públicos del Censo Educativo. Instituto Mexicano por la Competitividad, A.C. (IMCO). www.imco.org.mx/banner_es/datos-publicos-del-censo-educativo/

9

Teacher Unions in India

Diverse and Powerful

Tara Béteille, Geeta Gandhi Kingdon,
and Mohammad Muzammil

Introduction

This chapter describes the political power of school teachers in India, and the role played by teachers' unions in influencing education reform efforts in the country. India has done well in terms of rapidly expanding access to elementary education over the past 15–20 years. Today, 236 million students are enrolled in primary and secondary schools (grade 1–10), and are taught by 8.3 million teachers. The success in improving access to elementary schools is associated with two center-state programs: the District Primary Education Program and Sarva Shiksha Abhiyan (SSA). The Right of Children to Free and Compulsory Education Act 2009 (RTE) has also aimed to make schooling available to every child aged 6–14 years.

Unfortunately, India's tremendous success in expanding elementary-level schooling since the 1990s has not been accompanied by commensurate gains in student learning (Dundar *et al.*, 2014). This is not surprising. Access-oriented reforms tend to be politically popular and relatively easier to implement, with few opponents. They provide more jobs for teachers, administrators, service personnel, construction workers, and textbook and school equipment manufacturers – tangible resources that politicians are happy to distribute to their constituencies. In contrast, quality-enhancing reforms focus on accountability and cost-effectiveness. These reforms threaten many of the entities benefiting from expansionary policies, and are therefore frequently blocked by them (Grindle, 2004).

Improving quality in government schools in India is, of course, no easy task, given that the country has the largest number of school-age children relative to any other country, many of whom are first generation school-goers. Further, there is considerable variation in the linguistic and socio-economic background of students (and their teachers), all of which combine to make teaching in government schools in India a particularly challenging task.

These challenges in improving education quality and student learning in India are compounded by low teacher accountability: schools in large parts of India suffer from high rates of teacher absenteeism, with a national absenteeism rate of 25 percent – a problem similar to Mexico, also discussed in this book (Kremer et al., 2005; Muralidharan et al., 2014). This rate has not changed much over the past ten years, despite this being the era of major school reform in India. There are few adverse consequences for absenteeism: absentee teachers get full pay regardless of whether they do any work or whether that work has any impact on student learning. Many of these teachers are protected by powerful unions or politicians, and are difficult to discipline (Béteille, 2009; Kingdon and Muzammil, 2003). To make matters worse, teachers frequently have poor subject knowledge; oftentimes, only marginally better than the students they teach (Dundar et al., 2014; Kingdon and Banerji, 2009). In many ways, the rapid pace of expansion of the past has sown the seeds of low quality for the immediate future through the recruitment of large numbers of poorly qualified teachers.

As India aims to emerge as a key player in the global economy, it cannot afford to have the majority of its schools produce students who do not have basic skills. Its schools must work. For its schools to work, teacher performance and accountability are crucial. Education reforms and policy must emphasize accountability relationships that motivate good teachers, ensure they exert effort, and that they are effective in classrooms. Likewise, it is important that it be possible to weed out teachers who are ineffective and unlikely to improve.

Changing the status quo will not, however, be easy, because teachers in India are politically powerful. Teachers' political power and ability to maintain the status quo are all the more potent because of their access to multiple channels for exercising their power. Teachers influence the wider governance environment of schooling through their unions and union leaders, especially at the state level, and possibly, in a more far-reaching way, through their direct participation in politics, i.e. as teacher legislators with a say in education-related legislation. Ultimately, as we discuss in this chapter, teachers have vested interests in the status quo, and through multiple strategies they shape the school governance environment in a manner that helps them achieve working conditions consistent with their vested interests. And this has important consequences for student learning in the country, with teacher union membership being negatively correlated with student achievement (Kingdon and Teal, 2010).

Given the complexity and chaos of the teacher union landscape in India, this chapter will focus on drawing out commonalities in the functioning of these unions instead of focusing on union-specific issues. Our task is complicated not just by the large number of unions in the country, but also the scarce literature on this important aspect influencing education reform. Although the text that follows may miss the situation in entire states because of the absence of published research, interviews with people in the field suggest these states are unlikely to provide any major new insight on the themes discussed in this chapter. The chapter begins with a discussion of the history of school education reform in India. The next section provides a snapshot of teacher unions in India today, including a brief discussion of their historical progress in the context of education policy in India. Thereafter, we examine union power and the various mechanisms and strategies through which teachers exercise their influence over education reform efforts. The final section examines the effect of teachers' political power on education reform.

Historical Context of Education Policy and Role of Teachers' Unions

Teachers' unions in India have a long history, going back to the 1890s when India was still a British colony. Indeed, teachers' unions in India predate trade unions – the first trade union in India was established only in 1920. Available evidence suggests that the Madras Association of Women Teachers, covering the Presidency of Madras, was the first schoolteachers' union in the country, set up in 1890.[1] The main objective of the union was to stimulate an interest in the art of teaching, encourage its study, and promote sociability. Records of meetings suggest that these were usually lecture meetings, where teachers learned about issues as diverse as kindergarten teaching and the life of the queen (Madras Presidency, 1893). The next union to be established was the Madras Teachers' Guild in 1895, which included both male and female teachers. The South India Teachers' Union, established in 1909, was the first federal teacher organization, while in northern India, Uttar Pradesh was the first state to establish a state-level union (Gupta, 2013). In the east, the All Bengal Teachers' Association was among the first, founded in 1921.

With less than a fifth of the school-age population in school, and a colonial government whose education policy centered on supporting the colonial regime, teachers' unions in pre-Independence India were little more than small, professional groups with negligible political power. Whatever limited literature exists on this topic suggests that teachers, who were typically natives, viewed the union as the agency to help them fight unfair treatment at the hands of colonial school managers who dismissed them at will (Shrimali, 1951). The political feebleness of unions changed in the decades following Independence.

When India gained independence in 1947, less than 15 percent of the adult population was literate. The new (Congress) government emphasized the need for schooling to spread more widely, and made elementary education a Directive Principle of State Policy in the Constitution of India (1950). Education was also put on the State List, indicating that *states* were responsible for education provision, finance and regulation – not the central government. As we will

---

[1] The Madras Presidency was an administrative subdivision of British India, which at its greatest extent included most of southern India, including the modern day states of Tamil Nadu and Andhra Pradesh and parts of Odisha, Kerala and Karnataka, and the union territory of Lakshwadeep.

discuss, this is important from the perspective of teachers, as it meant the state government would determine teacher pay and terms of employment. As with other Directive Principles, the states were encouraged to provide elementary education to citizens *but not required* to do so because the Directive Principles are non-justiciable in nature.

Education provision in India since Independence has happened through three types of schools: government schools; private-aided schools and private-unaided schools. The first two types are funded by the government; the difference being that private-aided schools are managed privately. The level of autonomy private-aided schools have in determining school and teacher policy varies by state and has changed over time. Private-unaided schools are both funded and managed privately.

This chapter focuses on teachers funded by the government; that is, teachers in government schools and in private-aided schools, since it is their organization into unions that influences education reform and interactions with the state. Of the government-funded schools, the vast majority are state government schools, whose teachers are state government employees. Although some states such as Jharkhand also have teachers who are employees of local government, these form a small minority (less than 10 percent of the teaching force across the country).[2] State governments incur approximately 90 percent of education expenditure in their state (even in schools run by local governments), of which nearly 90 percent goes toward teacher salaries. As a result, teachers tend to organize themselves into unions at the state level much more frequently than at other levels. State-level teachers' unions tend to be fairly influential politically, since negotiations on employment terms and conditions are undertaken with the respective state government, and not the central government (as discussed subsequently). This being said, there are a number of national teacher unions with state-level branches and allies. The three largest national-level unions are: the All India Primary Teachers Federation (AIPTF); the All India Secondary Teachers Federation (AISTF); and the All India Federation of Teachers' Organizations (AIFTO).

In the decades following Independence, the Planning Commission, a central government entity entrusted with formulating India's five-year plans, established ambitious target dates for achieving universal elementary education. These targets were never met, and were continuously revised throughout the 1960s and 1970s. In 1966, the Sixth Education Commission of Independent India (1964–66) set the target date as no later than 1986, but even this had to be revised. This commission (the Kothari Commission) was the first education commission to look at every level of education holistically. It laid special emphasis on the importance of teachers in schools and argued in favour of teacher remuneration and working conditions being improved, recommendations that

---

[2] Local government in India comprises three layers of elected representatives: district-level (*Janpad*); block-level (*Panchayat Samiti*) and village level (*Village Panchayat*).

were likely to prove popular with unions. But the commission also asked for teachers to use their vacation time to complete training, and expected much greater accountability – issues which were likely to prove unpopular with unions. There is, however, no documented evidence of the reaction of the teachers' unions to the commission's recommendations. Their reactions, in any case, may have been minor for two reasons. First, there were not as many unions then as there are today. Second, the commission's recommendations were made by a central government body, and therefore not binding on states, who were ultimately responsible for school education.

By the mid-1970s it was becoming increasingly clear that a strategy that relied entirely upon states to achieve universal elementary education was at best going to lead to lop-sided development, and at worst, perpetual revision of targets. In 1976, the 42nd Constitutional Amendment put education on the Concurrent List of the Constitution of India, indicating shared responsibility between state governments and the central government in education provision, finance and regulation. The amendment gave more say to the central government in the governance of school education and in school accountability. The precise nature of these reforms was not articulated until nearly a decade later. Nevertheless, state-level teacher unions resented the amendment because it would reduce their power to influence the state's education agenda should the central government decide to intervene in that state's education affairs. As a result, teachers' unions across the country went on strike. For instance, the Uttar Pradesh secondary teachers' union (the Madhyamik Shikshak Sangh (MSS)) organized indefinite strikes and waged a *Jail Bharo Andolan* ('fill the jails' campaign) in December 1977 which continued until January 1978. In fact the central government had not yet adopted policies that might endanger a teacher's privileges or require accountability, but nonetheless unions across the country went on strike.

The increasing difficulty in introducing policies as envisioned in the 42nd Constitutional Amendment – due to teacher union opposition – continued through the 1980s. The report of the National Commission on Teachers (NCT, 1986) notes that the school governance environment created by teachers' unions and their political connections served to avert the proper use of teacher accountability measures. The commission rued the fact that union-backed teachers did not fear adverse repercussions if they were lax in their work. It also noted (NCT, 1986) that some school principals

> lamented that they had no powers over teachers and were not in a position to enforce order and discipline. Nor did the District Inspectors of Schools and other officials exercise any authority over them as the erring teachers were often supported by powerful teachers' associations. We were told that that there was no assessment of a teacher's academic and other work and that teachers were virtually unaccountable to anybody.

In 1986, the central government formulated the National Policy on Education, which set the stage for it to play an increasingly important role in elementary education by defining concrete steps. To carry out the policy the central government initiated a series of grant programs (known as centrally sponsored schemes) to assist states with the development of basic education. Even though the financial contribution of the center was small, it was strategic in that it influenced the policies of many state governments. The states most influenced were those under fiscal pressure – such as Rajasthan and Madhya Pradesh, which were among the poorest Indian states. The goals of these schemes were to expand and improve the quality of school education through two means: (1) improving school infrastructure; and (2) hiring more teachers. Both goals were in the interest of teachers, but implementation was poor, and in 1992 the national parliament approved an updated National Policy on Education which sharpened priorities for girls' education and for improved quality in education. It also emphasized the need for an integrated and decentralized approach to developing primary education systems, with a focus on building the capacity, responsibility and authority of local governments, known as the Panchayati Raj institutions.

The New Education Policy 1992 arrived against the backdrop of two important events. First, following the Jomtien Conference on Education for All in 1990, governments across the world, including India, vowed to intensify efforts towards meeting the basic learning needs of all children. Second, in 1991, the Government of India undertook a series of national structural reforms and fiscal adjustments to open up the economy. The reforms were precipitated by a balance of payments crisis, leading to bail-outs from the International Monetary Fund and loans from the World Bank, all conditional on the government undertaking measures aimed at improving fiscal discipline. The consequences for the social sector, including education, were important. The reforms in this area emphasized cost-effective interventions, as typified by the first externally financed project to improve education access and quality: the District Primary Education Program (DPEP). Part-financed by the World Bank, the European Union and the United Kingdom's Overseas Development Assistance, DPEP emphasized five key points: school infrastructure; in-service teacher training; decentralized school management; locally recruited teachers; and increased monitoring of dropout rates and student learning. The project was initially adopted in four states, but subsequently rolled out to 15 of the country's largest states.

There is little evidence to suggest that teachers' unions – whether at the national level or state level – were systematically consulted by the central government over the design and implementation of DPEP. This is in contrast to most developed countries, but also in contrast to the other developing country studied in this book, Mexico. With a history of top-down planning, heavy bureaucracy and a highly stratified social structure, the central government was unlikely to have felt that teachers needed to be consulted on the policies that applied to them. Teachers were expected to implement reforms and policies that had already been decided. There was nothing unique to the ruling

Congress Party about this top-down approach; as we will go on to describe, the Bharatiya Janata Party (BJP) government adopted the same approach several years later vis à vis the unions. As a study looking at the participation of teachers' organizations in education policy in the 1990s in India notes, there was no mechanism for automatic consultation between teacher unions and the government on education-related issues, such that unions were necessarily involved. When consultations did take place they tended to be ad hoc rather than part of a regular and professional exchange of views and opinions between government and unions (Frederiksson, 1999). Unions were sometimes asked to nominate members to sit on committees organized by national- and state-level organizations such as the National Council of Educational Research and Training and National University of Educational Planning and Administration concerning curriculum development, the code of professional ethics, teacher training, and so on. But this was only token involvement – carried out so that the government could claim that all key stakeholders had been consulted.

The story was different at the state level. In individual states, teachers' unions attempted to actively block aspects of the reforms proposed by DPEP – more specifically, aspects related to democratic decentralization and the hiring of local teachers. In Madhya Pradesh, where the impact of democratic decentralization on the school system was tremendous, the *Janpads* and *Gram Panchayats* were given administrative control of primary schools.[3] Teachers became employees of *Janpads*, rather than state governments. Policymakers believed that the *Panchayats* would protect the community's interests and monitor the school system more effectively because they were locally elected bodies representing the people (Sharma, 1999). Locally hired teachers were also expected to be more responsive to the needs of schools and their communities. As a result of the reforms there were dramatic changes in the contractual arrangements, working conditions and recruitment policies for teachers. The state government sought, over a period of time, to replace all regular primary schoolteachers – all of who were on "contracts for life" – with *shikshakarmis* (local education volunteers). New recruitment of teachers would be restricted to the *shikshakarmi* cadre. Relative to the regular cadre of teachers, *shikshakarmis* were less qualified, requiring only education up to the higher secondary level in order to teach in primary schools. Furthermore, they were hired on a contract for ten months each year and paid a basic stipend, approximately a tenth of the salary paid to regular teachers. Although there was discussion of putting well-performing *shikshakarmis* on regular contracts, the specifications of how and when this would happen were left vague by the government (Sharma, 1999).

The first set of protests against the *shikshakarmi* policy in Madhya Pradesh came from disgruntled teacher-applicants, who instituted legal cases challenging

---

[3] *Janpad* is the elected district-level of local government. *Gram Panchayat* is the elected village-level of local government.

the whole policy. The main complaint was that the new recruitment policy violated the fundamental rights enunciated in Article 16 of the Constitution. Article 16 emphasizes the principle of equality of opportunity for all citizens in matters relating to employment or appointment to office under the state, and lays down that no citizen can be ineligible for state office on the grounds of religion, race, caste, sex, descent or *place of birth*. Since the *shikshakarmi* recruitment procedure aimed to hire local candidates, from the *Panchayat*'s catchment area, it violated a citizen's fundamental rights. These applicants demanded the expansion of the catchment area for recruitment, which meant that the "local teacher" aspiration of the reforms would not be realized. Shortly thereafter, *shikshakarmis* formed their own union and began agitating for better service conditions, followed by a demand for regular jobs with wages equal to those of other (regular) teachers. They held demonstrations, meetings and took mass leave (Sharma, 1999). Burdened with litigation and teacher union pressure, the state government eventually redesigned the policy, making concessions on local recruitment and qualifications.

DPEP led the way for the Government of India's flagship program for universalizing elementary education, SSA. Similar to DPEP, it was a centrally sponsored scheme, with the central government providing the majority of funding in the first ten years. In these ten years, SSA was essentially an expansionary program, with states building more schools and hiring more teachers. Although there was an emphasis on quality, this was understood mainly in terms of more school inputs and more teacher training, support and supervision. Student learning was assumed to flow automatically from investing in inputs.

As with DPEP, teachers' unions were not systematically consulted in the design or implementation of SSA by the central government, now led by the BJP. And similar to DPEP, unions were much more active at the state level, with unions in states that were recruiting contract teachers demanding that the quality of the teaching force not be diluted by recruiting poorly qualified and low-cost contract teachers; and contract teacher unions in turn demanding regularization of the contract teaching force and invoking "equal work, equal pay".

In some states, as with Madhya Pradesh, the stance taken by the state government favored the contract teaching force; however, this was not true in all states. In Rajasthan, also an early adopter of the contract teacher scheme, the state government decided in 2008–09 to abolish the *Vidyarthi Mitra* scheme (similar to *shikshakarmi*, *Vidyarthi Mitra* literally translates to "student's friend" and is a contract teacher who is paid considerably less than a regular teacher, and not required to have the same qualifications). Subsequently, a handful of *Vidyarthi Mitra*s filed a petition in the Rajasthan High Court against the state government's decision. The court ruled in favor of the state government, declaring the scheme illegal, and as of 2014 no new recruitments have taken place under the scheme (Ramachandran *et al.*, 2015).

As SSA was being implemented, in 2002, the central government (still under the control of the BJP), passed an amendment to the Constitution making education a fundamental right; the state would henceforth guarantee education to all students aged 6–14 years, and make a greater allocation from the budget towards education. The amendment specified the need for legislation to describe the mode of implementation through a separate Education Bill. The Central Advisory Board of Education prepared the draft bill in 2005 (then under the control of the Congress Party), but the bill went through several iterations before finally becoming an Act in 2009. These iterations resulted from concerns and protests on a number of fronts, especially among civil society organizations and teachers' unions. Unions at the national level played an important role in giving the Act its current shape.

There was both independent lobbying by unions, and by unions organized under the National Coalition for Education (NCE), formed in 2002. The NCE was the official representative of the global campaign for education in India, and brought together four major national-level teachers' unions – AIPTF, AISTF, AIFTO and the All-India Association for Christian Higher Education – two civil society organizations, and a group of parliamentarians (the parliamentary forum on education) in order to campaign in support of issues related to education in India.[4] Ostensibly formed to campaign for education, the NCE's own membership was divided on two specific aspects of the bill: decentralization and teacher accountability (Grant, 2010). Teachers' union members far outnumbered other members, often giving them a much louder voice which they directed towards protecting their own interests and gaining a number of concessions in the RTE Act relating to accountability. As we will discuss subsequently, these relate to the role of school management committees (SMCs) in demanding accountability. Measures relating to student learning, for which teachers could have been held accountable, are strikingly absent.

Teachers' Unions in India: Characteristics, Interests and Strategies

There are several hundred unions for schoolteachers in India. While some are registered with the state government or central government, others are not. The consequences of *not* being registered from the perspective of union power are unclear. For instance, in the state of Rajasthan, no teacher union is registered. Yet the state government grants teachers two days' annual leave to attend union meetings (Ramachandran *et al.*, 2015).

At the time of writing, there was no centralized database to help estimate the number of teachers' unions operating in the country. In terms of type, broadly, most unions fall into categories defined by the following characteristics: geographical level (national level, state level and district level); school

---

[4] The NCE's main areas of focus included campaigning for the Right to Education Act, and, more recently, for including under the provisions of the Act children aged 0–6 years and 15–18 years.

TABLE 9.1. *Union Membership in India (%)*

	% member of union
National	2
State	27
Local	16
Not member	55

Source: Kremer et al. (2005)

level (primary, secondary and higher secondary); school type (government, private-aided and private-unaided); teacher contract type (regular teachers on permanent contracts and contract teachers on fixed-term contracts); and miscellaneous (subject teachers, special needs, and so on). States vary considerably in terms of the types of unions found. For instance, in Rajasthan, different levels of school have different unions, but there is also a general union, the Rajasthan Shikshak Sangh, which takes up common issues on behalf of all teachers. In West Bengal there are multiple unions for teachers in primary schools.

When looking at the number of teachers' unions and their range, it would appear that there is a teacher union to cater for every taste. Not all teachers, however, are members of teachers' unions. In fact, across India's 29 states and seven union territories, less than 50 percent of teachers are union members (Table 9.1), although, as will be discussed later, numbers vary by state. This is not surprising given that union membership is not compulsory. Furthermore, non-fee paying members can free-ride on many of the benefits that unions provide, such as lobbying for salary increases.

The majority of union members reported membership of a state-level union. Even though many teachers choose not to be members of unions, those who do are often members of multiple unions regardless of political ideology.[5]

Not being a union member does not mean a teacher will not support a union's stance. Similarly, being a fee-paying member of a union does not automatically mean that the teacher is actively involved in union activities. A recent study looking at teachers across India asked each teacher how active he/she was in teacher union activities, conditional on being a union member.[6] Only 18 percent of union members reported being very active, which was defined as attending at least one event/meeting per month. Approximately 36 percent said they were nominal members; that is, they paid their fees but did not attend events. A fifth reported attending fewer than two events in the past year. There are several reasons for such low participation rates. First, union leaders and

---

[5] The survey question was such that teachers could only choose one level of membership. In reality, they could be members of multiple unions at different levels.
[6] The data from the study reported here have not been formally published by the researchers, Karthik Muralidharan and Aakash Mohpal. We thank them for providing these statistics.

India: Diverse and Powerful

union activity tends to be concentrated in urban areas, suggesting that a large number of teachers do not have regular access to unions due to geographical distance. Second, teachers with little interest in union matters may be coerced into paying union fees given the 'public good' nature of the outcomes of union-led agitations.

Regardless of the reasons for their membership of a union, teachers believe unions will help them. As Figure 9.1 shows, when asked whether unions in three states (Rajasthan, Karnataka and Madhya Pradesh) helped teachers – regardless of their party affiliations – between 50 percent and 92 percent agreed that they did benefit from union support (Béteille, 2009). Likewise, union leaders believe they can rally teacher support when needed, whether those teachers are union members or not.

A recent study in Uttar Pradesh supports the above finding – showing that teachers seek help from their unions, and in large numbers (Kingdon and Muzammil, 2013). For instance, 44 percent of private-aided schoolteachers sought help from the teacher union at least once; and nearly 30 percent have sought help twice or more. Government schoolteachers are about 14 percentage points less likely to seek help from the union than the private-aided schoolteachers.

Of the national-level teachers' unions, the three mentioned previously (AIPTF, AISTF, and AIFTO) have been especially prominent over the years concerning issues relating to teachers and education reform. The first and largest, AIPTF (three million members), was established in 1954. Its first conference was inaugurated by India's first prime minister, Jawaharlal Nehru, and being a socialist state at the time the need to improve the working conditions of

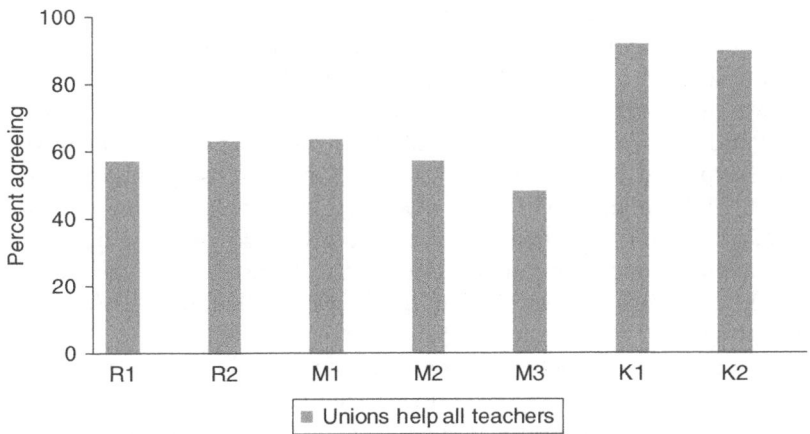

FIGURE 9.1. Unions Help Teachers Regardless of Party Affiliation
Source: Béteille, 2009. R1 and R2 are districts in Rajasthan; M1, M2 and M3 in Madhya Pradesh; and K1 and K2 in Karnataka.

teachers was widely accepted. The explicitly stated objectives of the AIPTF relate to improving the status of teachers and the quality of education. AISTF resembles AIPTF in its objectives. Its membership is 850,000 – less than a third of that of AIPTF – and is roughly proportionate to the number of schoolteachers at the secondary level. AIFTO, established in 1976, and with a membership of 1.2 million, is the only union that explicitly discusses in its charter the importance of professionalism in teaching, and the need for performance standards for teachers. As will be discussed in the next section, even though these unions support the notion of improving the quality of education, practice suggests they often oppose or jeopardize efforts to improve student performance. Importantly, none of them are explicitly organized along party lines in the sense that they do not consistently or visibly support any one political party.

All three national-level unions have state-level affiliates or branches – but not in all states. As a result, none of them are national federations in the true sense, and lack the kind of power that state-level unions have (whether affiliated with the national-level unions or not). This is partly understandable, since school education is primarily financed and regulated by state governments – notwithstanding the 42nd Constitutional Amendment and the RTE Act. There is much more to be gained in terms of a favorable employment contract by being powerful at the state level rather than at the national level. Even though national-level unions have played some role in the formulation of the RTE Act, as discussed below, the implementation of the Act is at the state-level and hence dependent on the support of state-level unions.

Although there has been little research on the internal structure of teachers' unions, it is unlikely that all members in a given union subscribe to the same point of view on important policy matters. Indeed, many of the larger unions at the state level are known to have internal factions. For instance, in 1972 Om Prakash Sharma won the union president election for Uttar Pradesh's secondary schoolteachers' union, MSS. Om Prakash Sharma was from Meerut District and was supported by the western districts of the state. His opponent, Maheshwar Pandey, who was defeated heavily in the election, was from the east and was supported by the eastern districts. Pandey subsequently formed a new group of MSS, called MSS (Pandey Group). There were two more splits in this union, as a result of which there are now four factions of the same union: the Sharma Group, the Pandey Group, the Thakurai Group and the Chandel Group. Similarly, in West Bengal, the All Bengal Teachers Association split multiple times, but into separate unions.

Although the number of teacher unions at the state level has grown consistently over the past few decades, there are huge variations across states in overall membership rates, with some states reporting under 10 percent membership, and some over 75 percent. What is important to note is that even when the number of teachers' unions in a given state is large – as in Punjab (26 unions) and Rajasthan (152 unions) – there are only a handful (typically between two

TABLE 9.2. *Teacher Responses on the Three Most Important Issues Their Unions Should Engage in*

Agenda item that trade union should undertake	% of teachers
Salary increment	24.7
Timely payment of salary	14.9
Insufficient number of teachers	8.3
Non-cooperation from parents/guardians	8.2
Deployment of an extra teacher	7.8
School infrastructure	6.7
Facilities	6.1
Training	5.4
Work environment (pension, holidays, etc.)	4.9
Transfer and promotion	4.9
Non-teaching activities	4.8
Teaching and learning materials	2.2
Non-cooperation from pupils	0.9
Other	0.1
Total	100

Source: Aslam *et al.* (2011)

and five) that are influential in terms of their organization, demands and threat potential.

State-level unions fight on similar issues to the national unions, and seek to protect their members' employment and working conditions. For instance, in Rajasthan, unions push for the following set of issues: making teacher pay and other benefits comparable with central government employees; securing additional benefits for teachers in rural areas; opposing the training of teachers during vacations; transparency in teacher transfer policy; and on matters relating to the involvement of teachers in non-academic activities (Ramachandran *et al.*, 2015). An analysis of teachers' unions lobbying in Uttar Pradesh over the past 50 years found that teachers fought exclusively for pay and service-related issues (Kingdon and Muzammil, 2013). A recent study in rural Bihar and Uttar Pradesh found that salary-related issues dominated the list of items that teachers felt their unions should engage in (Table 9.2). In Madhya Pradesh, teachers' unions went on strike between December 2012 and February 2013 in pursuit of demands that teachers be paid the same, regardless of whether they were government employees or contract teachers. In Odisha, the focus of teacher union campaigns has been lobbying for regular pay increments and restructuring the criteria for promotion (Ramachandran *et al.*, 2015).

An important feature of the teacher union landscape is that teachers' unions in India generally do not align themselves formally or permanently with any political party – unlike the situation in countries such as the United States or Germany where unions tend to align with liberal or left-wing parties. Instead, teachers' unions in most states have taken advantage of the political wave running through their state at election time, without permanently committing themselves to any political ideology or affiliation. As the chapter on Mexico suggests, the absence of formal allegiance with any particular party means teachers' unions can exploit the electoral weaknesses that parties may be facing. The exception is West Bengal, where there is a long history of leftist governments and where there is, in consequence, a somewhat different pattern of interaction between unions and political parties.[7] Although teachers' unions in the state are explicit about not backing or being backed by any political party, newspaper reports and general perception suggest otherwise. Chakravarty (2010) further notes from her own interviews with union officials that specific unions tend to be linked with specific parties. While the Communist Party of India (Marxist) backs the All Bangla Teachers' Association and All Bangla Primary Teachers' Association, the Sara Bangla Associations have the support of the Revolutionary Socialist Party. The Congress and Trinamul Congress reportedly backs the West Bengal Teachers' Association. The Headmasters' Association has members and followers of all ideologies, except that of the Communist Party of India (Marxist). The Bengal Primary Teachers' Association, which the media sees as being controlled by the Socialist Unity Center of India, calls itself anti-government. Utpal Ray, general secretary of the All Bengal Teachers' Association, asserts in an interview with Chakravarty that their teachers campaign on behalf of election candidates from the party that backs their association (Communist Party of India (Marxist)).

According to office bearers of the associations, political parties play no role in funding of teachers' unions, with the annual contributions of the members being sufficient. Additionally, unions publish examination question papers that also help raise money for the working of the union. Chakravarty notes that none of the unions were particularly forthcoming on what role the party actually plays, though interviews suggest the party dictates the level of forcefulness that the particular union adopts when making a certain demand. For example, if the municipal board is run by the opposition party, the level of aggression with which a demand is made differs from the situation where the board is run by the same party that backs the union.

The effectiveness with which unions are able to achieve their objectives depends upon their power, which in turn depends upon their political influence and the strategies they adopt. In general, teachers' unions in India do not have the kind of formal processes of contract negotiations with the government that exist in countries such as the United States. As a result, they adopt a number of indirect, though often coercive, mechanisms to achieve their goals. These

---

[7] Kerala is the other Indian state to have been ruled by Left parties historically, but the authors were unable to find literature on teachers unions in the state.

mechanisms can be categorized broadly into the following: (1) representation in the Upper House in the state; (2) election-time credible threats; (3) organized strikes; (4) court cases; and (5) direct involvement in politics.

Representation in the Upper House in the State

Seven states in India – the most populous ones – have an Upper House (Legislative Council).[8] This influences the nature of teacher politics in the state in an important way, since teachers at the secondary level of education (or higher) have guaranteed representation in the Legislative Council of the State Legislatures, as per the Constitution of India. The representation of (non-government) secondary schoolteachers in the Legislative Council of a state government is ensured by Article 171(3c) of the Constitution of India which provides that "as nearly as may be, one twelfth shall be elected by electorates consisting of persons who have been for at least three years engaged in teaching in such educational institutions within the State, not lower in standard than that of a secondary school, as may be prescribed by or under any law made by Parliament." Such representation is a direct outcome of teachers being traditionally revered for being learnèd and interested in the public good.

Not only can teachers jointly choose a twelfth of the members of the Upper House, a select category of them can also stand for election. In general, public sector employees who receive a salary from the government are disqualified from being elected as a member of the Lower or Upper House (Article 102 and 191(a) of the Constitution of India). But this condition does not hold true for teachers in the private-aided schools. In Uttar Pradesh, India's most populous state with 204 million people (nearly two-thirds the population of the United States), the combination of these provisions and a large private-aided school sector have allowed teachers to amass considerable political power. Approximately 45 percent of all secondary and higher secondary schools in the state are private-aided schools, and following Government Acts in 1971 schoolteachers in such institutions have been paid salaries directly from the state treasury and are de facto paid government employees – even though, by law, they are not deemed to be so. Thus, unlike government schoolteachers (and other government employees), private-aided schoolteachers can contest elections to the Lower House and the Upper House. This is important because it is in the State Legislature that laws regulating and governing education in the state are drawn up.

The consequence of such legal privilege is that approximately 17 percent of the membership of the Upper House in Uttar Pradesh comprises teachers – a high proportion given that teachers constitute only about 0.6 percent of the

---

[8] Andhra Pradesh, Bihar, Jammu and Kashmir, Karnataka, Maharashtra, Telengana and Uttar Pradesh.

adult population of the state. An average of 6.6 percent of the Lower House has been made up of teachers in the post-Independence period (Kingdon and Muzammil, 2013). This is a large enough proportion to exert substantial influence in legislative matters, including matters pertaining to the education sector and those that affect teachers' pay and working conditions.

There have been several attempts to abolish the guaranteed representation of teachers in the Upper House. The Chief Election Commissioner of India – in a letter to the law minister in 1965 – had suggested the abolition of teacher constituencies for election to state Upper Houses since "apart from there being no justification for singling out the teaching profession for special treatment, it seems to me undesirable that teachers should be dragged into party politics in this manner." The matter was also considered by the central government on seven occasions between 1957 and 1979 but there was no change in the status quo. Finally, in the early 1990s, a report of the Central Advisory Board on Education (CABE, 1992) stated:

the nature and extent of politicization of teachers through involvement in elections in the context of the constitutional provision for their representation in Legislative Councils came up for discussion in various aspects. An apprehension was expressed that extending voting rights to elementary (school) teachers would further aggravate the situation. The sufferers would be the children in particular and the elementary education system in general. Such a situation would not be in accordance with the spirit of the provisions of the Constitution [...] The Committee, therefore, is of the opinion that there is no need to retain the present provision of separate constituency for teachers in Legislative Councils.

While it expressed universally negative views about teacher representation on the Legislative Councils, CABE's recommendations have never been carried out. Thus, the special status of teachers that is afforded by the Constitution continues.

Election-Time Credible Threats

Teachers are able to make credible threats to politicians' fortunes ahead of, and on, polling day (Béteille, 2009). Teachers are important well before polling day for at least two reasons: (1) they can undertake informal campaigning work in the village community, and (2) they can influence the votes of family and friends. Regarding the first, Béteille (2009) notes widespread consensus among teachers in Rajasthan and Madhya Pradesh that they were well-positioned to undertake informal campaigning duties. Teachers, typically educated and high-caste, can create an environment in villages in favor of a politician; or conversely, they can damage the reputation of his/her opponent, given the low levels of literacy in many villages.

Additionally, teachers sometimes organize villagers' attendance at election rallies (Béteille, 2009). Note, however, that government schoolteachers, being government employees, are prohibited from formally campaigning in support of any party. That being said, Béteille's survey of approximately 2,400 government schoolteachers shows that in every district involved in the study, between 8 and 28 percent of teachers agreed that politicians used teachers, unofficially, as part of their campaigns.

Even if teachers do not actively campaign to sway villagers, Béteille (2009) argues that teachers are particularly attractive to politicians on account of their sheer numbers – they form the largest proportion of the government's employee base. Béteille notes:

> If each teacher influences the voting outcome of at least ten people from amongst his family and friends, it adds up to a sizeable amount for a constituency. Take the case of the state legislative constituency R2 Block in Rajasthan.[9] In the 2003 state elections, the winning candidate won with 38,304 votes, the runner up got 37,297 votes. The margin for victory was only 1,007 votes. R2 Block, and where the district headquarters for R2 are located, has approximately 2,000 government schoolteachers. If every teacher could influence even five votes, this would add up to almost ten times the margin required for victory.

Another study in Uttar Pradesh found that a remarkable 46 percent of all teachers (and 72.5 percent of private-aided secondary school teachers) said they discussed among themselves who they would vote for in an election and then voted for that candidate *en bloc* (Kingdon and Muzammil, 2013). Among those who say they vote *en bloc*, 53 percent of all teachers (and 68 percent of private-aided secondary school teachers) say their union motivates which way they should vote. Thus, many teachers' political/voting behavior seems to be dictated by their identity as teachers rather than being based on individual-level considerations such as personal political beliefs and values, how the party manifestos might affect their families, or indeed caste-based considerations. These results suggest that teachers, particularly in the private-aided and government school sectors, vote to elect candidates they believe will support teacher interests.

Teachers' political power also derives from their role on polling day (Béteille, 2009). Government schoolteachers man polling stations which are set up in public institutions such as schools and community halls. For a state or parliamentary election, a polling booth is typically staffed by four government employees, of which one is the presiding officer and three are polling officers. At least two of the four government officers are schoolteachers, given that schoolteachers are the largest employee base of the government. Inside the booth, the polling officers have two main functions: (1) to verify voters' papers to check they are genuine, and (2) to ensure the voting process is conducted

---

[9] In India, a Block is an administrative unit that is hierarchically above a village, but below a district.

legally. Teachers, Béteille (2009) notes, said that when it comes to verifying an illiterate voter's papers, they can decide whether or not such papers are in order, regardless of the reality. Once the potential voter leaves the booth, the polling booth person can then cast a *farzi* (non-genuine) vote under that person's name. Such potential for teachers to effectively "stuff the ballot boxes" gives them huge power over politicians who perceive that their political fortunes can be materially affected by teachers.

Next, when it comes to the voting process, polling booth staff can doctor voting outcomes when explaining the electronic voting machine to a voter. Béteille (2009) quotes the officer on special duty to a former chief minister of Madhya Pradesh: "Madam, have you ever seen one of these machines? People get confused, so they ask the *adhikari* (officer) how to operate it. And so he/she demonstrates [...] but that is it, the real vote has been cast. You can go on pressing, but the vote has been cast." He then went on to explain that this was the method adopted to defeat the previous (Congress) chief minister of Rajasthan, Ashok Gehlot, who had angered teachers as a result of his strict policies regarding reporting for work on time – a view echoed by teachers not just in his home state, Rajasthan, but also in the adjacent state of Madhya Pradesh. Whether teachers actually caused the chief minister to lose is difficult to establish; what is important is how widespread the view was that teachers had the power to affect the result so drastically, and that the electronic voting machine procedure could be abused in this manner. The power of teachers on election day itself, and not just in the lead-up, is also suggested by Béteille's survey of teachers in Rajasthan, Madhya Pradesh and Karnataka. When asked whether "teachers control the polling booth and hence control the fate of the election – they can make a politician win," up to 20 percent of teachers agreed with the statement in one district, while at least 8 percent agreed in another.

The threat – a credible one – of teachers being able to sway electoral outcomes should any politician undertake teacher-unfriendly measures, is reported in a number of other states too. In West Bengal, for instance, it has proved impossible to take absentee teachers to task because politicians fear that teachers could affect their political fortune (Sen, 2002). Chakravarty (2010) notes that politicians often introduce policies to appease the teaching community. She cites an article in the online edition of the *Telegraph*, West Bengal's leading newspaper (dated 23 March 2010) which describes how the state budget was designed to appease the teaching community with promises of more recruitment and higher salaries. The article states,

The CPM has in the past banked on the support of party-backed teachers' lobbies such as the All Bengal Teachers' Association and the West Bengal College and University Teachers' Association to win elections. The move to create such a large number of posts is also being seen in the context of the forthcoming elections.

The article then quotes a college principal as saying, "The announcements will give a boost to the CPM-backed teachers' lobbies, especially so as CPM supporters tend to be favored during any recruitment."

Organized Strikes and Threats

At the state level, teacher unions lead protests, which often turn into vendettas targeted at reform-minded politicians and government officials. As described above, the case of Ashok Gehlot is well known. But there are other instances too. In another incident, pertaining to Uttar Pradesh but reflective of happenings in other states such as Bihar and Madhya Pradesh, unions helped protect teachers from accountability pressures relating to the role of specific teachers in facilitating cheating in examinations (Kingdon and Muzammil, 2013). The district inspector of schools, Mr Umesh Tripathi, received death threats for seeking action against 81 teachers who he claimed were engaged in exam-related corruption. Teacher legislators in the Upper House alleged Tripathi had sent a list of the accused teachers to the district police chief to initiate action against them under the UP Control of Organised Crime Act. The teacher leader in the House (who was until recently also the Pro Tem chairman of the Upper House) said that this Act had not come into force and so the district inspector had no right to threaten teachers with it.

The matter became the subject of so much political pressure that Uttar Pradesh Legislative Assembly witnessed uproarious scenes on February 24, 2008. Teachers' leaders also criticized the secondary school education minister for allegedly shielding the district inspector of schools, who in turn had to clarify that he did not order any severe penal action against those concerned ("Confrontation between TU and GOUP Rises," *Hindustan*, February 25, 2008). At first the education minister was defiant, saying that he had not hurled abuse at teachers and that he had merely reminded them of their duty. "It is hurting them because they are guilty. Only those interested in politics are not keen to teach," he added. However, in the face of calls for the minister's removal by 92,000 secondary school teachers who marched in protest in every district of the state, burned his effigy, and threatened an examination boycott if he was not removed, the minister performed a *volte face*: far from defending the district inspector of schools' right to bring cheating teachers to book, the minister stated that he would protect the dignity and prestige of teachers by not implementing the proposed measure of frisking invigilating teachers as they entered examination halls. "We are fully conscious that the dignity of a teacher is bound to suffer if any such thing is allowed," he was quoted as saying in the *Times of India* on February 26, 2008. It was only then that MSS withdrew its examination boycott call (*Santusht*, March 2008).

An important illustration of national- and state-level unions collaborating through coordinated strike action comes from a protest relating to the Right to Education (RTE) Bill. Teachers across the country protested against those provisions of the bill that would give SMCs and the community more control over teacher recruitment and management. The NCE took the lead, although with the largest membership it was really the AIPTF calling the shots. They resorted to strikes, picketing and "fill the jail" campaigns. The AISTF also opposed the bill by organizing pickets and demonstrations. They demanded that the central government should not forward the bill to the states. The AISTF organized a sit-in before the national Parliament in 2006, and state-level unions such as the MSS in Uttar Pradesh started individual campaigns. They also organized seminars to educate the public about what they described as the likely negative effects of the bill. Likely as a result of all this pressure, the amended bill passed by Parliament in August 2009 *excluded* those provisions that had outraged the teacher unions: namely, school-based teacher cadres and more powers for the SMCs (Kingdon and Muzammil, 2013).

Court Cases Against the Government
Unions also pursue stalling tactics by filing cases against the state government in court. Cases generally relate to appointments, transfers (reassignments) and promotions. In several states, unions either file cases directly or help teachers file cases. In Tamil Nadu for instance, strong teachers' unions provide resources and support for teachers to litigate (Ramachandran *et al.*, 2015). In Mizoram, more than 200 cases have been filed in the courts in the last ten years with union help. These cases dealt with seniority issues of regular teachers, seniority of contract teachers, the regularization and absorption of contract teachers, and the new central provident fund scheme and service benefits (Ramachandran *et al.*, 2015).

Direct Involvement in Politics
Teachers at private-aided schools can take a leave of absence for the purposes of competing in elections to the Legislative Assembly. In West Bengal, several schoolteachers worked for CPI(M), and, having amassed considerable political power in rural areas, they were also members of the *Gram Panchayat* (Sen, 2002). This situation gave these teachers, and the CPI(M) Party they were aligned with (either by choice or through coercion), considerable power during the party's 34-year reign in the state. Often such participation in politics is illegal, but nobody would take these errant teachers to court for fear of retaliation by the party's "enforcers" (who have been known to resort to murder).

The Impact of Teachers' Unions on Education Policy and Practice

A number of teacher accountability measures exist in states across India. These include school inspections by the inspector of schools; school principals' annual entry into every teacher's character book/register; the use of the system of teacher transfers as a disciplining device; and provision for the suspension or withholding of salary increments of erring teachers (Kingdon and Muzammil, 2013). Interestingly, in states such as Uttar Pradesh, unions have consistently been opposed to the use of positive incentives such as performance-based pay or performance-based promotion. For instance, in 2003, primary schoolteachers in the state opposed the introduction of tests, the results of which would be used to partly determine salary levels. In addition to teacher accountability measures, there are also measures to ensure that schools function smoothly across the board. These include rules for teacher transfers from one school to another within the district, thereby harmonizing pupil-teacher ratios and avoiding an excess of teachers in some schools and a scarcity in others; and rules against corruption in the examination system. Yet none of these measures have any teeth: teachers' unions and politically powerful teachers have been able to defeat them by resorting to a number of tactics as described in the previous section, ranging from strikes and court cases, to criminal intimidation. This next section describes the main areas in which teachers' unions have been influential.

Increasing the Salaries of Teachers
Since Independence, seven Pay Commissions have been set up by the central government to review and make recommendations concerning the work and pay structure of all civil and military divisions. Every time there has been a Pay Commission to revise the payscales of central government employees, AIPTF (and its state-level counterparts) have lobbied to ensure that state governments make teacher payscales consistent with those of other central government employees. Most recently, unions across the states have lobbied to ensure that the payscales of all teachers are consistent with the Sixth Pay Commission's recommendations, or even more generous in the case of Punjab. Such lobbying has been productive for teachers. In Uttar Pradesh, for example, government regular teachers' mean pay was two-and-a-half times greater than that of private teachers' mean pay in the early 1990s (Kingdon, 1994); it was five times greater in the early 2000s (Singh and Sridhar, 2002); and 12 times greater in 2008 (Kingdon and Banerji, 2009). After Uttar Pradesh applied the Sixth Pay Commission's salary recommendations, regular teachers' salary in January 2009 (applied retrospectively from January 2006) nearly doubled in one go. In 2014 the mean salary of a government primary school regular teacher (with 15 years' teaching experience) was nearly 25 times the average salary of a similarly experienced teacher in a rural private-unaided primary school (Ramachandran *et al.*, 2015). Clearly, public sector teachers have been very successful in lobbying for higher pay. Indeed, teacher salaries are comparable (or higher) to those of other professionals with similar qualifications, including legislators (Dundar *et al.*, 2014).

Thwarting Measures to Ensure a Code of Conduct for Teachers
If teachers are central to the education of students, then their behavior should model what one would like to pass on to generations of students. However, this is much easier said than done in a system where most teachers are under-trained,

under-qualified and demotivated, and where the teaching profession is often seen as the last resort for unemployed (but educated) youth. While a code of conduct for teachers has been articulated in many policy documents, most recently in the RTE Act, implementation has proved difficult. The case of the defeat of Rajasthan's incumbent chief minister, Ashok Gehlot, in 2003 – for attempting to undertake strict accountability measures – is not unique. Kingdon and Muzammil (2013) cite the example of Uttar Pradesh where, in 2002, the then education minister Om Prakash Singh advocated a set of rules governing the conduct of teachers inside schools and out. He believed these would improve the quality of secondary education and would make teachers a guiding force for society. Kingdon and Muzammil cited an article in the *Times of India* (July 15, 2002) – according to which the minister had stated that there was already a code of conduct in place for university and college teachers, and that it would be a good idea to extend this to cover secondary school education too. The idea was to streamline the quality of education, and to make teachers realize that they must *turn up to classes, keep away from activities which might throw their profession into disrepute, and, above all, act as role models for their students* (emphasis added).

Teachers, however, rejected the proposal straightaway, saying "conduct can be improved through 'self-evaluation' and not by imposition of rules." "Besides," they pointed out, "politicians should first have a code of conduct for themselves, before designing one for teachers." Although the minister had given assurances that the code of conduct would be implemented only after a consensus was reached, teachers presented a united front in opposing it. Devi Dayal Shastri, a prominent union leader (MSS) and a member of the Legislative Council from Lucknow, said that "the code of conduct would not be appropriate for teachers as it projects the picture that teachers are at fault and the government is out to rein them in. Instead, the teachers should themselves conduct a self-evaluation." The president of MSS also decried the move to implement such a code, saying that "a code of conduct already exists in the community and […] the government should keep away from 'teaching' teachers about what they should do. Things like good conduct, inspiration and motivation come from within and cannot be imposed by the government," he pointed out. ("Govt, teachers clash over conduct code," *Times of India*, July 15, 2002).

In the southern state of Andhra Pradesh, Gupta (2013) notes that teachers in government schools threatened to go on strike when the introduction of biometric attendance systems (to replace the manual signing-in) was proposed. Introducing such a measure for teaching and non-teaching staff, the government argued, would lead to a greater level of accountability and discipline in schools. However, two of the major government teachers' unions in the state, the United Teachers' Forum and the Andhra Pradesh Teachers' Association, said the state government would be better focusing instead on providing basic amenities (including fresh drinking water and toilet facilities) in schools (Gupta, 2013). If the objective is to enhance learning outcomes for students, investing in teacher accountability is far more important than investing in infrastructure; but for these teacher unions, shielding their members from accountability measures was the primary concern, one that was conveniently masked by an otherwise secondary concern about building infrastructure.

Opposing Decentralization

Reforms aiming to increase the role of the community in school accountability began with DPEP in the mid-1990s and continued with SSA. At one end of the spectrum, as in Madhya Pradesh, village *Panchayats* were given the power to hire and fire teachers, while at the other end, as in Odisha, relatively powerless parents, typically illiterate, were asked to monitor higher caste and better-educated teachers. These measures were opposed tooth and nail in many states, especially in Madhya Pradesh. At the national level, however, the main opposition came when the draft bill of the Right to Education Act was circulated in 2005.

The bill comprised certain provisions for elementary schools, including school-based teacher cadres and the constitution of widely empowered SMCs for each school. The powers of SMCs in the draft bill included teacher appointments, salary disbursements to teachers, and the ability to take disciplinary action against teachers (e.g., cutting pay to penalise absence). The provision of a school-based cadre implies that once a teacher is appointed in a school he/she cannot easily seek a transfer to another school. These provisions had far-reaching implications: the first measure would ensure schools had the teachers they needed – no more and no less – while the second would make teachers more accountable to parents and the community.

The provisions, especially the one relating to SMCs, were vigorously opposed by all unions. Mr. D.V. Pandit, the general secretary of AIFTO, asserted, "The school management committee may not have the vital experience to supervise the work of teachers" (Chakravarty, 2010). In her study, Chakravarty found that almost all major unions in West Bengal agreed with this sentiment. The other objections voiced included the feasibility of ensuring parents' attendance at meetings, and their dedication to the work of the committee. As Chakravarty (2010) reports, according to Sudip Goswami – general secretary of the All Bangla Primary Teachers' Association – this was especially notable in light of the fact that parents could well belong to the lower strata of society and therefore face considerable difficulty in ensuring that their own children had enough to eat let alone having the ability to make provision for their schooling. Ashok Maiti, general secretary of the Headmasters' Association, reflected a commonly held perception about the literacy levels of parents compromising their ability to ensure adequate checks on teachers.

If SMC members had been trained to undertake school accountability-related roles effectively, then perhaps they might have been successful in carrying out such roles. But there is little evidence to suggest that the unions thought it important that the government should invest in training members of the

SMCs; it made more sense for the unions to devalue the SMCs in their entirety since their power would threaten absentee or non-performing teachers.

When the final version of the bill was enacted (2009), much of the power of SMCs had been watered down. In fact, Mr. R.C. Dabas, general secretary of the AIPTF, regarded this as one of the major achievements of his union (Gupta, 2013). In its current form, the Act envisages SMCs with parents forming 75 percent of the membership. The remaining 25 percent will comprise – in equal proportion – elected representatives of the local government, teachers from the school, and local educationalists and school students. The powers of the SMC, as originally envisaged, have been considerably reduced, and now comprise the following "(a) monitor the working of the school; (b) prepare and recommend a school development plan; (c) monitor the utilization of the grants received from the appropriate government or local authority or any other source; and (d) perform such other functions as may be prescribed" (taken from the wording of the Right to Education Act, 2009).

Ensuring a Stable Student-Teacher Ratio Across Schools

Across India, teachers belong to state-level, district-level or block-level cadres, depending on the state. This allows the government to move teachers from one school to another within the cadre in order to ensure a stable student-teacher ratio. This process of moving teachers to schools facing a deficit is known as "rationalization." Teachers themselves have little formal say in such decisions, and typically find ways of circumventing such efforts through informal or under-the-table mechanisms (Béteille, 2009).

Teachers' unions have opposed efforts to "rationalize" the teaching force, as a result of which many schools either have too many or too few teachers. Kingdon and Muzammil (2013) provide an example from the Kanpur District of Uttar Pradesh. In 2007 the district inspector of schools of Kanpur decided to rationalize staff across the district as a result of a situation arising in which there were excess teachers due to falling student enrolments. In one particular school, the pupil-teacher ratio had fallen greatly and as a result 37 teachers were surplus to requirements. As per the rules of the Uttar Pradesh government, teachers were required to move and were given the option to continue in other private-aided schools; but the affected teachers were adamant that they did not want to move.[10] The private-aided school teachers' union (MSS) supported the teachers by organizing a sit-in on the school premises. All prominent leaders of MSS, including the president and the secretary (both also teacher legislators), joined the protests against the management and the district education authorities and succeeded in stalling the implementation of the order (*Santusht* [monthly magazine of the MSS (Sharma Group) published from the head office of the MSS], August 2007).

---

[10] Female teachers and disabled teachers are exempt from the policy of rationalizing teacher numbers across schools.

In Rajasthan teacher transfers have been notoriously difficult to implement for political reasons and as a result of union pressure. Similar to the situation in Mexico, newspaper reports in Rajasthan suggest that transfers are seen more as a mechanism for rewarding politically useful teachers than as a means to correct imbalanced student-teacher ratios. In the summer of 2007, a handful of BJP legislators were upset by the way recent teacher transfers had been conducted. Every legislator had been promised a certain number of teacher transfers, but the state's leading daily newspaper, *Dainik Bhaskar*, reported that 80,000 transfer applications had been made that year (2008), of which 50,000 were for primary education. There were a total of 256,529 teachers in government schools in Rajasthan at the time. Given the large numbers, it is not surprising that the demands of many teachers were unmet. The teachers involved, believing that they had helped the BJP win the 2003 state election, were not going to let the matter go. A few days later the papers were reporting that the leader of the Rajasthan Shikshak Sangh (Pragati Sheel) state-level teachers' union – Mr Kesarlal Chaudhary – had said that teachers would teach the BJP a lesson in the forthcoming elections unless the party was able to give teachers what was rightfully theirs (*Dainik Bhaskar*, June 24, 2008, cited in Béteille, 2009).

With several similar threats coming in, including from BJP party workers, back-dated transfer decisions were made until early July 2008, by which time approximately 30,000 (out of 80,000 reported applications) had been completed (*Dainik Bhaskar*, July 4, 2008). This meant that a large number of teachers were unlikely to have their transfer requests met that year. As a result, office bearers of the BJP complained that many BJP loyalists had been disappointed by transfer outcomes, especially since they had promised teachers who were family members/friends that their transfer request would be processed. The unions and party workers made it clear that unless these transfers were done, it would be difficult to expect the support of these loyalists in the upcoming elections (*Dainik Bhaskar*, 15 July, 2008). As it turned out, the BJP lost the elections that year.

However, the unions are not all-powerful. A lot depends on the specific politician in power and the bureaucrats in office. Karnataka is a good example, having been able to pass the Regulation of Transfer of Teachers Act (2007) despite union opposition. This Act provides a foolproof technology-based system for undertaking teacher transfers. A recent study found the system has been working well, with patronage-based transfers and related corruption dramatically reduced as a result (Ramachandran *et al.*, 2015).

Regularizing Contract Teachers

A number of states, such as Punjab, Madhya Pradesh and Odisha, have strong contract teachers' unions, which, due to their sheer size, are politically powerful entities that have been able to successfully lobby for regularization of their teachers (Ramachandran *et al.*, 2015). When schools in India started hiring contract teachers in the 1990s, one key motivation was that these teachers would be easier to fire in case of poor performance – relative to regular government school teachers. In many states, in particular Madhya Pradesh, the unions of these teachers won several concessions. In Madhya Pradesh all teachers are hired on a contract basis for an initial period of three years, after which they are confirmed in their positions based upon three criteria: (1) the class(es) taught by the contract teacher must have attained the following exam pass rates – 50 percent pass for classes 1–5; 40 percent pass for classes 6–8; and 30 percent pass for classes 9–12; (2) they should have the requisite professional qualifications for the relevant grade; and (3) they should have completed three years of service without any disciplinary action or taking any leave without pay. One could argue that this system, despite its relatively low standards, is reasonable since it links regularization to performance. In reality, however, these criteria have not been adhered to and all contract teachers are regularized based upon union pressure or politicking. Indeed, the unionization of these teachers, and the fact that their leaders file court cases against the state government in order to stall the enactment of provisions contained in the contract, bears out the difficulty in designing a performance-based system in Indian schools.

Freeing Teachers from Non-Academic Work

Teachers' unions at the national level and at the state level have fought long and hard to free teachers from non-academic work. Such work, which could range from conducting a cattle census in the village to cooking meals for the midday meal scheme, clearly takes away time that the teacher has during the day to teach. The RTE Act has taken a strong stand on this, prohibiting the deployment of teachers for non-educational purposes with the exception of decennial population census duties, disaster relief duties, or duties relating to election to the local authority or the State Legislatures or the Parliament (RTE Act, 2009).

Teacher Eligibility Test

With the enactment of the RTE Act 2009 the central government authorized the National Council for Teacher Education as the academic authority for laying down the minimum qualifications for a person to be eligible for appointment as a teacher.[11] This resulted in the introduction of the Teacher Eligibility Test (TET) in 2011 as an eligibility criterion for teachers to be appointed. Across the states, teacher and union ire has been directed at the quality of the teacher eligibility test, a test mandated by the Act and meant to ensure that teachers have the necessary skillset to enter the profession. Passing the TET is a necessary but insufficient condition for entering the teaching profession. Unions assert that it only tests the theoretical knowledge of candidates, which may not be necessary for effective classroom teaching. Interestingly,

---

[11] MHRD notification, April 2010: www.mhrd.gov.in/sites/upload_files/mhrd/files/upload_document/5.pdf

over 99 percent of candidates failed to pass the Central Teacher Eligibility Test (CTET) in 2012 (Gupta, 2013), and in most states the TET pass rate has been scandalously low – less than 4 percent.

Educators agree with teachers that the exam does not properly measure teaching aptitude, competence, or critical thinking abilities. Nevertheless, there is no reason why 99 percent of teachers (as B.Ed. or equivalent degree-holders) should fail the exam, given both its basic syllabus (English, mathematics, environmental science, and child development and pedagogy), and its 60 percent pass score. Gupta (2013) argues that the failure of teachers is being obscured amid the resounding claims about the "uselessness" of the exam.

Discussion

With more than 200 million children in the school system – many of whom are learning little – and the skill demands of an ambitious growing economy, the need to improve the performance of schools could not be more urgent in India. At the same time, the fact that large numbers of teachers are indifferent, untrained, frequently absent, or enter teaching as a second-choice occupation, makes school reform difficult. Teachers are protected by powerful unions, especially at the state level, and over the course of time these unions have won several concessions for teachers in terms of their salaries, working conditions and accountability. Their concerted efforts to influence the RTE Act have led to the dilution of any form of teacher accountability contained within it. Indeed, the RTE Act, which is meant to ensure that all children between the ages of six and 14 years are educated, contains no concrete mechanisms via which to track whether its requirements are leading to learning gains among students, further weakening its hold on accountability.

Even though union membership rates vary considerably across states, even where membership rates are low, state-level unions are powerful because their leaders have political clout and connections. Importantly, our study suggests that regardless of union membership the teaching body generally believes that unions will come to their aid. That being said, the relationship between unions and individual teachers is not as clean as the accounts in the different sections above suggest. There are two issues that union leaders across the states have been fighting in favour of, even though they know that should policies be passed in support of them their vested interests will be harmed: (1) rationalizing teachers/transparent teacher transfer policies, and (2) freeing teachers from non-academic work. Transfer policies are important. In a system where schooling assignments are centrally determined, and where pay depends solely upon accrued experience, a teacher's working conditions can make a great difference to the overall benefit of their job. Transparent teacher transfer policies help the average teacher by ensuring mobility. Without a transparent process for managing transfers, teachers often resort to powerful middlemen to facilitate convenient transfers, albeit for a price. While teachers' unions in states such as Rajasthan have been publicly campaigning for transparent teacher policies, when asked in private whether such policies would be in their interest, they laughed and agreed that they would not. Furthermore, as a recent study in the state shows, union leaders often act as middlemen themselves, taking bribes and promising to connect teachers to powerful politicians who can grant transfer-related favors (Béteille, 2009). What would happen to this income if transfer policies suddenly became transparent? No wonder that transfers remain opaque and discretionary in all but one state.

As a result of their education and of their sheer numbers, teachers are frequently assigned tasks such as census work, assisting in polio vaccination programmes, and carrying out election-related duties. So when teacher unions campaign for teachers being exempted from non-academic work, they cannot be entirely serious. At the end of the day, it is teachers' political activities before and during polling that gives them their power and allows them to make credible threats against the ambitions of uncooperative politicians. Again, no wonder that little has changed in this regard – and teachers continue to perform election duty. The two instances discussed earlier suggest that teacher unions do not always act in the interest of teachers, since to do so in every regard would actually threaten their power.

As India attempts to reform its school system to meet the demands of a fast-growing economy, it will need to understand how it can design and implement better teacher management and accountability policies. In order to do so, we need to know more about the politics of education in India – not just at the national level, but in different states, districts, blocks and villages. As this chapter shows, teachers' unions are a central piece of the puzzle in understanding the political economy of education in India. We have, however, only been able to skim the surface of this landscape and the politics that underlie it. Much more needs to be known about the internal structure and functioning of teachers' unions across the country, and about how they interact with the education system, bureaucracy and politicians. Greater understanding of this will help in the design and implementation of more effective policies. We hope future research will help us understand this better.

References

Aslam, Monazza, Geeta Kingdon, and Shenila Rawal (2011). *Teacher Quality in South Asia*. Background paper for Dundar *et al*. (2014), *Student Learning in South Asia* (see separate reference).

Béteille, Tara (2009). *Absenteeism, Transfers and Patronage: The Political Economy of Teacher Labour Markets in India*. PhD thesis, Stanford University.

CABE (1992). Teachers' representation in the legislative councils, Report of the CABE Committee. New Delhi: Central Advisory Board of Education.

Chakravarty, Devkanya (2010). *Teacher Unions: Who, Where and What They Think*. Center for Civil Society. Working Paper No. 236.
Dundar, Halil, Tara Béteille, Michel Riboud, and Anil Deolalikar (2014). *Student Learning in South Asia: Challenges, Opportunities and Policy Priorities*. Directions in Development. The World Bank.
Frederiksson, Ulf (1999). *Education for All Assessment 2000: The Teachers' Perspective*.
Government of India (2009). The Right of Children to Free and Compulsory Education Act.
Grant, Laura (2010). *"The Second Freedom Struggle": Transnational Advocacy for EFA Case Study*. National Coalition for Education in India.
Grindle, M.S. (2004). *Despite the Odds: The Contentious Politics of Education Reform*. Princeton University Press.
Gupta, Saumya (2013). *Perspectives of Teachers' Union on Challenges to Education in India*. Center for Civil Society. Working Paper No. 304.
Kingdon, Geeta (1994). *An Economic Evaluation of School Management-Types in Urban India: A Case Study of Uttar Pradesh*. Dissertation. University of Oxford.
  (2010). *The Impact of the Sixth Pay Commission on Teacher Salaries: Assessing Equity and Efficiency Effects*. RECOUP Working Paper No. 29, Faculty of Education, University of Cambridge. May.
Kingdon, Geeta, and Rukmini Banerji (2009). *Addressing School Quality: Some Policy Pointers From Rural North India*. Briefing. Department for International Development.
Kingdon, Geeta, and Mohd. Muzammil (2003). *The Political Economy of Education in India: Teacher Politics in Uttar Pradesh*. Delhi: Oxford University Press.
  (2013). The school governance environment in Uttar Pradesh: Implications for teacher accountability and effort. *Journal of Development Studies* 49(2), February: 251–69. Also, see its fuller version, RECOUP Working Paper No. 31, Faculty of Education, University of Cambridge, May 2010.
Kingdon, Geeta, and Francis Teal (2010). Teacher unions, teacher pay and student performance in India: A pupil fixed effects approach. *Journal of Development Economics* 91(2), March: 278–88.
Kremer, Michael, Karthik Muralidharan, Nazmul Chaudhury, Jeffrey Hammer, and F. Hasley Rogers (2005). Teacher absence in India: A snapshot. *Journal of the European Economic Association* 3(2–3): 658–67.
Madras Presidency (1893). *Manual of Standing Information for the Madras Presidency*.
Muralidharan, Karthik, Jishnu Das, Alaka Holla, and Aakash Mohpal (2014). *The Fiscal Cost of Weak Governance: Evidence From Teacher Absence in India*. No. w20299. National Bureau of Economic Research.
NCT (1986) The Teacher and Society: Volume I. In *Report of the National Commission on Teachers, 1983–85*. New Delhi: Government of India Press.
Ramachandran, Vimala, Toby Linden, Tara Beteille, Sangeeta Dey, Sangeeta Goyal, and Prerna Goel (2015). *Teachers in the Indian Education System: A Nine State Study*. Draft. Government of India.
Sen, Amartya (2002) *The Pratichi Report*. Pratichi India Trust.
Sharma, Rashmi (1999). What manner of teacher? *Economic and Political Weekly*, June.

Shrimali, K.L. (1951). *Shikshak aur Bhartiya Loktantra* [The Teacher and Indian Democracy]. Udaipur: Vidya Bhawan Society.

Singh, Shailendra, and Kala Seetharam Sridhar (2002). Government and private schools: Trends in enrolment and retention. *Economic and Political Weekly* (2002): 4229–38.

10

The Comparative Politics of Education

Teachers Unions and Education Systems Around the World

Terry M. Moe

Country by country, the chapters of this book speak for themselves. When viewed collectively, however, they provide a rich empirical basis for gaining perspective on the bigger picture of teachers unions and education politics throughout the world. My aim in this final chapter is to begin moving in that direction—stepping back from the country-specific details and identifying some of the patterns, trends, and key comparisons that, in my view, help point the way toward a larger understanding. In the process, I also aim to show that a theoretical perspective directing analytic attention to vested interests—along the lines that Susanne Wiborg and I set out in the Introduction (see also Moe, 2015)—has much to offer in promoting such an understanding.

In addition to structuring our thinking in terms of vested interests, we believe important leverage can be gained by distinguishing between two institutional eras in the history of world education systems: an early period of institutional formation and a later period of performance-based institutional reform. Here in this overview chapter, I am most interested in exploring the politics of the modern era: the era in which all of us live, and whose fundamental features are likely to prevail for many decades to come. I will devote most of my attention to that time period. But the challenges faced by modern-day governments, as well as the politics that shape their agendas and decisions, are very much a function of political institutions and power structures inherited from the past—from the early era of institutional formation. So that is the place to begin.

The Era of Institutional Formation

It comes as no surprise that different nations developed their school systems at different times, at different rates, and in different ways (Green, 1990). Germany and France, for example, began to build bureaucratic national school systems more than 200 years ago, although the French approach was centralized and the German one was not. The United States saw the first stirrings of public education in the mid-1800s, but didn't develop a true nationwide, bureaucratic system—albeit a highly decentralized one—until the early 1900s, thanks to the concerted efforts of Progressive reformers. The modern Japanese system has its roots in the Meiji Restoration, whose leaders copied the centralized French system in the late 1800s; but after the devastation of the Second World War, its American occupiers imposed a new constitution and new political and education systems, and Japan was set on a different developmental path. The examples could easily go on, revealing vast differences across countries.

Yet there are also basic commonalities, distinctive of this early era, that are of great importance. In virtually every nation, education was being expanded to a much broader population of students—from the elites to the middle classes and ultimately to the poor—and expanded hierarchically as well, from primary schools to secondary schools, with the latter increasingly available to all students regardless of background or ability. Education for all became the norm, an expectation, a right. As enrollments dramatically increased, so did the resources that nations devoted to public education, which not only attracted huge absolute increases in public spending, but also absorbed a growing share of public budgets—and education rose from a novel and marginal undertaking to an imperative of government, a crucial function representing a big chunk of what government is and does.

As enrollments and resources soared, the numbers of teaching jobs rooted in the system expanded exponentially, and bureaucracies were developed and expanded—along, inevitably, with a growing number of bureaucratic jobs—to operationally govern and implement this new governmental imperative: by filling out the details of policy, generating rules and regulations, setting up and organizing the schools, and carrying out the various functions associated (in form if not substance) with actually educating children (e.g., Meyer et al., 1992).

This was a period, then, in which education systems became institutionalized as fundamental components of government. As this was happening, the new institutions generated an array of constituencies with vested interests—notably, teachers and bureaucrats, but also parents and students, as well as, in some countries (Mexico and India), politicians and local leaders who used education's vast sums of public money for purposes of patronage and simple corruption. The proliferation of vested interests was not, as we have emphasized, a bad thing in and of itself. It was a normal and inevitable thing, and a major force promoting the stability and entrenchment of the new institutions—for the most powerful of these vested interests, the ones that benefited the most from the systems' money, jobs, and services, had strong incentives to protect these institutions from disruption and change (Moe, 2015).

Politically, many aspects of this era might well be remarked upon. But one stands out as especially consequential and is its cardinal distinguishing feature. This was an era of an expanding institutional pie: the sheer size of the institution was growing, spending was going up, and ever-larger constituencies were benefiting from all this money and growth—for reasons that *had little to do with the systems' academic performance*. Parents and students had personal reasons to care about performance, of course; but they were politically weak, held back by collective action problems—and most importantly, with education extending to previously unserved clienteles, many were simply happy to be receiving any services at all. The business community had reason to care about performance too, as the expansion of education and its outcomes—basic literacy, basic skills, discipline—stood to promote a more productive workforce for commerce and industry. But *academic quality* was not the main issue. Simple service-provision was. As for education's key vested interests—teachers and government bureaucrats—their stakes in the system were rooted in jobs and money (and for the bureaucrats, control) that benefited them directly and quite substantially as individuals; and they would continue to get jobs and money (and control) as long as the system survived and attracted public funds, regardless of its performance in providing children with a high quality education.

This same historical period also corresponds to the emergence and institutionalization of the welfare state, and to state-building efforts across even the less developed nations—such as those in Latin America—that led to the emergence of an array of bureaucratic institutions capable (however incompetently and corruptly, in many cases) of delivering public services to ordinary citizens. During this time, then, the world was witnessing, almost everywhere, the rise of the bureaucratic, service-providing state. And for all of these systems, just as for education, the characteristic features had to do with the expansion of governments, the growth of spending, new rights and expectations on the part of the public, and new government promises and commitments (Fukuyama, 2014).

Around all these new programs and services—not just in education—new vested interests were being created: new mass constituencies that, for the first time, were receiving "modern" services from governments, and new constituencies of public workers, bureaucrats, and politicians who benefited from the jobs, money, and control that this expansion of government entailed. These were governmental systems that would now be protected by powerful new constituencies, and would become institutionalized for reasons that—as in education—had little to do with their performance. What mattered most was the sheer existence of these systems and their provision of new services (Moe, 2015; Pierson, 1993, 1994, 1996).

The Rise of the Teachers Unions
During this early era, the formation and institutional development of public school systems was accompanied by the organization of teachers into unions. And the rise of unions, in turn, was accompanied by pervasive union action in politics on behalf of teacher job interests. This was not a hit or miss thing. It happened in all the countries we studied.

In most of these countries, teacher organizations emerged in the late 1800s and early 1900s. In Germany and France, they arose much earlier. Why teachers were so successful at organizing remains to be fully explained. But it is clear that, as their education systems began to develop, they had strong and deep vested interests in their jobs. These interests gave them strong incentives to try to overcome the usual obstacles to collective action. And these same interests drove the political demands they were making at the time: what unionized teachers sought, above all else, were better wages, benefits, working conditions, and job security. More research (and theory) on the unions' emergence is surely needed. But the bottom line is that, as education systems developed, teachers did indeed *get* organized, and they became a forceful political presence in public education throughout the world.

For a long time, the United States was an outlier. As its school system was taking institutional shape in the late 1800s and early 1900s—in the form of a radically decentralized structure of local school districts (directly subject to state but not federal authority)—unions simply did not achieve take-off. They faced governments roundly hostile to public sector unions of all kinds, and laws that made collective bargaining and strikes by public workers illegal. That changed dramatically, but very late in the game, when states (outside the South) began passing public-sector labor laws during the 1960s and 1970s that legalized collective bargaining, made union organizing much easier, and led to an explosion in union membership among teachers and other public sector workers.

For the US, then, the basic institutions of public education were already well developed and entrenched by the time the teachers unions became a powerful force. Indeed, the unions rose to power just as the new era of performance-based reform was beginning—and they were immediately confronted with reformist demands for structural change and heightened performance. This was not true in other countries. Elsewhere in the world, the unions grew and developed as the institutions of public education grew and developed. They grew up together. And as we will see, the organization of these non-US systems is a reflection of that togetherness, with the unions woven into the warp and woof of their nations' education systems. But more on that later.

Another basic feature of the rise of teachers unions is that, almost everywhere, the mobilization process did not lead to the emergence of one sector-wide union that monopolized the representation of a nation's teachers. At least some measure of fragmentation has been the rule. In most countries, diverse unions initially arose to represent a dizzying array of teacher interests and clienteles—having to do, for example, with the level of schooling (elementary v. secondary), gender, religion (Catholic v. Protestant v. secular), ideology (left-aligned and militant v. more centrist and conciliatory), region (urban v. rural), and more. These internal divisions had to be overcome if the unions were to enhance their power in the education arena, and for the most part that is what happened. Over time, at least in the developed nations, virtually all the historic lines of cleavage dropped away, and consolidation occurred as unions put their main emphasis on what they all had in common: basic job interests.

Two forms of fragmentation remained, however, and still do to this day. One is a holdover from the past: the historical division between elementary and secondary teachers. This cleavage was actually based on job interests too—because elementary and secondary schools were different structural venues, across which teacher pay, prestige, training, and education often differed dramatically. The nature of those differing interests often brought the two groups into conflict.

The elementary-secondary division has worked itself out in different ways. In Sweden, Norway, and Denmark, for instance, elementary and secondary teachers have maintained separate unions into modern times, but the elementary unions—much larger than the secondary unions, and aligned with social democratic parties and the larger union movement—emerged as the major union power by far in education politics, and have been regarded (including by governments) as "the" teachers unions. In Germany, the same division is present within labor's ranks, but it is the (upper) secondary teachers who have the stronger hand, exercised through their potent union, the DPhV. As befits their higher levels of training and traditional status relative to elementary (and lower secondary) teachers, they have long identified with the educated elite; their vested interests are rooted in jobs and schools tied to a more advantaged population; and they are politically allied with the center-right party, the CDU. In Finland too, the secondary teachers have long had greater prominence and clout than the elementary teachers. But the difference there is that the two unions merged in 1973 into a single monopoly union that reflected the more elite, middle-class job priorities of the secondary teachers. Finland, I should note, is unique among developed nations in now having a single monopoly union representing its teachers.

A second form of union fragmentation is also quite common in developed nations—prevailing in the United States, England, France, and Japan. In these settings, there is more than one broadly based union, each of which represents the general job interests of the teachers they organize. The United States, after a late start, has two huge unions: the National Education Association (NEA) and the American Federation of Teachers (AFT). England has six different teachers unions—although two are by far the most prominent, the NUT and NASWUT. France has three, the FSU, the UNSA, and the SGEN—and the lowest membership levels in Europe. Japan had one dominant union, the Japan Teachers Union (JTU), for decades after the war; but the JTU's steps toward moderation during the 1990s (which I will discuss) led a militant faction to split off and form a rival union, Zenkyo, which has since competed with the JTU for members and influence.

The developing nations covered in this book, Mexico and India, are institutionally very different from the developed nations, and in many ways are still in flux as they move toward more modern, more democratic structures. In basic respects, their education systems resemble those of the developed nations during the early 1900s. Even so, teachers have still gotten organized in these settings, and their unions have long been central players in their politics of education.

India has countless numbers of teachers unions, fragmented along many lines. Three are prominent at the national level—the All India Primary Teachers' Federation, the All India Secondary Teachers' Federation, and the All India Federation of Teachers' Organizations—but the most important political action on education, in terms of both legislation and implementation, takes place at the state level; and at that level, the teachers unions are at once very powerful and, across the nation as a whole, very diverse. Mexico's government has until recently been monopolized by one party, the PRI—which, long ago (in 1943), used its great power to consolidate that country's hundreds of teachers unions to create one massive, monopolistic teachers union, the SNTE. That monopoly union has remained enormously powerful (and famously corrupt) ever since.

Finally, I should note that, during the early era of institutional formation, the union movement in education was generally quite successful at attracting teachers to join their organizations. This was a period of institutional growth: of governments, of education systems, of teachers unions. Across Scandinavia and most of Europe, the unionization of teachers hovered in the 80–100 percent range as late as the 1970s. In Japan it was slightly lower than that, but still quite high. And even in France and the United States, countries that are notorious for their low levels of union members overall, across occupations teachers still joined in huge numbers. Teacher unionization in France was at roughly 70 percent at that time. Comparable figures are not available for the US, and, indeed, the unions weren't even fully organized until the early 1980s, but data from later years suggest that a good guess for the 1970s would be about 50–60 percent. As for the developing nations: reliable figures are not available for India—but in Mexico, the union's government-granted monopoly assured that all teachers would automatically become dues-paying members, and this monopoly has remained in place for well over half a century.

Gaining Power and Getting Entrenched

As the unions grew in mass membership, financial resources, and organizational reach and capacity, they were increasingly in positions to exercise political power. They could fund political candidates and parties. They could mobilize voters and influence public opinion. They could organize strikes, call demonstrations, and create serious disruptions. They could facilitate patronage through control of jobs. They could use their connections to workers to administer various benefit programs. And much more. The unions, then, had a broad and impressive array of advantages to offer governments and parties.

They also had major weapons to unleash if they felt dissatisfied, betrayed, or excluded—particularly forms of disruption that are enormously threatening to governments. What governments want, above all else, is peace and normalcy—and these are things the unions can deny them very quickly and effectively.

Throughout the world, as a result, the teachers unions became central players in the politics of education, and thus in the decision making processes that shaped the policies and institutions of public schooling. Exactly how this happened varied from country to country, reflecting the specifics of their larger political systems, as well as their characteristic political approaches to the building of a bureaucratic, service-providing state—for education was not separate from all this, but an integral part of it. It also occasionally involved strikes, political battles, and power struggles. But the chapters speak to these sorts of details. What I want to focus on here are the kinds of *institutional* arrangements that emerged over time and the unions' role within them.

If one commonality stands out and deserves emphasis, it is this: the frequent reliance on *corporatist-like mechanisms* for incorporating the teachers unions into the institutional fabric of educational decision making. During the twentieth century, the Scandinavian governments developed as the world's paradigmatic examples of corporatism: a system of political decision making based on the incorporation of major social interests, particularly business and labor (and agriculture), through their regular, official involvement—mainly on various administrative boards, commissions, and councils—in national policy making, with decisions shaped by norms of compromise and consensus. The corporatist model, advanced by the power of the labor parties and strong unions, but also through historic compromises with business, agriculture, and the center-right parties, became the foundation for the Nordic welfare states, and served as a general mode of governance across all important realms of policy, including education policy.

The Nordic nations governed their education systems, then, by bringing teachers unions into the heart of the governmental process. The unions were extended an integral role in crafting education policy, including but by no means limited to matters of pay, benefits, and working conditions, and they were essential signers-on to virtually anything of importance that governments wanted to do in the realm of education. This does not mean that the unions always got what they wanted, for the corporatist system was based on compromise and consensus, and extreme demands—e.g., for much higher pay—were unlikely to be acceptable to other major interests that would have to foot the bill. Moderation was the norm. But the flip side was that the corporatist system effectively gave the teachers unions a veto over whatever government might want to do.

While the Nordics' approach to education is hardly surprising, the fact is that many other nations—not known as corporatist—have also approached the governance and politics of education in ways that bring the teachers unions inside the system as regular, ongoing participants. These are not truly corporatist systems. Yet they have important corporatist components that enmesh the unions in the governance of public education—making them, in key respects, insiders rather than outsiders, and giving them not only additional power over policy, but also deeper stakes in the system and stronger reasons for protecting it.

In Germany, for instance, the public schools are governed by the Länder (the states), and at that level the teachers unions are heavily involved as regular, inside participants within the education bureaucracies; similarly, at the school level, the teachers unions have a right of "codetermination" in school decision making, and they have a major presence (via teacher members) on formally established Staff Councils that make fundamental decisions on matters of hiring, work schedules, teacher evaluations, and other details of school organization. France, by contrast, has a highly centralized system of schools run by the national government; and the teachers unions are so deeply interwoven into the national department of education (the MEN) that Michael Dobbins refers to France's educational governance as one of "institutionalized coadministration" between the MEN and the unions—providing the unions with what amounts to a platform for self-regulation. The United Kingdom developed its education system very differently from Germany and France, governing the schools mainly through Local Education Authorities (LEAs, which are like school districts in the US); but at this local level, most LEAs and their teachers unions were bound together via what was called the "social partnership," and the unions participated as full fledged partners in local governance. At the national level, moreover, England developed corporatist-like mechanisms—such as the Burnham Commission (1919–87) to set national payscales, the School Council (1964–88) to deal with matters of curriculum and exams, and regularized modes of consultation in the policy process—through which the unions played insider governing roles as key decision makers.

Corporatist arrangements were not just restricted to the developed nations of the West. In Mexico, for instance, the ruling PRI gave the teachers union, the SNTE, a legal monopoly over the nation's teachers in 1943, as I have noted; and in the following decades, the SNTE colonized Mexico's Department of Education and essentially took control (with bureaucratic allies) of ongoing decisions about teacher pay, hiring, promotions, transfers, training, as well as broader matters of policy—giving union leaders extraordinary power not only over matters of education, but also over their own members, and enmeshing the union in a thoroughly corrupt system of patronage and symbiosis with governing politicians. Mexico is surely extreme in these respects. But corporatist arrangements in the governance of public education, in which the teachers unions are incorporated into education bureaucracies as insiders, is in fact the norm throughout most of Latin America. Here is what Grindle (2004: 122–3) has to say about Latin American education during this era of institutional formation:

> The 1950s and 1960s, when many countries expanded their educational systems [...] were important decades for the unions. During this period, the goals of the unions—to represent teachers in negotiations over salaries and conditions of work—coincided with government interests in labor peace and expansion of the teaching corps. Not surprisingly, corporatist relations with ministries of education developed as the unions were invited to help devise norms, regulations, and statutes [...] Indeed, ministries were often willing to accede to union demands and to union participation in policy decision making and implementation as budgets grew and there was need for interlocutors to ensure labor peace and cooperation in the sector. When they were unable to meet union demands for salary increments, they traded union quiescence for control over education policy and positions. Union colonization of ministries of education and control over teacher education, assignments, and promotions were common results of this relationship.

It is important to note that, outside of the Nordic nations, the kind of corporatism that prevailed on education did not follow the Nordic model of balance, consensus, and moderation. It was essentially a stunted version of that model, in which the teachers unions were allowed to share the exercise of public authority without any serious attempt to involve other social interests. These were arrangements, to use Michael Dobbins' phrase, of "teacher-dominated corporatism"—which reflected, and reinforced, the outsized power of the teachers unions in matters related to the structure and operation of the public schools.

Two major nations failed to engage in this teacher-dominated corporatism. The United States did not really have a union presence in education prior to the 1960s; and when the states then began to pass new labor laws, the emerging teachers unions had to fight and claw their way into local collective bargaining arrangements district by district—and this became their base of power, their source of members and money. They then quickly became institutionally entrenched at the local level, and used their enormous resources to become powerful players in state and national politics. Even after they consolidated their power and became the de facto leaders of the "education establishment" in American politics, however, they were never really insiders in the way their counterparts were in other countries. They were essentially outsiders, fighting to influence the officials who formally made governmental decisions. In collective bargaining, they struggled to influence local administrators and school boards (partly by trying to control local elections). In state and national politics, they participated actively in elections, put together formidable lobbying organizations, and in other ways tried to influence who got elected and what they did in office. Their power was (and is) considerable, but they exercised it from the outside in.

The other nation that departed from corporatist arrangements was Japan, where the teachers unions have not only been government outsiders, but have essentially been left out in the cold. From 1955 through 1993, Japanese government was monopolized by one party, the LDP—which was (as it is today) conservative and anti-union, and used its control over government to create a highly centralized education system run by the national Department of Education. The teachers union (the JTU), which allied itself with the Socialist Party and squared off against the LDP as an ardent opponent, was deliberately shut out of government—and indeed, at the national level, was not even recognized as a legal entity (and still isn't). The JTU wielded considerable clout in the politics of education nonetheless, in part because its local organization gave it the power to disrupt the operation of schools and interfere with policy implementation; and in part because national decision making was shaped by a norm of consensus, which the unions could torpedo even if they were not formally included in the policy process. But even so, the JTU was on the outside—a perpetual and strident opponent, never a participant.

Parties and Institutionalization

In every nation, the teachers unions grew to be key players in the politics of education. And the way they played the political game inevitably depended on the parties that organized politics and controlled the government. I do not want to dwell too much on the details of each system. But any effort to understand how the politics of education works and why educational institutions get established as they do must pay attention to the connection between the teachers unions and the political parties.

The Japanese case I just discussed provides a stark illustration of how crucial this nexus can be. Through no fault of its own, the JTU found itself in a political system monopolized by a conservative, anti-union party, and there was only so much the JTU could do to gain influence. As a strategic matter, it could take a conciliatory approach toward the LDP to eke out whatever benefits were possible. Or it could ally itself with the Socialist Party and Japan's progressive political forces more generally, including the broader labor movement, and try—election after election—to unseat the LDP and install a friendly government. The JTU chose the latter strategy; indeed, aside from the Socialist Party, it was the nationally acknowledged *leader* of the progressive, anti-LDP forces in politics—and its approach was not unreasonable, given how hostile the LDP was toward unions. But the approach turned out to be a loser. While the JTU was often in a position to block and disrupt, its oppositional strategy thrust it into the political wilderness, an outsider to the regularized governance and institutions of education.

In the other developed nations, the story is a much brighter one. A few simple generalizations help to convey the basics. Almost all teachers unions were allied with their nation's major left party; and during this era of institution-building, these parties either held the reins of government or played hugely influential roles in moving their nations toward the construction of welfare states. The education system and its unions were an integral part of all that, as governments expanded public education, spent more, and made the schools more inclusive. In this key respect, the teachers unions were on the winning side of politics—and history—as the bureaucratic state took form. They were also in a good position, as clients of the left parties, to benefit from the spending, jobs, benefits, enhanced working conditions, and job security that flowed naturally from a left agenda.

The center-right parties, moreover, were not ardent opponents of the welfare state as it took shape over the decades. It is true that they were more likely to be applying the brakes than the accelerator. But as modern bureaucratic institutions developed, most "conservatives" of this era did not seek to reverse course, and, indeed, basically signed on as more-reserved (or resigned) supporters of what the left parties were trying to do. Thus, although the center-right parties were often in control of government during the first three decades after the Second World War—in Germany, France, and England, for instance—the welfare state continued to thrive under their stewardship, as did its education systems. Throughout, the teachers unions were largely accepted by the center-right as established participants, and the various corporatist-like mechanisms were maintained. So, yes, the teachers unions were allies of the left parties, and they benefited from that alliance—but the center-right parties were not enemies bent on destroying them, eliminating their power, or transforming their institutions.

In terms of the major forces driving politics, then, the era of institutional formation could not have been much better for the teachers unions. As the chapters show, they had their struggles and setbacks. But the bigger picture is that they had very powerful political allies intent on creating—and successful at creating—a large, well-funded bureaucratic system, whose governance involved pervasive union participation; and their "opponents" were not real enemies, but just milder supporters of the same basic kind of system. This was a political-historical context thoroughly conducive to the growth and prosperity of the teachers unions—and to the institutionalization of their involvement and power in public education.

I want to emphasize, finally, that while the teachers unions benefited greatly from their alliances with parties of the left, unions and parties are different organizations with different agendas. In particular, it is important not to think that, because the parties of the left were strongly motivated by an egalitarian ideology, that the teachers unions were allied with them on ideological grounds and were themselves ideological in their approach to politics. As the book chapters show, their main concerns were material: better wages, benefits, working conditions, and job security—and their alliances with parties were means toward those ends.

Consider, for example, the educational issue that, for many of the nations studied here, stands out as the single most politically contentious issue of the era: comprehensive education. The fight for comprehensive education, vigorously led by parties of the left, was about the expansion of schooling beyond the primary grades to *all* children, without selection—and thus, about the democratization of secondary schooling, a vast increase in their enrolments, and an opening up to the lower classes of educational opportunities previously reserved for elites. The teachers unions were often strong proponents of comprehensive education, linking arms with their left-party allies to wage political battles on its behalf—fighting against the resistance of the center-right parties and their more affluent constituents.

It is easy to infer that the teachers unions were engaged in an egalitarian struggle on behalf of the disadvantaged and that this is what drove their behavior. While ideology may surely have had some resonance with union leaders (and members), there is much more to the story. Comprehensive education had major implications for the *jobs* of teachers—opening up huge numbers of new jobs in lower secondary schools to primary teachers, and raising their training and pay, while sharply diluting the differentials that had long worked to the great advantage (and higher social status) of secondary teachers. The teachers unions that were dominated by primary teachers pushed hard for comprehensive education in alliance with leftist political parties—but the teacher unions that represented secondary teachers were *opposed* to comprehensive education, and allied themselves with the center-right parties in fighting it. In Scandinavia, where the most powerful teachers unions were dominated by primary teachers, comprehensive education was widely adopted over the opposition of secondary school unions. But in Germany, the most powerful teachers union was (and is) the DPhV, representing upper secondary teachers—and it was (and continues to be) quite successful at blocking the efforts of Germany's Social Democrats and the GEW, the union representing primary and lower secondary teachers, to reform the nation's traditional tripartite system through a shift to comprehensive schooling.

It is important, then, to clearly distinguish the teachers unions from the left parties, and not to assume that teachers unions are proponents of egalitarian schooling. There is no data that can tell us, definitively, whether ideology actually plays much of a role in explaining what the unions do in politics. But it is clear, from this issue and from many others, that their job interests are consistently good predictors of their behavior—and that, for many unions, these interests can lead them to adopt political positions and enter into alliances that are actually opposed to the left parties and their ideological values.

Institutions and Power

The first thing scholars (and others) tend to ask when it comes to matters of union power is whether the unions have been successful at winning big wage gains for their members. In the case of teachers unions and the politics of education, this focus on wages is a mistake and threatens to be quite misleading.

For starters, I should note that, while it would surely be interesting to know what the impact of teachers unions on wages has actually been, country by country, social science provides no confident answers. Answers would require a great deal of complicated and very difficult research capable of sorting through all the obvious causality issues that would come up in the process. There is some research to indicate that the teachers unions have indeed increased wages (e.g., Hoxby, 1996), but some to suggest otherwise (e.g., Lovenheim, 2009); and there is not nearly enough research to truly clarify matters, even for the US, and surely not for cross-national purposes. Future work will hopefully lead to progress on these counts (see also Hirsch et al., 2013; Winters, 2011).

Research problems aside, though, there are compelling reasons why a focus on wage gains is likely to distract from the institutional reality of union power and its consequences for education systems. What it comes down to is this: there are major obstacles that stack the deck against big union wage gains, and in part for that reason, both governments and unions have acted to see that union power finds its rewards in *other* forms—forms that are ultimately institutional in nature.

A baseline problem for the unions is that, in all countries, money is scarce and a more-or-less continuous problem. This is the case not simply because economic growth and tax revenues don't always give nations the budgets they need, but more importantly, because there are so many competing programmatic needs and so many promises that have already been made that even powerful participants, like the teachers unions, find themselves up against powerful players in every *other* policy realm—and they are all fighting for bigger pieces of the same pie. They cannot all win, or win very much. This is especially true for teachers, because raising their wages across the board—which is always what the unions want—is one of the most expensive things governments can do, simply because there are so many teachers. As governments sought to expand their education systems, moreover—a very expensive thing to do—what money they had for education needed to go to *more* teachers (and buildings and supplies and bureaucracies), which reduced the amounts available to ratchet up salaries for each one of them.

In the United States, where union wage impacts have apparently been positive but modest, these financial facts of life are highly constraining. The local school districts are continually strapped for money; local (and state) citizens are resistant to paying higher taxes; the states have many programs and power groups competing for limited funds; and for most states public education is already their biggest budget item by far. The unions are in the position of trying to get blood out of a turnip. Plus, the teacher-student ratio has gone up monotonically over the decades (stabilizing in recent years); and with so many more teachers to pay, it is all the more difficult to raise salaries. The skyrocketing cost of benefits, magnified recently by the burdens of underfunded pension systems, only adds to those problems.

Other countries face similar budgetary realities that heavily constrain what they can do on wages. But in many of these nations—unlike the US—there is a second source of constraint that, when layered on top of the first, operates to put an even tighter lid on wage increases. This is that political institutions are often designed to moderate wage demands and give governments the institutional means of keeping them under control (e.g., Park and Young, 2014).

The Nordic corporatist systems were explicitly designed to encourage moderation in group demands, especially on matters involving major public expenditures, through mutual recognition (within corporatist decision venues) of what one group's gains might cost all the others, as well as the nation as a whole. In other countries not typically categorized as corporatist, there were also corporatist-like mechanisms that worked to promote moderation and tradeoffs. In England, for instance, the Burnham Committee was a venue for national collective bargaining and wage-setting that was designed through its membership and structure to encourage moderate outcomes (although these outcomes sometimes led to strikes). In Mexico, and indeed in many countries throughout Latin America, the incorporation of teachers unions into the educational bureaucracy and official committees gave them ample and wide-ranging non-wage arenas for exercising influence, with governments expecting moderation in wage demands in return (see, e.g., Grindle, 2004).

Another institutional means of moderation is the civil service system. With some exceptions, teachers unions around the world have fought to see that teachers remain outside their nations' civil service systems, with wages determined instead through collective bargaining between unions and employers (governments). But in some major cases—Germany and France, for example—teachers are part of the civil service for political reasons that go back in history: these two countries had well-developed bureaucratic systems well before most other nations, and their civil service systems were established much earlier as well. In both cases, the inclusion of teachers in the civil service helps governments to impose moderation on wages—as wage decisions are made for huge, diverse populations of public employees, and the latter are represented by federations or coalitions of public employee unions (or professional associations) rather than by occupation-specific groups like the teachers unions. The teachers unions do not advocate for themselves on wages, and are very limited in what they can accomplish.

Big wage gains, then, are almost always off the table. But to focus on that is to miss the forest for the trees. Governments still have incentives to respond to union power, and if they cannot do it through wages, they can allow the unions—essentially as part of an ongoing trade-off—to realize gains on many other dimensions of genuine importance to them. And the unions, for their part, can pursue these dimensions as their best opportunities for pursuing their job interests and reaping the rewards of power. The result is that the unions tend to win advantages and concessions in the form of things like job security, protective work rules, influence over policy, insider appointments to bureaucratic positions and decision making bodies, administration of government benefit programs, influence over hiring, transfers, promotions, and more. And these benefits, while potentially of enormous importance for education systems, *do not cost much money* in themselves. They take the form of rules and influence. They are *institutional*.

During the era of institutional formation, then, governments allowed teachers unions to gain positions of influence within education systems and the political governance structures surrounding them, and in the process, allowed them to play important roles in determining how those education systems would get structured, staffed, and operated. All of these elements may well have had consequences, some of them negative, for the academic performance of national education systems—although there is no well-developed research literature to demonstrate as much. Whatever the case, an accommodationist approach by governments was perhaps natural during this era, even easy—for in the politics of the time, the performance of the system did not matter that much. What mattered, politically, was the simple construction of institutional systems that could expand educational services to a broader population of children, and do it in a way that would help guarantee labor peace and system stability. Performance was not the main issue.

The Era of Performance-Based Reform

As public school systems and their political and power structures became institutionalized over the decades, similar processes were going on across policy realms as the bureaucratic, service-providing state took institutional shape throughout the world. The results, in the more advanced nations, were highly developed welfare states. But even in many developing nations, governments grew bigger and more bureaucratic, and their institutions grew more deeply entrenched (e.g., Fukuyama, 2014).

In general, nations were shifting away from more primitive, simplistic forms of government toward more modern administrative forms with greater capacity to expand public services—a major contrast to governments of the past, which often did little to provide for the needs of their citizens. In adopting these new institutions, however, nations had moved onto specific institutional paths that—due to all the usual forces associated with path dependence, including the protective power of vested interests—would be very difficult to change if the future presented them with new challenges that these established institutions might fail to meet (Moe, 2015; Pierson, 2004).

That is precisely what happened. As the twenty-first century approached, the nations of the world were plunged into a radically different environment for which at least some of their established institutions seemed to be a bad fit. Scholars of comparative politics began to talk about, study, and reorient their theoretical thinking around the "crisis of the welfare state"—which, with the ending of the postwar economic boom in the 1970s, the beginning of what seemed to be "permanent austerity," and heavy pressure on expansive (and expensive) social service programs, signaled the dawning of a new era (e.g., Huber and Stephens, 2001; Pierson, 1994, 1998).

As Pierson (1996) argued in his agenda-setting work on the topic, the politics of institutional expansion had given way to a distinctively different politics of retrenchment, with party divides less important than before, and governments seeking ways to pare back and restructure the welfare state in the face of powerful resistance from mass constituencies intent on keeping their benefits. Where the "new politics of the welfare state" leads, he argued, is rarely to retrenchment on a grand scale, and thus rarely to major institutional change. Path dependence is formidable—and change, when it comes, tends to be incremental, leaving the basic structure of the welfare state intact. Nonetheless, its political dynamics are different, and its institutions are under constant pressure.

An explosion of new research followed, along with considerable scholarly debate about the causes, consequences, and severity of the "crisis of the welfare state." On most topics, the literature is predictably mixed and contentious. Some scholars argue that left-right party differences are still fundamental to modern politics, and that much of the "old" politics still prevails (e.g., Huber and Stephens, 2001; Korpi and Palme, 2003). There is disagreement on the impact of globalization, whether it necessarily challenges the sustainability of welfare states, and whether other factors, such as demographics and the aging of populations, are far more important in this regard (e.g., Garrett and Mitchell, 2001; Rodrick, 1998; Swank, 2002). There is also debate over how "retrenchment" should be measured—in terms of spending, for example, or in terms of rules and structure—and thus over how much retrenchment has actually taken place and how significant it is (e.g., Klitgaard, 2007; Korpi and Palme, 2003; Starke, 2006). And these issues only touch on some of the highlights.

Scholarly battles notwithstanding, however, there is much consensus that a significant transition has taken place. Modern nations clearly do find themselves in a new institutional era: one in which they are under intense pressure to alter existing institutions. But those institutions—inherited from the past, and the unavoidable starting-point for moving into the future—are powerfully protected and resistant to change. For governments, parties, and interest groups alike, the politics of the new era is heavily focused on how to bring the inherited institutions into congruence with the new, more austere, more restrictive environment of modern times (Pierson, 1996, 1998).

My focus here is not on the welfare state per se. It is on public education systems, which, in advanced nations, are integral parts of the welfare state but must also be considered on their own terms in certain respects. While nations have been driven to consider retrenchments in their public pension systems, for example, or their healthcare systems or their systems of labor protections, public education is a different matter. It is subject to many of the same new-age pressures (as we will see), but it is *not* a target of retrenchment, at least as retrenchment is normally understood. Nations want *better* education systems, not smaller ones.

To understand how education, specifically, has been affected by the world's transition to a new institutional era, we need to appreciate the profound consequences of two modern developments. How consequential they have been for the welfare state as a whole is inevitably a matter of scholarly debate. But they are essential for understanding how nations in the new era—not just advanced nations, but developing nations as well—have sought to reform their education systems. The commonalities that these developments have induced across nations are striking and of universal relevance.

The first development has to do with the disruptive onset of globalization and rapid technological innovation, dating roughly from the late 1970s. In response to these new forces, nations throughout the world have grown increasingly concerned about their economic competitiveness. At the same time, they have grown acutely aware that human capital is an essential path to economic success, and convinced that the best way to expand and invest in human capital is to create education systems that are effective at promoting academic achievement (Goldin and Katz, 2009; Hanushek and Woessmann, 2015).

In the modern era, the simple provision of schools is no longer enough. Nor is the simple expansion of education to broader swaths of the population. Nations have increasingly sought to ensure that their children are learning as much as possible, that they are academically empowered to become highly productive members of the new "knowledge economy"—and thus that the schools are effective at providing a high quality education. The modern era, as a result, is an era of education reform—focused on school improvement, and on reforming traditional educational institutions to bring that improvement about. There are exceptions, of course, and the degree of reformist zeal varies across countries. But *performance-based reform* is the new normal. And this is true almost everywhere, even in nations such as Mexico and India where patronage and corruption are rampant, and the school systems remain very poorly developed.

International tests of student achievement, which allow for comparisons across nations, are now front page news. They are also a source of great consternation in countries that see themselves as falling behind. The United States has never stacked up well in such rankings, and this disturbing fact has regularly bolstered calls for reform. Other countries that in decades past thought of their education systems as especially good—Japan and Germany, for example—have experienced "PISA shock" after their rankings came in lower than expected, leading even in those contexts to reformist calls to action. Countries everywhere, regardless of their apparent place in the achievement hierarchy, have been vigorously jockeying for position, eager to get ahead, worried about their futures. Meantime, the few countries that have shown themselves to be high flyers on international tests, Finland in particular, have assumed the status of educational celebrities (see, e.g., Grek, 2009).

The question most on nations' minds is: what can they do—what specific reforms might actually work—to bring about better schools and higher achievement? The solution is not just to copy Finland—which, after all, is a tiny country of just five million people, ethnically homogeneous, high in income, and quite unlike almost all other countries of the world in its fundamentals. Much of its high academic achievement may be rooted in causes that have little or nothing to do with most aspects of its education system. What nations need, as they tackle the very real and ongoing challenges of reform, are more general models of what effective educational governance looks like and how it can be pursued—models that would directly apply to *them* and give them practical guidance as they try to improve.

Ideally, one might think, they would turn to social science for answers. And to some extent they have tried to. But over the decades, the social science of education—not unlike many other areas of social science—has been characteristically mixed, messy, and incapable of providing clear guidance. Lacking a definitive knowledge base, then, nations have largely taken their models of governance from elsewhere. In particular, they have been heavily influenced by a worldwide transformation that, over the last few decades, has changed the way nations approach governance across the full range of public policies. This worldwide transformation in governance is the second sea-change-inducing development that I referred to above—a key development that, despite all the differences across nations, has brought about important commonalities in their approach to education.

This second development dovetails historically with the first, and the two are quite related. At the same time that globalization and technological innovation were sweeping the world, disrupting economies, and rendering them increasingly interconnected and open, communism and socialism were revealing themselves to be horribly inefficient. Communism collapsed, and most communist countries became democracies (or something approximating democracies) with market economies. China, which remained communist (in some sense) in its politics, created a booming market economy that quickly fueled its exponential growth as a world leader. Belief in the efficacy of centrally planned, bureaucratically directed economies evaporated.

In the meantime, advanced democratic nations were grappling with the ongoing "crisis of the welfare state." There emerged a widespread recognition that many modern nations, through the best of intentions, had made vast promises to their citizens that were extraordinarily costly and that, over the long haul—especially with growing demographic imbalances (more seniors, fewer workers to support them)—may not be affordable. Nor would their economies save them, plagued as they were by slowing economic growth, lagging productivity, and fierce global competition. Indeed, it appeared that, if their economies were to do at least part of the job of bolstering the welfare state, they would need to be liberated from some of the heavy restrictions on business and labor markets imposed by the welfare state itself. Ordinary citizens, moreover—while happy to be receiving valuable benefits and services—expressed frustrations with how remote, out of touch, unresponsive, and bureaucratic their governments had become. They wanted a welfare state, but one that was institutionally less monolithic and rigid (e.g., Castles, 2004; Huber and Stephens, 2001; Pierson, 1996).

The upshot is that nations around the world—as symbolized early on by the Thatcher era in the United Kingdom (1979–89) and the Reagan era in the United States (1981–89), but often furthered by reform-oriented parties of the left—began moving toward less regulation, less bureaucracy, less reliance on top-down governance, and pervasive efforts to make the operation of governments more flexible, cost-effective, and performance-driven through reforms labeled as "neoliberal." Most prominent among these reforms were efforts to introduce greater decentralization, accountability, and choice (e.g., through the contracting out of public services and a proliferation of options)—modes of organization traditionally associated with business and markets, not government (e.g., Hebdon and Kirkpatrick, 2006; Hood, 1991; Osborne and Gaebler, 1992; Premfors, 1998).

Not all nations, of course, have moved in the same ways and with the same speed. And for the most part, change has been incremental and fiercely resisted by vested interests, leaving the welfare state very much in place. Even so, this movement has had impacts on governance systems throughout the world, including many of those in the developing nations—which are struggling to cope with the same harsh realities as the advanced nations, and are often induced to embrace the neoliberal ideas and mandates of major international sources of development money, notably the World Bank and the IMF (see, e.g., Hall and Lamont, 2013).

Some scholars, writing on the politics of globalization (including its effects on education), portray the influence of these ideas as an integral part of the growing international power of capitalism and its negative effects on governments, equality, and social responsibility (e.g., Applebaum and Robinson, 2005; Burbules and Torres, 2000). There are others, coming at it from the standpoint of the sociology of institutions, who argue that nations embrace these new arrangements not as a rational means of meeting new challenges, but rather because they are seeking legitimacy in the international arena by essentially copying the dominant governance ideas adopted by others (e.g., Meyer et al., 1992; Ramirez and Boli, 1987). I do not want to discount these notions. More research is surely needed to document what is actually happening and why.

Yet there are good reasons for thinking that these reforms are genuine efforts by governments to address very real problems (e.g., Schwartz, 2001). They may or may not ultimately prove successful. But the fact is, nations are living in a new environment that is radically different from the past—more competitive, more dynamic, more interconnected, with far more emphasis on knowledge, technology, and expertise—and they are struggling to adapt to it. They are also adapting to an environment of greater austerity, driving them to place much more emphasis on cost-effectiveness and bang for the buck. For the most part, there is nothing faddish, superficial, ephemeral—or irrational—about this. Nations are trying to reform the institutions of the past because *those institutions, as originally built, no longer seem to be a good fit with the environment of modern times.* They performed well enough for an earlier era, when much less was expected of them, and their job, in effect, was to provide a first-attempt institutional infrastructure for expanding services and creating an institutional capacity for active government. But nations now want institutions that can provide high quality, cost-effective performance—and the old institutions were simply not designed or expected to do that.

In education, three lines of institutional reform stand out. They essentially comprise a modern reformist syndrome common throughout the world, promoted by major international organizations active in education—notably, the World Bank and the OECD—and reflective of the larger worldwide influence of neoliberal ideas. The first is *decentralization*: an attempt to move away from national, top-down, bureaucratic governance of the schools by devolving authority to states, municipalities, and schools themselves. Much emphasis is placed on the need for autonomy and the greater flexibility, responsiveness, and local representation that is presumed to go along with it. The second is *accountability*: an attempt to inject principles of efficient management into government bureaucracy by putting the spotlight on performance, defining it through high standards, measuring it through student testing, subjecting teachers to performance-based evaluations, ridding the system of low performers, and building performance-based incentives into the organization of schooling. The third is a greater reliance on *choice and competition*: an attempt to get away from the problems of monopoly provision through greater diversity and autonomy on the supply side of schooling, more alternatives for families, and funding that follows children to their schools of choice (reforms that usually put little emphasis, I should add, on genuine privatization) (Astiz *et al.*, 2002; Blossing *et al.* 2014; Grindle, 2004; Hanushek and Woessmann, 2015; Jakobi, Martens, and Wolf, 2010; OECD, 1994, 2002; Wiborg, 2013; World Bank, 2003, 2011; Zadja, 2015).

I am not arguing here that these approaches to reform are wise or effective. The point to be made is simply that, however vast the differences across nations may seem to be, these nations are all bound up in a common political economy whose powerful contextual forces have tended to guide them in very similar directions—toward an emphasis on academic achievement and effective schools, toward specific lines of institutional change that depart from the top-down bureaucratic past, and toward a politics of performance-based reform that is threatening to vested interests.

Thinking About Performance-Based Reform

The teachers unions entered the modern era as formidable actors in their respective systems—well organized, politically active, embedded in existing institutions, and playing key roles in government decisions on education. But now they had a lot to *lose* as governments sought new ways of governing and organizing education—reforms that, if achieved, threatened to translate into less control over jobs and policy for the unions and far greater scrutiny of what teachers do and how well they do it. Indeed, the new emphasis on performance put the spotlight *squarely on teachers*. They are the ones in the classrooms, and it is largely *their* behavior that reformers aim to evaluate, motivate, and reorganize in pursuit of better schools. All of which is very threatening to teachers. And to their unions.

This tension is to be expected. All institutional systems give rise to vested interests. And whenever reformers attempt to bring about major change, one faultline is always the same: the reformers versus the vested interests. Other interests may be involved too. But this fundamental core will always be there. In the case of education, the chapters in this book show (as we will discuss) that this expectation is fully borne out. *For all of the countries studied here, reformers have had to contend with the opposition of the teachers unions.* Again, this is not to imply that the reformers were somehow "good" and the teachers unions somehow "bad." The point is an *analytical* one, backed by evidence, that strikes to the heart of the politics of education reform—and is essential for understanding it.

Not surprisingly, these battles between reformers and the teachers unions have played out differently across political contexts. If we are to get a handle on this variation and know what to expect, then, we need to have a simple way of characterizing these contexts: one that is analytically tractable and incisive—and well suited for understanding the politics of reform. In the welfare state literature, scholars have often oriented their theoretical orientation by reference to the three classic types of welfare states identified by Esping-Andersen (1990)—social democratic, conservative-corporatist, and liberal—in the expectation that institutional politics would work itself out in distinctively different ways across these three types. But research on welfare state reform is rather mixed in its support for this notion (e.g., Klitgaard, 2007). And as I will show, this book's country-studies do *not* bear it out in the case of education reform. We need to recognize, moreover, that all nations are not modern welfare states anyway, and we need to put ourselves in an analytic position to explore those that are not.

An alternative and very useful way to characterize political contexts is in terms of a simple universal: the extent to which a nation's governing institutions contain *formal veto points*—bicameralism, federalism, an independent executive, and the like—that put obstacles in the way of reform. The fewer the number of veto points, the greater the government's power to take action, and the greater the prospects for successful reform. The flip side is that the presence of veto points works to the great advantage of vested interests—because their goal in the politics of reform is mainly to block, and veto points make it much easier for them to do that (Huber and Stephens, 2001; Immergut, 1992, 2010; Klitgaard, 2007, 2010; Tsebelis, 2002).

A second factor of pivotal importance is the government's *commitment* to reform—which is necessary if governments are to *use* their power for reformist ends. Unlike the first, this factor is endogenous to ongoing politics, because what a government wants to do—meaning, which reforms it embraces and how much it is willing to invest in pursuing them—arises from its broader policy agenda, whether it governs alone or in coalition, how it is connected to voters and interest groups, and much more. Obviously, all this can get complicated. Yet there is a crucial simplifier at work here that is very helpful in structuring expectations—for the presence or absence of veto points is likely to have an important bearing on a government's commitment to reform.

Specifically, in a political system that places veto points in the way of government action, thus greatly advantaging the opponents of change, the government can anticipate that it is likely to lose or suffer painful political costs if it pursues major reform—and all else equal, these considerations will prompt it to shy away from such efforts in favor of incrementalism and compromise. *The less empowered the government, the less its commitment to major reform.* (This is but a reflection, I should note, of Bachrach and Baratz's (1962) well known "second face of power.") The converse is not, however, that in political systems that lack veto points governments will always be committed to major reform. For even in those systems, the vested interests may have plenty of raw political power, and the parties controlling government may actually be allied with them or have political reasons of their own for resisting a reform agenda. The converse, rather, is that when governments are empowered by the absence of veto points, they will simply be much *better positioned* to win should they seek to transform their institutions, and thus are *more likely* to be committed to major reform than governments that are more formally constrained.

When it comes to genuine institutional reform, then, political systems that lack veto points are doubly advantaged. Their governments are more likely to have *both* the power and the commitment to make reform a reality. Even in these cases there is no guarantee, because commitment is something of a wild card depending on the government's larger assessment—with an eye to constituencies, interest groups, and other opportunities—of whether major reform makes good political sense. But in general, if major reform is going to happen, it should tend to occur in these types of political systems, where the criteria of power and commitment are most likely to be jointly met.

Education Reform When Governments Are Formally Free to Act

Some 30 years ago, when the wheels of education reform first began churning worldwide, many may have thought that, if any nation could actually succeed in bringing transformative change to its public schools, it would be the United States. After all, the US was the paradigmatic liberal nation—wedded to markets, disdainful of big government and bureaucracy, known for its innovative energy in business and technology, and famous for weak unions. Surely it would leave the Europeans and the Scandinavians in the dust, mired in their "socialist" ideologies and welfare states and incapable of moving nimbly into the future.

But nothing of the sort actually happened. The US has failed miserably in bringing about a coherent, significant transformation of its education system. In the meantime, the stand-outs in world education reform, at least among the nations we have studied here, are two countries that few might expect to be at the forefront of institutional change: Sweden and England.

Sweden and England

As welfare states, Sweden and England are poles apart. Sweden is the paradigmatic social democratic welfare regime, while England is usually categorized as being a liberal regime (although its system is downright "socialist" by comparison to the United States). Yet despite their fundamental differences as welfare regimes, they have two big factors in common. One, their political systems *did not put formal veto points in their way*. And two, they were led by governments—of different parties, in succession, over time—that were firmly *committed* to a radical trajectory of change, and thus to taking advantage of the formal powers their political systems granted them.

Sweden entered the reform era as a highly centralized, fully corporatist welfare state. Its education system conformed to this same model, and during the 1960s and 1970s, the teachers union was at the peak of its power. In effect, Swedish governments—which, since 1932, had all been Social Democratic—did nothing in the realm of education unless the teachers union signed on. But then came the "crisis of the welfare state," and public disaffection with the Social Democrats and their legacy of centralized, bureaucratic government ran high. The center-right parties took control of government in 1976, initiating the process of decentralizing and deregulating the Swedish welfare state—and when the Social Democrats came back to power in 1982, this time in a much more competitive political setting (that has lasted to the present day), they shifted toward the political center and embraced the need for institutional reform. Over the next decades, control of government shifted back and forth between the Social Democrats and the center-right—but *both* were committed to reform. And together, over time, they brought about a profound restructuring of the Swedish welfare state.

In the realm of education, governance authority over the schools was officially shifted to the municipalities—in the late 1980s under the Social Democrats—and the locals were given substantial autonomy and encouraged to differentiate their schools in response to community needs. Collective bargaining too was shifted from the national to the local level (in 1995), allowing wages and working conditions to vary across regions and municipalities. Private schools had traditionally played almost no role in Sweden, enrolling less than 1 percent of the nation's students. But both sides of the political spectrum participated in the creation of a full-blown voucher system, in which students were allowed to enroll in private schools, called Free Schools, with government funding. The Free Schools, many of them run by for-profit companies, now enroll more than 10 percent of all Swedish students in the compulsory grades, and more than 25 percent at the upper secondary level.

The Swedish approach to reform involved, in effect, two very different forms of decentralization—one a devolution of authority within the structure of government, the other a market-based decentralization via the proliferation of hundreds of Free Schools that were largely *independent* of government, outside the formally bargained pay and work agreements, and less unionized. Together, these reforms entailed nothing less than a *destruction of the teachers union's traditional power base*, which was entirely rooted in centralized control, national-level institutions, and corporatist decision making. So why didn't the union use its pivotal positions within the Swedish corporatist system to veto them? And why didn't it use its raw power to get governments to back off?

The main teachers union, in alliance with the smaller academic (secondary) teachers union, *did* oppose these reforms, and, among other things, did launch protest actions—strikes—in an effort to defeat them. But it was politically isolated. Its key political partners, the Social Democrats, were fully supportive of bringing about a decentralization of the Swedish bureaucratic system, including its education system, and the association of municipal governments was supportive as well, as were the usual players on the center-right. The union had nowhere to go for political support and no formal veto points to take advantage of. Up against powerful governments committed to reform, it found itself in a weak and vulnerable position. In addition, the Social Democrats took tangible steps to compensate the union for its institutional losses by granting two of its most fervent wishes—for higher salaries and a much greater equalization of salaries between primary and academic teachers. This compromise helped to take the steam out of the union's opposition—an opposition that was destined to lose—and paved the way for a more peaceful path of institutional change.

But what about corporatism? Why didn't Sweden's much-vaunted system of group incorporation give the teachers unions a de facto veto in the ongoing practice of politics, as had long been the custom? Here the key is that these decision arrangements were always the informal creations of Swedish governments, which had good political reason to embrace them in the past but also had the formal authority to deviate from them if they wanted. And with Swedish governments on both sides of the political spectrum now thoroughly committed to major institutional reforms, they simply *did away* with some of the old-style arrangements that had given the teachers union a pivotal role in education policy. The new national working groups that formulated reform policy were purposely set up to *exclude* the union so that it could not stand in the way of change. The government's commitment to change—combined with its formal power to act—trumped corporatism.

The upshot is that, in a relatively short period of time, Sweden thoroughly transformed its educational institutions—and in doing so, it also transformed the surrounding structure of politics and power. The Swedish teachers union of today is a continuing and pervasive presence in Swedish education. But it is much less powerful than it used to be.

In England, education reform has been equally radical. And as in Sweden, the key to change was that successive governments of different parties were committed to reform, and they operated within a political system that did not put veto points in their way. Yet there is also an instructive difference between these two cases. For while the Swedish reform was fundamentally about decentralizing a centralized monolith, the English education system was *already decentralized* within the structure of government What, then, would the reformers in England do?

Here again, we gain analytic leverage by thinking in terms of vested interests. Both nations were dissatisfied with their existing education systems, which were inevitably protected by vested interests—and in both cases, the favored strategy was to weaken those interests and circumvent them in order to make real reform possible. In Sweden, the existing system was centralized, and so was the vested interests' power base—which led to a two-pronged strategy of decentralization: one within government, the other market-based. In England, by contrast, the existing system was already decentralized within government, with the vested interests powerfully entrenched at the *local* level via the "social partnership" between the LEAs and their unions. So what worked in Sweden would not work in England.

Given their situation, the reformist strategy in England involved aspects of *centralization*. The Thatcher government (1979–90) led the way. It abolished the quasi-corporatist Burnham Commission (for national collective bargaining) and Schools Council (for curriculum and assessment)—major blows to union power—and took unilateral control. The government would henceforth make its own decisions about teacher pay and working conditions. It would also impose a national curriculum and student assessments on the LEAs; require them to conduct annual performance evaluations; and require that they make test results public. In addition, the government abolished the LEAs' taxing authority and channeled a portion of education funding directly to the schools themselves. The national government, not the LEAs, would now be playing the pivotal role in guiding, operating, and funding public education.

Centralization was but one part of a two-part strategy. The second involved market-based decentralization, which, in the English context—unlike in Sweden—provided an especially disruptive means of undermining the *within-government* decentralization that represented the status quo. Under the Thatcher government, schools were allowed to "opt out" of LEA control, and funding was provided for new City Technology Colleges (specialized high schools of choice): steps intended to pave the way toward a much larger population of autonomous schools in future years.

The teachers unions, led by the National Union of Teachers (NUT), were staunchly opposed to all of these reforms—and militantly so. During the

Thatcher years, they launched a number of intense strikes (and work slowdowns and other industrial actions), and such disruptions have continued to the present day. Nonetheless, the governments that followed Thatcher—the Conservative government under Major (1990–97), the Labour governments of Blair and Brown (1997–2010), and the two Cameron governments—have all hewed to the same basic trajectory despite massive union efforts to stop them. There has been no reversal of course.

The Labour Party, which took power in 1997 after some 18 years of Conservative hegemony, had a chance to reverse course. But it did not. Like the Social Democrats in Sweden, it responded to the "crisis of the welfare state"—and to formidable electoral competition from the right—by moving toward the political center as New Labour, embracing markets and institutional innovation, and excluding the teachers unions from policy making. It further centralized power over the LEAs, subjecting them to new targets, plans, and monitoring; requiring much more rigorous performance management of teachers; and moving thousands of low-performing teachers out of the classroom. It also expanded the role of market-based decentralization by allowing failing public schools to convert to autonomous City Academies—and some 400 of these independent schools were ultimately created.

The two Cameron governments—the first in coalition with the Liberal Democrats (2010–15), the second in sole possession of power (beginning in May, 2015)—followed up by authorizing the conversion of existing public schools (not just those that were failing) into independent Academies, and the creation of entirely new, independent Free Schools. The result was an explosion in the number of independent schools of choice. By 2014, Academies accounted for more than *half* of all secondary schools in England, and more than 10 percent of elementary schools. The numbers, moreover, continue to rise. Increasingly, the LEAs are being marginalized, as are the unions, and their "social partnership" is left with fewer and fewer schools to control. For the schools that remain under their control, the government has continued on the same centralizing trajectory: enacting more rigid national requirements for teacher evaluations, and new requirements for performance-based pay. The NUT has launched waves of strikes, the most in modern history, to protest this massive move toward independent schools; and it has strongly opposed Cameron's new requirements on evaluation and performance pay. But to no avail.

Norway and Denmark

The Nordic countries have a lot in common. They are all social-democratic welfare states, and they share very similar political cultures, corporatist traditions, and deep beliefs in social equity. All these qualities would seem to generate resistance to neoliberal reform. Yet they did not prevent the governments of Sweden—empowered by the absence of veto points—from embracing neoliberal ideas and responding to the "crisis of the welfare state" with massive structural reforms, including radical reforms of education. It was a trail-blazer. What about Norway and Denmark (and Finland, which I will discuss later)?

Norway and Denmark have political systems very similar to Sweden's—with no veto points to get in their governments' way—and both countries have actually made considerable reforms to their education systems. But they have *not* been trail-blazers. Their reforms have been less extensive than Sweden's, they have taken much longer to achieve—and they are still in process, after all this time. Why?

A key reason is that, in both nations, the Social Democrats (Labor) did not choose to make early, sizeable strides toward the center, and thus were not on board with major neoliberal reforms, at least not until very recently. The governments in Norway and Denmark therefore lacked the kind of cross-party commitment to reform that would allow for effective, sustainable reforms over time. They had the formal power to act, but not—across parties—the continuing, broadly based political will to put that power to use.

In Norway, Labor had had an almost total lock on government (either alone or in coalition) from 1936 through 1981, but at that point—coinciding with the rise of neoliberalism worldwide—its politics became more competitive, and control of government has alternated between Labor and the center-right parties ever since. During the 1980s and 1990s, however, the historically weak center-right parties did not take aggressive action to transform the welfare state—in part, it would seem, because Norway's economy was boosted by vast oil revenues and thus was relatively shielded from the demands of austerity—and Labor did not have the same incentives to move to the center that the left parties in Sweden and England did. Labor remained wedded to its social democratic agenda, and it rejected neoliberal education reform.

Still, even during the 1980s and 1990s, some changes were afoot. Initial steps were taken to begin decentralizing education to the municipal level. But most dramatically, the Labor education minister Gudmund Hernes (1990–95) acted aggressively to break down the traditional corporatist arrangements in education policy, and he cut the teachers unions out of regular consultation—claiming that they "blocked policy reforms and killed new ideas," and saying that he wanted to "bring back the state" and "recapture education policy" (quotes taken from Wiborg's chapter on the Nordic countries). His own reforms as a Labor minister were only vaguely neoliberal, emphasizing standards, efficiency, and teacher education. But his weakening of the corporatist system in the interests of change, very much in the Swedish mold, was a precedent that made reform easier for those who wanted to bring it.

The center-right government that held power from 2001–05 wanted just that. It was committed to major change in a way that previous Norwegian governments had not been—and with no veto points in the way, it had the formal authority to follow through. It launched a radical decentralization (prompting a teachers union strike) that gave the municipalities authority over a full range of governance issues, including collective bargaining, and thus further undermined the traditional corporatist arrangements at the national level; it imposed a comprehensive new curriculum along with national tests; and it adopted a radical new voucher program patterned after Sweden's Free School reform. In the meantime, faced with an ever-more formidable center-right opposition, Labor finally took substantial steps toward the political center. The Labor coalition government that gained and held office from 2005–13 reversed the voucher law—a clear indication that it still was not fully on board the neoliberal bandwagon—but it embraced all the other neoliberal reforms, which the "old" Labor Party never would have done. And with the center-right victorious in the 2013 election, there is now—except on matters of privatization—a virtual consensus across parties on the direction of education reform. The prospect is for continued reform in the years ahead. Throughout, with the decline of corporatism and especially with Labor's move toward the center during the 2000s, the teachers unions have been marginalized in the policy process and weakened as a political force.

The details are different and more complicated for Denmark, where education was fairly decentralized well before the modern era and where choice and private schools have long (for more than 100 years) played a much greater role. An important part of the story is that the Social Democrats, like Labor in Norway, were very slow to embrace neoliberal reforms and prevented much movement in that direction for many years. But another key factor, in the Danish case, is that almost all governments over the last century or more have been minority governments, often in coalition, often short-lived. This has meant—despite the absence of formal veto points— that compromise and consensus-building have been the norm, governments *have been too weak* to carry out major reforms, and the Social Democrats had long had little political incentive to move to the center and become reformist.

Until the 2000s, as a result, not a lot happened to transform Danish education. In 2001, however, the reformist logjam was largely broken when the center-right parties won a majority of seats in parliament for the first time ever, signaling a shift in the balance of power. The center-right coalition government then moved ahead with neoliberal education reforms involving standards, testing, and choice—against the strong opposition of the teachers union, which was essentially excluded from the decision process. Meantime, the Social Democrats, faced with a more coherent and powerful reformist opposition, began moving to the center. When they took control of government in 2011, they embraced the same basic neoliberal approach to education; and the teachers unions remained marginalized in national decision making. The unions continue to wield power at the *local* level, where they have tried to establish corporatist-like arrangements with the municipalities to compensate for their national-level losses. But how that will play out remains to be seen. The bigger development is that, as in Norway, the teachers unions have seen a considerable diminishing of their overall political power during the 2000s.

Finland

Finland has much in common with the other Nordic countries culturally and historically. And like them, it has a political system without formal veto points. But in major respects it is also very different. It industrialized very late; its Social Democratic Party was for decades (until 1966) too weak to gain a role in government; and as a consequence its welfare state and corporatist system of decision making were not even developed until the 1970s and 1980s. Thus, at the time that Sweden, in particular, saw its mature welfare state as in crisis and demanding of major reform, Finland had a very young institutional system that had yet to become entrenched and problematic.

In the realm of education, Finland also stood apart from its neighbors. From the early 1900s, far higher percentages of its children were enrolled in secondary schools; its teachers were far better educated; and its secondary teachers—widely regarded as the protectors of Finnish culture, and high in status—identified with the social elites, were the dominant force among unionized teachers, were far more centrist in their political alliances and positions, and were *not* allied with the Social Democrats.

Going into the 1990s, Finland's education system was thoroughly corporatist and highly centralized, much like the systems that had earlier been developed in Sweden and Norway. It had a national curriculum, nationally uniform education laws, and a National Board of Education that strictly prescribed almost everything about the operation of the local schools. The teachers union was integrally involved in all educational policy decisions. But as was true in other Western nations—all of them concerned, in the modern era, with improving their schools to bolster human capital and economic competitiveness—neoliberal ideas were not without influence in Finnish education, and Finland did indeed pursue institutional reforms along neoliberal lines. Most important, with the onset of economic crisis in the early 1990s, center-right governments temporarily departed from the nation's corporatist decision arrangements to institute governmental reforms—and in the realm of education, although the center-right was allied with the teachers union, it circumvented them for a brief while to bring about a radical decentralization of education authority to the municipalities (which the union opposed), virtually freeing the schools from national prescriptions. In the late 1990s, a Social Democrat-led coalition moved to introduce more market-like arrangements, doing away with catchment areas for assigning kids to schools and adopting a system of public-school choice.

Yet in Finland, governments tended to be broad multiparty coalitions, and norms of consensus decision making were therefore strong—and corporatism, despite a short term decline, survived as the governing reality. Even though the decentralization of education was structurally transformative, the teachers union remained integrally involved through corporatist decision making arrangements at *both* levels, the national and the municipal, and well positioned to prevent reform from taking a significant upward trajectory. Its clout was bolstered, moreover, by the fact that, with the consolidation of separate teachers unions in the late 1980s, it became the monopoly representative of all teachers in Finland, and was thus better positioned than unions elsewhere to defend its turf. It also benefited because, unlike the teachers unions in other nations (except Germany), it was allied with the center-right parties—which, of course, are normally the most forceful political advocates for neoliberal reform. With these "reformist" parties politically interconnected with the reform-resistant teachers union, and with the Social Democrats even less supportive of neoliberalism, the political conditions were hardly ripe for major educational change in Finland.

The decentralization of the early 1990s, as a result, never really threatened the teachers union's interests. Indeed, the core aspect of educational decision making they cared about most—collective bargaining, which determined wages and important working conditions—remained centralized at the national level, quite unlike what had happened in Scandinavia. The school choice reform of the late 1990s, moreover, when it was actually implemented at the local level, was largely stifled by the unions and the municipalities to ensure that the vast majority of children attended the schools to which they were assigned.

The prospects for reform were deflated still further by the publication of the first PISA results in 2001—which showed, to everyone's great surprise, including the Finns—that Finland's academic performance was at the top of the international rankings. Very quickly, nations around the world turned their admiring eyes to Finland and tried to figure out why its education system was so successful. And although the answers are unclear to this day, the lesson to many Finns was that their system did not need to pursue serious reform, and was pretty much fine as it was. They did not rest entirely on their laurels, and did seek additional (if rather marginal) ways to improve what they already had: mainly through a new national curriculum, as well as a system of national testing (suggested by the OECD) to assess school effectiveness and student achievement levels. But tellingly, given the union's corporatist involvement in the reforms, there would be no public ranking of schools, and the assessment results would have no consequences for teacher evaluation or pay. The union was able to capitalize on the nation's success, moreover, by winning new raises for teachers, and by popularizing the notion that "trust" in teachers (which implies granting them lots of autonomy and not assessing them) and "collaboration" with teachers (which implies involving them in all educational decision making) are part of Finland's formula for quality schools.

The long honeymoon may be coming to an end, however. The most recent PISA scores have revealed signs of potential trouble—with small declines in test scores in 2009, followed by larger drops in 2012—and some in Finland are beginning to ask whether something needs to be done to get the system back on course. Reform is now being taken more seriously, and the teachers union—which still has a veto over key decisions—may find itself fending off pressures for change, at least in the near term.

Yet compared to other nations, Finland remains a story of resounding success. And that being the case, many readers of this book will probably want to know why Finnish students are achieving at such high levels. It is perhaps tempting to believe that this success is at least partly due to Finland's strong teachers union and its integral involvement in policy making. Such a conclusion, however, would be premature. The fact is, no one really knows why Finland has done so well on international tests, and it is not even remotely possible at this point to figure out the partial impact of the teachers union on student achievement controlling for all the other factors that make Finland so different from other nations, even its Nordic neighbors. If there is one specifically *educational* factor that stands out as the most plausible contributor to Finland's success—in addition to its affluence, homogeneity, and other *social* factors that work so greatly to its advantage—the most plausible candidate is that its teachers may be (on average) unusually high in quality, at least compared to the teachers in other nations. If so, the explanation would probably go back to the early 1900s, to the development and prominence of its secondary schools, and to the tradition of high-level teacher education (and elite status) that became well established from that time on.

But this is just a reasonable guess—and beyond the scope of this book, which is about politics and institutions, not the causes of academic performance. On the latter, I can only say that much more research is clearly needed to arrive at any confident conclusions.

Education Reform When Governments Are More Constrained

As the cases above illustrate, radical reform *can* happen, but all the pieces must fall into place. In political systems without veto points, governments have the formal power to take radical action, but they also need to be committed—across parties, over time—to a trajectory of reform that overcomes the inevitable opposition of vested interests. All five of the nations we just discussed had governments empowered by the absence of veto points, but their commitment to reform varied. England and Sweden had governments that were powerful *and* committed, and they achieved major reform. In Norway and Denmark, by contrast, reform was very much an issue, but the lack of cross-party commitment—due to the lesser willingness (compared to Sweden and England) of the left parties to move to the center and embrace neoliberal ideas—led to a slow and limited trajectory of change over the decades. Only recently has a broader consensus been achieved, leading to a ramp-up in reform. And in Finland, the continuation of corporatism, broad multiparty coalitions, and educational success relative to other nations have combined to keep reform—and the commitment to reform—very limited.

In the remaining countries studied in this book, governments had more limited formal power because their political systems placed veto points in the way of government action. The upside of these systems is that, if governments of the day somehow manage to adopt major reforms, the veto points work to their advantage in future years, making the reforms difficult to reverse through new legislation. The downside, however, is that reforms of real consequence are very difficult to achieve in the first place. And to make matters worse: because that is so, it is reasonable to believe that governments—knowing that the deck is stacked against them—are less likely to be truly committed to reform. They do not want to make enemies, only to lose. They do not want to waste their political capital on efforts that come up short. We should expect formal veto points and weak commitment to go hand in hand—magnifying the likelihood that major reform won't happen, or even be attempted in a serious, sustained way.

The United States

The United States entered the reform era facing a challenge very similar to England's. Its education system was decentralized, with vested interests fully entrenched at the local (and state) level. As we might expect, given this status quo, its reformers have followed a strategy of centralization combined with market-based decentralization—the same strategy that England has followed.

In the US, centralization has meant the historically unprecedented involvement of the federal government in imposing or (via incentives) encouraging accountability reforms at the state and local levels—notably through No Child Left Behind, Race to the Top, and their aftermath, including performance-based evaluations and Common Core (the US's limited version of national standards). Market-driven decentralization has taken the form of charter schools and (to a much lesser extent) vouchers and tax credit-based scholarships. Yet despite similar challenges and strategies, the US has not been even remotely as successful as England in bringing about major institutional change. Why?

In surface respects, as I said, the US might seem to be ideally suited for reform, as the premier liberal nation, committed to markets, and all the rest. Also, its interest group system is orders of magnitude bigger and more dynamic than those in other countries, including England, and the policy realm of public education is filled with countless reform groups—from philanthropists to business groups to advocacy groups, and much more. No other country even comes close to having such reformist activism arising from civil society.

Yet, ironically, this vibrant group universe is an endogenous outgrowth of a larger political system whose numerous built-in veto points—due to separation of powers and federalism—make it nearly impossible for reform groups to achieve the kind of change that they seek except in small increments. The US political system is an ideal set-up for vested-interest blocking. The teachers unions, with millions of members and enormous financial resources for political campaigns and lobbying, have been the vanguard of the opposition; and they have worked very effectively with their allies—most Democrats, the school districts, and various interest groups—to weaken and limit reformist gains.

Reformers have surely had their successes. Many of them. But almost all have been small, adopted in very different forms in different states and localities, and the overall impact of the reform movement has left the basic structure of the system intact after decades of continuing struggle. Charter schools, for example, have made major inroads in a handful of cities; but the brute fact is that, some 25 years after charters burst onto the reform scene, they enroll a paltry 6 percent of public school kids nationwide. Accountability reforms, advanced most forcefully by No Child Left Behind in 2001—the unions' single greatest political loss (occurring, not coincidentally, at the national level where they are weakest)—have put the spotlight on performance like never before. But NCLB had few real consequences for low-performing schools, none for teachers, and thus did little to actually hold anyone accountable for teaching children what they are supposed to know. It also had some basic technical flaws (such as the way it measured performance) that even supporters later recognized needed correction. Most important, though, it was besieged by the teachers unions and other political enemies—including, eventually, many Republicans who had initially been supporters, but who responded to the conservative shift in their party by re-embracing their traditional belief in local control. After years of wrangling and inaction, these strangest of political bedfellows came together—after Republicans took full control of Congress in 2015—to kill NCLB and pass new legislation that devolved all meaningful authority over school accountability to the state and local governments: which is precisely where the unions and the school districts—and their power to resist accountability—are the strongest.

President Obama's Race to the Top in 2009–10 succeeded in inducing many states to adopt reformist legislation—and most notably, in getting them to require performance-based evaluations of teachers. But in the years since, the teachers unions and the school districts have used their vantage points in the rule-writing and implementation processes to ensure that, despite the apparently "rigorous" new criteria and assessments, virtually all teachers are rated as satisfactory. Another key outgrowth of Race to the Top, Common Core academic standards in reading and math, are also in the cross-hairs of these same opponents—in alliance, once again, with Republicans who see Common Core as yet another instance of "federal overreach"—and many states are currently in the process of abandoning even this very limited step toward uniform national standards.

The sense among America's education reformers is that they have made great strides in recent years, and that they have got the unions and districts on the run. By comparison to past decades, there is something to that. The big picture, however, is that their reforms represent only marginal changes, layered on top of the existing system, that do not come close to constituting a coherent, significant whole, much less a transformation. All in all, and notwithstanding the pervasive activism and tumult reformers have managed to generate, the unions and the districts have been very successful over the years at stifling major change.

Two final points. The first is that, because power is so divided in the American separation of powers system, *government is not a coherent actor* in the same sense that it is in most other countries. No one is in charge. No one is in control. The "reformers" are sometimes public officials (like President Obama), sometimes philanthropic foundations, interest groups, nonprofits, or private individuals—and they are the key proponents of change. Not the government. It is *their* commitment to change that is most relevant. The second point is that, while American education reformers are numerous, active, and energetic, they are ultimately a very moderate bunch in terms of the kinds of reforms they actually push for in politics—because their proposals are inevitably tempered by the realities of a political system that is literally built to make change very difficult. In practice, then, their aims are almost always *incremental*—and when they are successful, that is what they get. In England and Sweden, reformist governments knew they could do better. They shot high, and they won. But in the United States, reformers know that they can't do that. The game is different. And what they get is different.

France and Germany

Like the rest of Europe and Scandinavia, France and Germany have parliamentary systems that stand in striking contrast to the American separation of powers system. Even so, both these countries have formal decision making arrangements that put veto points in the way of major institutional reform. France actually has a hybrid presidential-parliamentary form of government, in which government power is shared by the president and the prime minister, and two houses of parliament have shared roles in passing legislation. Germany has a parliamentary government with two houses, both with roles in legislation, and a federal system in which the Länder have important responsibilities—including virtually exclusive authority over the public schools. There is every reason to expect, then, that major educational reform would prove a difficult undertaking in both nations. And the facts bear this expectation out.

France has a famously centralized government and, as an integral part of it, a highly centralized education system. All primary and secondary school teachers are employees of the national government, and the national education bureaucracy is one of the largest bureaucracies in the world, exercising detailed central control over curriculum, personnel, training, and virtually all other matters related to the public schools. One would surely think, then, that as the era of performance-based reform took hold around the globe, France would have become a prime candidate for radical restructuring along neoliberal lines.

Since the mid-1970s, French governments have indeed tried to decentralize their education system—although not nearly as radically as the Swedes did. But the teachers unions, intricately woven into the warp and woof of the national education bureaucracy and long engaged in what amounts to professional self-regulation, strongly opposed any move away from centralized control. And although as a group the unions were fragmented and competitive with one another, they were united in defending their common turf, were strongly supported by France's larger (and highly ideological) union movement, and were highly militant in taking to the streets, gaining media attention, and influencing public opinion. Their tactics and power have consistently won out, in scenarios that have recurred many times. Throughout the 1980s, the 1990s, and into the 2000s, French governments have made numerous attempts to at least move in the direction of decentralization, including more autonomy for schools—and in all cases of any note, their efforts have been defeated.

Surprised and disappointed by their PISA standings in 2001, French governments also began to seek reform along a second front: greater accountability. The Sarkozy government proposed to change the existing system—in which teachers were evaluated every seven years, with no consequences for salaries or job security—by shifting to evaluations every three years that would indeed have such consequences. The teachers unions went on strike, supported by their allies in the union movement, and the proposal was defeated. The Socialist Hollande government, electorally supported by the teachers unions, subsequently offered a more modest proposal: for the evaluation of entire schools, rather than of individual teachers. But that too was vehemently opposed by the teachers unions, and was defeated.

In short, French governments have believed for decades that their education system is in need of fundamental change, and they have made attempts to do something about it—but those attempts have gone nowhere, again and again. The schools remain highly centralized, highly immune to neoliberal lines of reform—and securely protected by opponents whose militancy seems to have worked especially well in a governmental process constrained by formal vetoes.

Now consider the case of Germany. Needless to say, Germany and France are strikingly different in many respects, and it should come as no surprise that education reform in Germany has played out very differently than it has in France. But what the two countries have in common is that both have governments constrained by formal vetoes—and both have looked more like the United States than, say, Sweden or England, in bringing real change to their education systems.

Prior to the first PISA exam results in 2001, the worldwide pressures for education reform had generated no notable response from Germany. While many other nations scrambled during the 1980s and 1990s to improve their schools through structural reforms, German governments held back and embraced the status quo. There are perhaps many reasons for this non-response, but a few stand out. One is that the German education system, developed in the early 1800s, has long been an enormously influential model of public education throughout the world, and the Germans themselves were very proud of it and confident in its quality and efficacy. That pride and confidence continued well into the worldwide era of education reform—and German governments simply did not feel the need to change what they had. What they had, in their view, was already the best.

Another distinctly German factor that ran counter to reform was that its traditional concept of education, *Bildung*, on which its entire system was based, emphasized the holistic development of the individual through studies in the humanities, particularly history and the classics, and viewed education as the search for truth and freedom—and these things were not regarded as measureable through standardized tests. The neoliberal idea of accountability through data collection, testing, and the like, and indeed of restructuring to achieve the kind of academic "performance" that neoliberals typically had in mind, was foreign to the Germanic heritage. The resistance to measurement was more than just attitudinal. As an OECD (2010: 207) report recently put it, "The national government had no legal authority to measure student achievement or progress, the teachers were opposed, and the states had no interest in measuring these things."

And finally, a political factor loomed large. While there were at least some rumbles of educational concern among politicians and at least some receptivity to neoliberal reform ideas on the right, the Social Democrats did not accept these ideas. Their agenda mainly had to do with ending Germany's traditional tripartite structure of education, which streamed children into academic and nonacademic tracks at an early age, and moving toward comprehensive schools (as other European and Scandinavian nations had done), and they simply did not endorse the kinds of reforms that Sweden, England, the United States, and other nations were then pursuing (or trying to pursue). In a governmental system constrained by veto points, the opposition of the Social Democrats—backed by the GEW, the large union of primary and lower secondary teachers—meant that education reform was unlikely to gain traction during the 1980s and 1990s, even if some of the other players had seen the need for it.

The Germans entered the 2000s riding high, proud of their education system, and resistant to reform—but the publication of the first PISA results in 2001 confronted them with an astounding new reality:

> The results shocked the German nation [...] Germany came well below the average overall for all the countries tested. A substantial fraction of German students tested below Mexico [...] [M]ajor newspapers ran four, five and six-page special sections on the PISA results. The news and discussions of the results were all over the radio and television [...] Suddenly, educators could no longer make the case that what was most important about education could not be measured. If Germany was far behind in every important area of the curriculum, if Germany's education standards generally lagged those in the rest of the developed world ... something had to be done.
>
> (OECD, 2010: 208)

The sense of disappointment in German society was so deep and widespread that parties on both sides of the spectrum became strong advocates for education reform. The battle over comprehensive schooling continued, with the Social Democrats and the GEW arguing that reform along these lines would greatly improve the achievement of Germany's growing population of immigrant children—but they were defeated by the CDU and its teachers union ally, the powerful DPhV, just as in the past. And there continued to be little German enthusiasm for choice and privatization—again, as in the past.

Yet there was now substantial agreement, for the first time, on the need for accountability-related reforms, and the Social Democrats were on board. The teachers unions, moreover, were very aware of the massive public reaction to low PISA scores (which threatened the reputation of teachers) as well as the massive public support for reform, and they were willing to be accommodating in order not to appear obstructionist during these critical times. I should add that the vast majority of teachers are civil servants, who do not have the right to strike—so the militancy option is much-reduced by comparison to France.

The resulting reforms, although modest by comparison to what has happened in other nations, represent unusual changes for a nation long wedded to the status quo. Acting through their Council of Ministers—a collective body that allows the 16 Länder to come up with coordinated, uniform policies (and is yet another forum in which vetoes can be wielded)—the German states agreed to national standards and common annual assessments (tests). Transparency, accountability, and data collection would now be at the center of education policy—although none of the testing would have any bearing on teacher evaluations or pay. Indeed, the unions made sure that the tests would be carried out via a sampling procedure that rendered it impossible to connect student outcomes to teachers (OECD 2010: 213). Along with these nationwide reforms, some states also pursued decentralizing reforms that gave schools (via their principals) greater autonomy—e.g., in the hiring of teachers, the allocation of budgets—although here too the threat to the unions was modest, given the codetermination rights of teachers at the school level and the key role of School Councils in school-level decision making.

Thanks to the galvanizing force of PISA shock, the Germans left at least part of their tradition behind and achieved a modicum of institutional reform—which is a good bit more than can be said for France. Even so, the basic structure of German education remains much the same as before, and its reform efforts do not come close to rivaling what we have seen in England or Scandinavia.

Japan

Japan stands apart from every other developed nation that we have studied—because from the end of the Second World War to the present, some 65 years, its governments have been dominated by one party, the LDP, and that party has consistently shut the teachers unions out of governmental decision making. The education system, which was modeled after the French system, has been highly centralized during this entire period, with all-important policy and pay decisions made at the national level and great power concentrated in the Ministry of Education.

Although shut out, the Japanese Teachers Union (JTU) was nonetheless a forceful presence in education politics until the 1990s. It was the organizational vanguard of Japan's progressive political movement, allied with the Socialist

Party and other labor unions. And because it operated in a political system that offered various vantage points—a two-house parliament, a factionalized LDP, a strong norm of social consensus—it was able to use its power of disruption in both policy making and implementation to influence political outcomes, and in many cases to block policies it did not support.

The JTU's relation to reform, however, was different than elsewhere. In other countries, the teachers unions were typically wedded to the educational status quo, and they were often in the position of defending it from reformers. In Japan, by contrast, the JTU was *opposed* to the centralized structure of the education system—set up and controlled, as it was, by the LDP—and the union wanted it changed. The LDP and its Ministry of Education, meantime, knew that decentralization would mean putting greater power in the hands of the locally based unions—its political enemies—and it simply did not follow other nations in pursuing neoliberal reforms along those lines. The system has stayed centralized. And the unions have remained local and shut out.

Partly for this reason and partly for others, the LDP's approach to education reform has been fairly unique by international standards. Prime Minister Nakasone raced out of the gates in 1983, running on a platform of education reform and then actively pushing his agenda during the next several years. But most of it dealt with uniquely Japanese issues, and the neoliberal themes that guided reformist efforts in other nations were barely visible. Between the JTU and the Ministry of Education—each with its own, very different interests at stake—most of these proposals were blocked and very little happened.

The most important reform idea to survive and make it into policy—many years later—was that of "*yutori* education," which involved a reduction in the curriculum and study time, along with a diversification of classes, in order to lower the stress level of students and encourage greater creativity. These were reforms the JTU could support, because their by-product was more flexibility and time off for teachers. But almost as soon as the *yutori* reforms were adopted, Japan experienced its own version of PISA shock in 2004, as its international ranking dropped a few slots and the media went into a frenzy—prompting a public outcry for a return to stricter standards. The government then reversed course.

Neoliberal reforms have made minor headway in recent times. Local school boards have been allowed (since 1999) to adopt choice for primary and middle schools if they saw fit; but while choice has caught on in Tokyo, only some 11 percent of the municipalities have moved in this direction. A national system of tests has also been adopted for kids in grades 6 and 9—although the results are not made public, as the government wants to protect the myth that all kids attend equally good schools.

Overall, neoliberal reforms have not fared well in Japan. Nor have any reforms. The explanation, however, may well have little to do with the JTU. Since the mid-1990s, it has seen its more militant wing split off and form a separate (but smaller) union; it has moderated its policy positions considerably in order to broaden its appeal to both teachers and the dominant LDP—and despite its moderation, it has continued to be shunned by the LDP, and it has seen its membership drop off considerably (continuing a slide that began decades ago). Today the JTU is weaker than ever—and even at the local level, less able to disrupt than ever (due to its smaller membership)—yet the government shows no zeal for taking advantage of union weakness by ramping up its reform of education.

To understand Japan's immobilism, then, we probably need to look elsewhere: to a political system—two houses, a fragmented governing party, the norm of consensus—that makes change very difficult, to a powerful Ministry of Education with a vested interest in the status quo, and perhaps even to the conservatism of the Japanese public.

A Brief Summary: Reform in the Developed Nations

All of the nations discussed above are modern welfare states with well developed bureaucracies, and all have political systems that, by comparison to most of the rest of the world, are models of democracy. Politically and economically, they have a lot in common. And those commonalities are magnified by the shared environmental pressures they have faced during modern times to reform and improve their education systems—pressures that have pushed all of them, in greater or lesser degrees, along the same basic path. Yet institutional reform is ultimately a great challenge in almost any context. And as we have seen, commonalities notwithstanding, these nations remain very different in important respects, and their experiences with reform have varied considerably.

If there is one key pattern that stands out, though, it is that major education reform has only occurred in nations whose governments are formally powerful—unconstrained by formal veto points. In those nations, reform was resisted by the teachers unions (and other vested interests), but governments had the formal power to overcome that resistance to bring transformative institutional change. The vested interests lacked the formal venues that would allow them to block. Even in these powerful-government nations, however, change was hardly automatic. Governments had to be committed to change, across parties and over time—which happened from the beginning in England and Sweden, but was much-delayed in Norway and Denmark. Real reform, as a result, was a long time coming in the latter two cases. Still, in all these nations, major change did come—because powerful governments ultimately used their power to make it happen. Only in Finland—its governments weakened by broad multiparty coalitions, its commitment weakened by sky-high PISA scores—has reform been stifled, with the unions retaining their corporatist leverage. But even there, the education system was radically decentralized in the early 1990s: a genuine transformation of the structural status quo.

In the United States, France, Germany, and Japan, reformers have made little coherent progress. Further research may well show that a great many factors are responsible. Yet the simplest, most plausible explanation is that all these nations have governments that are highly constrained by veto points. They are not powerful. By comparison to the other nations we have discussed, they find it far more difficult to take strong, coherent action in pursuit of reform, and it is far more likely that vested interests will be able to block. Precisely because these governments are not powerful, moreover, and can foresee the great pitfalls that stand in their way, they have reason to be less committed to reform and thus less driven to use whatever power they possess to full advantage—and this appears to be borne out as well. In all four of these nations, governments are not only low in power but also low in commitment. And under these conditions, there seems to be little chance of transformative change. When change does come, theory suggests it should tend to be incremental, leaving the existing system intact and its vested interests fully entrenched in their usual niches. As the chapters of this book show, that is precisely what has happened in these nations. (I should add that, in Japan, where the teachers union had been frozen out of power for decades, they still succeeded in resisting many threatening reform proposals over the years—but preservation of the already-bad status quo was little consolation).

And finally, with the era of performance-based reform now well into its fourth decade, what can we say about the *trajectory* of union power? Are the teachers unions more or less powerful today than they were during the era of institutional expansion? The details vary across countries, of course, but the brute reality is that, with the possible exception of Finland—where the union achieved monopoly status in the 1980s and has worked closely with Finnish governments ever since—there are no countries in which the teachers unions have gained in power, some in which their power has held steady, and some in which their power has declined.

I should note that this finding is a useful contribution to the larger comparative literature on unions—which has found that, while there are variations across nations, unions have often experienced declines during the modern era due to the pressures of globalization, international competition, technological innovation, and economic weakness (Blanchflower, 2007; Pencavel, 2005; Western, 1999). That literature focuses mainly on private sector unions, and puts much emphasis on their membership levels. What our studies show, interestingly, is that while the teachers unions are in the public sector and thus largely shielded from the direct impacts of these "private" forces, they have actually not been shielded from the *indirect* impacts, which have been filtered through governments and their reformist attempts to respond to these pressures. The fate of the teachers unions turns on how, and how successfully, *governments* have been able to respond. Our studies also show that the fate of the unions in politics—which turns on their power—is not necessarily tied to their membership levels, and that the literature's focus on membership can be misleading.

In the case of education, our chapter studies reveal that there is a pattern to these dynamics. The teachers unions have seen their power decline markedly in

Sweden, England, Norway, and Denmark—all countries with powerful, committed governments that succeeded in carrying out major reforms that left the unions institutionally quite weakened. This occurred, moreover, even though union membership remains near 100 percent in the Scandinavian countries, and is 84 percent in England—big numbers for what are now considerably less potent organizations. Meantime, the teachers unions have done a much better job of holding their own in nations where governments are less powerful and less committed—and blocking is easier.

In Germany and France, the unions are arguably just as powerful as they were in the past, and structural reform has been minimal—even though, in Germany, the GEW organizes just 23 percent of teachers, and the DPhV just 12 percent, and in France only 30 percent of teachers are unionized (compared to 70 percent in 1970). Union density is not necessarily a good indicator of union blocking power.

In the United States, the NEA and the AFT are clearly on the defensive, fighting against a reformist surge, and they are somewhat weaker than in the past. Yet they are still huge and very powerful, and the American system gives them ample opportunity to defuse, undermine, and water down change.

Japan is an outlier of sorts, because it is the only country where the teachers union was excluded from policy making at the very outset of the reform; and unlike the unions in other countries, it had no stake in protecting the existing system and no niches from which to do so anyway. Still, things actually managed to go from bad to worse for the JTU over the decades—due to changes in the party system (which eliminated its Socialist allies), the continuing hegemony of the conservative LDP, and the split-off of Zenkyo to form a rival union. Membership, moreover, has declined precipitously, from some 80 percent in the 1950s to 34 percent today (27 percent for the JTU, 7 percent for Zenkyo).

The Developing Nations

Whatever obstacles these developed nations face in trying to change and improve their education systems, they pale in comparison to the problems faced by the poorer nations of the world. For them, the need for quality education is arguably far more pressing, yet the challenges of doing something about it are far more daunting. In part, of course, these difficulties arise from a sheer lack of resources, administrative capacity, infrastructure, and expertise. But it is of great consequence that these nations often have political systems that are (in varying degrees) corrupt, clientelistic, and in the grip of rent-seeking groups and power-holders. Their education systems, involving as they do huge sums of money and reservoirs of jobs, are highly valued terrain in which this kind of special-interest behavior thrives, and the incentives are especially strong to resist public-spirited change.

Mexico is an extreme example in some respects. But of all developing countries, its politics of education is probably the best studied and documented. And the evidence provides a vivid demonstration of how, even in a grossly deficient education system that weakens the economic and social well-being of the nation, power and vested interests make it virtually impossible to achieve the most obvious and basic reforms.

The Mexican education system has traditionally been governed through a union-dominated corporatism that is very common throughout Latin America. The teachers union was granted a "professional" monopoly over teachers, along with an official role in policy making and administration, by the PRI—which was itself a monopoly, controlling every Mexican government from 1929 through 2000. As a quasi-governmental actor, the union exercised vast control over hiring and firing, transfers, promotions, and other matters related to teacher jobs, allowing it to buy the dependence and loyalty of members. As part of all this, it was deeply involved in an array of corrupt or shady arrangements—among them, serving as a broker in an informal system that allowed teachers to buy and sell teaching jobs or pass them along to their children. In return for enormous rents and advantages bestowed on the union by the PRI, the union's leaders used their organizational leverage to guarantee labor peace and provide the PRI with money, poll workers, and vote-mobilizers for electoral campaigns—political manpower that was largely paid for by the government itself, for many of Mexico's "teachers" never actually set foot in a classroom, but spent their time working instead for the union or as political activists.

With the dawning of the modern era, Mexico's political leaders recognized that the nation's economic future was crucially dependent on a much-improved education system. But the prospects for change were grim. The entire political system, including the education system, was a tightly bound tangle of patronage, privilege, and corruption; and most of the key players had few incentives to depart from it. The formal structure of the government, moreover—a separation of powers presidential system combined with federalism, very much like the American system—made change all the more difficult even if leaders were to seriously try.

Still, there were two propitious signs that progress might be possible. One was the emergence of multi-party competition in 1988 that ended the PRI's guaranteed grip on power—and that prompted the teachers union, shortly thereafter, to cut loose from the PRI and pursue its alliances more strategically. The days of monopoly were over, and democracy seemingly had a chance. The second was that, in 1992, thanks to some strategic political maneuvers by President Salinas—who sought, for the first time, to cut the union and obstructive bureaucrats out of the loop—the government succeeded in adopting a major education reform that reversed Mexico's long-standing centralization of public schooling by decentralizing important responsibilities to the states. This move was intended to bring about a more flexible, more responsive education system—but also to lessen the union's powerful hold on the schools and fragment its organization (across states). In reform's timing and neoliberal direction, then, Mexico appeared to be moving along much the same path as other nations.

Yet Mexico was not Sweden, and the union was not facing a government powerful enough or committed enough to circumvent it. The union moved aggressively to colonize state education bureaucracies, and to make governors, state legislators, and mayors their political allies through the formidable electoral resources it could provide them—and it simply continued its powerful hold over the newly decentralized education system. When the PRI finally lost control of the national government in 2000 and PAN presidents took charge between then and 2012, the democratic transition was historic—but nothing much changed for Mexican education. As was true for many other countries, Mexico's abysmal PISA scores at that time heightened political recognition that something needed to be done and led (as elsewhere) to various efforts to promote accountability, data collection, and teacher evaluation. But the teachers union had made itself a key political ally of the PAN, and the party's presidents refused to confront the union, pursuing reform instead by bargaining with it and seeking mutually acceptable "accords." This strategy simply ensured that, in practice, little of real consequence would change. And little did. The union was too powerful at all stages of the game, from the design of policy through to its (alleged) implementation, and the governments were too weak and politically dependent.

The election of the PRI's Peña Nieto in 2012, however, may represent a critical juncture for Mexico's education system. Peña Nieto ran and won without the union's support. And he entered office at a time when the union had come under intense media scrutiny and criticism for its corrupt practices, political domination, and obstruction of reform—giving rise to public outrage, particularly among the growing middle class and business, and calls for action. Peña Nieto acted, and he did so not by bargaining or reaching accords with the union, but by taking it on directly—and winning. The union's president was sent to prison for corruption. Ambitious reforms were adopted to develop performance data on the schools, adopt genuine teacher evaluations, reform teacher hiring through new entry tests, eliminate the buying and selling of jobs, ensure merit-based promotions, and stop the practice of paying teachers to do union and political work.

But these are reforms on paper. In the trenches, there is massive resistance to them, both from the union and from state and local bureaucrats and politicians, and the union remains very powerful. It will not simply slink away, defeated, but will surely attempt to use its resources in the coming years to try to see that these reforms have little impact on everyday practice. For reformers this is a serious problem, and their gains are clearly at risk. Even so, the Peña Nieto reforms are a watershed in Mexican education—and may, with the attendant rise of the middle class and the reformist bent of business, reflect the coming of age of Mexico as a modern polity, much as the Progressive era did in the American context. But it is too early to tell.

The politics of education in India is not nearly as well studied as that of Mexico, and less is known about how education policies get made, how interest groups participate in state and national education bureaucracies, and exactly how the teachers unions engage in the exercise of influence throughout the nation. What we do know, however, has much in common with the politics of education in Mexico: it is fraught with corruption and patronage, and the teachers unions—although there are many of them, rather than just one—are key power-holders that are absolutely central to the way the education system functions (or most often, fails to function).

I won't go into detail here—readers are referred to the book's India chapter—but a few highlights get at these similarities. One of the biggest problems in Indian education—well known for some time, but still rampant—is that more than 25 percent of teachers are simply absent on any given day, and of those who do go to work, roughly half of them don't actually teach. The Indian education system is a big jobs program in which many are paid but few do any work—and there are virtually no serious systems of inspection or evaluation to hold anyone accountable, or even to keep track of what is going on. The teachers unions are extremely active in political campaigns, well represented in state legislatures, and benefit from a constitutional requirement that the upper houses in state legislatures allot one-twelfth of their seats to teachers. They are quite powerful. And they use that power to perpetuate India's no-work job arrangements, and to oppose serious efforts at reform. They also use their political connections with politicians—acting as brokers in a system of bribes and favors—to facilitate desirable job-transfers for their members. This is a system that greatly benefits union leaders, and makes members highly dependent on them.

India's political leaders at both the national and state levels have recognized the importance of education to the future of their nation, and they have sometimes moved to introduce accountability reforms, and to put greater authority in the hands of local school committees, in an effort to improve quality and effectiveness. But most of their efforts have been defeated, with unions leading the opposition; and even when reforms have been adopted, they have typically been weak and of little consequence. The system remains what it was—a big jobs program—entangled in corruption and patronage and largely immune to productive change.

Unlike in Mexico, moreover, there may well be no light at the end of the tunnel. Despite India's economic gains in recent decades, it remains a much poorer country—its GDP per capita is about one-third of Mexico's—and it is still struggling to expand even the most basic education to its deprived population of children. Quality can hardly become a priority when only 40 percent of the nation's kids even make it to secondary school. The middle class—and democracy—may soon come to the rescue of the Mexican education system, at least in dragging it beyond corruption and patronage. But these cleansing forces of development are unlikely to do anything comparable in India for a long time to come.

Paths to Future Research

The chapters of this book, taken together, shed informative new light on the politics of education across nations. But much more remains to be learned. My hope is that the empirical ground these studies have covered, along with the arguments I have made in attempting to bring coherence, meaning—and theoretical import—to what might otherwise have seemed a mass of country-specific detail, will spark interest and ideas (and perhaps dissent) in other scholars, and lead to productive new lines of research in future years.

The challenge is to build a genuine literature on the comparative politics of education. What the field needs, in my view, is a body of work that is self-consciously cumulative, guided by theory, and unified by a core set of substantive issues and problems. How best to proceed? There is, needless to say, no magic formula for progress. With so little now known about the politics of education, the job is huge—but the opportunities are countless.

My aim here is to keep the focus on fundamentals, and, with an eye toward what has been learned and argued in this book, to highlight targets of research and analytic modes of thinking that promise to be most productive at this early stage of the game. A great deal is "relevant" and well worth studying, and I surely don't want to close any doors. In what follows, I am simply pointing to certain avenues that, as I see it, warrant high priority.

Analytics

Two analytic components stand to be especially productive in shedding light on the politics of education. The first is a focus on *power*, along with the *interests* of those who wield it—for power is the driver of politics across all realms of policy, education included, and interests are the keys to understanding why the various actors want power and what they are trying to do with it. Research on education needs to come to grips with these fundamentals and bring them to the center of its theories and empirics. Who are the most powerful actors? How do they get power? How do they use it to shape policy, implementation, and schools? What are the interests that motivate them? These sorts of question are not currently at the heart of education research, nor have they ever been. But they need to be. (More generally on power and political institutions, see Moe, 2005.)

The second analytic component arises from a recognition that, while many interests are likely to be somehow relevant to the politics of education and thus worthy of study, *vested interests have a distinctively important role to play*—and future research needs to make them a special, continuing focus of theoretical and empirical attention. Vested interests are the inevitable outgrowths of all government institutions, including educational institutions. And when they involve valuable material benefits—as they surely do, for example, in the case of teacher jobs—they are likely to give rise to organized, politically active, potentially very powerful groups that are major forces in politics. Vested interests carry special weight, moreover, during times of institutional reform—the times in which we live—because they stand to be reform's most powerful opponents, and thus absolutely central to its politics. By training attention on vested interests, by recognizing their embeddedness in inherited institutions, and by understanding their distinctive nature as interest groups, researchers stand to gain great analytic leverage in understanding the politics of education reform and paving the way toward theories with genuine explanatory power (Moe, 2015).

To reiterate a point emphasized in the introductory chapter: there is nothing pejorative or negative in singling out vested interests for attention. Vested interests are an objective reality of great universal relevance across the world—and they are crucial to an understanding of all government institutions, their politics, and attempts at reform.

Beyond the Teachers Unions: Other Interests
In focusing on teachers unions, the chapters of this book have inevitably focused on what these groups do and the issues they care about most, and have paid less attention to other interests and other issues. In this overview chapter, I have naturally done the same. Indeed, I have simplified still further by framing the analysis in terms of two institutional eras and the commonalities they entail across nations. Any attempt to be truly comprehensive would obviously include a much broader range of contentious issues than it has been possible to cover here—among them, depending on the nation, clashes over race and ethnicity, religion, immigration, and acculturation. It would also include the much broader range of interest groups and constituencies that might become active in these sorts of clashes—churches, minority groups, and advocacy groups, for example.

All of this deserves study. But in keeping with a focus on fundamentals, what I want to do here is to argue that, however complex the terrain of education politics might get and however varied it might be from country to country, there are certain key actors that stand out as especially central to the politics of education—and thus as especially central to future research. When we get down to basics, these are the actors that demand attention.

Aside from teachers and their unions, the key vested interests in any nation's school system are likely to be the *administrative officials who populate the education bureaucracy*. They wield public authority, occupy pivotal positions in the making and implementation of policy—and their jobs, incomes, authority, and perquisites are deeply enmeshed in the existing system, which they have strong incentives to protect. That being so, they need to be brought under the spotlight of research. Among other things, scholars need to explore the obstacles that bureaucrats can represent for reformist parties: which may gain control of government, and thus titular control of the bureaucracy, yet find that bureaucrats still have ample resources and incentives for resisting the parties' reform agendas. Under what conditions are parties able to overcome bureaucratic resistance to reform their schools?

Bureaucrats are not the only official players with vested interests in existing education systems. In developing countries, especially, many *politicians and parties* may be using public education to generate valuable rents—in the form of money, patronage, nepotism, favors—that give them deep material stakes and vested interests in those systems, and strong incentives to protect and expand them. In most developed nations, as illustrated by the ones we've studied in this book, politicians and parties have been the key drivers of reform. But in the rest the world, this is probably more the exception than the rule. Scholars need to recognize as much in exploring the role that politicians and parties play in undermining and perverting education reform in precisely those nations that need it the most.

It seems likely that, almost everywhere, the pivotal players in the politics of education tend to be insiders: parties and politicians, bureaucrats, and the teachers unions (which are insiders in the sense that their members are government employees). But there are also basic types of actors arising from outside of government—from civil society—that are universally relevant to the politics of education. They too demand the serious, systematic attention of researchers regardless of the nations being explored.

The most obvious constituency is *parents*. Wherever there are schools, there are parents—who have vested interests in the kind of education their kids are receiving, are geographically on the scene, and have ample opportunity to learn what is going on in the classroom and with teachers. They are a latent group with great political potential. They can form their own organizations to concert their resources and take action in the political process. Or they can be mobilized by others to support a common cause. All the evidence (such as it is) suggests that—exceptions aside such as the relatively well-off American parents in suburban school districts, and Germany's parents of children in upper secondary schools—parents are rarely a major force in the politics of education, and almost never get organized in effective ways, disabled by their collective action problems (Haar, 2002; Moe, 2011). But it is also true that parents are rarely studied, and that what they actually do in the politics of education, and with what consequences, is very poorly understood. With parents such a ubiquitous presence in the education system, researchers clearly need to pay serious attention to them and fill in these yawning gaps in our knowledge.

A second basic constituency is *business*, which has a stake in every nation's human capital development and economic growth—and thus, has the potential to be an organized force in seeking to influence education policy, shape the nature of curriculum and training, and improve the schools. As I discussed in my chapter on the United States, however, the very concept of "business" is amorphous, and its political role is easily exaggerated. The fact is, business sectors (at least in developed nations) tend to be very diverse in their interests and political organization, and, in stark contrast to educational "stakeholders," they are only tangentially interested in education, which is but one of a huge number of policy dimensions (such as trade, regulation, and taxes) that concern them. That said, business groups may well exercise power in the realm of education when they achieve unity and focus on that topic—and whether, and under what conditions, they are able to do that clearly has an important bearing on the balance of political forces at work, and the direction that policy and reform ultimately take. The welfare state literature has already shown as much in the realm of vocational education and technical training (e.g., Busemeyer, 2014; Thelen, 2004)—although it has yet to focus on elementary and secondary education (except as these vocational realms impinge on it). With the rise of neoliberalism, the education literature has been filled with claims of business influence over these lower reaches of education; but much more research is needed before business's true role can be understood and, in particular, whether we can know if the power of business is a genuine counterweight to the power of vested interests.

A third constituency is the religious community—particularly in the developed world and Latin America, the Catholic Church and various Protestant churches. In almost all countries, churches played important roles in the early development of schools. In the United States, with its (fairly) strict constitutional separation of church and state, religion and schooling were slowly disentangled over time to yield a bifurcated system: with a large, secular public sector (enrolling roughly 85 percent of the students) and a much smaller, unsubsidized, lightly regulated, and largely religious private sector. But in most other nations, no strict separation occurred, and church-affiliated schools became integral parts of the "public" school system, often funded and highly regulated by the state. Clearly, religious organizations in these nations have strong incentives to care about government education policy, to get involved in the policy process and its implementation, and to exercise political power in trying to influence outcomes. Indeed, even in the US, certain government policies—for example, on charter schools and vouchers—have a direct bearing on the well-being of religious schools (charter schools threaten them, vouchers greatly benefit them), giving religious leaders incentives to influence those policies, and thus to wield power in politics if they can. The role that churches and other religious groups can, do, or should play in the politics of education is a potentially sensitive matter in many countries (it is surely quite sensitive in the US), and the reality of their involvement doubtless varies considerably from country to country. But whatever that reality may be, it stands to be genuinely important, and it has rarely been studied. It needs to be (see, e.g., Ansell and Lindvall, 2013; Glenn, 1989; Grzymala-Busse, 2015).

Finally, there is the *mass public*. In democracies, there is little doubt that the mass public can be a powerful political force—if it is paying attention, sees the issues in question as salient, and its preferences can affect the electoral prospects of parties and politicians. But when, and how often, these conditions are actually met in the realm of public education is another matter, and there is much for scholars to learn on this score. The literature on welfare state retrenchment and policy feedback has long argued that an aroused mass public can be very powerful when its vested interests in specific policy benefits are threatened—as, for example, when governments propose cutbacks of pension benefits (Campbell, 2003, 2012; Pierson, 1993, 1994). But such retrenchments are not the essence of the modern politics of education, which is about reforms intended to promote the performance of schools and teachers, not about cutbacks to the services or benefits that anyone will receive. Thus, whether the mass public plays a similarly powerful role in education politics remains to be seen. Clearly, performance-based reforms are no threat to the vast majority of ordinary citizens, and will not normally mobilize their opposition. Indeed, such proposals may well work the other way, with many citizens supporting government efforts to improve the schools—thus providing mass support for reform (if governments play their cards right); and to the extent the mass public is powerfully involved, special interests—including vested interests—will have a harder time getting their way. Only new research can settle the matter.

Power and Interests in Context: System-Level Influences

How interests come into play, and how much power they have, depends on the larger political system. The United States' presidential system is highly penetrated by interest groups, and the latter's political activities—in elections, in lobbying—are centered on separately influencing the countless political entrepreneurs who make up government. But the role of interest groups tends to be quite different in other developed nations, where parliamentary governments are controlled by parties, and parties are the key political actors. In these systems, interest groups may play important policy roles in the bureaucracy through various corporatist mechanisms (sanctioned by parties); but in the broader political arena where battles are waged and political agendas set, interest groups must often work through (or colonize) parties and shape party agendas in order to exercise power.

Scholars need to ask: how do these politically induced connections between parties and interest groups actually play out in the realm of education? How dependent are parties on interest group support, and which interest groups aside from the teachers unions really wield power over education? While the interest group universe in the US is thick with countless interest groups concerned with education, research may show that the relevant group universe in other nations is very thin indeed, with parties and bureaucrats influenced by teachers unions—and possibly business groups or locally dominant churches—but with few others (aside from experts) really involved in the consequential making of education policy.

What interest groups do may not be easy to observe. Much of what matters for public education, for example, may often occur within routine bureaucratic decision making processes that are internal to government and do not attract attention—even though power is being exercised. The bureaucracy, then, and particularly its corporatist aspects—which incorporate interest groups and are exceedingly common across both developed and less-developed nations—need to be recognized as an integral part of the politics of education, and pursued as a serious target of study by scholars. There are large scholarly literatures that can be drawn upon here for assistance: the literature on political control, for example, can help to shed light on the problems that parties face in controlling education's bureaucrats and the interest groups surrounding them (e.g., Gailmard and Patty, 2013; Moe, 2006, 2013; Strom *et al.*, 2006), and the literature on corporatism—and its weakening—can help to shed light on how and why interest groups wield power in these bureaucratic policy making contexts (e.g., Lijphart, 1991; Lindvall and Sebring, 2005; Schmitter, 1974).

Given the analysis of this book, one of the most rewarding questions facing scholars has to do with why, after decades of entrenchment, the teachers unions lost their grip on educational decision making in some nations, leading to radical reforms that the unions very much opposed. How could this have happened, in view of what scholars know about the durability and path dependence of political institutions? The answer appears to have a lot to do with the *power of governments*, as coherent actors, to overcome the predictable resistance of entrenched vested interests—and more fundamentally, with the conditioning effects that *formal veto points* have in determining whether governments actually have sufficient capacity *and* commitment to do that. The findings of this book are entirely consistent with this line of theoretical thinking, and contribute to the larger literature in comparative politics on the topic (Immergut, 1992, 2010; Tsbelis, 2002).

Our findings show that major reform occurs only in nations that have political systems that do not put formal obstacles in the way of government action. They also suggest that, in nations where the political process is encumbered by formal veto points, governments are less likely to push for major reform in the first place (knowing they are likely to lose), and instead are incremental and meliorist in approach. Much more research is needed to fully document and extend these findings. But in my view this is a particularly attractive line of research that, by putting the focus on simple fundamentals, stands to shed important light on when governments can succeed in carrying out major institutional reforms—and when they will want to.

At a still higher level of analysis, research is surely needed on the profound influence of the world political economy: the grandest systemic influence on public education. In the spotlight is the central notion here that, due to the dramatic shift in political economy that took place during the 1970s and 1980s, it is useful to think of worldwide educational institutions in terms of *two distinct eras*—an early era of educational expansion and institutional development, and a modern era of performance-based reform—whose *politics* were also distinctly and predictably different. In my view, this is a key analytic means of bringing order and coherence to what might otherwise seem to be an overwhelming diversity of national experiences across the globe—understanding them through a lens of common institutions, common problems, common politics. More research is clearly needed, however, to explore and document these commonalities in greater detail, to identify the exact mechanisms by which the worldwide political economy has brought them about, and to gain a better sense of how well the argument here stands up to further evidence or may need to be refined.

Performance
This book is about the politics of education across nations, with special attention to how power and vested interests have shaped the politics of institutional reform. These are profoundly important and difficult topics in themselves, and more than enough for one book to take on. Yet it goes without saying that, as reformers around the world have sought to reform their educational institutions, the purpose of their efforts has been to achieve higher levels of *performance*. As we look ahead, then, a comprehensive research agenda for the comparative politics of education would surely seek to connect the dots by seriously studying the *impacts* of these reforms on educational outcomes: including academic achievement, but potentially a host of other outcomes as well—from graduation rates to earning potential to technical skills to socialization, and, ultimately, to the human capital of the nation. How do various institutional reforms matter for these outcomes, and what difference does it make if reforms are blocked or weakened—which is normally what happens?

Susanne Wiborg and I have taken no position in this book about whether the reforms that modern governments have pursued—neoliberal reforms—are good for schools and children. And the country-specific chapters do not study performance. As researchers move in that direction, however—as we hope they will—two lines of inquiry stand out as especially attractive given what we have learned thus far.

The first has to do with the teachers unions and their impacts on educational outcomes. This is a topic of special importance because the unions are powerful actors in the politics and institutions of education; they use their power—when they can—to block reforms that threaten their interests; and their positions on reform issues are *not* determined by whether the reforms stand to be good for educational outcomes. As we have emphasized all along, this does not make them "bad" political actors. It makes them perfectly normal political actors, pursuing their interests in politics. But what it means is that there is strong reason, both theoretical and empirical, for believing that even the most productive and well-advised education reforms will tend to be opposed by the unions—and defeated, if possible, by their power—if those reforms threaten their fundamental job interests. Researchers need to explore these connections between interests, power, reform, and outcomes—to connect the dots—if we are to gain an understanding of the politics of institutional reform and its implications for performance.

The second line of research is broader in scope. As we've seen throughout this book, governments everywhere have pursued (with varying enthusiasm) neoliberal reforms of their education systems. But what impacts do these reforms actually have on schools and children? Does decentralization actually lead to better, more responsive schools? Do national standards, student testing, and performance-based evaluations of teachers improve academic achievement? And what about school choice? There is an existing research literature on these sorts of questions, but the issues themselves are complex and methodologically difficult to explore—problems that are only magnified by the fact that all these reforms can be designed and carried out in very different ways (e.g., Hanushek et al., 2013; Woessmann, 2007). As a result, most of what we need to know remains to be learned, and the literature is filled with mixed findings and controversy. Much progress needs to be made before we can gain a confident perspective on what institutional reform is actually accomplishing in the realm of education.

Conclusion

The reality for now is that political scientists rarely study education—and education researchers, most of them professors at education schools, rarely study politics. As a field of social science, the politics of education can barely be said to exist as a coherent body of theory and research.

This is unfortunate. Education could not be more important to the human capital, social well-being, and economic prosperity of nations—and its policies and institutions, as well as their ultimate impacts, are thoroughly and quite inevitably shaped by politics. This is true in the United States. It is true in Sweden. It is true in Mexico. It is true everywhere. And it could hardly be otherwise. So if we are to understand how education systems are designed, organized, and staffed, how their policies are crafted and implemented, how their schools are operated from day to day—and *whose interests they are really serving*—we need to understand their politics. There is so much to be learned, and so much to be gained, were scholars to enlist their energies and talents in the systematic study of the politics of education, and in building a robust body of cumulative, theoretically guided work that hangs together—and progresses—as a genuine field.

This book is an early step toward that goal. The teachers unions are not the be-all-and-end-all of education politics. But they are quite central to it—everywhere. And by studying them in political context, the various chapters presented here have been able to shed a good deal of light not only on the unions themselves, but also on fundamental matters of power, vested interests, institutions, and reform—matters that are ultimately essential to an understanding of education politics more generally. Our hope now is that others will build upon what we have done here, and will take up the challenge to move this field ahead. With so much left to be done, and with education so crucially important throughout the world, the journey going forward is exciting—and the payoffs to progress enormous.

References

Ansell, Ben, and Johannes Lindvall. 2013. The political origins of primary education systems: Ideology, institutions, and interdenominational conflict. *American Political Science Review* 107.3: 505–22.

Appelbaum, Richard P., and William I. Robinson, eds. 2005. *Critical Globalization Studies*. Psychology Press.

Astiz, M. Fernanda, Alexander W. Wiseman, and David P. Baker. 2002. Slouching towards decentralization: Consequences of globalization for curricular control in national education systems. *Comparative Education Review* 46.1: 66–88.

Bachrach, Peter, and Morton S. Baratz. 1962. The two faces of power. *American Political Science Review* 56.4: 947–52.

Blanchflower, David. 2007. International patterns of union membership. *British Journal of Industrial Relations* 45.1: 1–28.

Blossing, Ulf, Gunn Imsen, and Lejf Moos, eds. 2014. *The Nordic Education Model: "A School for All" Encounters Neo-Liberal Policy*. Springer.

Burbules, Nicholas C., and Carlos Alberto Torres, eds. 2000. *Globalization and Education: Critical Perspectives*. Psychology Press.

Busemeyer, Marius R. 2014. *Skills and Inequality: Partisan Politics and the Political Economy of Education Reforms in Western Welfare States*. Cambridge University Press.

Campbell, Andrea Louise. 2003. *How Policies Make Citizens: Senior Political Activism and the American Welfare State*. Princeton University Press.

2012. Policy makes mass politics. *Annual Review of Political Science* 15: 333–51.

Castles, Francis G. 2004. *The Future of the Welfare State: Crisis Myths and Crisis Realities*. Oxford University Press.

Fukuyama, Francis. 2014. *Political Order and Political Decay: From the Industrial Revolution to the Globalization of Democracy*. Macmillan.

Gailmard, Sean, and John W. Patty. 2013. *Learning While Governing*. University of Chicago Press.

Garrett, Geoffrey, and Deborah Mitchell. 2001. Globalization, government spending and taxation in the OECD. *European Journal of Political Research* 39.2: 145–77.

Glenn, Charles L. 1989. *Choice of Schools in Six Nations: France, Netherlands, Belgium, Britain, Canada, West Germany*. US Government Printing Office.

Goldin, Claudia Dale, and Lawrence F. Katz. 2009. *The Race Between Education and Technology*. Harvard University Press.

Green, Andy. 1990. *Education and State Formation*. Palgrave Macmillan UK.

Grek, Sotiria. 2009. Governing by numbers: The PISA "effect" in Europe. *Journal of Education Policy* 24.1: 23–37.

Grindle, Merilee S. 2004. *Despite the Odds: The Contentious Politics of Education Reform.* Princeton University Press.
Grzymala-Busse, Anna M. 2015. *Nations Under God: How Churches Use Moral Authority to Influence Policy.* Princeton University Press.
Haar, Charlene K. 2002. *The Politics of the PTA.* No. 22. Transaction Publishers.
Hall, Peter A., and Michèle Lamont, eds. 2013. *Social Resilience in the Neoliberal Era.* Cambridge University Press.
Hanushek, Eric A., Susanne Link, and Ludger Woessmann. 2013. Does school autonomy make sense everywhere? Panel estimates from PISA. *Journal of Development Economics* 104: 212–32.
Hanushek, Eric A., and Ludger Woessmann. 2015. *The Knowledge Capital of Nations: Education and the Economics of Growth.* MIT Press.
Hebdon, Robert, and Ian Kirkpatrick. 2006. Changes in the Organization of Public Services and Their Effects on Employment Relations. In Stephen Ackroyd, Rosemary Batt, Paul Thompson, and Pamela S. Tolbert, eds, *The Oxford Handbook of Work and Organization.* Oxford University Press.
Hirsch, Barry T., David A. Macpherson, and John V. Winters. 2013. Teacher salaries, state collective bargaining laws, and union coverage. Presented at the American Economic Association Meetings, San Diego, January 6.
Hood, Christopher. 1991. A public management for all seasons?. *Public Administration* 69.1: 3–19.
Hoxby, Caroline. M. 1996. How teachers' unions affect education production. *Quarterly Journal of Economics* 111.3: 671–718.
Huber, Evelyne, and John D. Stephens. 2001. *Development and Crisis of the Welfare State: Parties and Policies in Global Markets.* University of Chicago Press.
Immergut, Ellen M. 1992. The Rules of the Game: The Logic of Health Policy-Making in France, Switzerland, and Sweden. In Sven Steinmo, Kathleen Thelen, and Frank Longstreth, eds, *Structuring Politics. Historical Institutionalism in Comparative Analysis.* Cambridge University Press: 57–89.
  2010. Political Institutions. In Francis G. Castles, Stephan Leibfried, Jane Lewis, Herbert Obinger, and Christopher Pierson, eds, *The Oxford Handbook of the Welfare State.* Oxford University Press.
Jakobi, Anja P., Kersten Martens, and Klaus Dieter Wolf. 2010. *Education in Political Science: Discovering a Neglected Field.* Routledge.
Klitgaard, Michael Baggesen. 2007. Do welfare state regimes determine public sector reforms? Choice reforms in American, Swedish and German schools. *Scandinavian Political Studies* 30.4: 444–68.
  2010. Veto Points and the Politics of Introducing School Vouchers in the United States and Sweden. In Anja P. Jakobi, Kersten Martens, and Klaus Dieter Wolf, eds, *Education in Political Science: Discovering a Neglected Field.* Routledge.
Korpi, Walter, and Joakim Palme. 2003. New politics and class politics in the context of austerity and globalization: Welfare state regress in 18 countries, 1975–95. *American Political Science Review* 97.3: 425–46.
Lijphart, Arendt. 1991. Corporatism and consensus democracy in eighteen countries. *British Journal of Political Science* 21.1: 235–46.
Lindvall, Johannes, and Joakim Sebring. 2005. Policy reform and the decline of corporatism in Sweden. *West European Politics* 28.5: 1057–74.

Lovenheim, Michael F. 2009. The effect of teachers' unions on education production: Evidence from union election certifications in three midwestern states. *Journal of Labor Economics.* 27.4: 525–87.
Meyer, John W., Francisco O. Ramirez, and Yasemin Nuhoğlu Soysal. World expansion of mass education, 1870–1980. *Sociology of Education* (1992): 128–49.
Moe, Terry M. 2005. Power and political institutions *Perspectives on Politics* 3.2: 215–33.
   2006. Political control and the power of the agent. *Journal of Law, Economics, and Organization* 22.1: 1–29.
   2011. *Special Interest: Teachers Unions and America's Public Schools.* Brookings Institution.
   2013. Delegation, Control, and the Study of Public Bureaucracy. In Robert Gibbons, and John Roberts, eds, *Handbook of Organizational Economics.* Princeton University Press.
   2015. Vested interests and political institutions. *Political Science Quarterly* 130.2: 277–318.
Organisation for Economic Cooperation and Development (OECD) 1994. *School: A Matter of Choice.* Paris: OECD.
Organisation for Economic Cooperation and Development (OECD) 2002. *What Works in Innovation in Education. School: A Choice of Direction.* Paris: OECD/CERI (Centre for Educational Research and Innovation).
Organisation for Economic Cooperation and Development (OECD). 2010. *Strong Performers and Successful Reformers in Education: Lessons from PISA for the United States.* Paris: OECD/CERI (Centre for Educational Research and Innovation).
Osborne, David, and Ted Gaebler. 1992. *Reinventing Government: How the Entrepreneurial Spirit is Transforming the Public Sector.* Plume.
Park, Sung Ho, and Kevin L. Young. 2014. Wage moderation in the public sector: The experiences of 11 EMU countries in the recent economic crisis, 2008–2010. *Economic and Industrial Democracy:* 36.4: 575–609.
Pencavel, John. 2005. Unionism viewed internationally. *Journal of Labor Research* 26.1: 65–97.
Pierson, Paul. 1993. When effect becomes cause: Policy feedback and political change. *World Politics* 45.4: 595–628.
   1994. *Dismantling the Welfare State?: Reagan, Thatcher and the Politics of Retrenchment.* Cambridge University Press.
   1996 The new politics of the welfare state. *World Politics* 48.2: 143–79.
   1998. Irresistible forces, immovable objects: Post-industrial welfare states confront permanent austerity. *Journal of European Public Policy* 5.4: 539–60.
   2004. *Politics in Time: History, Institutions, and Social Analysis.* Princeton University Press.
Premfors, Rune. 1998. Reshaping the democratic state: Swedish experience in comparative perspective. *Public Administration* 76.1: 142–59.
Ramirez, Francisco O., and John Boli. 1987. The political construction of mass schooling: European origins and worldwide institutionalization. *Sociology of Education* 60.1: 2–17.
Rodrik, Dani. 1998. Why do more open economies have bigger governments? *Journal of Political Economy* 106.5: 997–1032.

Schmitter, Philippe C. 1974. Still the century of corporatism? *The Review of Politics* 36.1: 85–131.
Schwartz, Herman. 2001. Round up the Usual Suspects!: Globalization, Domestic Politics, and Welfare State Change. In Paul Pierson, ed., *The New Politics of the Welfare State*. Princeton University Press: 17–44.
Starke, Peter. 2006. The politics of welfare state retrenchment: A literature review. *Social Policy & Administration* 40.1: 104–20.
Strom, Kaare, Wolfgang C. Muller, and Torbjorn Bergman, eds. 2006. *Delegation and Accountability in Parliamentary Democracies*. Oxford University Press.
Swank, Duane. 2002. *Global Capital, Political Institutions, and Policy Change in Developed Welfare States*. Cambridge University Press.
Thelen, Kathleen. 2004. *How Institutions Evolve: The Political Economy of Skills in Germany, Britain, the United States, and Japan*. Cambridge University Press.
Tsebelis, George. 2002. *Veto Players: How Political Institutions Work*. Princeton University Press.
Western, Bruce. 1999. *Between Class and Market: Postwar Unionization in the Capitalist Democracies*. Princeton University Press.
Wiborg, Susanne. 2013. Neo-liberalism and universal state education: The cases of Denmark, Norway and Sweden 1980–2011. *Comparative Education* 49.4: 407–23.
Winters, John V. 2011. Teacher salaries and teacher unions: A spatial econometric approach. *Industrial and Labor Relations Review* 64.4: 747–64.
Woessmann, Ludger. 2007. International evidence on school competition, autonomy, and accountability: A review. *Peabody Journal of Education* 82.2–3: 473–97.
World Bank. 2003. *World Development Report 2004: Making Services Work for Poor People*. World Bank.
   2011. *Learning for All: Investing in People's Knowledge and Skills to Promote Development*. World Bank.
Zajda, Joseph. 2015. *Second International Handbook on Globalisation, Education and Policy Research*. Springer.

Index

absence of veto points, 17, 290, 294, 296, 299
absenteeism, 227, 240
   teacher, 215, 226, 234, 240, 256
academic achievement, 3, 285, 288, 319, 320
academic performance, 132, 271, 283, 298, 299
academic standards, 43, 166, 167, 173, 301
Academies, 57, 80–2, 84, 294
   City, 78, 294
accountability, 39–40, 42–3, 44–5, 133, 239–40, 243, 247, 303–4
   reforms, 19, 30, 32, 300–1, 305, 312
   school, 33, 35, 39, 44, 243, 261, 301
   teachers, 240, 243, 247, 258–9, 261, 265
achievement, academic, 3, 285, 288, 319, 320
activists, 28, 36–7, 50, 90
Ad Hoc Council on Education, see AHCE, 196
administration, 43, 72, 100, 161, 193, 208, 223, 282
   civil, 144–5, 166
administrative committees, 95, 96
advanced nations, 2, 210, 283, 284–5, 287
AFT (American Federation of Teachers), 8, 15, 25–6, 27, 34, 43, 273, 309
Agreement for the Modernization of Education (ANMEB), 222–3
agreements, 147, 151–2, 163–4, 171, 173, 178, 222, 228
   national, 80, 81, 161, 171, 175, 222
AHCE (Ad Hoc Council on Education), 196–7, 198, 202
aided school teachers, 249, 253, 258, 262
aided schools, 255, 258, 262
AIFTO (All India Federation of Teachers Organizations), 242, 247, 249–50, 261, 274

AIPTF (All India Primary Teachers Federation), 242, 247, 249–50, 258, 259, 262, 274
AISTF (All India Secondary Teachers Federation), 242, 247, 249–50, 258, 274
alliances, 92, 93, 133–4, 170, 224, 228–9, 232, 279–80
   political, 221, 224–6, 297
allies, 37–9, 40, 42, 45, 196, 197, 278, 279
   political, 25, 91, 103, 207, 225, 232, 311
American Federation of Teachers, see AFT, 8
arbitration, 70, 74, 125, 219
Association of Municipalities, 161, 168, 170–1, 173
associations, 66, 135, 146, 148, 176–7, 181, 184–5, 252
   professional, 25, 117, 125, 282
autonomy, 103, 173, 181, 185, 218, 288, 303, 305
   local, 39, 101, 199
   school, 44, 57, 97, 105, 106, 108, 185, 293
   teacher, 83, 133

backwardness, 215
bargaining, see collective bargaining, 8
bargaining power, 61, 83, 101, 144, 223
basic education, 3, 116, 225, 228, 244, 312
basic skills, 215, 240, 271
behavior, 5, 7, 16, 28, 45, 255, 259, 280
benefits, 5–6, 28, 206, 225–6, 251, 278–9, 281, 316–17
   fringe, 102, 219, 223, 225
   pension, 206, 317
blocking, 24–52
   force, 177–8
   power, 42, 210, 212, 309

325

brokers, 222, 226, 310, 312
  electoral, 219
budgets, 35, 83, 99–100, 170, 176, 179, 277, 281
bureaucracy, 16, 20, 88, 266, 270, 287, 315, 317–18
  education, 216, 219–20, 223, 276, 302, 311, 312, 314
  ministerial, 87, 123–4, 125–6
bureaucratic institutions, 14, 271, 279
bureaucrats, 201–2, 205, 208, 210, 212, 270–1, 315, 317
Burnham Committee, 62–3, 69, 70–1, 73–5, 79, 83, 282
business community, 35–6, 271
business groups, 35, 37, 300, 316, 317
business leaders, 36, 39, 45, 231–2, 233

California, 27, 38, 41, 47, 50
California Teachers Association, 27, 49
Cameron governments, 80, 294
capital, human, 1–3, 35, 231, 285, 297, 315, 319–20
capitalism, 9, 11, 287
  welfare, 10
cartels, 151, 154
CATE (Council for the Accreditation of Teacher Education), 76
CCE (Central Council on Education), 196
CDU (Christian Democrat Union), 122–3, 129, 131, 273, 304
central control, 19, 57, 71–2, 204, 302
Central Council on Education (CCE), 196
central government employees, 251, 259
central governments, 56, 75, 88, 201–2, 242–4, 246–7, 258, 259
centralization, 71–2, 87–8, 94, 95, 100, 103–4, 293, 300
  France, 98–102
centralized control, 77, 292, 302
centralized education systems, 87, 98–9, 107, 180, 278, 302
centralized power, 162, 175, 218, 294
center parties, 150, 155, 159, 161, 163, 174
center-left parties, 150, 156
center-right governments, 159, 165
center-right parties, 160, 273, 275, 279–80, 291, 295, 296, 298
Chakravarty, D., 252, 256, 261
change, institutional, 17, 18, 35, 37, 50, 51, 288, 291
charter schools, 30, 31–2, 42, 47–8, 50, 52, 300–1, 316

charters, 47–9, 204, 250
children, 2, 6, 44–6, 48, 128–9, 147–8, 172–3, 319–20
  disadvantaged, 33, 36, 39, 46–7, 78
choice, 44–6, 47, 209, 211, 288, 293–4, 296, 306
  movement, 38, 45
  parental, 73, 134, 168, 178–9
  school, 17–18, 19, 33, 44, 171, 172, 178–9
Christian Democrat Union, see CDU, 122
cities, 26, 30–1, 32, 193, 197, 199, 202, 204
  large, 26, 27, 179, 193
City Academies, 78, 294
civil servant status, 62, 116–17, 120, 121–2, 128, 134, 175
civil servants, 115, 117, 118–19, 120–1, 124, 127–8, 136, 184
civil service, 92, 146, 282
civil society, 234, 247, 300, 315
  groups, 227, 231–2
class size reduction, 38
classroom teachers, 26, 79, 215, 226
classroom teaching, 154, 171, 173, 264
classrooms, 40–1, 181–2, 226, 231, 289, 294, 310, 315
clergy, 115, 146–7
coalition governments, 57, 80, 82, 83, 172, 173, 174, 202–3
coalitions, 4, 39–40, 80, 82, 290, 294–5, 296, 297
  multiparty, 18, 297, 299, 307
codetermination rights, 124, 305
collective agreements, 79, 151, 171, 172, 173–4
collective bargaining, 24–5, 28, 51, 61–2, 125–6, 127–8, 151–2, 205
  national, 176, 282, 293
  national bargaining rights, 56, 62, 73
  process, 151, 175, 179
  United States, 27–9
co-management, 87, 101
  competitive union, 91
communism, 205, 286
competition, 42, 46, 48, 57, 59, 95–6, 167, 171
  electoral, 217, 220, 222, 226, 294
  international, 35, 37, 207, 308
  multi-party, 216, 221, 224, 234, 310
competitive elections, 222, 226, 233
competitive union co-management, 91
comprehensive education, 2, 67–8, 148, 152, 154, 156, 182–3, 279–80
  England, 66–8

Index

France, 97–8
  reforms, 157, 158, 177
  Scandinavia, 152–4
  systems, 121, 133, 149, 152, 156, 165–6, 169
  teachers, 153, 154, 158, 182–3
compromise, 57, 199–200, 202, 206, 275, 290, 292, 296
concessions, 30, 42, 223, 228, 246, 247, 264, 265
conferences, 79, 200, 201, 249
  national, 194, 199–200, 201
conflict, 12, 57, 103, 183, 198, 208, 273
  political, 208, 221
confrontation, 76, 162, 173, 195, 198, 199, 204, 257
Congress, 43–4, 46, 230, 241, 252, 256, 301
consensus, 43, 65–7, 160, 209, 254, 260, 275, 277
  norm of, 278, 307
consensus-building, 193, 296
conservative parties, 80, 118, 123, 128, 146, 148, 165, 195
conservatives, 36, 49, 77, 159, 161, 174, 205, 279
constituencies, 31, 32, 42, 45, 118, 254–5, 314–15, 316
consultations, 77, 79, 83, 92, 124, 154, 158, 245
contract teachers, 246, 248, 251, 258, 263–4
contracts, 31, 81, 88, 171, 179, 207, 245, 264
control, 19–20, 46–7, 161–2, 222–3, 256–7, 271, 276–8, 294–5
  central, 19, 57, 71–2, 204, 302
  centralized, 77, 292, 302
  direct, 207, 219
  local, 39, 42, 43–4, 301
  local authority, 57, 73, 78, 81
  union, 226–7, 230
core subjects, 154, 166–7
corporate politics, 170, 185
corporate system, 128, 144, 147–8, 152, 157
corporatism, 145, 155, 159, 166, 174, 176, 184, 216
  teacher-dominated, 93, 277
corporatist governance, 144, 150, 159
corporatist relationships, 216–17, 218–19, 220, 233, 234
corporatist systems, 151, 159, 166, 225, 275–6, 295, 297
  Nordic, 282, 292
corruption, 1, 5, 231–2, 234, 257, 259, 310, 311–13

Council for the Accreditation of Teacher Education (CATE), 76
courts, 46, 48, 49, 50, 52, 121, 246, 258
credible threats, 253, 254–7, 266
crisis of the welfare state, 3, 16, 35, 283–4, 286, 291, 294
CSU (Christian Social Union), 123
curricula, 57–8, 60, 75–6, 173, 175, 180, 193, 209–10
  national, 76, 81, 83, 166, 167, 210, 297, 298
  reforms, 180, 210

data collection, 304, 305, 311
DBB (Deutscher Beamtenbund), 117, 118–19, 122
decentralization, 98–101, 103–4, 136, 162, 185, 216–17, 222–3
  India, 261–2
  laws, 99
  market-based, 292, 293–4, 300
  Mexico, 221–3
  process, 160–1, 162–3, 169, 175, 179, 185
  reforms, 18, 160, 161–2, 168, 174, 221, 222–3
decision-making powers, 72, 136, 170, 184
democracy, 203, 208, 216, 220, 307, 310, 312, 317
  local, 2, 27, 171
  social, 144–5, 149, 155, 165, 184
democratic pressures, 230, 231, 235
democratization, 12, 89, 131, 216, 226, 280
Democrats, 25, 34–5, 43, 46–7, 49, 51–2, 300
  Liberal, 80, 294
  Social, 122–3, 128–30, 147–50, 160–1, 172–3, 291–2, 296–8, 304–5
denationalization, 95, 101, 105
Denmark, 18, 144, 148, 150, 152–3, 158–60, 169–74, 184, 294–5
deregulation, 90, 104, 105, 161, 197, 291
Deutscher Beamtenbund, see DBB, 117
Deutscher Philologenverband, see DPhV, 115
developed nations, 13–14, 15, 17, 19, 271, 272–4, 315–16, 317
  reforms, 307–9
developing nations, 12, 19–20, 273–4, 283, 285, 287
  reforms, 309–13
devolution, 99, 169–70, 171, 185, 292
direct control, 207, 219
disadvantaged children, 33, 36, 39, 46–7, 78
discipline, 92, 216, 240, 243, 260, 271
  fiscal, 244
  professional, 69–70

disputes, 74, 75, 98, 125, 168, 173–4, 175
disruption, 192, 193, 196, 205, 274–5, 278, 306, 307
dissidents, 218, 220, 222, 233–4
District Primary Education Program, see DPEP, 239
diversity, 14, 36, 87, 89, 95, 97, 105, 211
DPEP (District Primary Education Program), 239, 244, 245, 246, 261
DPhV (Deutscher Philologenverband), 115, 117–24, 125–6, 128–9, 131–2, 134–6, 273, 280
DPJ (Democratic Party of Japan), 203, 207, 208–9, 212

early selection, 114, 122–3, 135
economic growth, 1–2, 35, 207, 208–9, 234, 281, 286, 315
educated elites, 116, 120, 124, 135, 273
education bureaucracy, 216, 219–20, 223, 276, 302, 311, 312, 314
education governance, 16, 91, 99, 132, 276, 286
education policy, 89–90, 91–2, 125, 127, 136, 192–3, 207, 241
  France, 97, 108
  Germany, 114, 126
  national, 158, 207, 232
education politics, 9, 14, 152, 269, 273, 314, 317, 320–1
education reform, see reforms, 3
Education Reform Act 1988, 73, 75
education systems, 1, 3–5, 8–10, 13–14, 16–19, 104–6, 269–70, 285–6
  centralized, 87, 98–9, 107, 180, 278, 302
  public, 2, 15, 88, 94, 115, 121, 284
education unions, see unions, 26
educational equality, 101, 106
educational institutions, 2, 5, 6, 10–11, 66, 197, 314, 319
elections, 20, 125–6, 219, 250, 253–5, 256, 263–4, 277–8
  competitive, 222, 226, 233
  general, 67, 70, 75, 208
  municipal, 177
  parliamentary, 108, 128, 255
  presidential, 220, 224
electoral brokers, 219
electoral competition, 217, 220, 222, 226, 294
electoral defeats, 123, 129, 130, 161, 208
electoral support, 51, 149, 204, 219

elementary education, 58, 63, 147, 239, 241–4, 246
elementary schooling, duration, 115, 123, 126, 128–9, 131, 135
elementary schools, 58, 64, 116, 118–19, 122, 128–9, 148, 211–12
  six-year, 128–9, 196
  teachers, 59, 61–2, 64, 65, 116, 126–7, 145–6, 155–8
elementary teachers, see elementary schools, teachers, 59
elites, educated, 116, 120, 124, 135, 273
employees, 124, 128, 168, 172, 206–8, 221, 223, 242
  government, 251, 253–4, 255, 259, 315
employers, 59, 62, 66, 73–4, 80–1, 83, 171, 172
  of teachers, 66, 73, 161, 185
employment conditions, 116, 122, 125–7, 132, 136, 161–2
enemies, political, 32, 301, 306
England, 13–14, 17–18, 19, 57–9, 291, 293, 294–5, 299–300
  beginnings of teacher unionism, 58–9
  Burnham Committee, 62–3, 69, 70–1, 73–5, 79, 83, 282
  Cameron governments, 80–3, 294
  comprehensive education, 66–8
  Education Reform Act 1988, 73, 75
  interwar period, 62–5
  iron triangle, 65–6
  militancy over work and pay conditions, 70–1
  New Labour, 57, 74, 77–80, 203
  NUT (National Union of Teachers), 57, 59–66, 67–70, 74–5, 79–80, 81–4, 293
  NUWT (National Union of Women Teachers), 62
  Ofsted, 76, 78–9
  payment by results, 60
  performance management
    pay and working conditions, 79–80
  Review Body, 75, 79–80, 82, 83
  self-government, 69–70
  standards, 77–8
  teachers unions, 56–84
  Thatcherism, 56, 77, 293
  working conditions, 60–1
enrollments, 45, 46, 48–9, 131, 270, 280
environment, 16, 254, 283, 287–8
equality, 167, 194, 246, 287

Index

educational, 101, 106
social, 10, 154
equalization, 154–5, 162
equity, social, 1–2, 7, 12, 46, 294
evaluations, 41, 102–3, 133–4, 215–19, 221, 226, 227–9, 303
  institutional, 103, 106
  performance-based, 41, 43, 50, 133–4, 288, 293, 300, 301
  teacher, 40, 43, 51–2, 226, 227–30, 232–3, 298, 311
examinations, 57, 66, 68, 75–6, 91, 199, 205, 264–5
exclusive representation, 25–6, 119
expansion, 12, 15, 97, 99, 132, 271, 284, 285
expectations, 52, 263, 270, 271, 289, 302

factions, 90, 94, 96, 147, 218, 222, 250
families, 6, 11, 44–5, 47–8, 73, 80, 115, 254–5
federal government, 43–4, 127, 136, 221, 222, 228, 230, 233
federalism, 289, 300, 310
federalism reforms, 127, 136
Fédération de l'éducation nationale, *see* FEN, 89
Fédération Générale de l'Enseignement, *see* FGE, 88
Fédération Syndicale Unitaire, *see* FSU, 90
FEN (Fédération de l'éducation nationale), 89–91, 93–4, 97
FGE (Fédération Générale de l'Enseignement), 88–9
finance, 161, 197, 218, 241, 243
financial resources, 51, 133, 217, 229, 234, 274, 300
findings, 15, 38, 217, 249, 308, 318
Finland, 18–19, 144–5, 146–7, 155–9, 176–8, 179–82, 184–5, 297–9
  education reform, 297–9
  governments, 18, 176, 178, 308
  teacher union, 146–7, 149, 155–8, 174–82
  teacher unions, 146, 174
fiscal discipline, 244
flexibility, 105, 207, 209–10, 288, 306
Florida, 38, 42, 46, 50
formal power, 127, 291, 292, 295, 299, 307
formal veto points, 17, 19, 289, 291, 292, 296–7, 300, 318
fragmentation, 36, 94, 95, 119, 123, 127, 136, 272–3
France, 13–14, 87, 90–1, 104–5, 106–8, 273–4, 276, 302–3
  comprehensive schools, 97–8

decentralization
  administrative efficiency
    and educational performance, 104–7
  education policy, 97, 108
  educational centralization, 98–102
  governments, 92, 100, 106, 108, 302–3
  historical development, 88–90
  Hollande government, 103, 107, 108
  impact of teacher unions on education policy, 97–104
  internal union structures and relationships to state and partisan actors, 90–4
  Sarkozy government, 91, 103, 105, 107, 303
  SGEN (Syndicat Général de l'Éducation Nationale), 89, 91, 94, 96, 103, 273
  SNI (Syndicat National des Instituteurs), 88, 89, 93, 97–8
  teacher unions, 87–108
  vested interests
    guiding principles
      and strategies, 94–7
  working and institutional conditions, 102–4
Free Schools, 80–1, 82, 84, 163, 168, 292, 294, 296
freedom, 173, 175, 182, 185, 304
fringe benefits, 102, 219, 223, 225
FSU (Fédération Syndicale Unitaire), 90, 91, 93–5, 101, 273
fundamental rights, 246, 247
funding, 4–5, 32–3, 72–3, 174, 176, 177, 179, 293

general elections, 67, 70, 75, 208
Georgia, 41, 46
Germany, 13–14, 106, 114–16, 123–4, 126–7, 132, 133–6, 302–4
  CDU (Christian Democrat Union), 122–3, 129, 131, 273, 304
  CSU (Christian Social Union), 123
  DBB (Deutscher Beamtenbund), 117, 118–19, 122
  DPhV (Deutscher Philologenverband), 115, 117–24, 125–6, 128–9, 131–2, 134–6, 273, 280
  education policy, 114, 126
  federalism reforms, 127, 136
  GEW (Gewerkschaft Erziehung und Wissenschaft), 114, 118–22, 125–6, 128, 130, 131, 132–5, 304
  Gymnasium, 114, 116–17, 120, 122–3, 124, 125–6, 129–31, 134–6
  Hauptschule, 114, 119, 122, 124, 129, 130–1

Germany (*Cont.*)
  Länder, 118, 122, 126–7, 128
  Realschule, 114, 119, 122, 124, 129, 130–1
  reunification, 119–20
  teacher unions, 114–36
  teachers, 104, 116, 120, 136
  Volksschule, 116, 117
GEW (Gewerkschaft Erziehung und Wissenschaft), 114, 118–22, 125–6, 128, 130, 131, 132–5, 304
Gewerkschaft Erziehung und Wissenschaft, *see* GEW, 8
ghost teachers, 226, 231, 232
globalization, 2, 10, 11, 16, 35, 284–5, 286, 287
goals, 39, 42, 129, 133, 194, 196, 244, 252
  policy, 96–7, 120, 227
  shared, 96, 195
governance, 3, 9, 155, 160, 275–6, 279, 286
  corporatist, 144, 150, 159
  education, 16, 91, 99, 132, 221, 276, 286
  school, 136, 240, 243
government employees, 251, 253–4, 255, 259, 315
government institutions, 3, 5–6, 181, 314
government intervention, 67, 70, 76, 173–4, 185
governmental power, 145–6, 148, 150, 302
governments, 69–74, 75–7, 169–75, 269–72, 281–4, 289–92, 293–5, 305–9
  central, 56, 75, 88, 201–2, 242–4, 246–7, 258, 259
  center-right, 159, 165
  Conservative, 57, 64, 71, 161, 294
  Finland, 18, 176, 178, 308
  France, 92, 100, 106, 108, 302–3
  Labor, 66–7, 70, 77, 294
  local, *see* local governments, 29
  Mexico, 274, 310
  minority, 150, 159, 296
  national, 24, 33, 60, 100, 205, 276, 302, 304
  parliamentary, 30, 302, 317
  right-wing, 159–60, 163, 167, 184, 205
  social democratic, 150, 152, 160
  state, 222–3, 227, 229, 233–4, 242–4, 245–6, 247, 258–9
  Sweden, 291, 292
  United States, 4–5, 20, 24, 27, 30, 34
governors, 31, 39, 81, 83, 204, 219, 223, 233
grades, 125, 131, 152–4, 157, 163, 169, 239, 306
grammar schools, 58, 63–4, 66, 68, 73

growth, 37, 62, 71, 76, 91, 227, 271, 279
  economic, 1–2, 35, 207, 208–9, 234, 281, 286, 315
  rapid, 194, 232
Gymnasium, 114, 116–17, 120, 122–3, 124, 125–6, 129–31, 134–6

Hamburg, 128–9
Hauptschule, 114, 119, 122, 124, 129, 130–1
head teachers; *see also* principals, 79, 82, 84, 95, 99, 101, 103
high schools, 193, 196, 208, 209, 211, 293
higher education, 9–10, 11, 69, 76, 78, 89, 116, 156
higher secondary education, 12, 120, 127
hiring, *see* recruitment, 221
history, 62, 63, 66, 162, 166, 241, 244, 279
Hollande government, 103, 107, 108
human capital, 1–3, 35, 231, 285, 297, 315, 319–20

ideology, 7, 15, 45, 83, 108, 203, 252, 280
  neoliberal, 56, 71, 287, 288, 297, 299
  political, 248, 252
implementation, 133–4, 215–16, 228–9, 233, 244, 246–7, 260, 313
  policy, 57, 77, 92, 145, 174, 179, 278
  problems, 228, 229
incentives, 6, 28–30, 37–9, 44–5, 47, 49, 309–10, 315
  strong, 1, 6, 25, 29, 270, 272, 314–15, 316
inclusive education system, 121, 122
income children, low, 46
independence, 62, 122, 199, 204, 241–2
independent schools, 122, 130–1, 294
India, 13, 19–20, 239–43, 247–9, 252–4, 263–5, 273–4, 312–13
  code of conduct for teachers, 259–61
  Constitution, 241, 243, 253
  contract teachers, 263–4
  court cases against government, 258
  decentralization, 261–2
  direct teacher involvment in politics, 258
  election-time credible threats, 254–7
  historical context, 241–7
  impact of teacher unions on education policy and practice, 265
  non-academic work, 264, 265
  organized strikes and threats, 257–8
  representation in state upper houses, 253–4
  Right to Education (RTE), 239, 257, 261

Index

SMCs (school management committees), 247, 257–8, 261–2
SSA (Sarva Shiksha Abhiyan), 239, 246–7, 261
student-teacher ratios, 262–3
teacher salaries, 259
teacher unions, 239–66
TET (Teacher Eligibility Test), 264, 265
union characteristics
  interests and strategies, 247–52
industrial relations, 15, 72, 206
INEE (National Institute of Education Evaluation), 227–8, 229, 230–1, 233
information, 21, 40–1, 81, 227, 229, 231
information technology, 41, 52, 125
initial teacher training, 76, 78, 167, 198
in-service teacher training, 244
insiders, 16, 276–7, 282, 315
inspections, 58, 76, 78, 161, 163, 181, 258, 312
Institute for Competitiveness (IMCO), 232
institutional change, 17, 18, 35, 37, 50, 51, 288, 291
institutional evaluations, 103, 106
institutional formation, 2, 3, 15–16, 269–71, 274, 277
institutional reform, 17, 288, 290–1, 292, 302, 305, 307, 318–20
Institutional Revolutionary Party, see PRI, 216
institutionalization, 15, 271
  and parties, 278–80
institutionalized interchanges, 91, 93, 176
institutions, 2–3, 5–6, 270–1, 278–9, 283–4, 287, 289–90, 319–21
  bureaucratic, 14, 271, 279
  educational, 2, 5, 6, 10–11, 66, 197, 314, 319
  government, 3, 5–6, 181, 314
  political, 269, 281, 313, 318
  and power, 280–3
interest groups, 34, 35–7, 91–2, 134–5, 145–6, 290, 314, 317–18
interest representation, 72, 127, 216
international competition, 35, 37, 207, 308
international standards, 102, 107, 306
international tests, 215, 285, 299
internationalization, 11, 197
inter-union politics, 69, 74, 95, 104
intervention, government, 67, 70, 76, 173–4, 185
interwar period, 57, 62–3, 65, 145, 147, 148–9, 152, 183

England, 62–5
iron triangle, 56, 58, 65, 72, 83, 165

Japan, 19, 194–5, 198–9, 205, 206–7, 208–10, 211–12, 305–8
  collapse of Japan Socialist Party and realignment of parties, 202–3
  decline of teacher unionism, 212
  DPJ (Democratic Party of Japan), 203, 207, 208–9, 212
  education reform, 209–12
  government structure and education system, 192–3
  JSP (Japan Socialist Party), 192, 195, 202–3, 207
  JTU (Japanese Teachers Union), 192, 193–6, 197–200, 202–4, 207–10, 212, 278, 305–6
    confrontation with government under 1955 system, 195–6
    formation, 193–5
    influence on education policy, 207–12
    new strategy of compromise, 199–202
    relationship with DPJ, 208–9
    road to division, 198–9
  LDP (Liberal Democratic Party), 19, 195, 197, 202–3, 207–8, 278, 305–7, 309
  prefectures, 193, 197, 198–200, 202, 204, 205, 211
  reforms, 305–7
  schools, 197, 200, 201, 210
  teacher unions, 192–212, 273
  teachers' interests and ambiguous role of unions, 204–7
  Zenkyo, 198–200, 201, 204, 206, 210, 211, 212, 309
Japan Communist Party, see JCP, 198
Japan Socialist Party, see JSP, 192
Japanese Teachers Union, see JTU, 19
JCP (Japan Communist Party), 198, 204
job interests, 6–7, 8, 27, 28, 33, 273, 280, 282
job security, 17, 41, 79, 133, 136, 162, 279, 282
JSP (Japan Socialist Party), 192, 195, 202–3, 207
JTU (Japanese Teachers Union), 192, 193–6, 197–201, 202–4, 207–11, 212, 278, 305–6
  confrontation with government under 1955 system, 195–6
  formation, 193–5
  influence on education policy, 207–12

new strategy of compromise, 199–202
relationship with DPJ, 208–9
road to division, 198–9

Karnataka, 249, 256, 263
knowledge transfer, 117, 127

Labor governments, 66–7, 70, 77, 294
labor markets, 75, 83, 148, 151
Labor parties, 165–6, 167, 275, 294, 296
labor unions, *see* unions, 87
Länder, 120, 123, 127–32, 134, 135–6
Latin America, 8, 12, 217, 223, 271, 276, 282, 310
LDP (Liberal Democratic Party), 19, 195, 197, 202–3, 207–8, 278, 305–7, 309
leaders, 2, 7, 8, 193, 198, 262, 265, 270
  dissident, 219, 220
  local, 32, 270
  national, 220, 223
  political, 10, 310, 312
  school, 79, 82
  union, *see* union leaders, 20
LEAs, *see* local education authorities, 18
left parties, 16, 34, 123, 278–9, 280, 295, 299
left-of-center parties, 203
legislation, 42, 44, 60, 172, 174, 300, 301, 302
legislators, 37, 127, 219, 259, 263
  teacher, 240, 257, 262
less-developed nations, 13–14, 16, 318
Liberal Democratic Party, *see* LDP, 19
Liberal Democrats, 80, 294
liberalization, 197
literacy, 77–8, 177, 180, 254, 271
  mathematical, 180
  scientific, 104, 180
local authorities, 56–7, 58, 65–7, 72–4, 75, 80–1, 82–3, 99–100
local authority control, 57, 73, 78, 81
local autonomy, 39, 101, 199
local control, 39, 42, 43–4, 301
local democracy, 2, 27, 171
local education authorities (LEAs), 60, 63, 67–8, 70, 72–3, 76–7, 276, 293–4
local elections, 30, 277
local governments, 43–4, 72, 74, 75, 77, 170, 171, 242
  as weak bargainers, 29–33
local negotiations, 28, 168, 175
local representation, 185, 288
local school boards, 25, 32, 59, 60, 63, 306
local school districts, 28, 33, 272, 281

local taxation, 61–2
local union branches, 164, 170, 176, 179
local unions, 18, 28, 192, 196, 212
Louisiana, 46
low-income children, 46
lower secondary education, 98, 102, 127, 130, 153, 280
lower secondary teachers, 126, 280, 304

Madhya Pradesh, 244, 245–6, 249, 251, 254, 256–7, 261, 264
mainstream reforms, 37–8
management, 45, 99–100, 215, 258, 262
  effective, 39
  performance, 78–9, 133, 294
  resources, 92, 101
  school, 95, 100, 103, 125, 200, 244
managers, 60, 79, 81, 164, 200–1, 206
market reforms, 180
market-based decentralization, 292, 293–4, 300
market-oriented education policies, 160
markets, 3, 45, 71, 162, 287, 290, 300
  free, 45, 46
mathematical literacy, 180
mayors, 31, 32, 219, 311
media, 43, 47, 50, 104, 177, 209, 232, 306
  attention, 217, 232, 303
membership, 25, 26, 49, 90, 198–9, 247–8, 250–2, 308–9
Mexico, 13–14, 19–20, 215–35, 310–12
  authoritarian roots of union power, 217–20
  Constitution, 218, 230
  decentralization, 221–3
  democratic pressures and limits of union power, 230–4
  education system, 310, 312
  governments, 274, 310
  INEE (National Institute of Education Evaluation), 227–8, 229, 230–1, 233
  Institute for Competitiveness (IMCO), 232
  new partisan alliances, 224–6
  PAN (National Action Party), 221, 225, 230, 311
  political transition and struggle for education reform, 220–1
  PRI (Institutional Revolutionary Party), 216–20, 221, 224, 230, 233, 234, 274, 310–11
  SNTE (Sindicato Nacional de Trabajadores de la Educación), 215–18, 220–4, 225–6, 227–8, 230–5, 274, 276
  teacher hiring and evaluation, 226–9

Index

teachers, 216, 217, 220, 234
middle classes, 20, 58, 63, 135–6, 270, 273, 311, 312
middle schools, 68, 148, 152, 306
militant unions, 75, 205, 208
minimum standards, 197, 209
ministerial bureaucracy, 87, 123–4, 125–6
minority governments, 150, 159, 296
mixed commissions, 219, 223, 227, 228, 234
mobility, upward, 1–2, 45, 98
moderation, 16, 30, 273, 275, 277, 282, 307
money, 20, 28, 36–8, 44–5, 60–1, 270–1, 281, 309–10
monopolies, 19–20, 153, 155, 182–3, 216, 273, 274, 310
monopoly unions, 15, 20, 273–4
multiparty competition, 216, 221, 224, 234, 310
multiple veto points, 19, 27, 34, 125
multi-tiered school system, 122–3, 130–1, 135
municipal elections, 177
municipalities, 160–2, 163, 168, 170–7, 178–9, 185, 291, 296–8
 see also local governments, 107
 association of, 161, 168, 170–1, 173

Nakasone, Yasuhir, 196–7, 198, 199, 202, 306
NAS (National Association of Schoolmasters), 62, 64, 74
National Action Party (PAN), 221, 225, 230, 311
national agreements, 80, 81, 161, 171, 175, 222
National Association of Schoolmasters (NAS), 62, 64, 74
national bargaining rights, 56, 62, 73
National Coalition for Education, see NCE, 247
national collective bargaining, 176, 282, 293
national conferences, 194, 199–200, 201
national curricula, 76, 81, 83, 166, 167, 210, 297, 298
National Education Association, see NEA, 25
national education policy, 158, 207, 232
national flags, 197, 200, 202
national government, 24, 33, 60, 100, 205, 276, 302, 304
National Institute of Education Evaluation, see INEE, 227

national standards, 19, 43, 168, 173, 185, 300, 301, 305
National Union of Teachers, see NUT, 57
NCE (National Coalition for Education), 247, 258
NCLB (No Child Left Behind), 4, 9, 19, 33, 40, 42–4, 300–1
NEA (National Education Association), 25–6, 27, 34, 43, 273, 309
negotiations, 60, 68, 70, 74, 128, 145, 150–2, 223
 local, 28, 168, 175
neoliberal ideology, 56, 71, 287, 288, 297, 299
neoliberal reforms, 3, 17, 19, 36, 294–6, 298, 306, 319–20
New Labour, 57, 74, 77–80, 203
New Orleans, 31–3, 48
New York, 26, 31–2, 40–1, 48
No Child Left Behind, see NCLB, 4
non-cooperation, 193, 200, 208, 251t. 9.2.
Nordic countries
 see also Denmark; Finland; Norway; Sweden, 282
 comprehensive education, 152–4
 corporatist systems, 282, 292
 decline of teacher union power, 158–82
 interwar period, 147–9
 social democracy
  corporatism and political integration of teacher unions, 149–58
 teacher unions, 144–85
Norway, 144, 147–9, 152–3, 158–60, 165–9, 184–5, 294–5, 296–7
NUT (National Union of Teachers), 57, 59–66, 67–70, 74–5, 79–80, 81–4, 293
NUWT (National Union of Women Teachers), 62

OECD (Organisation for Economic Cooperation and Development), 100, 102, 103–4, 106, 126–7, 132–3, 209–11, 304–5
Ofsted, 76, 78–9
opposition parties, 129, 172, 202, 220, 252
Organization for Economic Cooperation and Development, see OECD, 82
organizational resources, 224
organizational unity, 69–70
outliers, 5, 19, 144, 272, 309
outsiders, 167, 276, 277, 278

PAN (National Action Party), 221, 225, 230, 311
parental choice, 73, 134, 168, 178–9
parents, 6, 80–1, 93, 124, 133–4, 211, 261–2, 315
parliamentary elections, 108, 128, 255
parliamentary governments, 30, 302, 317
parliamentary systems, 17–18, 302, 319
parliaments, 121, 123, 125, 169, 171, 176–7, 178, 179
parties, 8, 195–6, 203–4, 224–5, 252, 278–9, 315, 317
    center, 150, 155, 159, 161, 163, 174
    center-left, 150, 156
    center-right, 160, 273, 275, 279–80, 291, 295, 296, 298
    conservative, 80, 118, 123, 128, 146, 148, 165, 195
    and institutionalization, 278–80
    labour, 165–6, 167, 275, 294, 296
    left, 16, 34, 123, 278–9, 280, 295, 299
    left-of-center, 203
    opposition, 129, 172, 202, 220, 252
    reformist, 298, 315
    right-wing, 165, 169, 174
    socialist, 89, 91, 160, 167, 195, 202, 278, 305
partisan politics, 10–11, 95
patrimonial power, 215–17, 220–1, 228, 231, 234–5
patronage, 1–2, 215–35, 312–13
payrolls, 215, 219, 221, 222, 226–7, 231–2
pedagogical methods, 98, 100
pedagogy, 153–4, 167, 183, 265
    progressive, 153–5, 157
pension benefits, 206, 317
performance, 3, 28–9, 82, 103–4, 163–4, 264–5, 271, 288–9
    academic, 132, 271, 283, 298, 299
    future research directions, 319–20
    management, 78–9, 133, 294
performance-based evaluations, 41, 43, 50, 133–4, 288, 293, 300, 301
performance-based reform, 3, 16–20, 283–90, 302, 308
policy goals, 96–7, 120, 227
policy implementation, 57, 77, 92, 145, 174, 179, 278
political alliances, 221, 224–6, 297
political allies, 25, 91, 103, 207, 225, 232, 311

political enemies, 32, 301, 306
political ideology, 248, 252
political institutions, 269, 281, 313, 318
political leaders, 10, 310, 312
political parties, *see* parties, 2
political power, 4, 6, 7, 25, 34–5, 146–7, 239, 240–1
political pressures, 19, 79, 159, 257
political processes, 1, 4, 34, 134, 315, 318
political scientists, 2, 9–10, 13, 155, 320
political setbacks, 216–17, 230, 231, 234
political support, 25, 31, 216, 219, 222, 224, 226, 292
political systems, 17, 19, 144, 149–50, 290–1, 299–300, 307, 309–10
politicians, 20, 177–8, 239–40, 254–5, 256, 270–1, 311–12, 315
politicization, 215, 232, 254
politics, 3–10, 11–14, 20–1, 33–5, 278–9, 288–90, 312–15, 319–20
    education, 9, 14, 152, 269, 273, 314, 317, 320–1
    interest, 58, 160, 185
    inter-union, 69, 74, 95, 104
    national, 24, 159, 165, 277
    partisan, 10–11, 95
    patronage, 215–35
    teacher, 68, 253
United States, 4–5, 9, 277
power, 3–4, 8–10, 17–21, 51–40, 56–7, 182–5, 307–10, 317–20
    bargaining, 61, 83, 101, 144, 223
    bases, 18, 45, 49, 67, 176, 182, 292, 293
    blocking, 42, 210, 212, 309
    centralized, 162, 175, 218, 294
    formal, 127, 291, 292, 295, 299, 307
    governmental, 145–6, 148, 150, 302
    and institutions, 280–3
    and interests in context, 317–19
    patrimonial, 215–17, 220–1, 228, 231, 234–5
    political, 4, 6, 7, 25, 34–5, 146–7, 239, 240–1
    teacher union, 136, 144–5, 155, 158, 160
    union, 208, 217, 230
    veto, 92, 124–5, 136, 178
prefectures, 193, 197, 198–200, 202, 204, 205, 211
preparation time, 81, 132, 172, 174
presidential candidates, 225–6, 224–5

Index

presidential elections, 220, 224
presidential systems, 310, 317
pressures, 30, 33, 40, 208, 209, 210, 307, 308
   democratic, 230, 231, 235
PRI (Institutional Revolutionary Party), 217–21, 216–20, 221, 224, 230, 233, 234, 274, 310–11
primary education; *see also* elementary education, 10, 12, 129, 221, 263
primary school teachers, 82, 88, 98, 152–5, 157, 183, 280
primary schools, 78, 97–8, 147, 148, 152, 154, 245, 259
principals, 81, 169–70, 173–4, 175, 208, 215, 219, 221
private schools, 11, 45, 88, 134, 145, 171, 291, 296
private sector, 25, 88, 147, 168, 178, 198, 206–7, 308
private-aided schools, 242, 253, 255
privatization, 169, 172
privileges, 59, 95, 101–2, 122, 126, 243, 310
   legal, 216, 253
productivity, 1, 37, 163–4, 179, 286
profession, 69, 76–7, 115–20, 153–4, 157–8, 183, 206, 226
professional associations, 25, 117, 125, 282
professional development, 81, 164, 180, 202
professional discipline, 69–70
professional self-regulation, 92, 302
progressive pedagogy, 153–5, 157
promotions, 194, 216, 217, 219, 221, 251, 276–7, 282
protests, 101, 218–19, 222, 229, 233–4, 245, 247, 257
psychology, educational, 153, 158
public education, 2–3, 24–5, 90–1, 215, 219, 270, 272, 317–18
   systems, 2, 15, 88, 94, 115, 121, 284
public school systems, 2, 35, 165, 215–17, 221, 227, 231, 271
public school teachers, 134, 215, 218
public schools, 4, 33, 38–9, 44–8, 58, 276–7, 294, 302
public sector, 124, 127, 161, 162, 168, 205, 206–7, 210–11
   unions, 49, 90, 92, 155, 202, 203, 272
   workers, 25, 70, 151, 168, 205, 253, 272
public services, 100–1, 103, 161, 165, 169, 172, 175, 283

public spending, 182, 225, 270
public support, 125–6, 169, 196, 305
public teaching service, 92, 107–8
pupils, 60, 63, 82, 97–9, 102, 163–4, 168–9, 180
   secondary, 88, 107

qualifications, 114, 116, 122, 154, 167, 168, 246, 264
qualified teacher status, 65, 76, 80
quasi-market regulation, 169, 170

Race to the Top (RTT), 41, 47, 50, 300, 301
radical reforms, 57, 67, 71–2, 295, 299, 318
Rajasthan, 244, 246, 247–9, 250–1, 254–5, 256, 263, 266
Realschule, 114, 119, 122, 124, 129, 130–1
recruitment, 57–8, 99–100, 221, 226–7, 230–1, 245–6, 256–7, 276
reformers, 33, 36–9, 48–9, 50, 51–2, 289, 300, 302
reformist parties, 298, 315
reforms, 31–3, 35–8, 131–4, 209–11, 288–93, 297–300, 303–8, 319–21
   accountability, 19, 30, 32, 300–1, 305, 312
   blocking, 104, 125–6, 133, 135, 166, 196, 197, 295
   comprehensive school, 157, 158, 177
   curricula, 180, 210
   decentralization, 18, 160, 161–2, 168, 174, 221, 222–3
   developed nations, 307–9
   developing nations, 309–13
   Finland, 297–9
   institutional, 17, 288, 290–1, 292, 302, 305, 307, 318–20
   Japan, 305–7
   mainstream, 37–8
   major, 17, 19, 33, 34–5, 290, 296–7, 300, 318
   market, 180
   neoliberal, 3, 17, 19, 36, 294–6, 298, 306, 319–20
   performance-based, 3, 16–20, 283–90, 302, 308
   radical, 57, 67, 71–2, 295, 299, 318
   United States, 300–2
   when governments are formally free to act, 290–9
   when governments are more constrained, 299–307
regular teachers, 245–6, 248, 258–9, 264

regularization, 246, 258, 263–4
relationships
  antagonistic, 107–8
  corporatist, 216–17, 218–19, 220, 233, 234
religion, 1, 3, 15, 246, 272, 314, 316
religious groups, 93, 316
religious schools, 46, 316
remuneration, 57, 82, 103, 115–17, 164, 169
rents, 217, 225–6, 234, 310, 315
representation, 69, 74, 118, 216, 220, 253–4, 272
  exclusive, 25–6, 119
  interest, 72, 127, 216
  local, 185, 288
  monopoly of, 120, 218
  union, 193, 219, 227
representatives, 35, 62, 156, 162, 192, 195, 201–3, 219–20
  union, 8, 92–3, 128, 170, 173–4
Republicans, 39, 42–3, 44, 46, 49, 301
resources, 34–5, 45, 161, 177, 216–17, 220, 234, 270
  allocation, 161, 169, 170
  financial, 51, 133, 217, 229, 234, 274, 300
  management, 92, 101
  organizational, 224
responsive education system, 197, 310
retrenchment, 9, 16, 284, 317
Review Body, 75, 79–80, 82, 83
rewards, 103, 263, 281, 282
Right to Education (RTE), 239, 247, 250, 257, 260, 261, 262, 264–5
rights, 28, 60, 121, 124, 136, 195, 204–5, 263
  codetermination, 124, 305
  fundamental, 246, 247
right-wing governments, 159–60, 163, 167, 184
right-wing parties, 165, 169, 174
RTE, see Right to Education, 239
RTT, see Race to the Top, 41

salaries; see also remuneration, 61–2, 103–4, 106–7, 154, 161–3, 168, 205–6, 259
salary increments, 25 lt. 9.2., 258, 277
salary scales, 62, 92, 154, 216
Sarkozy government, 91, 103, 105, 107, 303
Sarva Shiksha Abhiyan, see SSA, 239
Schleswig-Holstein, 128–9
school accountability, 33, 35, 243, 261, 301
  United States, 39–44
school autonomy, 44, 57, 97, 105, 106, 108, 185, 293

school boards, 27, 39, 58, 60–1, 64, 125, 169–70, 185
  local, 25, 32, 59, 60, 63, 306
school choice, 17–18, 19, 33, 35, 171, 172, 178–9
  United States, 44–9
school closures, 96, 97, 107, 108
school districts, 28, 30, 32–3, 38–9, 44, 45, 133–4, 300–1
  local, 28, 33, 272, 281
school governance, 136, 240, 243
school headmasters, see head teachers, 95
school inspections, see inspections, 58
school leaders, 79, 82
school management, 95, 100, 103, 125, 200, 215–44
school management committees, see SMCs, 247
school policy, 60, 119, 123, 129, 133–5, 136, 145, 165
school principals, see principals, 29
school structure, 63, 115, 124, 125, 130–2, 134–5, 152
school systems, 134, 136, 148–9, 245, 265, 266, 269, 272
  comprehensive, 121, 133, 149, 152, 156, 165–6, 169
  multi-tiered, 122–3, 130–1, 135
  secondary, 3, 63, 124, 149
  tripartite, 114–16, 121, 122, 129, 131, 132
school types; see also *individual school types*, 15, 57, 66, 88, 123, 130, 132, 135
schools, 31–3, 41–2, 72–3, 76–81, 82–4, 169–71, 172–6, 257–62
  aided, 255, 258, 262
  bad, 44–5
  charter, 30, 31–2, 42, 47–8, 50, 52, 300–1, 316
  effective, 47, 288
  independent, 122, 130–1, 294
  Japan, 197, 200, 201, 210
  low-performing, 42, 77, 301
  middle, 68, 148, 152, 306
  primary, 78, 97–8, 147, 148, 152, 154, 245, 259
  private, 11, 45, 88, 134, 145, 171, 291, 296
  private-aided, 242, 253, 255
  public, 4, 33, 38–9, 44–8, 58, 276–7, 294, 302
  religious, 46, 316
  secondary, see secondary schools, 57
  voluntary, 58, 61
schoolteachers, see teachers, 6

Index

science, 35, 40, 65–6, 67, 114, 118, 177, 215
scientific literacy, 104, 180
secondary education, 2, 9–10, 11–13, 59, 63–5, 67, 114, 260
  higher/upper, 12, 120, 127
  lower, 98, 102, 127, 130, 153, 280
secondary school systems, 3, 63, 124, 149
secondary schools, 57, 58, 63–4, 116–17, 119, 146–8, 154, 156
  lower, 97–8, 280
secondary teachers, 59, 64–5, 102, 107, 116–18, 146–7, 155–7, 273
selection, 67, 98, 121, 219, 280
  early, 114, 122–3, 135
self-government, 57
  England, 69–70
self-regulation, professional, 92, 302
seniority, 28–9, 31, 32, 50, 101, 103, 154, 205
setbacks, political, 216–17, 230, 231, 234
SGEN (Syndicat Général de l'Éducation Nationale), 89, 91, 94, 96, 103, 273
shared goals, 96, 195
Sindicato Nacional de Trabajadores de la Educación, *see* SNTE, 215
skills, 10, 99, 104, 132, 166, 167, 319
  basic, 215, 240, 271
SMCs (school management committees), 247, 257–8, 261–2
SNI (Syndicat National des Instituteurs), 88, 89, 93, 97–8
SNTE (Sindicato Nacional de Trabajadores de la Educación), 215–18, 220–4, 225–6, 227–8, 230–5, 274, 276
Social Compromise for Education Quality, 227
social democracy, 144–5, 149, 155, 165, 184
Social Democrats, 122–3, 128–30, 147–50, 160–1, 172–3, 291–2, 296–8, 304–5
social equality, 10, 154
social equity, 1–2, 7, 12, 46, 294
social partnership, 18, 65, 276, 293, 294
social science, 9–10, 11, 91, 280, 286, 320
socialist parties, 89, 91, 160, 167, 195, 202, 278, 305
South India Teachers Union, 241
Soviet Union, 156, 174
SPD, *see* Social Democrats, 17
spending, 6, 12, 34, 37–8, 219, 271, 279, 284
  public, 182, 225, 270
SSA (Sarva Shiksha Abhiyan), 239, 246–7, 261
standards, 39, 65, 69, 71, 78–9, 165–6, 209, 295–6
  England, 77–8

international, 102, 107, 306
minimum, 197, 209
national, 19, 43, 168, 173, 185, 300, 301, 305
raising, 59, 77, 80
state governments, 222–3, 227, 229, 233–4, 242–4, 245–6, 247, 258–9
state legislatures, 20, 40, 233, 253, 264, 312
state level, 40, 42, 240, 244–5, 246, 247, 250, 264–5
state-level union sections, 218, 220, 224, 233
state-level unions, 241, 248, 250–1, 257–8
status quo, 2, 3, 67–8, 177–8, 240, 303, 305–6, 308
stratification, 66, 88, 97, 114, 126
strikes, 62, 82, 87, 95–6, 101, 105, 208, 243
student learning, 38, 239–40, 244, 246–7
subject teachers, 145, 153, 157, 248
subjects (taught), 78, 82, 153, 157, 164, 168, 171, 216
  core, 154, 166–7
support, 38, 39–40, 43, 47, 49, 206, 248–50, 306
  political, 25, 31, 216, 219, 222, 224, 226, 292
  public, 125–6, 169, 196, 305
  union, 62, 172, 203, 223, 249–50, 311
Sweden, 17–19, 146–8, 152–3, 158–9, 160–4, 165, 166, 168–9, 173, 291–5
  governments, 291, 292
  welfare state, 291
Syndicat Général de l'Éducation Nationale, *see* SGEN, 89
Syndicat National des Instituteurs, *see* SNI, 88

tax credits, 46–7
taxation, local, 61–2
teacher autonomy, 83, 133
teacher categories, 65, 68, 152–3, 154, 157, 162
teacher education, *see* teacher training, 37
teacher evaluations, 40, 43, 51–2, 226, 227–30, 232–3, 298, 311
teacher hiring, *see* recruitment, 57
teacher legislators, 240, 257, 262
teacher payrolls, *see* payrolls, 215
teacher politics, 68, 253
teacher quality, 38, 40, 50
teacher salaries, *see* salaries, 38
teacher strikes, *see* strikes, 62
teacher training, 78, 123, 153, 155, 157, 167, 180–1, 245
  colleges, 152, 201

initial, 76, 78, 167, 198
in-service, 244
university-based, 157, 183
teacher transfers, *see* transfers, 16
teacher unionism, *see* unionism, 7
teacher-dominated corporatism, 93, 277
teacher-pupil ratios, 106, 168, 262
teachers
  absenteeism, 215, 226, 234, 240, 256
  accountability, 240, 243, 247, 258–9, 261, 265
  aided school, 249, 253, 258, 262
  bad, 28, 38, 40, 49
  classroom, 26, 79, 215, 226
  comprehensive school, 153, 154, 158, 182–3
  contract, 246, 248, 251, 258, 263–4
  elementary school, 59, 61–2, 64, 65, 116, 126–7, 145–6, 155–8
  ghost, 226, 231, 232
  head, 79, 82, 84, 95, 99, 101, 103
  lower secondary, 126, 280, 304
  Mexico, 216, 217, 220, 234
  private school, 145, 176, 178
  public school, 134, 215, 218
  regular, 245–6, 248, 258–9, 264
  secondary, 59, 64–5, 102, 107, 116–18, 146–7, 155–7, 273
  subject, 145, 153, 157, 248
  uncertified, 62, 163
  university-educated, 145, 152–3, 154–5, 177, 181, 183
  unqualified, 70, 81
  upper secondary, 98, 126, 153, 161–2, 182, 280
teaching profession, *see* profession
tests, international, 215, 285, 299
Thatcherism, 56, 77, 293
threats, credible, 253, 254–7, 266
transfers, 92, 98, 218, 219–20, 258–9, 261, 263, 265–6
transition, 59, 62, 63, 147, 220, 284, 311
transparency, 82, 215, 227, 229, 232, 305
tripartite school system, 114–16, 121, 122, 129, 131, 132

uncertified teachers, 62, 163
union branches, 177, 179
  local, 164, 170, 176
union control, 226–7, 230
union leaders, 96, 198, 205, 219–20, 223–4, 225–6, 248–9, 265–6

national, 218–19, 229
union members, 28, 96, 119, 125, 182, 248, 249, 274
union membership, *see* membership, 25
union power, 24, 27, 144–5, 158, 160, 217, 280–1, 282
union representation, 193, 219, 227
union representatives, 8, 92–3, 128, 170, 173–4
union support, 62, 172, 203, 223, 249–50, 311
unionism, 87, 89, 90, 93, 94, 97, 104, 115–16
  France, 87–108
unionization, 25, 90, 264, 274
unions
  England, 56–84
  Finland, 146–7, 149, 155–8, 174–82
  France, 87–108
  Germany, 114–36
  India, 239–66
  influence, 73, 124, 159, 209
  Japan, 192–212, 273
  local union branches, 164, 170, 176, 179
  Mexico, 235
  militant, 75, 205, 208
  monopoly, 15, 20, 273–4
  Nordic countries, 144–85
  patrimonial power, 216–17, 221, 228, 235
  power gain and entrenchment, 274–8
  public sector, 49, 90, 92, 155, 202, 203, 272
  rise, 271–4
  state-level, 241, 248, 250–1, 257–8
  United States, 24–52
United States, 4–5, 25, 51–2, 92–3, 252–3, 273–4, 290–1, 316–17
  collective bargaining, 27–9
  Democrats, 25, 34–5, 43, 46–7, 49, 51–2, 300
  formative era of education, 24–7
  governments, 4–5, 20, 24, 27, 30, 34
  local governments as weak bargainers, 29–33
  mainstream reforms, 37–8
  NCLB (No Child Left Behind), 4, 9, 19, 33, 40, 42–4, 300–1
  NEA (National Education Association), 25–6, 27, 34, 43, 273, 309
  organization of schools, 27–9
  politics, 4–5, 9, 277
  politics of blocking, 33–5
  recent developments, 49–51
  reform movement, 35–7

Index

reforms, 300–2
Republicans, 39, 42–3, 44, 46, 49, 301
school accountability, 39–44
school choice, 44–9
teachers unions, 24–52
universities, 65, 76, 78, 114, 116, 146, 181
university-educated teachers, 145, 152–3, 154–5, 177, 181, 183
unqualified teachers, 70, 81
upper secondary schools, 148, 152, 155, 157, 170, 175, 183, 253
upper secondary teachers, 98, 126, 153, 161–2, 182, 280
upward mobility, 1–2, 45, 98
Uttar Pradesh, 241, 243, 249–51, 253, 255, 257–60, 262

vested interests, 5–7, 16–17, 19–21, 32–3, 118–22, 234–5, 270–2, 313–15
veto points, 37, 289–90, 293, 295, 299–300, 302, 304, 308
  absence of, 17, 290, 294, 296, 299
  formal, 17, 19, 289, 291, 292, 296–7, 300, 318
  multiple, 19, 27, 34, 125
veto powers, 92, 124–5, 136, 178
vice-principals, 201, 208
villages, 254, 261, 264, 266

vocational education, 9, 11–12, 316
vocational training, 114, 170
Volksschule, 116, 117
voluntary schools, 58, 61
voters, 202, 256, 290
votes, 8, 74, 123, 125, 207, 222, 225, 254–6
voucher schemes, 45–7, 160, 163, 170, 300, 316

wages, *see* salaries, 16, 18, 28, 107, 121, 164, 246, 280–2
Washington, 31, 32, 44, 46–8, 205
welfare capitalism, 10
welfare state, 9–12, 13, 15–16, 17, 278–9, 284–5, 286–7, 291
  crisis, 3, 16, 35, 283–4, 286, 291, 294
West Bengal, 248, 250, 252, 256, 258, 261
Wisconsin, 25, 26, 46, 49
women, 62–3, 64, 118, 145, 194, 225, 241
working conditions, 16–17, 174, 175, 249, 251, 265, 291, 293
  England, 60–1
World Bank, 13, 244, 287, 288

yutori reforms, 209–10, 306

Zenkyo, 198–200, 201, 204, 206, 210, 211, 212, 309